Publications of the
National Bureau of Economic Research, Inc.

Number 48

Value of Commodity Output since 1869

Officers

Shepard Morgan, *Chairman*
C. Reinold Noyes, *President*
Boris Shishkin, *Vice-President*
George B. Roberts, *Treasurer*
W. J. Carson, *Executive Director*
Martha Anderson, *Editor*

Directors at Large

Chester I. Barnard, *President, New Jersey Bell Telephone Company*
Arthur F. Burns, *Columbia University*
Oswald W. Knauth, *New York City*
H. W. Laidler, *Executive Director, League for Industrial Democracy*
Shepard Morgan, *Vice-President, Chase National Bank*
C. Reinold Noyes, *New York City*
George B. Roberts, *Vice-President, National City Bank*
Beardsley Ruml, *Chairman, Board of Directors, R. H. Macy & Company*
Harry Scherman, *President, Book-of-the-Month Club*
George Soule, *President, Pilot Press, Inc.*
N. I. Stone, *Consulting Economist*
J. Raymond Walsh, *WMCA Broadcasting Company*
Leo Wolman, *Columbia University*

Directors by University Appointment

E. Wight Bakke, *Yale*
C. C. Balderston, *Pennsylvania*
W. L. Crum, *Harvard*
Corwin D. Edwards, *Northwestern*
G. A. Elliott, *Toronto*
Guy Stanton Ford, *Minnesota*
H. M. Groves, *Wisconsin*
Clarence Heer, *North Carolina*
Wesley C. Mitchell, *Columbia*
Paul M. O'Leary, *Cornell*
W. W. Riefler, *Institute for Advanced Study*
T. O. Yntema, *Chicago*

Directors Appointed by Other Organizations

Percival F. Brundage, *American Institute of Accountants*
Arthur H. Cole, *Economic History Association*
Frederick C. Mills, *American Statistical Association*
Boris Shishkin, *American Federation of Labor*
Warren C. Waite, *American Farm Economic Association*
Donald H. Wallace, *American Economic Association*

Research Staff

Arthur F. Burns, *Director of Research*

Moses Abramovitz
Harold Barger
Morris A. Copeland
Daniel Creamer
Solomon Fabricant
W. Braddock Hickman
F. F. Hill
Thor Hultgren

Simon Kuznets
Clarence D. Long
Ruth P. Mack
Frederick C. Mills
Wesley C. Mitchell
Geoffrey H. Moore
Raymond J. Saulnier
George J. Stigler

Leo Wolman

Value of Commodity Output since 1869

William Howard Shaw

NATIONAL BUREAU OF ECONOMIC RESEARCH

1947

↑ 946446

Copyright, 1947, by
National Bureau of Economic Research, Inc.
1819 Broadway, New York 23

All Rights Reserved

Printed in the U. S. A. by E. L. Hildreth & Company; bound
by H. Wolff, New York

Contents

Preface xiii

PART I
SUMMARY

A	Definitions	4
B	The Estimates	7
C	Movements over Time	8
	1 Rates of Growth and Changes in Composition	8
	2 Variations from Decade to Decade	14
	a Variations in absolute figures	15
	b Variations in shares	16
	3 Behavior during Business Cycles	18
	a Variations in amplitude	18
	b Variations in conformity	25
	4 Summary	28

PART II
ESTIMATES OF THE VALUE OF OUTPUT

A	Census of Manufactures	79
	1 Census Commodity Data	81
	2 Mixed Commodities	82
	3 Comparisons with Other Estimates	83
	a Kuznets' estimates for 1919	83
	b Census net value of manufactured products, 1899	89
B	Intercensal Estimates	92
	1 The Data	92
	a State materials	92
	b Miscellaneous sources	96
	2 Selection and Evaluation	97
C	Nonmanufactured Commodities	101
	1 Nonmanufactured Foods	101
	a Products of farms	101
	b Products of fisheries	102
	c Products of mines	103
	2 Nonmanufactured Fuels	103
	a Products of mines	103
	b Products of forests	103

	3 Construction Materials	104
	a Products of forests	104
	b Products of mines	104
D	Derivation of the Estimates since 1919	104
	1 Adjustments to Kuznets' Estimates for 1919–1933	104
	2 Estimates for Years since 1933	105
	a Perishable	105
	b Semidurable	106
	c Consumer durable	106
	d Producer durable	106
	e Construction materials	107

Part III
EXPORTS AND IMPORTS

A	Exports	269
B	Imports	272
C	Changes in Relative Importance of Exports and Imports	272

Part IV
PRICE INDEXES

A	Problems of Constructing Price Indexes	287
B	Adequacy of the Price Indexes	288
INDEX		303

TABLE

1 Classification of Commodities   5

2 Value of Finished Commodities destined for Domestic Consumption, Major Commodity Groups, Producers' Current and 1913 Prices   9

3 Value of Finished Commodities, Averages of 1879 and 1889, 1929 and 1939, Major and Minor Commodity Groups, Producers' Current Prices   13

4 Value of Finished Commodities and Price Indexes, Major Commodity Groups, Producers' Current and 1913 Prices, and Price Indexes   15

5 Value of Finished Commodities, Major Commodity Groups,

CONTENTS vii

Producers' Current and 1913 Prices, Percentage Shares, Averages for Successive Decades — 17
6 Value of Finished Commodities and Price Indexes, Major Commodity Groups, Producers' Current and 1913 Prices, Averages of Specific Cycle Relatives for Cycles before and after World War I — 23
7 Value of Finished Commodities and Price Indexes, Major Commodity Groups, Index of Conformity, 13 Reference Cycles, 1891–1938 — 26
8 Value of Finished Commodities and Price Indexes, Complete Cycle Indexes of Conformity — 27

I-1 Value of Output of Finished Commodities and Construction Materials, Exports, Imports, and Values Destined for Domestic Consumption, Current Prices, 1869, 1879, 1889–1919 — 30
I-2 Value of Finished Commodities and Construction Materials Destined for Domestic Consumption, 1919–1939, Current Prices — 66
I-3 Value of Finished Commodities and Construction Materials Destined for Domestic Consumption, 1869, 1879, 1889–1939, 1913 Prices — 70
II-1 Value of Manufactured Commodities, Census Years, 1869–1919 — 108
II-2 Mixed Commodities and their Allocation, Census Years, 1869–1919 — 174
II-3 Industrial Composition of the Census of Manufactures, 1869–1919 — 200
II-4 Value of Products Reported for Eight States by the United States Census of Manufactures and by State Agencies, Census Years, 1889–1919 — 202
II-5 Value of Product, Selected Industries, Reported by United States Census of Manufactures and by State Agencies, 1909 — 208
II-6 Composition of Interpolating Series by Minor Commodity Groups — 213

II-7 Percentage Changes in Census Year Ratios of Interpolating and Complementary Series to Minor Commodity Group Totals	242
II-8 Differences in the Year-to-Year Percentage Changes in the Interpolating Series, Frequency Distribution by Minor Commodity Groups	245
II-9 Value of Nonmanufactured Food Products Destined for Consumption in Farm Households or for Sale to Ultimate Consumers, 1869, 1879, 1889–1919	247
II-9a Value of Fruit, Nut, and Vegetable Crops Produced and Destined for Consumption in Farm Households or for Sale to Ultimate Consumers, 1869, 1879, 1889–1919	249
II-9b Value of Fluid Milk Produced and Destined for Consumption in Farm Households or for Sale to Ultimate Consumers, 1869, 1879, 1889–1919	250
II-9c Value of Eggs Produced and Destined for Consumption in Farm Households or for Sale to Ultimate Consumers, 1869, 1879, 1889–1919	251
II-9d Value of Fish Catch Destined for Sale to Ultimate Consumers, 1869, 1879, 1889–1919	252
II-10 Value of Nonmanufactured Fuels Destined for Sale to Ultimate Consumers, 1869, 1879, 1889–1919	262
II-11 Value of Nonmanufactured Construction Materials, 1869, 1879, 1889–1919	264
III-1 Classification of Import and Export Series by Minor Commodity Groups	275
III-2 Export Values before Application of Reduction Percentages, 1869, 1879, 1889–1919	280
IV-1 Price Indexes 1869, 1879, 1889–1939	290

CHART

1 Indexes of Output of Finished Commodities and Construction Materials in 1913 Prices and of Output in Manufacturing, Mining, and Agriculture, 1899–1919	3
2 Values, Major Groups of Finished Commodities Destined for Domestic Consumption, 1869, 1879, 1889–1939	10
3 Amplitude of Expansion and Contraction in Successive Specific Cycles between 1889 and 1939 Major Commodity Groups; Current and 1913 Prices, and Price Indexes	19

Preface

IN 1933, at the request of the Committee on Credit and Banking of the Social Science Research Council, the National Bureau began its research on the flow of commodities. Four volumes stemming from this project—*National Income and Capital Formation* (1937) and *Commodity Flow and Capital Formation,* Vol. One (1938), by Simon Kuznets; *Capital Consumption and Adjustment* (1938), by Solomon Fabricant; and *Outlay and Income in the United States* (1943), by Harold Barger—contain detailed estimates for the various segments of the flow of commodities and services since 1919. A fifth, *National Product since 1869,* by Simon Kuznets, gives decade estimates for broad categories back to 1869.

This volume too is an outgrowth of the original project. As first conceived, it was designed to be a comprehensive report on the flow of commodities since 1869, particular attention being given to basic estimates for years before 1919. But because of the War and other commitments, the scope of the study had to be narrowed considerably. Estimates of commodity output at producers' prices alone were completed. Since they constitute an integrated body of new data and provide a wealth of detail essential to a better understanding of how our economic system functions, it was decided to publish them separately.

Although the estimates in this volume have been integrated with those in Parts I and II of *Commodity Flow and Capital Formation,* Volume One, little has been done to revise those for the 1930's. The decision to concentrate on the earlier period was made in order to avoid duplicating the intensive work on the recent period in progress at the Department of Commerce. In 1940 it, with the cooperation of the National Bureau, took over the task of estimating currently the flow of commodities and services and of compiling official series back to 1919.

Final results of the Department of Commerce studies are not yet available, although articles summarizing preliminary estimates since 1929 for various segments of the major project have been published from time to time in the *Survey of Current Business.* When completed, the Department of Commerce estimates will supplant the estimates since 1919 published in this and other National Bureau volumes. In combination with those in this volume for the years before 1919 they will provide a continuous record covering three quarters of a century.

To Simon Kuznets who suggested this historical study I owe a debt beyond words. Throughout the preparation of this volume he has been an unfailing guide and source of inspiration. Without the intelligent help of David L. Rolbein it would have been much more difficult to collect and synthesize the extremely detailed statistics required for the estimates. As senior research assistant he showed comprehension and judgment far beyond the usual. I am also deeply indebted to Arthur F. Burns for his painstaking and highly constructive criticism of Part I and to Harold Barger, Solomon Fabricant, Frederick C. Mills, Carl Shoup, and N. I. Stone for many valuable suggestions. Finally, appreciation is due Martha Anderson for her skillful editing, and to H. Irving Forman for the charts.

Part I

Summary

THE ESTIMATES in this volume serve many purposes. To the economic historian they give threads of detail with which the pattern of development during the late 19th and early 20th century can be woven. To the practicing economist they give added insight into the workings of the commodity producing economy, particularly concerning its end products. And to the theorist they give empirical aid in testing hypotheses.

A few examples will illustrate the wide range of application. First, finished commodities constitute important components of gross national product.[1] Their total value, even as measured at prices received by producers rather than at final cost to users, accounts for at least one-third of gross national product—most of the commodity elements of consumer expenditures and of capital formation. And, as shown in Section C, these elements vary markedly over time.

Of course the conclusions that can be drawn from an analysis of the covered third are not necessarily applicable to gross national product as a whole. We need merely list the components *not* covered by the present estimates to make this clear: distributive costs, consumer services, new construction, changes in business inventories, changes in the foreign balance, and the product of government. The heterogeneity of this list, encompassing as it does segments that not only differ widely in cyclical reactions but may even have conflicting trends, is obvious.

Second, the totals of manufactured finished commodities and construction materials, in current prices, approximate the net values of manufactures.[2] As such they provide a continuous series on manufacturing activity unmarred by the varying amounts of duplication present in gross value totals.

Third, an index of the grand total of finished commodities and construction materials, in constant prices, corresponds to a composite index of industrial production for four basic industries: agriculture, mining, fishing, and manufactures. Since this composite probably reflects a coverage as comprehensive as any of the directly constructed annual produc-

[1] For the definition of finished commodities see Section A.
[2] See Part II, Section A 3b for a direct comparison with net values of manufactures.

tion indexes before 1919, it is of particular interest to compare it with them. Three indexes, running back to 1899 and representing the net output of manufactures, agriculture, and mining, can be found in recent publications of the National Bureau.[3] These have not been consolidated into one; but even in their separate form, they make possible a rough comparison.

Although it is not strictly equivalent to a composite production index for the three industries, the index of the grand total in constant prices is close enough to warrant the belief that it should be between the extremes of the directly constructed indexes.[4] We test this belief in Chart 1. In view of the conceptual differences as well as the crudities of estimation the correspondence is good. Not only are the longer movements fairly corroborative but even the shorter ones reveal few disturbing divergences.

The annual movements differ most in the years between 1914 and 1919. It is of course exceedingly difficult to measure production in times of violent change; and this difficulty alone probably accounts for the disagreement in these years. However, it is pertinent to point out with respect to the striking divergence of 1918–19 that the rise in our index is due chiefly to the consumer durable group and to the ship and boat component of the producer durable (Table I 3). These products are not covered adequately in the direct index of manufacturing output. In fact, the annual index Fabricant used to interpolate his comprehensive index for 1914 and 1919 is mainly one of industrial materials.[5]

These comments do not mean that our index is necessarily a good index of industrial production for the war years. At best it is an approxima-

---

[3] Solomon Fabricant, *The Output of Manufacturing Industries, 1899–1937* (1940), p. 44; Barger and Landsberg, *American Agriculture, 1899–1939: A Study of Output, Employment and Productivity* (1942), p. 20; Barger and Schurr, *The Mining Industries, 1899–1939: A Study of Output, Employment and Productivity* (1944), p. 14.

[4] The differences are numerous but hardly of a magnitude to invalidate a rough comparison. As mentioned above, our index includes the output of the fishing industry. In addition, it reflects the contribution of the trade, public utility, finance, etc., industries to the extent that their services are included in the value of finished commodities and construction materials measured at producers' prices. Conversely, our index excludes products that constitute materials and supplies for industries other than the covered four. For example, the output of containers and fuel used in retail trade is not reflected.

Finally, there are the differences that might be expected to stem from the statistical crudities inherent in all global estimates for the years before 1919.

[5] The relation between an index of industrial materials and of industrial production is puzzling. Apparently the two do not diverge appreciably except in times of violent change. See Geoffrey H. Moore, Production of Industrial Materials in World Wars I and II, National Bureau *Occasional Paper 18* (March 1944).

SUMMARY

tion, and its adequacy for this purpose can be judged only by studying our interpolating series (Part II, Sec. B2) and our price deflators (Part IV).

As a fourth illustration of the usefulness of the estimates, we may cite the detail given for consumer commodities. For the eight census years in

CHART 1

Indexes of Output of Finished Commodities and Construction Materials in 1913 Prices and of Output in Manufacturing, Mining, and Agriculture, 1899–1919

1899 : 100

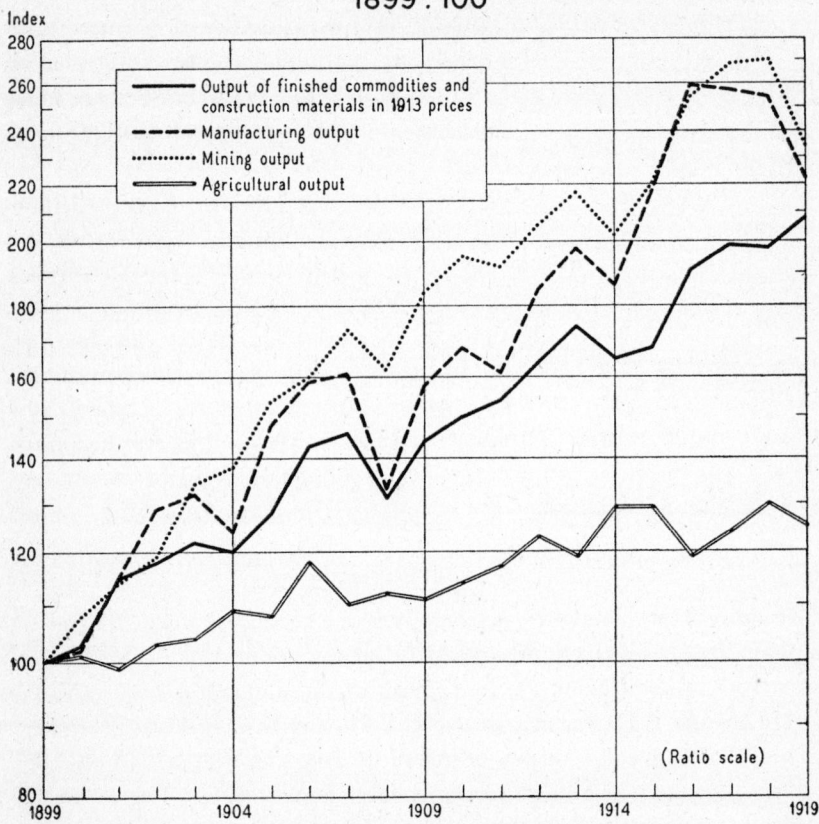

1869–1919, values of output are shown on a comparable basis for several hundred commodities (Table II 1). Annual estimates since 1889, in both current and constant prices, are shown for almost thirty distinct groups—ranging from food and clothing to automobiles and household appliances (Tables I 1 and I 3). Such detail is especially useful to students of welfare economics.

Finally, the series on producer durable commodities and construction materials provide data helpful in studying the longer run aspects of capital formation. For example, they make it possible to test some of the assumptions underlying the hypothesis of secular stagnation in the United States economy.[6]

As we use the concepts set forth by Simon Kuznets in *Commodity Flow and Capital Formation,* Volume One, it is necessary here only to review briefly the definitions implicit in them and to summarize the system of classification (Sec. A). In Section B the estimates of the total values of domestic output and of the amounts destined for domestic consumption, in both current and constant prices, are outlined with cross-references to the more elaborate discussion in Parts II, III, and IV. Because of the newness of the estimates the discussion embodies a complete description of their derivation.

In Section C the movements over time of the values of finished commodities destined for domestic consumption together with those of the corresponding price indexes are investigated. Attention is concentrated on the totals and on four major groups: consumer perishable, semidurable, and durable, and producer durable. The longer run developments, since 1879, are analyzed by examining changes in decade averages; the shorter run, since 1889, by examining simple measures of cyclical amplitude and of relative conformity to business cycles. Our conclusions—which emphasize the importance, for economic analysis, of commodity classification by durability—are summarized in Section C5.

A DEFINITIONS

The concepts developed by Kuznets embrace a comprehensive scheme of commodity classification designed to differentiate end or finished products from others (Table 1). End products, those under A I 1a, A II 1a, A III 1a, and B III 1a, may be produced in any basic industry: farming, fishing, mining, construction, or manufacturing. They embrace both consumer commodities and producer durable commodities. The latter are defined as machinery and equipment intended for multiple use in production and with an average life of three or more years.

The term 'end' or 'finished' does not apply solely to the degree of processing; it reflects also the use to which an article is put. Flour, for instance, is classified as finished if it is to be consumed by households, by

---

[6] For example, see George Terborgh, *The Bogy of Economic Maturity* (Machinery and Allied Products Institute, Chicago, 1945).

TABLE 1
Classification of Commodities

A Consumer

I PERISHABLE	II SEMIDURABLE	III DURABLE

1 At Destination
  a Finished: bread, coal used by households, etc., in hands of households
	1 At Destination
	  a Finished: shoes, clothing, etc., in hands of households
		1 At Destination
		  a All finished: passenger cars, jewelry, furniture in hands of households
		
		  aa Residential building
		  bb All other

b Unfinished: none	b Unfinished: none	b Unfinished: none

2 In Circulation
  a Finished: same as under A I 1a, but in hands of producers & distributors
	2 In Circulation
	  a Finished: same as under A II 1a, but in hands of producers & distributors
		2 In Circulation
		  a Finished: same as under A III 1a, but in hands of producers & distributors

b Unfinished: raw materials, fuels, supplies used for production, transportation, & distribution yielding A I 1a	b Unfinished: raw materials, fuels, supplies used for production, transportation & distribution yielding A II 1a	b Unfinished: raw materials, fuels, supplies used for production, transportation & distribution yielding A III 1a

B Producer

I PERISHABLE	II SEMIDURABLE	III DURABLE

None	None	1 At Destination
		  a Finished: industrial, farm machinery, buildings, trucks, etc., in hands of business units who will use them
		  b Unfinished: none
		2 In Circulation
		  a Finished: same as under B II 1a, but in hands of producers & distributors
		  b Unfinished: raw materials, fuels, supplies, etc., used for production, transportation & distribution, yielding B III 1a

DURABLE: Commodities that, without marked change and retaining their essential physical identity, are ordinarily employed in their ultimate use three or more years. Examples: a building, a steam engine or dynamo; an automobile or truck; a bed, table, or chair.

NONDURABLE: Commodities that, without marked change and retaining their essential physical identity, are ordinarily employed in their ultimate use less than three years. Nondurable commodities are further classified into:

SEMIDURABLE: Commodities that, without marked change and retaining their essential physical identity, are ordinarily employed in their ultimate use from six months to three years. Examples: automobile tires, clothing, shoes.

PERISHABLE: Commodities that, without marked change and retaining their essential physical identity, are ordinarily employed in their ultimate use less than six months. Examples: bread, cigarettes.

AT DESTINATION: Commodities that have reached either the household or the producing units where they will find their ultimate use. Examples: bread in the household larder; truck in the hands of the firm using it.

IN CIRCULATION: Commodities that are still in process of production, transportation, or distribution and have not yet reached the units where they will find their ultimate use. Examples: clothing in department store; coal in factory bin.

FINISHED: Commodities, whether durable or nondurable, in the form in which, without significant alteration, they are employed in their ultimate use. Examples: shoes, furniture, machinery.

UNFINISHED: Commodities that, whether ultimately durable or nondurable, are not yet in the form in which they are employed in their ultimate use. Examples: raw cotton; structural steel beams.

CONSUMER: Commodities, whether finished or unfinished, that when finished and at their destination, are used by households or large ultimate consuming units. Examples: flour, bread, raw wool, clothing.

PRODUCER: Commodities, whether finished or unfinished, that, when finished and at their destination, are used by business agencies in the production process. Examples: industrial machinery; steel used therein.

Source: *Commodity Flow and Capital Formation,* Vol. One, p. 6. Minor changes have been made.

institutions, by service establishments such as hotels, or by governmental agencies;[7] it is classified as unfinished if it is to be consumed by a factory engaged in making bread or other products for which flour is a raw material. A barrel of apples destined for home consumption is included in our estimates of finished commodities, whereas a similar barrel of apples shipped to a commercial bakery is excluded.

With these definitions as a guide, the data were classified by minor commodity groups (Table I 1). The criteria for grouping were durability and budgetary use. Because of its significance in economic analysis, grouping by durability was adopted as the basic classification.

Perishable commodities include those usually lasting less than six months; semidurable those usually lasting from six months to three years;

[7] Ideally, commodities going to institutional and service purchasers and governmental agencies should be treated separately; but the data preclude segregation or even a satisfactory estimate of the amounts involved. In most years the output of finished commodities destined for these groups has been small, but during the 1914–18 War purchases by the federal government alone of food, clothing, and other supplies were substantial. That the repercussions of these purchases were felt also in later years is indicated by government receipts of more than a billion dollars from the resale of commodities during the early 1920's. This was a realization of approximately 50 percent on the original cost (J. M. Clark, *The Costs of the World War to the American People;* Yale University Press, 1931, p. 54). Although these resales are not covered in our estimates, they are reflected indirectly in the composition of output during the early 1920's.

SUMMARY

3.2 percent.[12] The difference reflects the long term rise in prices. But even the lower rate means a doubling of output every 22 years. Meanwhile, population was growing at an average annual rate of only 1.3 percent; it rose less than twofold in the entire 60 years.

The rates of growth for both durable groups considerably exceed those for the nondurable, and that for the consumer durable is highest of all (Table 2). Growing at an average annual rate of 5 percent, consumer

TABLE 2

Value of Finished Commodities destined for Domestic Consumption Major Commodity Groups, Producers' Current and 1913 Prices

Average Annual Rate of Growth, 1879–1939, and Percentage Shares, 1879, 1939, 1879–1888, and 1929–1938*

	PERISH-ABLE	CONSUMER SEMI-DURABLE	DURABLE	PRODUCER DURABLE	ALL FINISHED COMMODITIES
	\multicolumn{5}{c}{VALUE IN PRODUCERS' CURRENT PRICES}				
Av. annual rate of growth, 1879–1939	+3.7	+3.7	+5.0	+4.3	+4.0
Percentage Shares					
1879	58.0	24.1	8.8	9.1	100.0
1939	51.8	18.4	16.0	13.8	100.0
Absolute change	−6.2	−5.7	+7.2	+4.7	
Average 1879–88*	57.8	22.6	9.3	10.4	100.0
Average 1929–38	54.1	18.6	14.9	12.4	100.0
Absolute change	−3.6	−4.0	+5.6	+2.0	
	\multicolumn{5}{c}{VALUE IN PRODUCERS' 1913 PRICES}				
Av. annual rate of growth, 1879–1939	+2.9	+2.9	+4.7	+3.6	+3.2
Percentage Shares					
1879	60.5	21.3	9.6	8.6	100.0
1939	52.8	16.0	18.1	13.1	100.0
Absolute change	−7.7	−5.3	+8.5	+4.5	
Average 1879–88*	59.6	20.4	10.0	10.0	100.0
Average 1929–38	52.2	17.9	17.5	12.4	100.0
Absolute change	−7.4	−2.5	+7.5	+2.4	

* The averages for 1879–88 in this and certain subsequent tables are based on rough interpolations of the 1879 and 1889 Census year estimates. The interpolations are not believed accurate enough to warrant their presentation as annual series in Tables I 1 and I 3.

durable commodities in current prices gained more than one-third again as rapidly as nondurable.

By removing the long term price rises of some 10 to 20 percent, measurement in 1913 prices reduces the rates of growth of all groups. Nevertheless, since the calculated price indexes for durable commodities rose less than those for nondurable, the intergroup differences are bigger. The 4.7 percent rate for consumer durable commodities in 1913 prices, which

[12] Average annual rates of growth were computed by using Glovers' method to fit exponential curves to the original data.

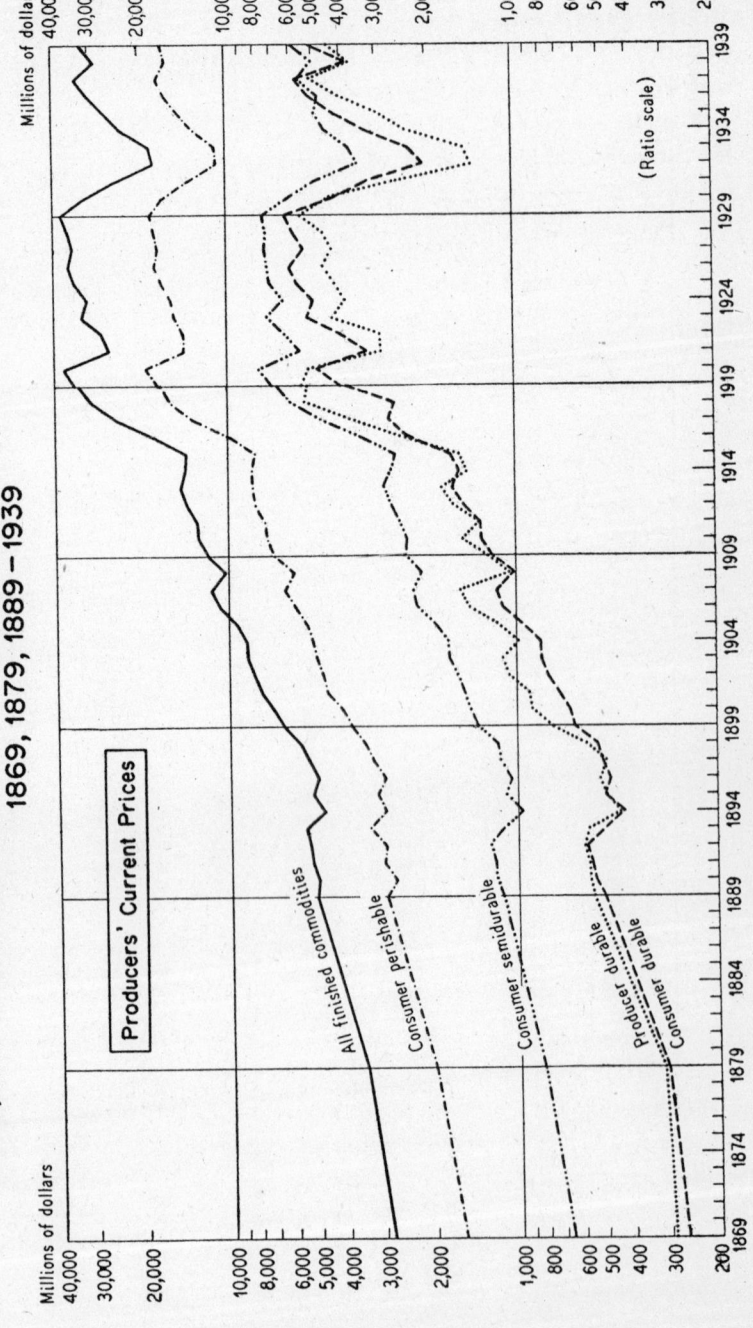

CHART 2

Values, Major Groups of Finished Commodities Destined for Domestic Consumption
1869, 1879, 1889-1939

SUMMARY

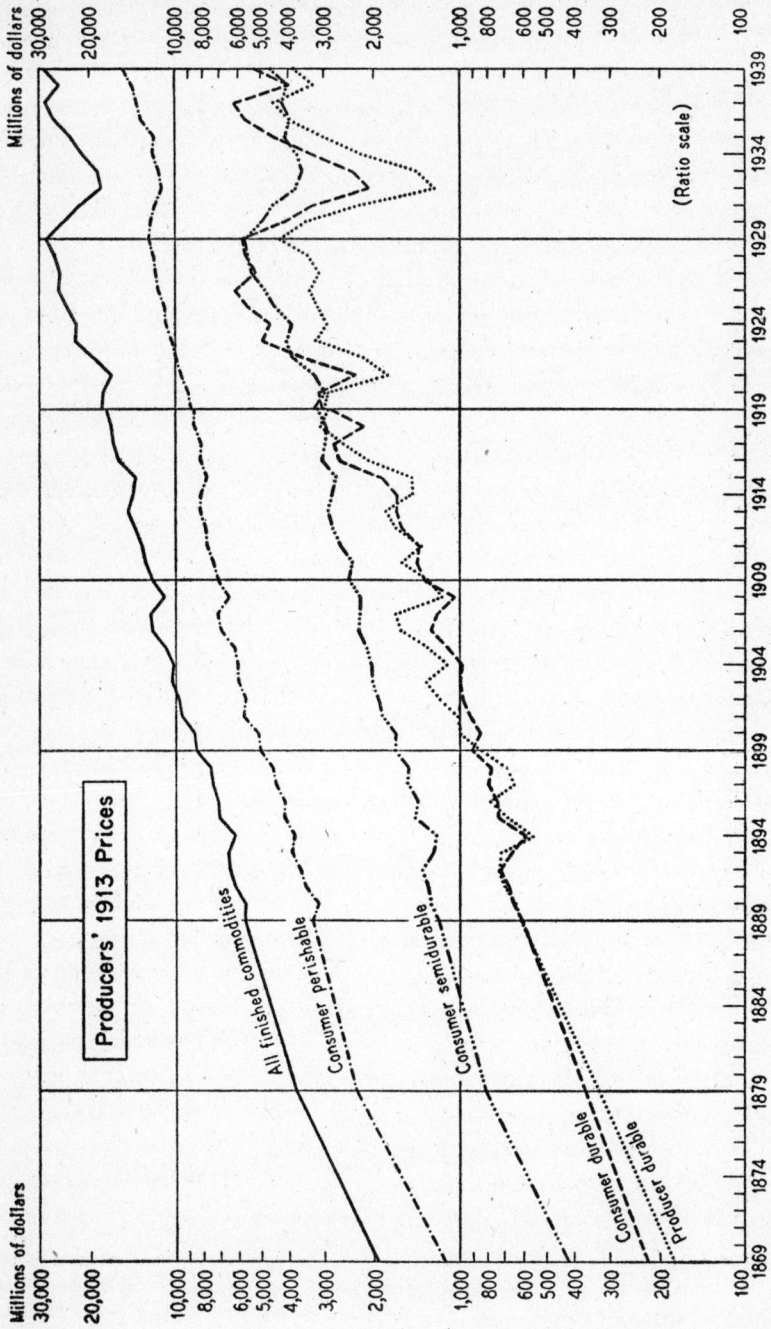

is only slightly below that in current prices, is almost two-thirds higher than the rates for the nondurable groups, which fall far short of the corresponding rates in current prices.

The higher rates of growth for the durable groups mean that these categories increased in relative importance during the six decades. In current prices the share of consumer durable commodities alone rose from 8.8 percent of all finished commodities in 1879 to 16.0 percent in 1939; in 1913 prices from 9.6 to 18.1 percent; that of producer durable rose from 9.1 to 13.8 and 8.6 to 13.1 percent in current and 1913 prices respectively.[13] Similar shifts are observed when the averages for 1879-88 are compared with those for 1929-38 although, since the interval 1929-38 includes the great depression, they are somewhat less pronounced.

From these shifts in composition it may be inferred that the structure of the commodity producing economy changed considerably. Some understanding of the changes is gained through study of the more detailed commodity classification in Table 3.

It is apparent immediately that most of the expansion in total consumer durable commodities was due not to older products but to three new classes: automotive equipment, household electrical appliances, and radios. To some extent these new classes superseded older ones—motor vehicles and parts taking the place of horse-drawn vehicles; electrical appliances, of nonelectrical; radios, of musical instruments and phonographs. But their values soon exceeded the peaks reached by the older classes. The value of passenger cars and replacement parts alone averaged more than $2.6 billion or almost 8 percent of the average for all finished commodities in 1929 and 1939. The contribution of electrical appliances and radios was smaller; but even they averaged $535 million in 1929 and 1939, or about 1.5 percent of the average value for all commodities.

In addition to altering the composition of the consumer durable group, the growth of the automotive industry was reflected in the other major commodity groups: in the perishable group, by the pronounced rise in manufactured petroleum products, in the semidurable, by that in tires and tubes, and in the producer durable group, by the more obvious increases in trucks and tractors and by the partly concealed increases in the machinery group that must have resulted from the demand for special automotive machinery and tools. No automotive products were made in 1879 and

[13] If all groups were measured at final cost to users, the share of the producer durable group would be smaller since transportation charges and distributive mark-ups are relatively less important than for other groups. Measurement at producers' prices instead of final cost would thus seem to overstate slightly the share of producer durable commodities. But the effects on the relative movements of the various groups are probably very small.

TABLE 3
Value of Finished Commodities
Averages of 1879 and 1889, 1929 and 1939
Major and Minor Commodity Groups, Producers' Current Prices

	MILLIONS OF DOLLARS		PERCENTAGE SHARES	
	1879 AND 1889	1929 AND 1939	1879 AND 1889	1929 AND 1939
Consumer Perishable, Total	2,450.9	17,419.8	57.52	50.04
1a Food & kindred prod., mfd.	1,198.6	9,279.8	28.13	26.66
1b Food & kindred prod., nonmfd.	836.6	3,770.6	19.63	10.83
2 Cigars, cigarettes, & tobacco	161.1	1,283.8	3.78	3.69
3 Drug, toilet, & household preparations	61.0	934.0	1.43	2.68
4 Magazines, newspapers, stationery & supplies & misc. paper prod.	77.7	641.2	1.82	1.84
5a Fuel & lighting prod., mfd.	49.6	1,219.6	1.16	3.50
5b Nonmfd. fuels	66.4	290.8	1.56	0.84
Consumer Semidurable, Total	980.6	6,662.9	23.01	19.14
6 Dry goods & notions	272.4	766.2	6.39	2.20
7 Clothing & personal furnishings	459.5	3,993.4	10.78	11.47
8 Shoes & other footwear	204.9	929.2	4.81	2.67
9 Housefurnishings (semidurable)	24.2	403.0	0.57	1.16
10 Toys, games, & sporting goods	19.6	216.4	0.46	0.62
11 Tires & tubes		354.6		1.02
Consumer Durable, Total	401.8	5,704.0	9.43	16.39
12 Household furniture	79.3	531.6	1.86	1.53
13a Heating & cooking apparatus & household appliances, except electrical	31.0	317.5	0.73	0.91
13b Electrical household appliances & supplies		255.2		0.73
13c Radios		280.2		0.80
14 Housefurnishings (durable)	77.2	625.8	1.81	1.80
15 China & household utensils	38.8	255.5	0.91	0.73
16 Musical instruments	21.2	79.9	0.50	0.23
17 Jewelry, silverware, clocks & watches	58.9	332.8	1.38	0.96
18 Printing & publishing: books	26.8	169.9	0.63	0.49
19 Luggage	8.9	55.2	0.21	0.16
20a Passenger vehicles, motor		2,149.9		6.18
20b Motor vehicle accessories		490.4		1.41
20c Passenger vehicles, horse-drawn, & accessories	44.6	*	1.05	*
21 Motorcycles & bicycles	1.0	20.8	0.02	0.06
22 Pleasure craft	1.2	22.7	0.03	0.07
23 Ophthalmic products & artificial limbs	1.6	74.4	0.04	0.21
24 Monuments & tombstones	11.4	42.2	0.27	0.12
Producer Durable, Total	427.8	5,025.3	10.04	14.44
25a Industrial machinery & equipment	141.6	1,802.8	3.32	5.18
25b Tractors		140.1		0.40
26 Electrical equipment, industrial & commercial	7.5	789.0	0.18	2.27
27 Farm equipment	75.6	465.9	1.77	1.34
28 Office & store machinery & equipment	5.9	194.4	0.14	0.56
29 Office & store furniture & fixtures	20.8	235.7	0.49	0.68
30 Locomotives & rr. cars	61.8	199.9	1.45	0.57
31 Ships & boats	22.0	158.8	0.52	0.46
32a Business vehicles, motor		471.3		1.35
32b Business vehicles, horse-drawn	23.2	*	0.54	*
33 Aircraft		73.4		0.21
34 Professional & scientific equipment	2.2	80.2	0.05	0.23
35 Carpenters & mechanics' tools	17.1	102.0	0.40	0.29
36 Misc. subsidiary durable equipment	50.2	311.8	1.18	0.90
All Finished Commodities	4,261.0	34,812.0	100.00	100.00

* Included with farm equipment.

1889; their average value for 1929 and 1939 constituted at least 15 percent of the average for all finished commodities.

This tremendous growth takes on added significance when it is recalled that passenger cars and the larger electrical appliances are commodities that can be sold in large quantities only when purchasing power and the standard of living are relatively high. Moreover, to the degree that their purchase can be readily postponed, their production is subject to rather violent cyclical fluctuations. If they make up a large segment of all finished commodities, the fluctuations in their output can have serious repercussions on manufacturing and in turn on the economy as a whole.

Other intragroup shifts also influenced the major groups during the long period. In recent decades the relatively greater consumption of packaged foods and the marked rise in drug, toilet, and household preparations all helped to maintain the share of the perishable group. In the semidurable group the increased production of ready-made clothing accounts for the relative stability of the clothing group and for the decline in the relative standing of dry goods. The share of the shoe group declined; while that of light housefurnishings increased. Within the consumer durable group many of the old-line commodities at least held their own.

Notable in the producer durable group is the long term rise in the output of electrical equipment. From an average of $7 million for 1879 and 1889, or less than .2 percent of the average for all finished commodities, it rose to an average of almost $800 million for 1929 and 1939, or 2.3 percent of the average total. This rise, together with the increases in machinery and trucks and tractors, more than balanced a sizable decline in the relative importance of railroad equipment and is chiefly responsible for the larger share of the producer durable group in recent decades.

2 Variations from Decade to Decade

In the preceding section we emphasized the longer run changes in the pattern of output by making comparisons at the beginning and end of the period covered by the estimates. Here we show the development of these changes through the decades by examining the inter-decade variations.

Ten-year averages are long enough to dampen cyclical and random fluctuations yet short enough to reveal the relative persistence of trends. True, the end years of the decades may be in different phases of business cycles, thereby failing to minimize the influence of cyclical fluctuations. But ex-

SUMMARY

perimentation with other time units indicated movements similar to those in the decade averages.[14]

a *Variations in absolute figures*

For the total value of finished commodities in current prices, the change in the decade averages is less than 14 percent from 1879–88 to 1889–98, rises sharply during the following three decades to a high of 96 percent from 1909–18 to 1919–28, then turns decidedly negative from 1919–28 to 1929–38 (Table 4).

TABLE 4
Value of Finished Commodities and Price Indexes
Major Commodity Groups, Producers' Current and 1913 Prices, and Price Indexes
Percentage Change in Decade Averages

	1879–88 TO 1889–98	1889–98 TO 1899–1908	1899–1908 TO 1909–18	1909–18 TO 1919–28*	1919–28 TO 1929–38	MEAN CHANGE	AVERAGE DEVIATION
VALUE IN PRODUCERS' CURRENT PRICES							
Consumer Perishable	14.5	68.4	82.2	77.0	−11.0	46.2	35.6
Consumer Semidurable	9.6	58.9	81.7	111.9	−27.4	46.9	44.7
Consumer Durable	19.4	70.8	108.7	174.4	−19.0	70.9	56.6
Producer Durable	11.9	106.0	103.4	92.0	−21.7	58.3	50.6
All Finished Commodities	13.6	70.4	87.3	96.5	−17.1	50.1	41.5
PRICE INDEXES							
Consumer Perishable	−12.5	6.2	38.4	36.8	−25.9	8.6	23.2
Consumer Semidurable	−17.9	4.7	31.6	48.5	−32.5	6.9	26.5
Consumer Durable	−16.4	14.3	16.0	20.5	−16.9	3.5	16.1
Producer Durable	−17.9	13.2	26.8	31.0	−24.2	5.8	21.5
All Finished Commodities	−14.7	6.1	33.8	34.0	−25.6	6.7	21.7
VALUE IN PRODUCERS' 1913 PRICES							
Consumer Perishable	31.6	56.6	31.1	31.8	18.6	33.9	9.0
Consumer Semidurable	33.8	49.8	37.5	49.9	2.7	34.7	13.2
Consumer Durable	41.9	47.1	80.6	138.4	−6.1	60.4	39.3
Producer Durable	36.8	81.9	51.0	56.9	1.8	45.7	21.1
All Finished Commodities	33.6	56.7	39.7	52.2	8.4	38.1	13.7

* The changes from the averages for 1909–18 to those for 1919–28 are slightly distorted because the data for the years before 1919 are not strictly comparable with those after 1919. However, the distortions are too small to affect conclusions drawn from comparing the changes in the decade averages.

[14] E.g., when we used peak years of business cycles as terminal years and stayed as close to decades as possible, we found that the periods varied from 8 to 12 years in length. The movements of the averages for these periods resembled those of the averages for the decades upon which this discussion is based.

Likewise, a more complex analysis based on overlapping decades also gives similar results (see *Occasional Paper 3*, pp. 14–25).

Since the changes in the decade averages for the price index of all finished commodities more or less parallel those of the total in current prices, we must expect fluctuations in the latter to reflect fluctuations in the price index. The extent to which they do during the period as a whole is indicated by comparing the mean average decade changes. For the total in current prices the mean average decade change is 50 percent, for the total in 1913 prices, 38 percent.

The changes in the decade averages for the four major commodity groups show both similarities and differences in behavior. There is marked correspondence between the patterns of commodity values and of the price indexes. The sustained rises through the first four decades as well as the sharp declines from 1919-28 to 1929-38 for each group in current prices are paralleled by the movements in the decade changes of the price indexes. Consequently, for all groups the decade changes for the values in 1913 prices fluctuate less than do those for the values in current prices.

But the degree to which the movements in the price indexes affect the series in current prices differs among the groups. The effect is smallest on the consumer durable group. In fact, despite the narrower fluctuations in the decade changes for each group, the intergroup variability for the series in 1913 prices is wider than for the series in current prices. While the order of increasing variability (perishable, semidurable, producer durable, consumer durable) is the same for the values in both current and 1913 prices, the average deviations in the latter range from 9 to 39 percent; from 36 to 57 percent in the former.

b *Variations in shares*

The decade variations in the percentage shares are substantial for the shares in current prices and even more so for the shares in 1913 prices (Table 5). However, in interpreting the variations, the interdependence of the percentages must not be forgotten. We summarize the major movements in the shares of all groups, but we believe that the greater part of what may be termed the generating changes has its source in the durable, i.e., that variations in the shares of the nondurable reflect primarily fluctuations in the values of durable commodities destined for domestic consumption.

In current prices the decade average share of the perishable group hovers around 58 percent through 1899-1908. Sizable declines then take place, especially from 1909-18 to 1919-28. And although the average share of perishable commodities recovers somewhat in the final decade, which includes years of severe depression, it does not return to the 1909–18 level. In 1913 prices the long term relative decline in the perishable share is accentuated; from an average of 60 percent for 1879–88, it falls almost continuously to 48 percent for 1919–28.

TABLE 5

Value of Finished Commodities
Major Commodity Groups, Producers' Current and 1913 Prices
Percentage Shares, Averages for Successive Decades

	1879–1888	1889–1898	1899–1908	1909–1918	1919–1928	1929–1938
		VALUE IN PRODUCERS' CURRENT PRICES				
Percentage Shares						
Consumer Perishable	57.8	58.2	57.5	56.0	50.4	54.1
Consumer Semidurable	22.6	21.8	20.3	19.7	21.2	18.6
Consumer Durable	9.3	9.8	9.8	10.9	15.2	14.9
Producer Durable	10.4	10.2	12.4	13.4	13.1	12.4
Absolute Changes from Decade to Decade						
Consumer Perishable		+0.4	−0.7	−1.5	−5.6	+3.7
Consumer Semidurable		−0.8	−1.5	−0.6	+1.5	−2.6
Consumer Durable		+0.5	0.0	+1.1	+4.3	−0.3
Producer Durable		−0.2	+2.2	+1.0	−0.3	−0.7
		VALUE IN PRODUCERS' 1913 PRICES				
Percentage Shares						
Consumer Perishable	59.6	58.7	58.7	55.1	47.7	52.2
Consumer Semidurable	20.4	20.4	19.5	19.2	18.9	17.9
Consumer Durable	10.0	10.6	10.0	12.9	20.2	17.5
Producer Durable	10.0	10.3	11.9	12.8	13.2	12.4
Absolute Changes from Decade to Decade						
Consumer Perishable		−0.9	0.0	−3.6	−7.4	+4.5
Consumer Semidurable		0.0	−0.9	−0.3	−0.3	−1.0
Consumer Durable		+0.6	−0.6	+2.9	+7.3	−2.7
Producer Durable		+0.3	+1.6	+0.9	+0.4	−0.8

The pattern of the average share of the semidurable group is less clear. In current prices it declines slightly and without interruption through 1909–18, rises during the next decade, then declines further. In 1913 prices it declines moderately but continuously.

The more striking shifts in composition are the larger shares of the durable groups, especially consumer durable. In current prices its average share rises from less than 10 percent in the early decades to more than 15 in the later. But this substantial gain is not evenly distributed: the greater part occurs in the single decade 1919–28. For 1909–18 the average share is 11 percent; for 1919–28, 15. Moreover, despite the severe curtailment in production during the depression of the 1930's, the share of the consumer durable group continues to average about 15 percent of total output during 1929–38.

In 1913 prices the rise in the share of the consumer durable group is even more marked. After hovering around 10 percent through 1899–1908, it increases to 13 for 1909–18, and to 20 for 1919–28. Even though the ensuing decline is more severe than that in the current price shares, the group still averages 17.5 percent during 1929–38.

In all six decades the average percentage shares in 1913 prices are higher than those in current prices. The difference is especially marked for 1919–28 when consumer durable commodities constitute one-fifth of the total in 1913 prices, but less than one-sixth of the total in current prices.

The average share of producer durable commodities in current prices declines very slightly from 1879–88 to 1889–98. It then increases fairly sharply during the next two decades, reaching a peak above 13 percent in the interval that included the first World War. Following 1909–18, successive declines bring it to 12 percent by 1929–38. Correction for price changes has little effect either on the size or on the movements of the shares. However, in 1913 prices the peak share is attained not during 1909–18 but during 1919–28.

To summarize: until 1919–28 the total of finished commodities destined for domestic consumption does not change appreciably in composition. The concentration of the gain in the average share of durable goods in this decade emphasizes how much large scale production of automobiles and electrical appliances affected the economy. The decade averages for 1929–38 reveal the first major interruption to the long term rise in the relative importance of durable commodities. Whether this interruption was a consequence of the extraordinary acceleration in the 1920's or the beginning of a period in which the durable groups will no longer better their position—war and immediate postwar activity excepted—cannot now be determined. The longer run comparisons, however, do suggest that the experience of the 1930's was a distinct departure from the trend to that time.

3 Behavior during Business Cycles

How did the output series and the price indexes behave during business cycles? What were the fluctuations and how well did the series conform to cyclical turning points? Were there any long term tendencies in the amplitude of fluctuation or in the apparent conformity?

a *Variations in amplitude*

To calculate amplitude we first marked off the trough and peak years for

SUMMARY

CHART 3
Amplitude of Expansion and Contraction in Successive Specific Cycles between 1889 and 1939
Major Commodity Groups; Current and 1913 Prices, and Price Indexes

A VALUES IN CURRENT PRICES

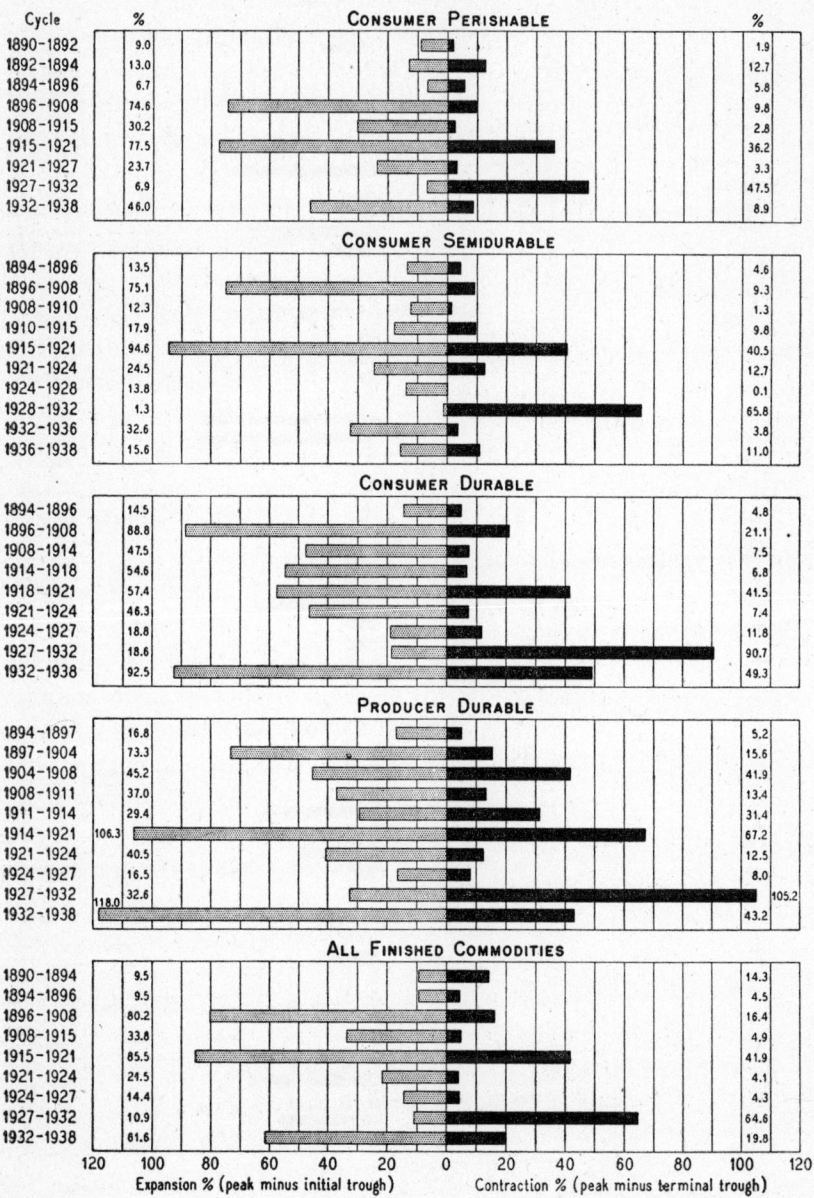

CHART 3 *(Continued)*

Amplitude of Expansion and Contraction in Successive Specific Cycles between 1889 and 1939
Major Commodity Groups; Current and 1913 Prices, and Price Indexes

B PRICE INDEXES

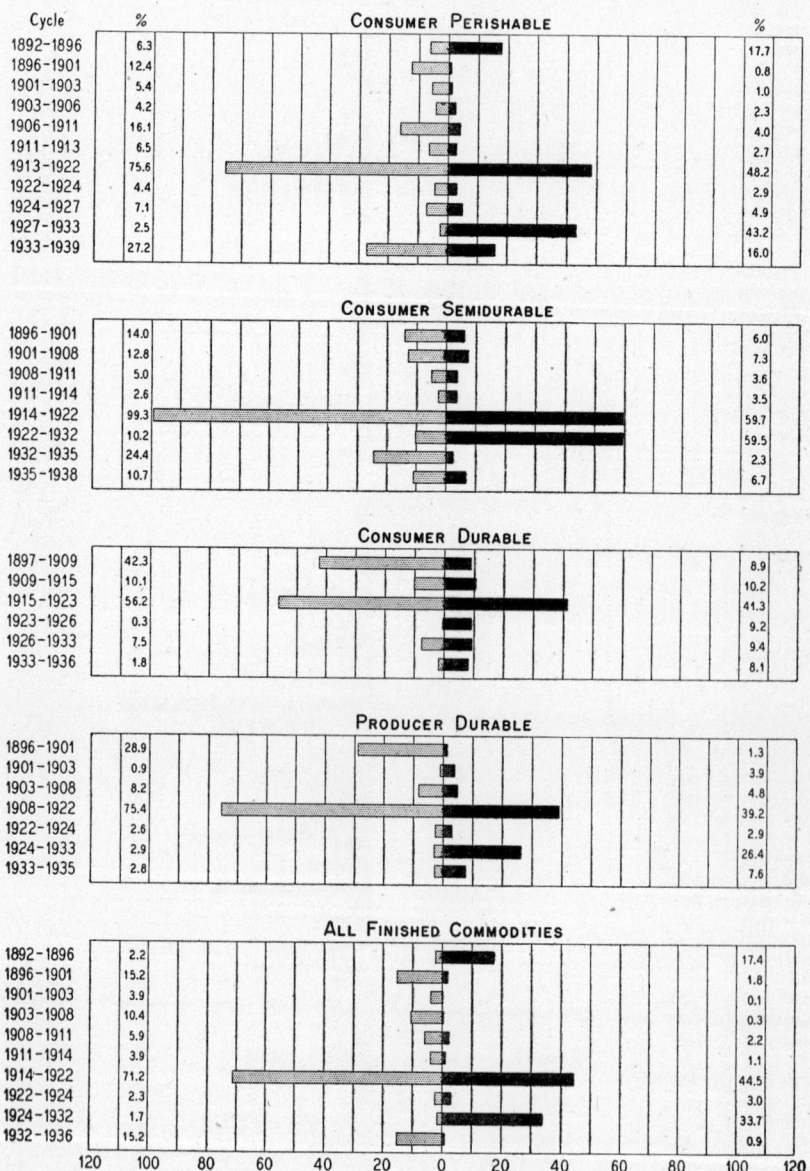

CHART 3 *(Concluded)*
Amplitude of Expansion and Contraction in Successive Specific Cycles between 1889 and 1939
Major Commodity Groups; Current and 1913 Prices, and Price Indexes

C VALUES IN 1913 PRICES

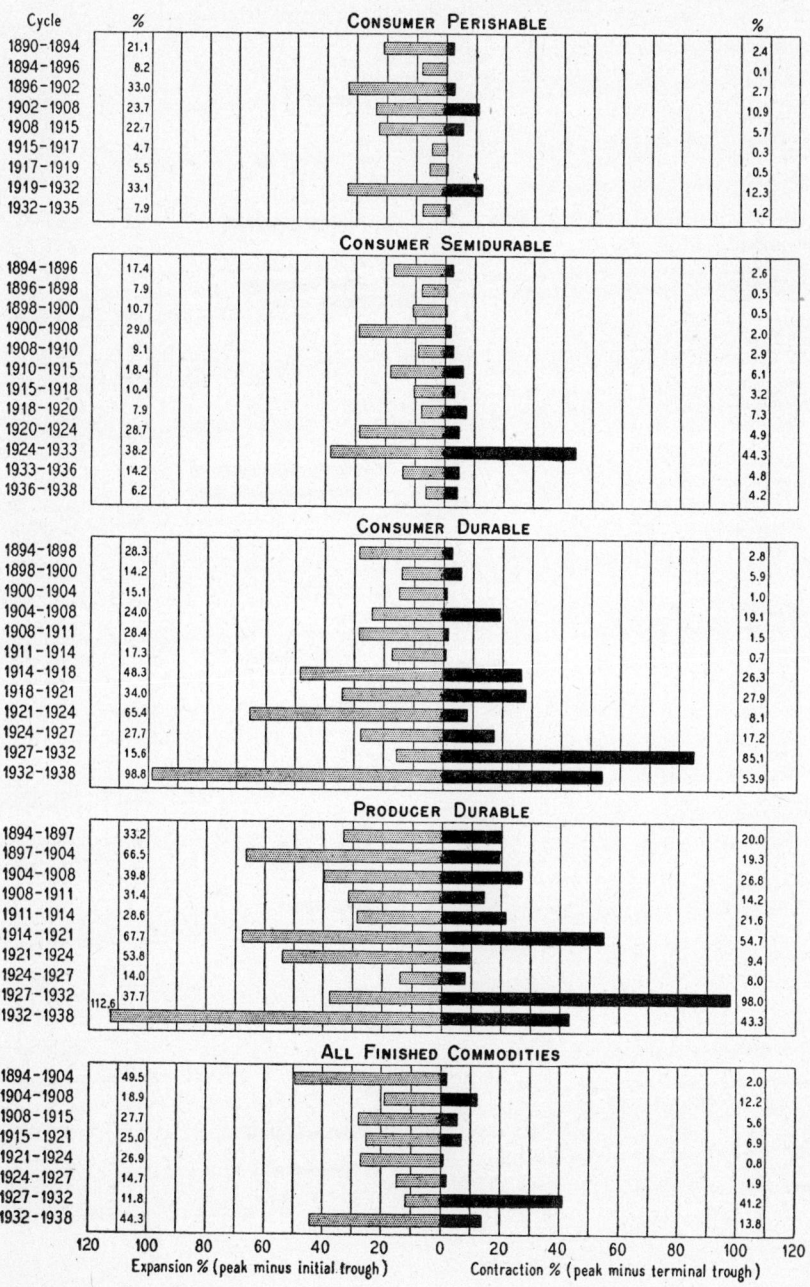

each series. Then, measuring from trough to trough, we expressed the values at the initial trough, the peak, and the terminal trough of each cycle as percentages of the average value for the entire cycle.[15] The differences among these percentages, or specific cycle relatives, indicate the relative rises and falls during expansions and contractions as well as the total swings from trough to trough.

The cyclical behavior of the commodity series and price indexes, as revealed by the specific cycle relatives (Chart 3), confirms the conclusion obvious from our discussion of the broader changes: that as a whole the period is characterized essentially by expanding output and rising prices. For the total values in current and 1913 prices and for the price index of all finished commodities, the differences between the average standing at the trough and peak years of most cycles show that the increases from initial trough to peak are much greater than the declines from peak to terminal trough. The major exceptions, of course, are in the cycles that include the great contraction of the 'thirties. This contraction is responsible for the decisive interruption in that decade to the long term rises.

The main reason for the markedly greater increases from initial troughs to peaks in nearly all cycles prior to the 'thirties is obvious. Expansions usually lasted longer than contractions. If the relative rises and falls are computed on a per year basis, the differences narrow considerably. In fact, there are fairly numerous instances of a higher *rate* of contraction.

Comparison of the average measures of amplitude for the cycles preceding and following World War I (Table 6) suggests certain long run tendencies. The average total swings for all finished commodities in current prices and for the corresponding price index are decidedly higher in the later cycles. But the averages for all finished commodities in 1913 prices differ only negligibly—the effect of removing the influence of the variations in the price index.

More striking than the changes in total swings are those in the average rises and falls. Since changes in the rises and falls can offset one another,

---

[15] This is a simplified description. For example, to avoid overweighting the trough years, the value for each trough year is given one-half weight, for when cycles are measured from trough to trough the terminal trough of one cycle is always the initial trough of the succeeding cycle. For a complete description see *Measuring Business Cycles* by Arthur F. Burns and Wesley C. Mitchell (National Bureau of Economic Research, 1946).

In interpreting our results the reader should keep in mind the limitations of annual series for measuring cyclical behavior. Mild contractions, for example, are likely to be concealed when the secular trend is rising. Moreover, since annual series average and cancel fluctuations within each year, the amplitude tends to be less than in monthly or quarterly data.

TABLE 6

Value of Finished Commodities and Price Indexes
Major Commodity Groups, Producers' Current and 1913 Prices
Averages of Specific Cycle Relatives for Cycles before and after World War I*

	PREWAR CYCLES AVERAGE				POSTWAR CYCLES AVERAGE			
	No.	Rise	Fall	Total Swing	No.	Rise	Fall	Total Swing
		VALUE IN PRODUCERS' CURRENT PRICES						
Consumer Perishable	5	26.7	6.6	33.3	3	25.5	19.9	45.4
Consumer Semidurable	4	29.7	6.2	35.9	5	17.5	18.7	36.2
Consumer Durable	3	50.3	11.1	61.4	4	44.0	39.8	83.8
Producer Durable	5	42.3	21.5	63.8	4	51.9	42.2	94.1
All Finished Commodities	4	33.3	10.0	43.3	4	27.1	23.2	50.3
		PRICE INDEXES						
Consumer Perishable	6	8.4	4.8	13.2	4	10.2	16.8	27.0
Consumer Semidurable	4	8.6	5.1	13.7	3	15.1	22.8	37.9
Consumer Durable	2	26.2	9.6	35.8	3	3.2	8.9	12.1
Producer Durable	3	12.7	3.3	16.0	3	2.8	12.3	15.1
All Finished Commodities	6	6.9	3.8	10.7	3	6.4	12.5	18.9
		VALUE IN PRODUCERS' 1913 PRICES						
Consumer Perishable	5	21.7	4.4	26.1	2	20.4	6.8	27.2
Consumer Semidurable	6	15.4	2.4	17.8	4	21.8	14.6	36.4
Consumer Durable	6	21.2	5.2	26.4	4	51.9	41.1	93.0
Producer Durable	5	39.9	20.4	60.3	4	54.5	39.7	94.2
All Finished Commodities	3	32.0	6.6	38.6	4	24.4	14.4	38.8

* The war year cycles are excluded from the averages.

there can be large differences in the expansions and contractions measured separately even when total swings are much the same.

The averages in Table 6 well illustrate this point. Average rises in the later cycles are smaller than in the earlier; average falls are much bigger. Indeed, the differences between the average falls are far greater than those between the total swings.

The striking increases in average contractions—from 12 to 23 percent for all finished commodities in current prices, from 4 to 12 percent in the corresponding price index, and from 7 to 14 percent for the total measured in 1913 prices—are due to the inclusion of the severe decline of 1929–32 in the postwar cycle averages. When that contraction is excluded, the apparent tendency toward progressively severe contractions in the later cycles disappears (Chart 3).[16]

In fact, if the contractions in the later cycles are averaged excluding the 1929–32 decline, the averages are slightly smaller than those of the earlier cycles for the commodity totals and considerably smaller for the

---

[16] However, even the continuance of approximately similar amplitudes has significant implications. For, *ceteris paribus,* contractions of the same relative magnitude give rise to graver problems of unemployment as an economy becomes more industrialized.

price index. The average contraction for all finished commodities in current prices is reduced to 9, that for the price index to 2, and that for the total in 1913 prices to 6 percent.

Whatever tendency there may be toward progressively severe contractions originates chiefly in the consumer durable group. As noted above, its share was appreciably larger after World War I. And it is this group whose average fall increased most—threefold for the value in current prices and sevenfold for the value in 1913 prices.[17]

Table 6 also reveals striking intergroup differences in amplitude. In the prewar sets of cycles, the average total swings are much wider for the durable group valued in current prices than for the nondurable. But except for a wide average swing in the price index for the consumer durable group—due chiefly to a large average rise—the intergroup differences in the average swings for the price indexes are small.

The average swings for the groups valued in 1913 prices, narrower than the corresponding swings in the groups valued in current prices, reflect the removal of the influence of variations in the price indexes. Since the narrowing is especially notable in the average swing for the consumer durable group, only the producer durable is left with a swing considerably wider than those for the other groups in 1913 prices.

In the postwar cycle averages, the intergroup differences are even more marked. The average total swings for the durable groups valued in current prices are about twice those for the nondurable. But for the price indexes the opposite is true. The swings for the nondurable groups are at least twice those for the durable. Consequently, for the groups valued in 1913 prices the average total swings for the durable are almost three times as wide as for the nondurable.

Finally, comparison of the average rises and falls in the prewar and postwar cycles reveals an interesting development common to all groups, both for the measures in current and 1913 prices and for the price indexes. In the earlier sets of cycles the average rises are much greater than the average falls. In the later sets the average rises still exceed the falls for the groups valued in current and 1913 prices but by a considerably smaller margin. For the price indexes the average falls are greater than the average rises.

[17] The greater part of these increases can be traced to the rise in the importance of passenger car output.

b Variations in conformity

To measure the consistency with which a series responds to 'reference' cycle expansions and contractions, we use indexes of conformity.[18] First, we credit a series with +100 for every rise during an expansion or decline during a contraction, with −100 for every decline during an expansion or rise during a contraction, and with 0 when there is no change; then we take an arithmetic mean of all the entries.

The conformity indexes for the complete business cycle are based on the total average swings.[19] They are usually higher than simple averages of the corresponding expansion and contraction indexes, because when total swings are considered, a series may be said to conform to the complete cycle not only when there is conformity during both expansion and contraction, but also when a per year rise during the contraction is less than during the expansion, or when a per year decline during the expansion is less than during the contraction.

In a growing economy—characterized mainly by expansions—there is some reason to expect more consistency in the rises of production series during expansions than in the declines during contractions. The behavior of the conformity indexes for the thirteen cycles in 1891–1938 fulfills this expectation. For the total value of finished commodities in current prices there is perfect conformity during expansions but an index of only +38 during contractions. A similar though less close correspondence is revealed by the indexes of the total value in 1913 prices.

Changes in the price index of all finished commodities, however, consistently conform more closely during contractions, which suggests that prices may be more sensitive to declining phases of business cycles.

The conformity indexes calculated for complete cycles indicate that the turning points of all three series for total finished commodities agree fairly well with reference cycle dates. Even the conformity index for prices is fairly high; while the index of +84 for the total value in 1913

---

[18] The reference cycle dates, i.e., the turning points in the business activity of the economy as a whole, established in the National Bureau study of business cycles, give the following trough and peak years: trough—1891, 1894, 1896, 1900, 1904, 1908, 1911, 1914, 1919, 1921, 1924, 1927, 1932, and 1938; peak—1892, 1895, 1899, 1903, 1907, 1910, 1913, 1918, 1920, 1923, 1926, 1929, and 1937.

[19] Separate indexes are computed from trough to trough and from peak to peak. The final index is an arithmetic mean of the separate indexes, each weighted by the number of cycles covered. For further details see Burns and Mitchell, *op. cit.*

prices, which exceeds slightly that for the total value in current prices, implies almost perfect positive conformity.

TABLE 7

Value of Finished Commodities and Price Indexes
Major Commodity Groups
Index of Conformity, 13 Reference Cycles, 1891–1938

	REFERENCE EXPANSION	REFERENCE CONTRACTION	COMPLETE CYCLE
VALUE IN PRODUCERS' CURRENT PRICES			
Consumer Perishable	+85	−8	+92
Consumer Semidurable	+100	+23	+76
Consumer Durable	+100	+38	+84
Producer Durable	+85	+69	+76
All Finished Commodities	+100	+38	+76
PRICE INDEXES			
Consumer Perishable	+69	+23	+50
Consumer Semidurable	+31	+62	+68
Consumer Durable	+8	−8	−4
Producer Durable	−8	0	+12
All Finished Commodities	+23	+54	+60
VALUE IN PRODUCERS' 1913 PRICES			
Consumer Perishable	+100	−23	+60
Consumer Semidurable	+85	+23	+44
Consumer Durable	+100	+69	+84
Producer Durable	+85	+69	+76
All Finished Commodities	+85	+38	+84

Among the commodity groups the differences in the conformity indexes for contractions are pronounced. For the values in current prices the index for producer durable products implies conformity in 11 of 13 contractions, that for consumer durable in 9, that for semidurable in 8, and that for perishable in only 6.

But the complete cycle indexes of conformity are high for all four groups valued in current prices. In fact, perishable commodities conform most closely, which indicates not only that there was conformity during expansions but also that, although *absolute* declines did not always take place during contractions, the rates of increase usually slackened.

The conformity indexes for the group price indexes do not behave at all like those for the groups valued in current prices. They are considerably higher for the nondurable groups than for the durable. Clearly during the thirteen cycles included in the analysis the price indexes for durable commodities responded less consistently to business cycles than those for nondurable.

Intergroup differences in the fluctuations of the price indexes affect only slightly the conformity indexes for the groups valued in 1913 prices.

SUMMARY

The indexes for the expansions and contractions approximate those for the groups valued in current prices. Similarly, the complete cycle indexes for neither the durable groups nor the total value of finished commodities in 1913 prices differ appreciably. However, the complete cycle indexes for nondurables are considerably below those for groups valued in current prices.

When the measures of conformity for the six reference cycles from 1914 to 1938 are compared with those for the seven from 1891 to 1914 few striking changes are revealed (Table 8). The conformity of the total

TABLE 8

Value of Finished Commodities and Price Indexes
Complete Cycle Indexes of Conformity
7 Cycles, 1891 to 1914, and 6 Cycles, 1914 to 1938

	7 CYCLES 1891 TO 1914	6 CYCLES 1914 TO 1938
VALUE IN PRODUCERS' CURRENT PRICES		
Consumer Perishable	+86	+100
Consumer Semidurable	+71	+82
Consumer Durable	+100	+64
Producer Durable	+71	+82
All Finished Commodities	+71	+82
PRICE INDEXES		
Consumer Perishable	+14	+82
Consumer Semidurable	+43	+100
Consumer Durable	0	−9
Producer Durable	0	+27
All Finished Commodities	+43	+82
VALUE IN PRODUCERS' 1913 PRICES		
Consumer Perishable	+86	+27
Consumer Semidurable	+72	+9
Consumer Durable	+100	+64
Producer Durable	+57	+100
All Finished Commodities	+100	+64

value of finished commodities in current prices is slightly higher, and of the total in 1913 prices, decidedly lower, during the last six cycles. Only the conformity index for the price index for all finished commodities increased appreciably.

The changes are somewhat greater in the measures for the separate commodity groups. For all groups in current prices, except consumer durable, the conformity indexes are higher in the recent six cycles. The price indexes for the nondurable groups also conform better; but those for the durable do not conform well in either set of cycles. For the values in 1913 prices the conformity indexes are considerably lower for the nondurable groups and slightly lower for the consumer durable in recent cycles. For the producer durable group alone is there indication of closer conformity.

Thus with respect to the closeness with which the turning points of the values and price indexes for the four groups conform to reference cycle dates there is considerable inter-group variation as well as several fairly striking differences between the measures for the cycles from 1891 to 1914 and from 1914 to 1938. Most notable is the markedly lower conformity of the nondurable groups in 1913 prices during the later set of cycles.

4 Summary

The main findings of the analysis of movements over time can be summarized as follows:

a) Except for the final decade, 1879–1939 was characterized by a notable increase in the value of finished commodities destined for domestic consumption, whether measured in current prices or adjusted for changes in prices (a rough measure of physical volume). In 1879 the total in current prices was $3.4 billion; in 1913 prices, $3.8; in 1939 it was $31.9 billion and $29.1 billion respectively. In contrast to these increases of 940 and 770 percent, population rose some 260 percent.

b) Differences in rates of growth among the commodity groups are reflected by appreciable changes in the composition of total finished commodities. Especially striking was the increase in the share of consumer durable commodities. From an average of some 10 percent during the early decades it reached an average of almost 20 percent during the recent. The percentage share of producer durable commodities increased from about 10 to 13. In 1879 the two durable groups combined constituted less than one-fifth of total finished output; in 1939, almost one-third.

c) The extraordinary increase in durable commodities can be credited largely to the automotive and electrical industries.

d) During the 1930's there was a decided interruption to the longer term trends.

e) Variations from one decade to the next in the price index of all finished commodities are closely related to variations in the total value in current prices and account for a large part of them. As a result, the decade changes for the total in 1913 prices not only are usually lower than those for the total in current prices, but also are subject to smaller fluctuations.

f) Price adjustments affected the decade changes for the perishable and semidurable groups in 1913 prices most, reducing considerably both the changes and their variability from decade to decade; the decade changes for the consumer durable group were least affected.

g) The counter movement of the shares of the nondurable groups in 1913 prices to the decade rises and declines in the price index of all finished commodities, and the parallel movements of the shares of the durable groups, indicate that during periods of sharp price variations commodities for which demand is more postponable expand or contract more rapidly than commodities for which demand is less postponable.

h) The measures of cyclical amplitude revealed wide fluctuations in the total value of finished commodities in both current and 1913 prices and in the over-all price index.

i) The amplitude measures for the four commodity groups differed considerably. The expansions and contractions, particularly the contractions, in the durable groups were much greater than in the nondurable.

j) Although too few cycles were represented to warrant definitive conclusions, there was some evidence of increasingly severe contractions in the later cycles, apparently stemming chiefly from the greater relative importance of the consumer durable group. This may be symptomatic of a tendency toward more violent cyclical fluctuations in the industrial sectors of the economy. However, the evidence rests mainly upon the inclusion of the sharp contraction of 1929–32.

k) The turning points of both total value series, as well as of the price index of all finished commodities, conformed rather consistently to the business cycle dates.

l) Inter-group variations in conformity were not large except for the price indexes. The price indexes for the nondurable groups conformed much better than those for the durable.

m) For the groups valued in current prices, little change in conformity was revealed by a comparison of the measures for the earlier and later cycles. The price indexes for the nondurable groups, however, did conform sufficiently better in later cycles to increase the conformity in the price index for all finished commodities. The measures for the groups valued in 1913 prices showed less conformity for the nondurable and consumer durable groups and more for the producer durable.

TABLE I 1

Value of Output of Finished Commodities and Construction Materials,
Exports, Imports, and Values Destined for Domestic Consumption,
Current Prices, 1869, 1879, 1889–1919
(thousands of dollars)
Major and Minor Commodity Groups

PERISHABLE

	OUTPUT	EXPORTS	IMPORTS	DOMESTIC CONSUMPTION
	1a FOOD & KINDRED PRODUCTS, MANUFACTURED			
1869	681,620	49,921	41,402	673,101
1879	1,067,608	141,218	36,545	962,935
1889	1,607,913	209,220	35,571	1,434,264
1890	1,350,188	236,750	42,046	1,155,484
1891	1,498,842	231,980	41,656	1,308,518
1892	1,433,612	224,535	42,370	1,251,447
1893	1,705,938	188,186	37,547	1,555,299
1894	1,513,381	210,620	35,106	1,337,867
1895	1,581,907	173,974	35,785	1,443,718
1896	1,584,429	179,996	31,754	1,436,187
1897	1,794,586	197,368	36,461	1,633,679
1898	1,920,558	239,855	27,203	1,707,906
1899	2,160,531	246,026	41,000	1,955,505
1900	2,283,754	246,099	46,230	2,083,885
1901	2,583,019	264,313	46,249	2,364,955
1902	2,614,382	268,452	57,202	2,403,132
1903	2,689,316	229,551	56,897	2,516,662
1904	2,750,169	205,713	57,035	2,601,491
1905	3,026,731	229,931	59,873	2,856,673
1906	3,309,214	253,390	65,213	3,121,037
1907	3,564,065	247,267	72,904	3,389,702
1908	3,137,822	228,816	65,677	2,974,683
1909	3,728,926	193,860	82,589	3,617,655
1910	3,917,026	175,936	82,366	3,823,456
1911	4,116,154	204,190	68,110	3,980,074
1912	4,464,489	205,880	83,685	4,342,294
1913	4,582,235	225,050	84,763	4,441,948
1914	4,601,972	226,952	109,793	4,484,813
1915	4,680,578	416,292	77,792	4,342,078
1916	5,802,898	496,901	74,151	5,380,148
1917	7,520,597	677,054	82,132	6,925,675
1918	9,724,309	1,246,755	106,046	8,583,600
1919	10,840,581	1,587,669	59,464	9,312,376
	1b FOOD & KINDRED PRODUCTS, NONMANUFACTURED			
1869	686,161	1,699	14,620	699,082
1879	701,258	1,883	17,132	716,507
1889	936,291	11,546	31,894	956,639
1890	953,590	8,023	45,874	991,441
1891	1,053,215	10,330	36,337	1,079,222
1892	1,036,877	10,550	35,939	1,062,266
1893	1,153,361	7,277	36,626	1,182,710

SUMMARY 31

	OUTPUT	EXPORTS	IMPORTS	DOMESTIC CONSUMPTION
1894	1,000,622	20,397	32,041	1,012,266
1895	1,058,072	10,614	31,558	1,079,016
1896	909,162	12,322	30,698	927,538
1897	1,017,143	13,989	28,950	1,032,104
1898	1,107,365	15,117	29,142	1,121,390
1899	1,141,120	16,307	36,077	1,160,890
1900	1,233,618	19,013	34,527	1,249,132
1901	1,396,984	16,069	39,955	1,420,870
1902	1,495,358	22,883	46,836	1,519,311
1903	1,489,980	26,925	55,887	1,518,942
1904	1,582,566	27,348	59,696	1,614,914
1905	1,505,925	25,450	59,574	1,540,049
1906	1,677,370	26,672	68,940	1,719,638
1907	1,833,134	27,028	80,817	1,886,923
1908	1,869,381	27,100	73,418	1,915,699
1909	2,057,156	31,694	87,060	2,112,522
1910	2,252,147	36,217	90,172	2,306,102
1911	2,183,253	48,705	101,194	2,235,742
1912	2,351,904	51,659	110,286	2,410,531
1913	2,255,898	52,365	112,379	2,315,912
1914	2,314,780	51,749	117,065	2,380,096
1915	2,281,731	68,668	97,262	2,310,325
1916	2,651,111	77,305	119,814	2,693,620
1917	3,832,010	82,025	157,252	3,907,237
1918	4,212,043	95,405	164,165	4,280,803
1919	4,714,256	215,361	210,120	4,709,015

2 CIGARS, CIGARETTES & TOBACCO

1869	72,208	1,444	3,921	74,685
1879	117,401	1,993	4,268	119,676
1889	197,414	3,450	8,564	202,528
1890	209,856	3,617	9,136	215,375
1891	223,420	3,851	6,981	226,550
1892	226,685	3,485	7,287	230,487
1893	215,940	3,619	6,171	218,492
1894	216,555	3,453	5,016	218,118
1895	201,241	3,771	4,909	202,379
1896	192,341	4,247	4,922	193,016
1897	197,195	4,469	4,595	197,321
1898	227,178	4,622	4,308	226,864
1899	266,180	4,681	5,872	267,371
1900	303,729	5,163	5,410	303,976
1901	326,208	4,838	6,561	327,931
1902	321,771	4,972	8,299	325,098
1903	342,383	5,451	9,077	346,009
1904	333,940	5,666	10,958	339,232
1905	351,547	5,979	11,624	357,192
1906	390,297	6,264	14,097	398,130
1907	397,080	5,798	13,880	405,162
1908	393,225	5,227	11,757	399,755
1909	421,995	5,427	13,938	430,506
1910	452,127	5,144	16,983	463,966
1911	449,714	5,198	15,856	460,372

Table I 1 cont.

	OUTPUT	EXPORTS	IMPORTS	DOMESTIC CONSUMPTION
1912	458,101	6,126	16,938	468,913
1913	498,027	7,380	16,165	506,812
1914	494,375	7,474	13,988	500,889
1915	473,193	6,860	12,280	478,613
1916	517,823	11,114	15,685	522,394
1917	628,823	16,617	17,292	629,498
1918	871,610	29,216	21,585	863,979
1919	1,024,458	44,687	20,274	1,000,045

3 Drugs, Toilet, & Household Preparations

	OUTPUT	EXPORTS	IMPORTS	DOMESTIC CONSUMPTION
1869	37,866	1,146	957	37,677
1879	41,707	1,693	367	40,381
1889	82,915	2,615	1,329	81,629
1890	91,417	2,977	1,630	90,070
1891	99,429	2,751	1,223	97,901
1892	106,081	3,118	1,767	104,730
1893	105,821	3,082	2,133	104,872
1894	103,628	3,182	2,449	102,895
1895	112,800	3,953	2,451	111,298
1896	114,541	3,938	2,086	112,689
1897	116,707	4,082	2,926	115,551
1898	124,789	4,239	1,861	122,411
1899	137,712	5,395	2,242	134,559
1900	138,624	5,548	3,121	136,197
1901	157,889	5,492	2,792	155,189
1902	176,240	5,997	3,772	174,015
1903	186,282	7,208	4,038	183,112
1904	185,702	7,618	4,173	182,257
1905	220,338	8,938	4,352	215,752
1906	230,758	9,655	4,257	225,360
1907	256,132	10,542	3,707	249,297
1908	241,117	10,873	3,883	234,127
1909	256,366	10,543	4,467	250,290
1910	275,110	11,508	3,232	266,834
1911	286,963	13,181	5,009	278,791
1912	298,326	14,428	5,532	289,430
1913	304,949	15,279	5,269	294,939
1914	300,088	15,930	4,825	288,983
1915	346,821	20,640	4,789	330,970
1916	435,917	21,409	6,177	420,685
1917	532,053	27,171	6,641	511,523
1918	665,474	35,491	6,116	636,099
1919	691,307	40,437	9,260	660,130

4 Magazines, Newspapers, Stationery & Supplies & Misc. Paper Products

	OUTPUT	EXPORTS	IMPORTS	DOMESTIC CONSUMPTION
1869	28,807	288	2,032	30,551
1879	60,073	589	1,977	61,461
1889	91,038	990	3,815	93,863
1890	93,631	1,028	4,731	97,334
1891	97,310	948	4,808	101,170
1892	106,605	886	3,554	109,273
1893	95,962	1,177	3,542	98,327

SUMMARY

	OUTPUT	EXPORTS	IMPORTS	DOMESTIC CONSUMPTION
1894	91,224	1,234	2,935	92,925
1895	92,434	1,198	2,840	94,076
1896	87,810	1,261	3,408	89,957
1897	90,924	1,274	2,919	92,569
1898	101,592	1,198	2,797	103,191
1899	111,221	1,462	3,271	113,030
1900	120,428	1,838	3,700	122,290
1901	133,078	2,105	3,926	134,899
1902	149,661	2,629	4,231	151,263
1903	152,168	2,630	4,642	154,180
1904	158,706	3,295	4,318	159,729
1905	170,737	3,660	5,400	172,477
1906	182,949	4,005	5,370	184,314
1907	194,280	4,506	6,879	196,653
1908	154,032	4,072	6,802	156,762
1909	204,230	4,439	10,760	210,551
1910	207,366	5,027	7,527	209,866
1911	208,259	4,954	8,020	211,325
1912	228,778	5,630	10,456	233,604
1913	241,481	6,975	9,439	243,945
1914	251,537	6,101	8,971	254,407
1915	256,400	6,399	5,582	255,583
1916	358,284	9,605	3,540	352,219
1917	415,928	11,663	3,266	407,531
1918	457,019	14,083	2,557	445,493
1919	479,837	25,298	4,144	458,683

5a FUEL & LIGHTING PRODUCTS, MANUFACTURED

	OUTPUT	EXPORTS	IMPORTS	DOMESTIC CONSUMPTION
1869	29,699	338	...	29,361
1879	39,887	209	...	39,678
1889	59,652	128	...	59,524
1890	75,573	141	...	75,432
1891	62,818	148	...	62,670
1892	52,332	195	...	52,137
1893	54,220	214	...	54,006
1894	62,147	245	...	61,902
1895	96,012	259	...	95,753
1896	93,060	290	...	92,770
1897	62,642	261	...	62,381
1898	64,230	289	...	63,941
1899	88,053	324	...	87,729
1900	100,606	274	...	100,332
1901	85,000	293	...	84,707
1902	90,099	395	...	89,704
1903	112,030	508	...	111,522
1904	109,870	628	...	109,242
1905	95,038	618	...	94,420
1906	103,444	569	...	102,875
1907	128,940	483	...	128,457
1908	126,054	265	...	125,789
1909	125,064	318	...	124,746
1910	121,235	262	...	120,973

Table I 1 cont.

	OUTPUT	EXPORTS	IMPORTS	DOMESTIC CONSUMPTION
1911	119,314	250	...	119,064
1912	141,410	231	825	142,004
1913	190,605	228	927	191,304
1914	159,581	277	1,051	160,355
1915	141,454	447	690	141,697
1916	261,990	1,076	1,589	262,503
1917	424,665	1,189	2,241	425,717
1918	579,049	1,580	3,215	580,684
1919	631,825	2,128	971	630,668

5b Nonmanufactured Fuels

1869	49,736	...	...	49,736
1879	55,462	...	...	55,462
1889	77,243	...	...	77,243
1890	80,178	...	...	80,178
1891	88,850	...	...	88,850
1892	98,487	...	...	98,487
1893	100,652	...	...	100,652
1894	90,346	...	...	90,346
1895	92,881	...	...	92,881
1896	91,870	...	...	91,870
1897	89,039	...	...	89,039
1898	86,030	...	...	86,030
1899	101,823	...	...	101,823
1900	105,025	...	...	105,025
1901	131,960	...	...	131,960
1902	102,169	...	...	102,169
1903	182,296	...	...	182,296
1904	160,834	...	...	160,834
1905	166,992	...	...	166,992
1906	161,334	...	...	161,334
1907	196,484	...	...	196,484
1908	181,255	...	...	181,255
1909	175,822	...	...	175,822
1910	194,838	...	...	194,838
1911	205,907	...	...	205,907
1912	213,980	...	...	213,980
1913	235,320	...	...	235,320
1914	226,924	...	...	226,924
1915	220,541	...	...	220,541
1916	261,675	...	...	261,675
1917	366,888	...	...	366,888
1918	416,532	...	...	416,532
1919	444,533	...	...	444,533

PERISHABLE, TOTALS

1869	1,586,097	54,836	62,932	1,594,193
1879	2,083,396	147,585	60,289	1,996,100
1889	3,052,466	227,949	81,173	2,905,690
1890	2,854,433	252,536	103,417	2,705,314
1891	3,123,884	250,008	91,005	2,964,881

SUMMARY

	OUTPUT	EXPORTS	IMPORTS	DOMESTIC CONSUMPTION
1892	3,060,679	242,769	90,917	2,908,827
1893	3,431,894	203,555	86,019	3,314,358
1894	3,077,903	239,131	77,547	2,916,319
1895	3,235,347	193,769	77,543	3,119,121
1896	3,073,213	202,054	72,868	2,944,027
1897	3,368,236	221,443	75,851	3,222,644
1898	3,631,742	265,320	65,311	3,431,733
1899	4,006,640	274,195	88,462	3,820,907
1900	4,285,784	277,935	92,988	4,100,837
1901	4,814,138	293,110	99,483	4,620,511
1902	4,949,680	305,328	120,340	4,764,692
1903	5,154,455	272,273	130,541	5,012,723
1904	5,281,787	250,268	136,180	5,167,699
1905	5,537,308	274,576	140,823	5,403,555
1906	6,055,366	300,555	157,877	5,912,688
1907	6,570,115	295,624	178,187	6,452,678
1908	6,102,886	276,353	161,537	5,988,070
1909	6,969,559	246,281	198,814	6,922,092
1910	7,419,849	234,094	200,280	7,386,035
1911	7,569,564	276,478	198,189	7,491,275
1912	8,156,988	283,954	227,722	8,100,756
1913	8,308,515	307,277	228,942	8,230,180
1914	8,349,257	308,483	255,693	8,296,467
1915	8,400,718	519,306	198,395	8,079,807
1916	10,289,698	617,410	220,956	9,893,244
1917	13,720,964	815,719	268,824	13,174,069
1918	16,926,036	1,422,530	303,684	15,807,190
1919	18,826,797	1,915,580	304,233	17,215,450

SEMIDURABLE

	OUTPUT	EXPORTS	IMPORTS	DOMESTIC CONSUMPTION
		6 DRY GOODS & NOTIONS		
1869	170,831	2,272	55,919	224,478
1879	227,534	3,359	38,956	263,131
1889	223,295	3,474	61,852	281,673
1890	227,606	3,389	75,339	299,556
1891	232,346	3,162	60,070	289,254
1892	235,491	2,795	64,468	297,164
1893	207,326	4,521	56,558	259,363
1894	176,943	4,660	37,571	209,854
1895	201,127	4,469	69,091	265,749
1896	173,175	5,298	47,671	215,548
1897	189,519	5,786	48,543	232,276
1898	194,816	6,169	38,711	227,358
1899	218,944	6,502	43,337	255,779
1900	233,520	6,361	44,784	271,943
1901	235,671	9,740	45,150	271,081
1902	260,569	11,281	49,422	298,710
1903	264,243	9,964	47,803	302,082
1904	255,137	9,787	39,716	285,066
1905	281,649	11,101	47,766	318,314

Table I 1 cont.

	OUTPUT	EXPORTS	IMPORTS	DOMESTIC CONSUMPTION
1906	306,550	12,177	53,807	348,180
1907	330,357	11,993	57,148	375,512
1908	266,334	11,542	40,659	295,451
1909	328,914	13,643	52,763	368,034
1910	317,247	17,348	49,627	349,526
1911	301,748	19,222	43,813	326,339
1912	329,767	21,525	54,911	363,153
1913	324,073	21,837	46,411	348,647
1914	320,294	25,109	42,600	337,785
1915	348,257	62,586	31,341	317,012
1916	498,794	74,775	37,541	461,560
1917	682,477	94,700	32,514	620,291
1918	931,500	99,137	22,416	854,779
1919	985,642	137,817	43,034	890,859

7 Clothing & Personal Furnishings

	OUTPUT	EXPORTS	IMPORTS	DOMESTIC CONSUMPTION
1869	214,072	691	16,421	229,802
1879	343,607	656	15,283	358,234
1889	525,921	450	35,342	560,813
1890	546,361	525	43,000	588,836
1891	570,082	653	33,821	603,250
1892	597,341	516	36,006	632,831
1893	533,079	684	34,547	566,942
1894	453,609	662	25,182	478,129
1895	501,417	840	41,615	542,192
1896	507,092	926	43,308	549,474
1897	555,880	1,117	42,061	596,824
1898	582,882	1,315	26,620	608,187
1899	719,035	1,737	26,353	743,651
1900	794,269	1,982	25,077	817,364
1901	812,763	2,533	27,719	837,949
1902	862,456	3,249	33,568	892,775
1903	952,763	4,440	33,472	981,795
1904	964,577	4,965	32,973	992,585
1905	1,069,235	5,872	36,370	1,099,733
1906	1,274,677	6,968	46,992	1,314,701
1907	1,291,482	7,902	51,831	1,335,411
1908	1,254,852	6,257	38,392	1,286,987
1909	1,421,529	7,495	45,687	1,459,721
1910	1,367,962	9,104	49,489	1,408,347
1911	1,526,644	10,323	43,723	1,560,044
1912	1,625,003	13,285	44,950	1,656,668
1913	1,689,693	14,151	46,053	1,721,595
1914	1,574,867	18,795	42,028	1,598,100
1915	1,550,203	46,278	29,989	1,533,914
1916	2,039,326	45,599	31,617	2,025,344
1917	2,618,117	34,347	38,934	2,622,704
1918	3,360,770	42,914	43,250	3,361,106
1919	3,866,186	85,318	37,059	3,817,927

SUMMARY

	OUTPUT	EXPORTS	IMPORTS	DOMESTIC CONSUMPTION
		8 SHOES & OTHER FOOTWEAR		
1869	185,644	376	...	185,268
1879	174,060	375	...	173,685
1889	236,711	654	...	236,057
1890	250,492	676	...	249,816
1891	244,861	700	...	244,161
1892	264,693	886	...	263,807
1893	234,342	792	...	233,550
1894	228,969	927	...	228,042
1895	237,225	1,258	...	235,967
1896	230,370	1,499	...	228,871
1897	247,937	1,637	...	246,300
1898	263,769	1,844	...	261,925
1899	296,256	3,396	...	292,860
1900	294,355	4,545	...	289,810
1901	333,390	6,004	...	327,386
1902	332,462	6,608	...	325,854
1903	360,039	7,531	...	352,508
1904	376,803	7,866	...	368,937
1905	405,231	9,298	...	395,933
1906	459,197	10,271	...	448,926
1907	466,925	12,553	...	454,372
1908	462,807	10,658	...	452,149
1909	480,283	12,382	...	467,901
1910	500,633	14,601	...	486,032
1911	516,545	15,715	...	500,830
1912	548,874	17,763	278	531,389
1913	602,583	19,048	265	583,800
1914	541,027	17,816	590	523,801
1915	557,250	36,926	315	520,639
1916	746,695	41,445	280	705,530
1917	899,964	37,013	403	863,354
1918	1,076,441	33,720	466	1,043,187
1919	1,258,542	71,327	346	1,187,561
		9 HOUSEFURNISHINGS		
1869	12,966	123	...	12,843
1879	16,309	90	...	16,219
1889	31,349	123	888	32,114
1890	33,356	122	1,248	34,482
1891	34,146	126	1,329	35,349
1892	36,000	168	1,122	36,954
1893	35,077	173	1,014	35,918
1894	31,815	150	751	32,416
1895	35,569	122	980	36,427
1896	34,020	146	1,625	35,499
1897	34,756	147	1,046	35,655
1898	34,831	130	1,162	35,863
1899	41,370	188	1,280	42,462
1900	48,498	193	1,504	49,809
1901	47,972	214	1,634	49,392
1902	51,853	222	1,607	53,238

Table I 1 cont.

	OUTPUT	EXPORTS	IMPORTS	DOMESTIC CONSUMPTION
1903	52,275	249	1,845	53,871
1904	51,228	254	1,895	52,869
1905	54,273	314	1,782	55,741
1906	67,707	331	2,134	69,510
1907	66,287	404	2,358	68,241
1908	58,366	420	2,176	60,122
1909	73,431	455	2,067	75,043
1910	80,805	575	2,765	82,995
1911	77,680	655	2,958	79,983
1912	82,329	604	3,807	85,532
1913	92,143	556	3,932	95,519
1914	86,850	453	3,593	89,990
1915	84,437	924	2,323	85,836
1916	110,236	1,018	2,948	112,166
1917	154,355	1,868	4,194	156,681
1918	198,817	3,107	4,179	199,889
1919	212,906	4,344	3,467	212,029

10 Toys, Games & Sporting Goods

	OUTPUT	EXPORTS	IMPORTS	DOMESTIC CONSUMPTION
1869	13,028	1,743	1,724	13,009
1879	15,965	2,040	3,035	16,960
1889	18,964	807	4,109	22,266
1890	19,085	702	4,904	23,287
1891	21,304	719	4,261	24,846
1892	21,572	706	4,153	25,019
1893	25,202	706	3,947	28,443
1894	20,434	630	2,624	22,428
1895	23,403	863	3,889	26,429
1896	21,870	736	4,280	25,414
1897	21,090	664	4,373	24,799
1898	20,003	704	4,108	23,407
1899	23,778	918	4,092	26,952
1900	24,798	1,415	5,597	28,980
1901	30,235	1,014	7,262	36,483
1902	31,784	1,087	7,087	37,784
1903	33,713	1,306	7,735	40,142
1904	35,285	1,661	7,675	41,299
1905	39,779	1,974	8,463	46,268
1906	43,512	2,762	9,627	50,377
1907	52,937	3,318	11,280	60,899
1908	38,686	2,665	7,234	43,255
1909	47,844	3,639	8,723	52,928
1910	47,773	3,704	10,334	54,403
1911	51,756	4,070	11,036	58,722
1912	54,108	5,223	10,432	59,317
1913	58,672	6,623	11,940	63,989
1914	61,898	6,249	11,445	67,094
1915	80,311	13,088	6,260	73,483
1916	150,735	40,101	2,412	113,046
1917	282,547	86,758	2,682	198,471
1918	154,115	30,201	1,903	125,817
1919	161,292	18,992	4,146	146,446

SUMMARY

	OUTPUT	EXPORTS	IMPORTS	DOMESTIC CONSUMPTION
		11 TIRES & TUBES		
1869	...	...	...	...
1879	...	...	...	...
1889	...	...	...	...
1890	...	...	...	...
1891	...	...	...	...
1892	...	...	...	...
1893	...	...	...	...
1894	...	...	...	...
1895	7,906	...	...	7,906
1896	10,485	684	...	9,801
1897	18,713	610	...	18,103
1898	19,590	579	...	19,011
1899	13,309	593	...	12,716
1900	8,420	626	...	7,794
1901	6,900	701	...	6,199
1902	6,270	808	...	5,462
1903	5,278	1,010	...	4,268
1904	6,677	940	...	5,737
1905	10,470	1,139	...	9,331
1906	13,784	1,320	...	12,464
1907	17,221	1,585	...	15,636
1908	18,940	1,439	...	17,501
1909	25,182	1,774	...	23,408
1910	38,402	2,406	...	35,996
1911	48,704	3,253	...	45,451
1912	62,550	4,221	...	58,329
1913	91,634	4,999	...	86,635
1914	97,012	4,264	...	92,748
1915	118,397	13,546	...	104,851
1916	174,099	18,027	...	156,072
1917	346,190	17,068	...	329,122
1918	507,524	16,236	...	491,288
1919	546,339	30,929	...	515,410
		SEMIDURABLE, TOTALS		
1869	596,541	5,205	74,064	665,400
1879	777,475	6,520	57,274	828,229
1889	1,036,240	5,508	102,191	1,132,923
1890	1,076,900	5,414	124,491	1,195,977
1891	1,102,739	5,360	99,481	1,196,860
1892	1,155,097	5,071	105,749	1,255,775
1893	1,035,026	6,876	96,066	1,124,216
1894	911,770	7,029	66,128	970,869
1895	1,006,647	7,552	115,575	1,114,670
1896	977,012	9,289	96,884	1,064,607
1897	1,067,895	9,961	96,023	1,153,957
1898	1,115,891	10,741	70,601	1,175,751
1899	1,312,692	13,334	75,062	1,374,420
1900	1,403,860	15,122	76,962	1,465,700
1901	1,466,931	20,206	81,765	1,528,490

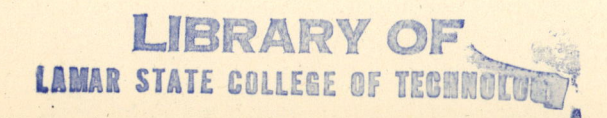

TABLE I 1 *cont.*

	OUTPUT	EXPORTS	IMPORTS	DOMESTIC CONSUMPTION
1902	1,545,394	23,255	91,684	1,613,823
1903	1,668,311	24,500	90,855	1,734,666
1904	1,689,707	25,473	82,259	1,746,493
1905	1,860,637	29,698	94,381	1,925,320
1906	2,165,427	33,829	112,560	2,244,158
1907	2,225,209	37,755	122,617	2,310,071
1908	2,099,985	32,981	88,461	2,155,465
1909	2,377,183	39,388	109,240	2,447,035
1910	2,352,822	47,738	112,215	2,417,299
1911	2,523,077	53,238	101,530	2,571,369
1912	2,702,631	62,621	114,378	2,754,388
1913	2,858,798	67,214	108,601	2,900,185
1914	2,681,948	72,686	100,256	2,709,518
1915	2,738,855	173,348	70,228	2,635,735
1916	3,719,885	220,965	74,798	3,573,718
1917	4,983,650	271,754	78,727	4,790,623
1918	6,229,167	225,315	72,214	6,076,066
1919	7,030,907	348,727	88,052	6,770,232

CONSUMER DURABLE

	OUTPUT	EXPORTS	IMPORTS	DOMESTIC CONSUMPTION

12 Household Furniture

	OUTPUT	EXPORTS	IMPORTS	DOMESTIC CONSUMPTION
1869	58,365	997	1,089	58,457
1879	66,306	1,283	176	65,199
1889	95,179	2,394	611	93,396
1890	97,221	2,406	461	95,276
1891	102,312	2,454	615	100,473
1892	116,728	2,378	642	114,992
1893	102,451	2,668	421	100,204
1894	84,641	2,593	383	82,431
1895	95,937	2,522	550	93,965
1896	92,694	2,747	261	90,208
1897	91,245	3,111	286	88,420
1898	91,819	2,734	314	89,399
1899	106,740	3,102	446	104,084
1900	109,594	3,301	649	106,942
1901	121,132	3,298	887	118,721
1902	131,665	3,466	1,181	129,380
1903	142,218	4,013	1,044	139,249
1904	145,181	3,653	876	142,404
1905	163,693	4,185	1,310	160,818
1906	193,193	4,428	1,538	190,303
1907	188,808	5,127	1,398	185,079
1908	155,705	4,001	860	152,564
1909	195,231	4,324	1,100	192,007
1910	206,565	5,294	1,097	202,368
1911	208,403	5,389	1,047	204,061
1912	225,509	6,186	1,216	220,539
1913	241,906	6,418	1,237	236,725

SUMMARY 41

	OUTPUT	EXPORTS	IMPORTS	DOMESTIC CONSUMPTION
1914	225,430	3,984	1,068	222,514
1915	214,320	2,719	716	212,317
1916	273,968	3,231	946	271,683
1917	303,748	3,801	626	300,573
1918	331,594	2,868	254	328,980
1919	498,005	3,828	541	494,718

13a Heating & Cooking Apparatus & Household Appliances, except Electrical

	OUTPUT	EXPORTS	IMPORTS	DOMESTIC CONSUMPTION
1869	26,509	102	...	26,407
1879	23,075	83	...	22,992
1889	39,220	283	...	38,937
1890	38,156	232	...	37,924
1891	39,375	253	...	39,122
1892	39,091	205	...	38,886
1893	35,532	236	...	35,296
1894	31,211	241	...	30,970
1895	35,772	289	...	35,483
1896	45,915	304	...	45,611
1897	51,094	361	...	50,733
1898	46,790	449	...	46,341
1899	59,757	524	...	59,233
1900	62,481	567	...	61,914
1901	71,333	656	...	70,677
1902	79,419	869	...	78,550
1903	79,885	1,057	...	78,828
1904	74,450	898	...	73,552
1905	86,885	1,115	...	85,770
1906	104,828	1,441	...	103,387
1907	102,737	1,490	...	101,247
1908	85,316	1,142	...	84,174
1909	95,095	1,300	...	93,795
1910	98,792	1,474	...	97,318
1911	105,958	1,820	...	104,138
1912	133,727	2,266	...	131,461
1913	127,066	2,166	...	124,900
1914	112,133	1,663	...	110,470
1915	121,489	2,081	...	119,408
1916	144,575	2,113	...	142,462
1917	196,990	2,783	...	194,207
1918	218,924	2,134	...	216,790
1919	266,576	3,124	...	263,452

13b Electrical Household Appliances & Supplies

	OUTPUT	EXPORTS	IMPORTS	DOMESTIC CONSUMPTION
1869	...	...	...	...
1879	...	...	...	...
1889	...	...	...	...
1890	...	...	...	...
1891	...	...	...	...
1892	...	...	...	...
1893	...	...	...	...
1894	...	...	...	...
1895	...	...	...	...

Table I 1 cont.

	OUTPUT	EXPORTS	IMPORTS	DOMESTIC CONSUMPTION
1896	...	...	...	...
1897	...	...	...	...
1898	...	...	...	...
1899	1,858	...	...	1,858
1900	2,384	...	...	2,384
1901	2,550	...	...	2,550
1902	3,236	...	...	3,236
1903	3,753	...	...	3,753
1904	3,298	...	...	3,298
1905	4,737	...	...	4,737
1906	8,021	...	...	8,021
1907	10,181	...	...	10,181
1908	7,722	...	...	7,722
1909	11,816	...	...	11,816
1910	16,312	...	...	16,312
1911	15,734	...	...	15,734
1912	19,657	...	...	19,657
1913	22,121	...	108	22,229
1914	18,256	...	516	18,772
1915	22,924	...	818	23,742
1916	40,671	...	564	41,235
1917	58,605	...	188	58,793
1918	67,468	...	69	67,537
1919	84,244	...	280	84,524

14a Floor Coverings

	OUTPUT	EXPORTS	IMPORTS	DOMESTIC CONSUMPTION
1869	22,124	...	3,625	25,749
1879	30,337	...	939	31,276
1889	43,967	...	2,373	46,340
1890	48,065	...	1,989	50,054
1891	56,382	...	4,036	60,418
1892	52,198	...	3,970	56,168
1893	42,652	...	3,971	46,623
1894	37,710	...	2,892	40,602
1895	45,042	...	4,653	49,695
1896	33,902	...	5,622	39,524
1897	37,681	...	6,403	44,084
1898	38,015	23	5,630	43,622
1899	46,987	32	7,544	54,499
1900	48,871	42	7,222	56,051
1901	50,805	71	8,633	59,367
1902	60,560	38	10,919	71,441
1903	65,001	67	11,602	76,536
1904	61,987	56	8,842	70,773
1905	66,985	69	11,411	78,327
1906	77,958	72	13,907	91,793
1907	77,491	108	15,733	93,116
1908	58,657	105	12,736	71,288
1909	78,992	138	14,190	93,044
1910	84,458	120	13,259	97,597
1911	81,116	158	12,194	93,152

SUMMARY

	OUTPUT	EXPORTS	IMPORTS	DOMESTIC CONSUMPTION
1912	88,899	153	12,425	101,171
1913	90,952	122	11,384	102,214
1914	80,142	87	11,806	91,861
1915	78,597	121	6,676	85,152
1916	103,995	279	7,068	110,784
1917	114,409	392	7,740	121,757
1918	116,588	1,141	4,647	120,094
1919	151,397	1,437	8,543	158,503

14b Misc. Housefurnishings

	OUTPUT	EXPORTS	IMPORTS	DOMESTIC CONSUMPTION
1869	14,356	...	...	14,356
1879	25,425	...	...	25,425
1889	51,280	31	...	51,249
1890	53,861	29	...	53,832
1891	54,482	25	...	54,457
1892	56,448	11	...	56,437
1893	53,546	36	...	53,510
1894	48,345	34	...	48,311
1895	52,973	26	...	52,947
1896	51,147	38	...	51,109
1897	51,967	44	...	51,923
1898	51,929	110	...	51,819
1899	61,179	126	...	61,053
1900	70,946	213	...	70,733
1901	69,570	186	...	69,384
1902	75,516	157	...	75,359
1903	76,235	236	...	75,999
1904	75,688	223	...	75,465
1905	78,596	219	...	78,377
1906	94,251	270	...	93,981
1907	89,978	276	...	89,702
1908	75,985	192	...	75,793
1909	91,416	270	...	91,146
1910	98,379	324	...	98,055
1911	94,700	312	...	94,388
1912	98,504	543	...	97,961
1913	107,696	562	...	107,134
1914	99,298	452	...	98,846
1915	97,013	750	...	96,263
1916	125,043	968	...	124,075
1917	167,914	1,101	...	166,813
1918	203,165	3,178	...	199,987
1919	218,861	2,209	...	216,652

15 China & Household Utensils

	OUTPUT	EXPORTS	IMPORTS	DOMESTIC CONSUMPTION
1869	18,620	599	7,996	26,017
1879	20,291	694	11,642	31,239
1889	28,464	953	18,849	46,360
1890	30,037	906	20,195	49,326
1891	32,385	1,019	20,379	51,745
1892	31,313	1,044	22,586	52,855
1893	24,011	1,207	20,656	43,460

Table I 1 cont.

	OUTPUT	EXPORTS	IMPORTS	DOMESTIC CONSUMPTION
1894	23,685	960	16,581	39,306
1895	22,225	1,038	24,736	45,923
1896	31,137	1,167	21,034	51,004
1897	33,669	1,269	18,580	50,980
1898	37,270	1,353	16,057	51,974
1899	43,676	1,955	19,164	60,885
1900	49,194	2,251	22,560	69,503
1901	51,413	2,262	24,341	73,492
1902	56,094	2,387	24,816	78,523
1903	64,239	2,587	29,177	90,829
1904	65,439	2,815	29,057	91,681
1905	81,347	3,195	30,582	108,734
1906	93,117	3,631	33,115	122,601
1907	90,279	4,009	34,398	120,668
1908	71,665	3,444	25,335	93,556
1909	79,503	3,704	27,074	102,873
1910	90,304	4,505	28,341	114,140
1911	94,920	5,079	26,892	116,733
1912	104,837	6,699	24,236	122,374
1913	109,362	4,237	25,117	130,242
1914	106,457	3,476	22,908	125,889
1915	119,072	6,273	13,345	126,144
1916	160,745	9,788	9,921	160,878
1917	221,549	10,565	10,734	221,718
1918	197,961	10,269	9,893	197,585
1919	235,629	17,272	11,783	230,140

16 Musical Instruments

	OUTPUT	EXPORTS	IMPORTS	DOMESTIC CONSUMPTION
1869	10,095	214	916	10,797
1879	14,060	606	876	14,330
1889	26,911	842	2,122	28,191
1890	31,903	1,034	2,079	32,948
1891	32,449	979	1,496	32,966
1892	34,380	1,322	1,511	34,569
1893	23,043	995	1,117	23,165
1894	19,892	854	823	19,861
1895	27,251	922	1,606	27,935
1896	22,375	1,015	1,482	22,842
1897	24,222	1,027	1,334	24,529
1898	27,654	1,276	1,417	27,795
1899	34,156	1,568	1,647	34,235
1900	42,822	1,690	1,227	42,359
1901	50,258	2,879	1,467	48,846
1902	58,540	2,761	1,443	57,222
1903	65,920	2,741	1,922	65,101
1904	58,472	2,560	1,820	57,732
1905	71,865	2,604	1,801	71,062
1906	81,772	2,605	1,983	81,150
1907	88,436	2,856	2,222	87,802
1908	63,641	2,346	1,719	63,014
1909	77,368	2,527	1,971	76,812
1910	80,528	4,956	2,011	77,583

SUMMARY 45

	OUTPUT	EXPORTS	IMPORTS	DOMESTIC CONSUMPTION
1911	84,571	5,446	2,196	81,321
1912	97,972	5,210	2,420	95,182
1913	107,340	5,417	2,438	104,361
1914	93,432	3,703	1,852	91,581
1915	92,550	3,759	1,381	90,172
1916	120,593	5,623	1,279	116,249
1917	141,020	7,716	1,412	134,716
1918	150,431	7,334	1,134	144,231
1919	256,485	10,728	2,505	248,262

17 Jewelry, Silverware, Clocks & Watches

	OUTPUT	EXPORTS	IMPORTS	DOMESTIC CONSUMPTION
1869	35,396	577	6,758	41,577
1879	37,980	1,583	6,909	43,306
1889	58,974	2,682	18,164	74,456
1890	73,257	2,394	19,369	90,232
1891	72,021	2,504	17,171	86,688
1892	74,266	1,802	17,869	90,333
1893	59,890	2,258	14,018	71,650
1894	52,176	1,870	7,995	58,301
1895	59,768	2,138	11,587	69,217
1896	52,571	2,327	8,252	58,496
1897	58,318	2,491	7,781	63,608
1898	65,269	2,643	11,385	74,011
1899	80,859	2,842	19,069	97,086
1900	88,106	3,328	15,196	99,974
1901	82,596	3,489	24,527	103,634
1902	94,773	3,509	25,697	116,961
1903	97,890	3,834	26,468	120,524
1904	100,576	3,861	24,168	120,883
1905	113,344	4,340	35,056	144,060
1906	136,897	5,016	42,103	173,984
1907	153,322	5,169	32,783	180,936
1908	114,940	3,762	17,439	128,617
1909	135,936	4,060	43,992	175,868
1910	146,268	4,770	44,651	186,149
1911	148,460	5,571	43,203	186,092
1912	155,477	5,842	41,216	190,851
1913	157,660	5,418	43,777	196,019
1914	133,081	3,777	25,330	154,634
1915	121,330	4,925	27,646	144,051
1916	173,828	6,647	54,482	221,663
1917	184,503	7,363	42,043	219,183
1918	176,490	7,040	25,494	194,944
1919	304,810	11,931	116,861	409,740

18 Printing & Publishing: Books

	OUTPUT	EXPORTS	IMPORTS	DOMESTIC CONSUMPTION
1869	8,341	165	264	8,440
1879	19,145	313	290	19,122
1889	34,409	891	1,138	34,656
1890	33,447	950	1,386	33,883
1891	32,525	876	1,770	33,419
1892	33,753	834	1,979	34,898
1893	33,439	1,131	1,980	34,288

Table I 1 cont.

	OUTPUT	EXPORTS	IMPORTS	DOMESTIC CONSUMPTION
1894	27,729	1,183	1,815	28,361
1895	34,859	1,153	1,880	35,586
1896	33,956	1,222	1,906	34,640
1897	33,292	1,228	1,666	33,730
1898	40,340	1,172	1,594	40,762
1899	44,516	1,326	1,826	45,016
1900	43,931	1,577	1,994	44,348
1901	46,984	1,750	2,169	47,403
1902	48,884	2,129	2,395	49,150
1903	51,075	2,095	2,524	51,504
1904	53,312	2,285	2,580	53,607
1905	56,555	2,592	2,756	56,719
1906	55,672	2,837	3,112	55,947
1907	56,986	3,309	3,086	56,763
1908	53,919	3,012	2,930	53,837
1909	62,930	3,147	3,144	62,927
1910	61,131	4,091	3,292	60,332
1911	59,639	4,047	3,522	59,114
1912	67,162	4,666	3,852	66,348
1913	78,603	4,794	3,980	77,789
1914	68,588	4,312	3,811	68,087
1915	74,031	3,902	3,182	73,311
1916	78,396	4,913	3,219	76,702
1917	92,345	5,389	2,820	89,776
1918	102,898	5,552	1,868	99,214
1919	132,699	8,809	3,467	127,357

19 Luggage

	OUTPUT	EXPORTS	IMPORTS	DOMESTIC CONSUMPTION
1869	7,745	71	...	7,674
1879	7,270	155	...	7,115
1889	10,849	180	...	10,669
1890	13,648	212	...	13,436
1891	14,108	170	...	13,938
1892	15,756	152	...	15,604
1893	13,061	130	...	12,931
1894	11,185	104	...	11,081
1895	9,021	104	...	8,917
1896	9,309	98	...	9,211
1897	8,935	98	...	8,837
1898	8,904	106	...	8,798
1899	12,727	135	...	12,592
1900	12,134	106	...	12,028
1901	13,235	104	...	13,131
1902	15,043	180	...	14,863
1903	16,015	170	...	15,845
1904	19,091	191	...	18,900
1905	20,367	221	...	20,146
1906	24,127	247	...	23,880
1907	27,979	298	...	27,681
1908	23,854	208	...	23,646
1909	28,703	248	...	28,455
1910	32,786	...	...	32,786

SUMMARY

	OUTPUT	EXPORTS	IMPORTS	DOMESTIC CONSUMPTION
1911	36,061	...	...	36,061
1912	34,359	421	...	33,938
1913	34,544	521	...	34,023
1914	26,768	317	...	26,451
1915	26,319	425	...	25,894
1916	40,065	424	...	39,641
1917	37,169	471	...	36,698
1918	52,513	341	...	52,172
1919	64,864	705	...	64,159

20a PASSENGER VEHICLES, MOTOR

	OUTPUT	EXPORTS	IMPORTS	DOMESTIC CONSUMPTION
1869	...	...	...	...
1879	...	...	...	...
1889	...	...	...	...
1890	...	...	...	...
1891	...	...	...	...
1892	...	...	...	...
1893	...	...	...	...
1894	...	...	...	...
1895	...	...	...	...
1896	...	...	...	...
1897	...	...	...	...
1898	...	...	...	...
1899	4,390	218	...	4,172
1900	6,273	297	...	5,976
1901	8,156	367	...	7,789
1902	10,361	1,070	...	9,291
1903	12,957	1,643	...	11,314
1904	23,279	1,898	...	21,381
1905	38,450	2,824	...	35,626
1906	60,962	4,481	6,238	62,719
1907	90,667	5,489	4,408	89,586
1908	133,519	4,769	3,419	132,169
1909	157,345	7,224	4,187	154,308
1910	212,627	11,688	2,842	203,781
1911	222,750	16,257	2,689	209,182
1912	332,521	23,840	2,652	311,333
1913	397,982	26,741	1,562	372,803
1914	419,903	20,890	571	399,584
1915	574,826	37,260	257	537,823
1916	919,627	46,482	522	873,667
1917	1,051,705	55,173	185	996,717
1918	800,655	37,997	39	762,697
1919	1,363,521	76,813	158	1,286,866

20b MOTOR VEHICLE ACCESSORIES

	OUTPUT	EXPORTS	IMPORTS	DOMESTIC CONSUMPTION
1869	...	...	...	...
1879	...	...	...	...
1889	...	...	...	...
1890	...	...	...	...
1891	...	...	...	...
1892	...	...	...	...
1893	...	...	...	...

TABLE I 1 *cont.*

	OUTPUT	EXPORTS	IMPORTS	DOMESTIC CONSUMPTION
1894	...	...	...	...
1895	...	...	...	...
1896	...	...	...	...
1897	...	...	...	...
1898	...	...	...	...
1899	...	...	...	...
1900	...	...	...	...
1901	...	...	...	...
1902	...	...	...	...
1903	...	...	...	...
1904	2,451	...	...	2,451
1905	4,280	...	...	4,280
1906	7,136	...	692	7,828
1907	11,031	677	907	11,261
1908	17,014	666	947	17,295
1909	20,930	1,016	1,227	21,141
1910	28,123	2,136	932	26,919
1911	29,250	3,435	508	26,323
1912	43,684	4,808	454	39,330
1913	51,908	6,423	627	46,112
1914	54,525	5,841	1,194	49,878
1915	77,181	16,935	753	60,999
1916	127,980	24,399	390	103,971
1917	152,452	32,219	244	120,477
1918	119,970	34,220	67	85,817
1919	210,834	43,248	374	167,960

20c Passenger Vehicles, Horse-Drawn, & Accessories

1869	36,111	445	...	35,666
1879	35,966	892	...	35,074
1889	56,043	2,004	...	54,039
1890	62,346	1,898	...	60,448
1891	64,458	2,094	...	62,364
1892	64,908	1,610	...	63,298
1893	60,193	1,654	...	58,539
1894	52,508	1,601	...	50,907
1895	46,780	1,626	...	45,154
1896	41,229	1,912	...	39,317
1897	42,741	1,851	...	40,890
1898	45,100	1,586	...	43,514
1899	55,640	2,158	...	53,482
1900	52,863	2,773	...	50,090
1901	66,759	2,667	...	64,092
1902	61,822	2,987	...	58,835
1903	60,218	3,514	...	56,704
1904	61,080	3,255	...	57,825
1905	64,942	3,697	...	61,245
1906	66,621	4,270	...	62,351
1907	68,229	4,462	...	63,767
1908	52,728	3,883	...	48,845
1909	53,691	3,864	...	49,827
1910	58,381	5,051	...	53,330

SUMMARY

	OUTPUT	EXPORTS	IMPORTS	DOMESTIC CONSUMPTION
1911	51,385	5,471	22	45,936
1912	46,760	5,205	2	41,557
1913	42,383	2,251	5	40,137
1914	37,103	1,550	16	35,569
1915	31,572	1,047	22	30,547
1916	31,846	817	16	31,045
1917	39,783	997	6	38,792
1918	35,839	576	12	35,275
1919	27,230	863	20	26,387

21 Motorcycles & Bicycles

	OUTPUT	EXPORTS	IMPORTS	DOMESTIC CONSUMPTION
1869	...	...	...	...
1879	...	...	...	...
1889	1,907	...	...	1,907
1890	...	...	...	...
1891	...	...	...	...
1892	...	...	...	...
1893	...	...	...	...
1894	...	...	...	...
1895	14,067	...	...	14,067
1896	18,657	3,796	...	14,861
1897	33,928	6,903	...	27,025
1898	34,857	7,092	...	27,765
1899	23,690	4,820	...	18,870
1900	13,585	3,061	...	10,524
1901	10,292	2,599	...	7,693
1902	8,990	2,581	...	6,409
1903	6,307	2,099	...	4,208
1904	4,100	1,622	...	2,478
1905	6,722	1,320	...	5,402
1906	6,299	1,405	...	4,894
1907	7,628	1,083	...	6,545
1908	5,606	702	...	4,904
1909	6,280	681	...	5,599
1910	8,024	729	...	7,295
1911	10,179	962	188	9,405
1912	12,959	1,211	249	11,997
1913	23,072	1,499	277	21,850
1914	17,668	1,753	262	16,177
1915	16,698	3,432	46	13,312
1916	20,514	4,313	88	16,289
1917	20,961	4,470	199	16,690
1918	22,623	3,710	6	18,919
1919	28,887	9,922	16	18,981

22 Pleasure Craft

	OUTPUT	EXPORTS	IMPORTS	DOMESTIC CONSUMPTION
1869	550	...	...	550
1879	920	...	...	920
1889	1,460	...	...	1,460
1890	1,454	...	...	1,454
1891	1,589	...	...	1,589
1892	1,462	...	...	1,462
1893	1,395	...	...	1,395

TABLE I 1 cont.

	OUTPUT	EXPORTS	IMPORTS	DOMESTIC CONSUMPTION
1894	1,036	...	...	1,036
1895	1,315	...	...	1,315
1896	1,201	...	...	1,201
1897	1,195	...	...	1,195
1898	1,399	...	...	1,399
1899	2,065	...	...	2,065
1900	2,698	...	...	2,698
1901	3,742	...	...	3,742
1902	3,539	...	...	3,539
1903	3,584	...	...	3,584
1904	3,149	...	...	3,149
1905	3,783	...	...	3,783
1906	4,320	...	...	4,320
1907	6,055	...	...	6,055
1908	3,654	303	...	3,351
1909	4,738	437	...	4,301
1910	4,844	407	...	4,437
1911	4,827	544	...	4,283
1912	4,752	881	...	3,871
1913	4,801	711	...	4,090
1914	4,121	505	...	3,616
1915	4,207	844	...	3,363
1916	4,504	518	...	3,986
1917	4,835	1,514	...	3,321
1918	5,165	3,664	...	1,501
1919	5,496	359	...	5,137

23 Ophthalmic Products & Artificial Limbs

	OUTPUT	EXPORTS	IMPORTS	DOMESTIC CONSUMPTION
1869	386	...	...	386
1879	752	...	...	752
1889	2,296	...	...	2,296
1890	2,625	...	...	2,625
1891	2,936	...	...	2,936
1892	3,225	...	...	3,225
1893	3,303	...	...	3,303
1894	3,302	...	...	3,302
1895	3,674	...	...	3,674
1896	3,806	...	...	3,806
1897	3,951	...	...	3,951
1898	4,285	...	...	4,285
1899	4,806	...	...	4,806
1900	4,729	...	...	4,729
1901	5,218	...	...	5,218
1902	5,698	...	...	5,698
1903	5,814	...	...	5,814
1904	5,644	...	...	5,644
1905	7,099	...	...	7,099
1906	7,874	...	...	7,874
1907	9,360	...	...	9,360
1908	9,307	...	...	9,307
1909	10,477	...	...	10,477
1910	10,653	...	...	10,653

SUMMARY

	OUTPUT	EXPORTS	IMPORTS	DOMESTIC CONSUMPTION
1911	10,928	...	...	10,928
1912	10,557	...	...	10,557
1913	12,304	...	...	12,304
1914	15,476	...	...	15,476
1915	20,172	...	...	20,172
1916	23,904	...	...	23,904
1917	36,514	...	...	36,514
1918	71,119	...	...	71,119
1919	45,041	...	...	45,041

24 MONUMENTS & TOMBSTONES

	OUTPUT	EXPORTS	IMPORTS	DOMESTIC CONSUMPTION
1869	6,581	...	...	6,581
1879	7,543	...	...	7,543
1889	15,247	...	...	15,247
1890	17,265	...	...	17,265
1891	16,722	...	...	16,722
1892	16,568	...	...	16,568
1893	11,938	...	...	11,938
1894	14,868	...	...	14,868
1895	13,789	...	...	13,789
1896	13,354	...	...	13,354
1897	16,629	...	...	16,629
1898	17,459	...	...	17,459
1899	20,323	...	...	20,323
1900	18,426	...	...	18,426
1901	23,164	...	...	23,164
1902	27,868	...	...	27,868
1903	25,888	...	...	25,888
1904	25,689	...	...	25,689
1905	28,658	...	...	28,658
1906	34,468	...	...	34,468
1907	38,315	...	...	38,315
1908	40,937	...	...	40,937
1909	38,405	...	...	38,405
1910	42,568	...	...	42,568
1911	42,385	...	...	42,385
1912	40,250	...	...	40,250
1913	42,146	...	...	42,146
1914	40,977	...	...	40,977
1915	37,513	...	...	37,513
1916	37,895	...	...	37,895
1917	42,284	...	...	42,284
1918	50,036	...	...	50,036
1919	73,361	...	...	73,361

CONSUMER DURABLE, TOTALS

	OUTPUT	EXPORTS	IMPORTS	DOMESTIC CONSUMPTION
1869	245,179	3,170	20,648	262,657
1879	289,070	5,609	20,832	304,293
1889	466,206	10,260	43,257	499,203
1890	503,285	10,061	45,479	538,703
1891	521,744	10,374	45,567	556,837
1892	540,096	9,358	48,557	579,295
1893	464,454	10,315	42,163	496,302

Table I 1 cont.

	OUTPUT	EXPORTS	IMPORTS	DOMESTIC CONSUMPTION
1894	408,288	9,440	30,489	429,337
1895	462,473	9,818	45,012	497,667
1896	451,253	14,626	38,557	475,184
1897	488,867	18,383	36,050	506,534
1898	511,090	18,544	36,397	528,943
1899	603,369	18,806	49,696	634,259
1900	629,037	19,206	48,848	658,679
1901	677,207	20,328	62,024	718,903
1902	742,008	22,134	66,451	786,325
1903	776,999	24,056	72,737	825,680
1904	782,886	23,317	67,343	826,912
1905	898,308	26,381	82,916	954,843
1906	1,057,516	30,703	102,688	1,129,501
1907	1,117,482	34,353	94,935	1,178,064
1908	974,169	28,535	65,385	1,011,019
1909	1,148,856	32,940	96,885	1,212,801
1910	1,280,743	45,545	96,425	1,331,623
1911	1,301,266	54,491	92,461	1,339,236
1912	1,517,586	67,931	88,722	1,538,377
1913	1,651,846	67,280	90,512	1,675,078
1914	1,553,358	52,310	69,334	1,570,382
1915	1,729,814	84,473	54,842	1,700,183
1916	2,428,149	110,515	78,495	2,396,129
1917	2,866,786	133,954	66,197	2,799,029
1918	2,723,439	120,024	43,483	2,646,898
1919	3,967,946	191,248	144,548	3,921,240

PRODUCER DURABLE

	OUTPUT	EXPORTS	IMPORTS	DOMESTIC CONSUMPTION

25a Industrial Machinery & Equipment

1869	112,685	4,456	2,170	110,399
1879	102,746	5,296	1,171	98,621
1889	192,229	11,715	3,969	184,483
1890	195,358	13,532	3,740	185,566
1891	195,477	14,560	4,536	185,453
1892	206,408	14,282	4,341	196,467
1893	195,374	14,156	3,645	184,863
1894	169,817	13,803	1,712	157,726
1895	206,170	15,952	2,903	193,121
1896	228,752	22,103	3,147	209,796
1897	204,955	24,631	1,955	182,279
1898	223,085	30,807	2,645	194,923
1899	302,428	37,821	2,915	267,522
1900	385,018	42,872	5,468	347,614
1901	359,110	32,880	4,027	330,257
1902	402,763	37,230	5,728	371,261
1903	439,245	38,961	5,633	405,917
1904	367,144	44,005	4,007	327,146
1905	452,672	52,538	4,574	404,708
1906	560,889	62,710	6,421	504,600

SUMMARY 53

	OUTPUT	EXPORTS	IMPORTS	DOMESTIC CONSUMPTION
1907	575,514	71,234	6,647	510,927
1908	381,844	55,306	4,681	331,219
1909	492,396	55,427	9,917	446,886
1910	575,620	74,155	10,981	512,446
1911	553,793	87,290	10,087	476,590
1912	603,893	97,557	10,720	517,056
1913	642,115	106,764	8,040	543,391
1914	532,850	79,967	7,326	460,209
1915	650,654	118,076	4,183	536,761
1916	1,102,515	201,112	4,568	905,971
1917	1,588,535	233,675	3,257	1,358,117
1918	1,798,080	227,419	5,177	1,575,838
1919	1,745,940	309,953	4,464	1,440,451

25b Tractors

1869	...	...	...	...
1879	...	...	...	...
1889	...	...	...	...
1890	...	...	...	...
1891	...	...	...	...
1892	...	...	...	...
1893	...	...	...	...
1894	...	...	...	...
1895	...	...	...	...
1896	...	...	...	...
1897	...	...	...	...
1898	...	...	...	...
1899	...	...	...	...
1900	...	...	...	...
1901	...	...	...	...
1902	...	...	...	...
1903	...	...	...	...
1904	...	...	...	...
1905	...	...	...	...
1906	...	...	...	...
1907	...	...	...	...
1908	...	...	...	...
1909	...	...	...	...
1910	...	...	...	...
1911	...	...	...	...
1912	13,118	5,001	...	8,117
1913	8,220	3,802	...	4,418
1914	17,651	972	...	16,679
1915	24,030	1,303	...	22,727
1916	32,036	6,209	...	25,827
1917	67,239	16,521	...	50,718
1918	161,004	24,402	...	136,602
1919	172,667	20,026	...	152,641

26 Electrical Equipment, Industrial & Commercial

1869	...	...	...	...
1879	1,935	...	...	1,935
1889	13,056	...	...	13,056

Table I 1 cont.

	OUTPUT	EXPORTS	IMPORTS	DOMESTIC CONSUMPTION
1890	21,847	...	...	21,847
1891	23,728	...	...	23,728
1892	22,651	...	...	22,651
1893	16,551	...	...	16,551
1894	15,800	...	...	15,800
1895	19,984	...	...	19,984
1896	20,483	...	...	20,483
1897	25,287	917	...	24,370
1898	36,845	2,524	...	34,321
1899	59,208	3,143	...	56,065
1900	73,492	5,286	...	68,206
1901	76,009	7,499	...	68,510
1902	90,623	10,043	...	80,580
1903	101,965	10,030	...	91,935
1904	87,071	11,133	...	75,938
1905	98,123	13,216	...	84,907
1906	136,767	16,841	...	119,926
1907	145,286	17,760	...	127,526
1908	95,942	12,773	...	83,169
1909	124,397	13,211	...	111,186
1910	161,672	17,235	...	144,437
1911	153,423	19,936	...	133,487
1912	186,266	24,137	...	162,129
1913	206,579	29,430	...	177,149
1914	168,075	21,085	...	146,990
1915	185,555	25,342	...	160,213
1916	295,586	41,644	...	253,942
1917	382,526	57,339	...	325,187
1918	401,567	61,699	...	339,868
1919	456,602	90,948	...	365,654

27 Farm Equipment

	OUTPUT	EXPORTS	IMPORTS	DOMESTIC CONSUMPTION
1869	51,064	1,068	...	49,996
1879	69,930	2,656	...	67,274
1889	88,479	4,589	...	83,890
1890	92,701	3,696	...	89,005
1891	79,091	3,760	...	75,331
1892	80,123	4,722	...	75,401
1893	76,907	5,700	...	71,207
1894	64,110	5,426	...	58,684
1895	65,337	6,016	...	59,321
1896	52,117	5,549	...	46,568
1897	64,906	6,494	...	58,412
1898	96,194	10,610	...	85,584
1899	115,756	16,392	...	99,364
1900	118,871	18,310	...	100,561
1901	129,533	19,146	...	110,387
1902	173,467	20,601	...	152,866
1903	145,986	25,789	...	120,197
1904	149,907	24,693	...	125,214
1905	155,953	25,750	...	130,203

SUMMARY

	OUTPUT	EXPORTS	IMPORTS	DOMESTIC CONSUMPTION
1906	189,725	29,259	...	160,466
1907	191,886	30,295	...	161,591
1908	166,666	28,999	...	137,667
1909	197,837	31,351	...	166,486
1910	206,447	35,874	...	170,573
1911	209,778	41,615	...	168,163
1912	233,720	46,433	...	187,287
1913	260,740	58,293	...	202,447
1914	214,639	27,367	526	187,798
1915	235,562	30,959	533	205,136
1916	291,892	55,084	323	237,131
1917	305,204	55,695	449	249,958
1918	359,194	58,091	727	301,830
1919	394,974	54,531	3,356	343,799

28 OFFICE & STORE MACHINERY & EQUIPMENT

	OUTPUT	EXPORTS	IMPORTS	DOMESTIC CONSUMPTION
1869	3,207	117	...	3,090
1879	3,822	195	...	3,627
1889	8,557	335	...	8,222
1890	9,004	307	...	8,697
1891	9,344	314	...	9,030
1892	10,178	359	...	9,819
1893	9,919	372	...	9,547
1894	8,892	292	...	8,600
1895	11,081	388	...	10,693
1896	12,677	1,063	...	11,614
1897	11,643	1,936	...	9,707
1898	13,002	2,406	...	10,596
1899	17,989	3,684	...	14,305
1900	23,890	4,141	...	19,749
1901	23,330	4,397	...	18,933
1902	27,198	5,304	...	21,894
1903	31,001	7,135	...	23,866
1904	26,911	6,633	...	20,278
1905	36,038	8,066	...	27,972
1906	48,107	9,335	...	38,772
1907	52,841	10,169	...	42,672
1908	37,359	9,437	...	27,922
1909	51,148	11,057	...	40,091
1910	61,127	12,771	...	48,356
1911	60,134	16,383	...	43,751
1912	68,300	18,095	...	50,205
1913	73,588	18,193	...	55,395
1914	63,704	12,852	...	50,852
1915	73,133	10,089	...	63,044
1916	114,208	15,438	...	98,770
1917	154,687	14,202	...	140,485
1918	169,113	11,304	...	157,809
1919	153,406	27,972	...	125,434

29 OFFICE & STORE FURNITURE & FIXTURES

	OUTPUT	EXPORTS	IMPORTS	DOMESTIC CONSUMPTION
1869	13,631	...	...	13,631
1879	15,870	...	...	15,870

Table I 1 cont.

	OUTPUT	EXPORTS	IMPORTS	DOMESTIC CONSUMPTION
1889	25,585	...	...	25,585
1890	25,793	...	...	25,793
1891	26,783	...	...	26,783
1892	30,138	...	...	30,138
1893	26,078	...	...	26,078
1894	21,230	...	...	21,230
1895	23,700	...	...	23,700
1896	22,542	...	...	22,542
1897	21,831	46	...	21,785
1898	21,600	177	...	21,423
1899	24,677	453	...	24,224
1900	27,625	415	...	27,210
1901	30,600	395	...	30,205
1902	33,856	294	...	33,562
1903	38,175	355	...	37,820
1904	38,639	413	...	38,226
1905	43,694	594	...	43,100
1906	51,453	705	...	50,748
1907	50,035	889	...	49,146
1908	41,040	683	...	40,357
1909	49,290	716	...	48,574
1910	50,947	801	...	50,146
1911	49,784	1,045	...	48,739
1912	55,594	1,343	...	54,251
1913	55,748	1,427	...	54,321
1914	51,831	1,004	...	50,827
1915	44,283	1,006	...	43,277
1916	53,320	1,767	...	51,553
1917	63,312	2,055	...	61,257
1918	68,400	2,731	...	65,669
1919	90,923	4,514	...	86,409

30 Locomotives & Railroad Cars

	OUTPUT	EXPORTS	IMPORTS	DOMESTIC CONSUMPTION
1869	41,645	876	...	40,769
1879	37,548	1,265	...	36,283
1889	90,844	3,545	...	87,299
1890	85,943	4,416	...	81,527
1891	91,466	3,901	...	87,565
1892	92,994	2,080	...	90,914
1893	107,820	3,746	...	104,074
1894	49,698	2,264	...	47,434
1895	56,836	3,132	...	53,704
1896	79,023	3,814	...	75,209
1897	72,042	4,304	...	67,738
1898	89,317	7,255	...	82,062
1899	121,414	7,350	...	114,064
1900	139,042	9,032	...	130,010
1901	136,720	9,334	...	127,386
1902	165,318	7,534	...	157,784
1903	200,950	6,397	...	194,553
1904	170,561	7,821	...	162,740
1905	226,109	11,795	...	214,314

SUMMARY

	OUTPUT	EXPORTS	IMPORTS	DOMESTIC CONSUMPTION
1906	315,633	16,225	...	299,408
1907	372,329	21,172	...	351,157
1908	143,923	6,844	...	137,079
1909	133,861	6,822	...	127,039
1910	292,753	9,502	...	203,251
1911	176,040	14,325	...	161,715
1912	319,787	16,355	...	303,432
1913	444,604	22,059	...	422,545
1914	211,319	8,118	...	203,201
1915	164,033	21,833	...	142,200
1916	403,513	40,097	...	363,416
1917	667,792	57,206	...	610,586
1918	775,093	41,121	...	733,972
1919	550,424	89,487	...	460,937

31 Ships & Boats

	OUTPUT	EXPORTS	IMPORTS	DOMESTIC CONSUMPTION
1869	11,524	...	...	11,524
1879	19,399	...	...	19,399
1889	24,704	...	...	24,704
1890	24,554	...	...	24,554
1891	26,945	...	...	26,945
1892	24,895	...	...	24,895
1893	23,866	...	...	23,866
1894	17,800	...	...	17,800
1895	22,661	...	...	22,661
1896	20,781	...	...	20,781
1897	20,747	...	...	20,747
1898	24,368	...	...	24,368
1899	36,072	...	...	36,072
1900	46,883	...	...	46,883
1901	64,654	...	...	64,654
1902	60,835	...	...	60,835
1903	61,280	...	...	61,280
1904	53,583	...	...	53,583
1905	55,624	...	...	55,624
1906	54,845	...	...	54,845
1907	66,280	...	...	66,280
1908	34,400	...	...	34,400
1909	38,167	...	...	38,167
1910	40,844	...	...	40,844
1911	42,748	...	...	42,748
1912	44,392	...	...	44,392
1913	47,577	...	...	47,577
1914	43,493	...	...	43,493
1915	66,788	...	...	66,788
1916	103,715	...	...	103,715
1917	243,763	...	...	243,763
1918	805,333	...	...	805,333
1919	1,389,509	...	...	1,389,509

32a Business Vehicles, Motor

	OUTPUT	EXPORTS	IMPORTS	DOMESTIC CONSUMPTION
1869	...	...	...	...
1879	...	...	...	...

TABLE I 1 cont.

	OUTPUT	EXPORTS	IMPORTS	DOMESTIC CONSUMPTION
1889	...	...	...	...
1890	...	...	...	...
1891	...	...	...	...
1892	...	...	...	...
1893	...	...	...	...
1894	...	...	...	...
1895	...	...	...	...
1896	...	...	...	...
1897	...	...	...	...
1898	...	...	...	...
1899	...	...	...	...
1900	...	...	...	...
1901	...	...	...	...
1902	...	...	...	...
1903	...	...	...	...
1904	1,351	...	...	1,351
1905	1,516	...	...	1,516
1906	1,754	...	...	1,754
1907	2,309	...	...	2,309
1908	3,506	...	...	3,506
1909	7,754	427	...	7,327
1910	13,205	695	...	12,510
1911	26,901	987	...	25,914
1912	51,342	1,470	...	49,872
1913	48,752	1,687	...	47,065
1914	45,165	8,986	...	36,179
1915	128,442	59,839	...	68,603
1916	164,542	52,948	...	111,594
1917	225,845	36,755	...	189,090
1918	444,155	27,164	...	416,991
1919	379,931	35,918	...	344,013

32b BUSINESS VEHICLES, HORSE-DRAWN

1869	18,065	...	...	18,065
1879	17,951	...	...	17,951
1889	28,393	...	...	28,393
1890	31,969	...	...	31,969
1891	33,470	...	...	33,470
1892	34,145	...	...	34,145
1893	32,094	...	...	32,094
1894	28,389	...	...	28,389
1895	25,677	...	...	25,677
1896	22,972	...	...	22,972
1897	24,187	...	...	24,187
1898	25,937	...	...	25,937
1899	32,544	...	...	32,544
1900	31,376	...	...	31,376
1901	40,213	...	...	40,213
1902	37,893	...	...	37,893
1903	37,569	...	...	37,569
1904	38,922	...	...	38,922
1905	43,127	...	...	43,127

SUMMARY

	OUTPUT	EXPORTS	IMPORTS	DOMESTIC CONSUMPTION
1906	46,226	...	...	46,226
1907	49,546	...	...	49,546
1908	40,170	...	...	40,170
1909	42,971	...	...	42,971
1910	48,322	...	...	48,322
1911	44,153	...	...	44,153
1912	41,913	...	...	41,913
1913	39,854	...	...	39,854
1914	36,859	...	...	36,859
1915	34,019	...	...	34,019
1916	37,367	...	...	37,367
1917	51,061	...	...	51,061
1918	50,594	...	...	50,594
1919	42,518	...	...	42,518

33 AIRCRAFT

	OUTPUT	EXPORTS	IMPORTS	DOMESTIC CONSUMPTION
1869	...	...	...	...
1879	...	...	...	...
1889	...	...	...	...
1890	...	...	...	...
1891	...	...	...	...
1892	...	...	...	...
1893	...	...	...	...
1894	...	...	...	...
1895	...	...	...	...
1896	...	...	...	...
1897	...	...	...	...
1898	...	...	...	...
1899	...	...	...	...
1900	...	...	...	...
1901	...	...	...	...
1902	...	...	...	...
1903	...	...	...	...
1904	...	...	...	...
1905	...	...	...	...
1906	...	...	...	...
1907	...	...	...	...
1908	...	...	...	...
1909	...	...	...	...
1910	...	...	...	...
1911	...	...	...	...
1912	446	113	...	333
1913	276	61	...	215
1914	437	253	...	184
1915	3,588	2,960	...	628
1916	1,499	114	...	1,385
1917	22,390	1,100	...	21,290
1918	175,257	607	...	174,650
1919	8,610	215	...	8,395

34 PROFESSIONAL & SCIENTIFIC EQUIPMENT

	OUTPUT	EXPORTS	IMPORTS	DOMESTIC CONSUMPTION
1869	1,632	9	...	1,623
1879	1,659	42	...	1,617

Table I 1 cont.

	OUTPUT	EXPORTS	IMPORTS	DOMESTIC CONSUMPTION
1889	3,473	571	...	2,902
1890	3,799	616	...	3,183
1891	3,851	642	...	3,209
1892	3,953	468	...	3,485
1893	3,621	658	...	2,963
1894	3,175	664	...	2,511
1895	3,866	882	...	2,984
1896	4,286	1,117	...	3,169
1897	3,990	1,268	...	2,722
1898	4,570	1,364	...	3,206
1899	6,375	2,341	...	4,034
1900	8,042	2,790	...	5,252
1901	7,649	2,638	...	5,011
1902	8,902	1,384	...	7,518
1903	9,775	1,996	...	7,779
1904	8,221	1,865	...	6,356
1905	10,323	2,085	...	8,238
1906	13,678	2,937	...	10,741
1907	14,970	3,174	...	11,796
1908	10,229	2,215	...	8,014
1909	13,693	1,278	...	12,415
1910	14,333	1,684	...	12,649
1911	15,216	1,850	...	13,366
1912	15,275	1,972	865	14,168
1913	18,671	1,804	791	17,658
1914	24,877	1,782	578	23,673
1915	32,922	3,722	230	29,430
1916	39,700	7,427	211	32,484
1917	62,005	5,138	176	57,043
1918	123,479	4,557	285	119,207
1919	80,108	6,092	524	74,540

35 Carpenters' & Mechanics' Tools

	OUTPUT	EXPORTS	IMPORTS	DOMESTIC CONSUMPTION
1869	10,856	310	...	10,546
1879	14,323	898	...	13,425
1889	22,652	1,975	108	20,785
1890	25,270	1,831	152	23,591
1891	26,494	1,901	92	24,685
1892	26,267	1,838	135	24,564
1893	24,303	1,886	95	22,512
1894	18,510	2,019	71	16,562
1895	21,048	2,012	92	19,128
1896	20,869	2,353	89	18,605
1897	19,119	2,377	69	16,811
1898	22,329	2,636	75	19,768
1899	27,863	3,479	89	24,473
1900	30,511	3,714	123	26,920
1901	32,752	3,629	88	29,211
1902	39,943	4,358	137	35,722
1903	42,848	5,292	142	37,698
1904	40,332	5,726	113	34,719
1905	44,669	6,772	...	37,897

SUMMARY

	OUTPUT	EXPORTS	IMPORTS	DOMESTIC CONSUMPTION
1906	50,696	7,252	...	43,444
1907	62,286	9,635	...	52,651
1908	43,203	7,553	...	35,650
1909	54,817	7,100	...	47,717
1910	57,767	8,703	...	49,064
1911	52,603	10,749	...	41,854
1912	61,110	12,554	...	48,546
1913	66,148	12,516	...	53,632
1914	58,510	8,864	...	49,646
1915	68,515	11,551	...	56,964
1916	115,111	17,583	...	97,528
1917	156,622	24,947	...	131,675
1918	231,791	21,206	...	210,585
1919	208,007	33,205	...	174,802

36 MISC. SUBSIDIARY DURABLE EQUIPMENT

	OUTPUT	EXPORTS	IMPORTS	DOMESTIC CONSUMPTION
1869	31,456	73	...	31,383
1879	37,260	148	...	37,112
1889	63,613	331	...	63,282
1890	66,845	374	...	66,471
1891	69,945	420	...	69,525
1892	75,671	730	...	74,941
1893	72,078	350	...	71,728
1894	61,363	368	...	60,995
1895	65,155	398	...	64,757
1896	68,306	451	...	67,855
1897	64,600	426	...	64,174
1898	69,793	398	...	69,395
1899	84,441	518	...	83,923
1900	92,710	906	...	91,804
1901	90,382	859	...	89,523
1902	103,763	970	...	102,793
1903	111,764	1,338	...	110,426
1904	110,299	1,587	...	108,712
1905	117,624	1,975	...	115,649
1906	137,525	2,308	...	135,217
1907	160,385	2,494	...	157,891
1908	159,492	2,137	...	157,355
1909	157,387	2,833	...	154,554
1910	155,129	3,526	...	151,603
1911	150,891	3,810	...	147,081
1912	157,161	4,402	...	152,759
1913	166,063	4,388	...	161,675
1914	177,055	6,026	...	171,029
1915	160,311	19,681	...	140,630
1916	218,585	12,968	...	205,617
1917	302,145	10,595	...	291,550
1918	370,905	10,178	...	360,727
1919	360,043	10,778	...	349,265

PRODUCER DURABLE, TOTALS

	OUTPUT	EXPORTS	IMPORTS	DOMESTIC CONSUMPTION
1869	295,765	6,909	2,170	291,026
1879	322,443	10,500	1,171	313,114

Table I 1 cont.

	OUTPUT	EXPORTS	IMPORTS	DOMESTIC CONSUMPTION
1889	561,585	23,061	4,077	542,601
1890	583,083	24,772	3,892	562,203
1891	586,594	25,498	4,628	565,724
1892	607,423	24,479	4,476	587,420
1893	588,611	26,868	3,740	565,483
1894	458,784	24,836	1,783	435,731
1895	521,515	28,780	2,995	495,730
1896	552,808	36,450	3,236	519,594
1897	533,307	42,399	2,024	492,932
1898	627,040	58,177	2,720	571,583
1899	828,767	75,181	3,004	756,590
1900	977,460	87,466	5,591	895,585
1901	990,952	80,777	4,115	914,290
1902	1,144,561	87,718	5,865	1,062,708
1903	1,220,558	97,293	5,775	1,129,040
1904	1,092,941	103,876	4,120	993,185
1905	1,285,472	122,791	4,574	1,167,255
1906	1,607,298	147,572	6,421	1,466,147
1907	1,743,667	166,822	6,647	1,583,492
1908	1,157,774	125,947	4,681	1,036,508
1909	1,363,718	130,222	9,917	1,243,413
1910	1,678,166	164,946	10,981	1,524,201
1911	1,535,464	197,990	10,087	1,347,561
1912	1,852,307	229,432	11,585	1,634,460
1913	2,078,935	260,424	8,831	1,827,342
1914	1,646,465	177,276	8,430	1,477,619
1915	1,871,835	306,361	4,946	1,570,420
1916	2,973,589	452,391	5,102	2,526,300
1917	4,293,126	515,228	3,882	3,781,780
1918	5,933,965	490,479	6,189	5,449,675
1919	6,033,662	683,639	8,344	5,358,367

FINISHED COMMODITIES, TOTALS

1869	2,723,582	70,120	159,814	2,813,276
1879	3,472,384	170,214	139,566	3,441,736
1889	5,116,497	266,778	230,698	5,080,417
1890	5,017,701	292,783	277,279	5,002,197
1891	5,334,961	291,240	240,581	5,284,302
1892	5,363,295	281,677	249,699	5,331,317
1893	5,519,985	247,614	227,988	5,500,359
1894	4,856,745	280,436	175,947	4,752,256
1895	5,225,982	239,919	241,125	5,227,188
1896	5,054,286	262,419	211,545	5,003,412
1897	5,458,305	292,186	209,948	5,376,067
1898	5,885,763	352,782	175,029	5,708,010
1899	6,751,468	381,516	216,224	6,586,176
1900	7,296,141	399,729	224,389	7,120,801
1901	7,949,228	414,421	247,387	7,782,194
1902	8,381,643	438,435	284,340	8,227,548
1903	8,820,323	418,122	299,908	8,702,109

SUMMARY

	OUTPUT	EXPORTS	IMPORTS	DOMESTIC CONSUMPTION
1904	8,847,321	402,934	289,902	8,734,289
1905	9,581,725	453,446	322,694	9,450,973
1906	10,885,607	512,659	379,546	10,752,494
1907	11,656,473	534,554	402,386	11,524,305
1908	10,334,814	463,816	320,064	10,191,062
1909	11,859,316	448,831	414,856	11,825,341
1910	12,731,580	492,323	419,901	12,659,158
1911	12,929,371	582,197	402,267	12,749,441
1912	14,229,512	643,938	442,407	14,027,981
1913	14,898,094	702,195	436,886	14,632,785
1914	14,231,028	610,755	433,713	14,053,986
1915	14,741,222	1,083,488	328,411	13,986,145
1916	19,411,321	1,401,281	379,351	18,389,391
1917	25,864,526	1,736,655	417,630	24,545,501
1918	31,812,607	2,258,348	425,570	29,979,829
1919	35,859,306	3,139,194	545,177	33,265,289

CONSTRUCTION MATERIALS, MANUFACTURED

	OUTPUT	EXPORTS	IMPORTS	DOMESTIC CONSUMPTION
1869	319,892	583	5,489	324,798
1879	363,318	912	3,503	365,909
1889	704,498	3,456	11,144	712,186
1890	1,063,136	4,374	11,706	1,070,468
1891	930,845	4,204	13,361	940,002
1892	1,155,106	4,358	14,093	1,164,841
1893	923,778	4,223	13,514	933,069
1894	860,171	4,384	11,232	867,019
1895	873,243	4,892	12,822	881,173
1896	745,940	6,505	11,922	751,357
1897	820,214	8,946	9,723	820,991
1898	799,994	13,394	9,222	795,822
1899	863,637	19,240	11,319	855,716
1900	1,054,551	20,989	13,287	1,046,849
1901	1,124,750	18,149	12,596	1,119,197
1902	1,272,752	20,670	18,541	1,270,623
1903	1,220,868	21,984	20,059	1,218,943
1904	1,178,712	24,422	12,986	1,167,276
1905	1,349,281	28,626	13,376	1,334,031
1906	1,636,883	32,357	18,321	1,622,847
1907	1,791,362	39,040	17,799	1,770,121
1908	1,531,888	29,793	11,767	1,513,862
1909	1,704,712	32,084	14,075	1,686,703
1910	1,755,867	40,971	13,149	1,728,045
1911	1,692,997	49,010	11,373	1,655,360
1912	1,901,226	58,251	11,939	1,854,914
1913	2,136,520	67,074	13,753	2,083,199
1914	1,787,078	42,572	14,150	1,758,656
1915	1,775,392	53,474	10,944	1,732,862
1916	2,389,745	90,903	10,686	2,309,528
1917	2,812,341	120,488	10,999	2,702,852
1918	2,929,454	113,841	9,031	2,824,644
1919	3,366,352	157,444	15,585	3,224,493

Table I 1 cont.

	OUTPUT	EXPORTS	IMPORTS	DOMESTIC CONSUMPTION

CONSTRUCTION MATERIALS, NONMANUFACTURED

1869	49,210	4,803	8,187	52,594
1879	78,120	4,391	4,596	78,325
1889	128,717	10,756	8,710	126,671
1890	147,779	11,239	9,521	146,061
1891	137,166	10,512	9,318	135,972
1892	172,910	14,191	11,989	170,708
1893	143,738	13,726	11,261	141,273
1894	143,794	14,121	7,393	137,066
1895	153,584	13,902	12,311	151,993
1896	134,822	17,352	11,464	128,934
1897	151,618	20,257	11,079	142,440
1898	152,387	18,994	8,542	141,935
1899	163,510	23,580	10,654	150,584
1900	193,455	28,106	10,491	175,840
1901	200,441	25,718	12,349	187,072
1902	232,441	26,296	16,845	222,990
1903	248,819	36,543	16,159	228,435
1904	248,168	35,768	14,578	226,978
1905	260,246	33,729	17,535	244,052
1906	312,621	47,871	23,502	288,252
1907	370,250	54,033	25,160	341,377
1908	327,720	41,545	20,102	306,277
1909	324,004	42,752	24,549	305,801
1910	344,895	48,299	25,088	321,684
1911	325,042	59,894	22,295	287,443
1912	338,650	67,265	27,802	299,187
1913	347,938	74,602	27,855	301,191
1914	308,858	48,611	24,943	285,190
1915	284,287	31,675	25,208	277,820
1916	321,041	32,498	29,684	318,227
1917	362,466	40,759	33,997	355,704
1918	402,013	52,386	43,179	392,806
1919	508,371	73,958	44,254	478,667

CONSTRUCTION MATERIALS, TOTALS

1869	369,102	5,386	13,676	377,392
1879	441,438	5,303	8,099	444,234
1889	833,215	14,212	19,854	838,857
1890	1,210,915	15,613	21,227	1,216,529
1891	1,068,011	14,716	22,679	1,075,974
1892	1,328,016	18,549	26,082	1,335,549
1893	1,067,516	17,949	24,775	1,074,342
1894	1,003,965	18,505	18,625	1,004,085
1895	1,026,827	18,794	25,133	1,033,166
1896	880,762	23,857	23,386	880,291
1897	971,832	29,203	20,802	963,431
1898	952,381	32,388	17,764	937,757

Table I 1 concl.

	OUTPUT	EXPORTS	IMPORTS	DOMESTIC CONSUMPTION
1899	1,027,147	42,820	21,973	1,006,300
1900	1,248,006	49,095	23,778	1,222,689
1901	1,325,191	43,867	24,945	1,306,269
1902	1,505,193	46,966	35,386	1,493,613
1903	1,469,687	58,527	36,218	1,447,378
1904	1,426,880	60,190	27,564	1,394,254
1905	1,609,527	62,355	30,911	1,578,083
1906	1,949,504	80,228	41,823	1,911,099
1907	2,161,612	93,073	42,959	2,111,498
1908	1,859,608	71,338	31,869	1,820,139
1909	2,028,716	74,836	38,624	1,992,504
1910	2,100,762	89,270	38,237	2,049,729
1911	2,018,039	108,904	33,668	1,942,803
1912	2,239,876	125,516	39,741	2,154,101
1913	2,484,458	141,676	41,608	2,384,390
1914	2,095,936	91,183	39,093	2,043,846
1915	2,059,679	85,149	36,152	2,010,682
1916	2,710,786	123,401	40,370	2,627,755
1917	3,174,807	161,247	44,996	3,058,556
1918	3,331,467	166,227	52,210	3,217,450
1919	3,874,723	231,402	59,839	3,703,160

TABLE I 2

Value of Finished Commodities and Construction Materials Destined for Domestic Consumption, 1919–1939, Current Prices
(thousands of dollars)

Major and Minor Commodity Groups

PERISHABLE

	1a	1b	2	3	4	5a	5b	Total
1919	9,468,184	4,720,193	1,008,426	667,799	439,785	668,442	419,537	17,392,366
1920	10,301,363	4,696,308	1,195,453	765,572	675,942	1,044,758	556,763	19,236,159
1921	6,548,683	4,182,375	1,053,013	562,200	474,541	714,859	487,270	14,022,941
1922	6,837,567	3,842,954	1,002,084	624,630	499,880	888,365	363,935	14,059,415
1923	7,554,580	4,012,858	1,050,287	698,511	550,665	746,408	562,680	15,175,989
1924	7,981,306	3,948,038	1,073,172	718,564	563,026	781,255	508,231	15,573,592
1925	8,684,029	4,335,814	1,094,381	766,951	615,724	990,095	383,535	16,870,529
1926	9,039,831	4,467,357	1,127,181	783,252	632,763	1,220,742	513,433	17,784,559
1927	8,827,346	4,360,159	1,164,465	851,852	648,365	958,917	452,490	17,263,594
1928	9,111,712	4,466,948	1,168,706	932,335	661,617	1,153,328	416,413	17,911,059
1929	9,463,859	4,358,277	1,243,643	984,225	683,894	1,237,843	412,250	18,383,991
1930	8,497,505	3,996,827	1,141,773	891,004	644,826	1,052,219	366,321	16,590,475
1931	6,730,217	3,133,447	1,154,860	808,997	573,535	740,195	290,470	13,431,721
1932	5,183,047	2,408,083	1,006,624	624,395	492,635	830,587	209,529	10,754,900
1933	5,509,525	2,451,067	910,650	626,039	470,082	707,244	198,282	10,872,889
1934								12,987,200
1935	7,884,900	3,183,600	1,096,400	727,700	527,200	952,200	199,700	14,571,700
1936								16,239,000
1937	9,402,300	3,683,000	1,274,100	818,400	601,900	1,335,000	180,600	17,295,300
1938								15,721,600
1939								16,073,500

	6	7	*SEMIDURABLE* 8	9	10	11	Total
1919	806,498	3,932,894	1,254,220	324,008	155,758	546,556	7,019,934
1920	903,647	4,382,800	1,368,185	390,505	148,768	678,885	7,872,790
1921	607,447	3,345,292	953,478	277,869	124,132	323,471	5,631,689
1922	681,505	3,865,376	993,021	307,112	131,050	335,786	6,313,850
1923	861,944	4,347,380	1,128,185	377,336	167,101	348,349	7,230,295
1924	700,713	3,743,890	1,061,702	358,420	154,588	382,047	6,401,360
1925	816,023	4,149,219	1,044,769	404,763	164,168	555,080	7,134,022
1926	803,547	4,186,562	1,073,947	438,057	177,185	616,305	7,295,603
1927	798,550	4,360,191	1,077,625	396,921	182,502	574,874	7,390,663
1928	769,146	4,385,648	1,074,909	401,547	200,920	551,028	7,383,198
1929	791,023	4,516,366	1,081,922	416,525	214,645	437,821	7,458,302
1930	574,443	3,767,824	860,326	347,767	182,197	336,882	6,069,439
1931	549,354	3,087,850	705,078	256,621	149,092	273,418	4,931,413
1932	317,473	2,183,439	546,333	187,512	96,893	194,469	3,526,119
1933	390,376	2,274,581	597,258	218,197	95,773	196,653	3,772,838
1934							4,501,600
1935	576,000	3,039,100	693,400	273,700	140,300	215,100	4,937,600
1936							4,775,800
1937	712,900	3,258,600	828,300	340,100	190,200	261,200	5,591,300
1938							4,852,700
1939							5,490,600

1a Food and kindred products, mfd.
1b Food and kindred products, nonmfd.
2 Cigars, cigarettes & tobacco.
3 Drug, toilet & household preparations.
4 Magazines, newspapers, stationery & supplies & misc. paper products.
5a Fuel & lighting products, mfd.
5b Fuel & lighting products, nonmfd.
6 Dry goods & notions.
7 Clothing & personal furnishings.
8 Shoes & other footwear.
9 House furnishings.
10 Toys, games & sporting goods.
11 Tires & tubes.

	12	13a	13b	13c	14	15	CONSUMER DURABLE 16	17	18	19	20a	20b	21	22	23	24	TOTAL
1919	508,977	242,496	65,099	14,250	430,211	201,678	241,952	427,832	128,214	70,351	1,292,559	282,574	23,951	13,938	58,187	73,361	4,075,630
1920	620,526	345,579	82,779	16,992	574,756	265,721	264,181	383,229	140,018	78,152	1,628,275	313,403	20,843	14,724	67,797	82,286	4,899,261
1921	466,622	186,500	63,208	12,173	374,607	166,755	166,406	263,083	121,989	51,032	1,115,450	169,470	10,184	9,373	46,552	46,930	3,270,334
1922	501,097	239,228	58,554	26,941	469,966	167,693	187,681	327,026	124,892	52,574	1,546,095	243,440	8,914	6,177	48,604	47,619	4,056,501
1923	578,917	322,047	76,329	50,334	600,043	238,956	215,089	388,063	130,707	69,208	2,188,767	355,793	16,305	12,142	58,478	65,564	5,366,742
1924	613,977	322,215	83,371	139,291	547,099	181,524	178,482	363,900	144,991	57,750	1,922,517	337,247	12,979	14,003	48,553	66,443	5,034,342
1925	622,852	346,135	106,293	168,157	603,970	240,079	173,632	384,315	149,752	66,411	2,340,180	444,269	11,331	15,008	46,563	66,785	5,785,732
1926	638,239	364,299	137,471	206,663	591,567	271,643	189,273	398,868	155,386	66,381	2,504,326	440,191	11,879	22,358	46,613	63,831	6,108,988
1927	625,527	339,393	146,286	181,546	584,651	229,335	176,214	387,643	172,141	65,889	1,967,840	419,814	10,146	17,780	49,692	61,913	5,435,810
1928	629,252	314,153	152,735	298,689	627,548	275,659	148,606	396,273	179,656	67,901	2,294,934	411,660	12,035	17,378	48,655	60,970	5,936,104
1929	600,353	347,330	176,707	366,004	643,333	274,033	111,860	402,699	192,280	70,282	2,566,950	407,584	10,560	26,238	52,114	63,635	6,311,962
1930	441,445	254,183	159,998	230,588	402,728	196,438	103,399	263,766	174,305	44,537	1,538,016	326,067	9,241	24,640	48,285	54,938	4,272,574
1931	333,211	206,199	144,389	154,738	373,596	185,857	48,714	178,784	141,488	29,351	1,074,111	273,083	7,746	16,763	40,299	43,550	3,251,879
1932	205,394	122,989	82,249	94,226	252,006	138,862	35,044	108,534	102,859	18,401	603,235	211,944	4,607	9,315	32,033	25,705	2,047,403
1933	226,882	147,052	110,257	98,015	311,638	150,392	24,083	116,014	92,090	19,082	725,288	228,247	7,456	4,822	39,099	20,846	2,321,263
1934																	3,307,200
1935	323,700	237,500	217,800	167,400	468,300	204,800	31,500	189,500	131,100	31,000	1,688,300	463,600	16,800	14,100	50,100	21,300	4,256,800
1936																	5,158,000
1937	478,700	341,000	332,600	218,000	640,900	241,600	52,000	272,600	161,600	42,500	2,212,900	594,600	30,800	25,400	70,900	26,000	5,742,100
1938																	3,747,300
1939																	4,973,100

12 Household furniture.
13a Heating & cooking apparatus & household appliances, except electrical.
13b Electrical household appliances & supplies.
13c Radios.
14 Housefurnishings.
15 China & household utensils.
16 Musical instruments.
17 Jewelry, silverware, clocks & watches.
18 Printing & publishing: books.
19 Luggage.
20a Motor vehicles.
20b Motor vehicle accessories.
21 Motorcycles & bicycles.
22 Pleasure craft.
23 Ophthalmic products & artificial limbs.
24 Monuments & tombstones.

PRODUCER DURABLE

	25a	25b	26	27	28	29	30	31	32a	33	34	35	36	TOTAL	TOTAL F.C.*	TOTAL C.M.†
1919	1,434,257	171,571	460,831	394,646	156,407	100,327	560,725	1,381,258	344,303	9,957	62,046	120,621	347,553	5,544,502	34,032,432	3,508,100
1920	1,635,837	197,416	557,922	270,570	160,576	135,133	563,274	808,130	332,892	8,679	74,833	128,701	403,020	5,276,983	37,285,193	4,777,100
1921	922,822	49,624	406,625	248,088	113,989	115,536	313,591	272,693	170,448	6,097	48,792	62,126	208,645	2,939,076	25,864,040	2,956,700
1922	1,085,240	43,351	415,814	160,696	132,350	136,805	265,553	93,646	237,183	8,760	51,723	87,819	245,091	2,964,031	27,393,797	3,568,900
1923	1,510,912	63,549	598,057	315,529	182,020	201,301	635,534	73,086	321,809	11,490	64,722	115,396	302,096	4,395,501	32,168,527	4,647,300
1924	1,303,761	52,051	655,000	265,858	179,166	229,460	481,054	67,395	323,445	10,868	65,953	106,413	208,031	3,948,455	30,957,749	4,465,300
1925	1,486,386	70,310	666,171	306,493	196,431	236,065	353,121	55,701	389,619	10,549	74,890	109,849	300,387	4,255,972	34,046,255	4,950,400
1926	1,606,767	87,356	776,403	355,410	200,103	242,344	399,288	86,454	377,237	17,591	86,510	110,166	321,857	4,667,486	35,856,636	5,111,500
1927	1,476,027	91,262	741,181	340,365	201,156	248,957	318,474	70,824	302,334	19,367	87,660	104,201	318,368	4,320,176	34,410,243	4,845,200
1928	1,644,055	104,072	894,950	356,514	213,623	245,824	245,105	60,386	318,287	51,070	92,130	131,587	304,919	4,662,522	35,892,883	4,793,800
1929	2,017,154	121,773	1,000,050	386,524	217,784	288,661	347,603	78,160	510,829	55,988	109,569	124,577	369,717	5,628,389	37,782,644	5,007,500
1930	1,457,840	95,393	722,249	338,478	165,306	203,483	352,737	94,869	372,973	28,807	91,571	99,794	304,683	4,328,183	31,260,671	3,779,800
1931	938,238	19,589	499,507	163,403	116,502	151,721	78,029	81,961	246,984	30,028	48,560	53,852	199,916	2,628,290	24,243,303	2,552,100
1932	525,764	15,844	215,547	70,868	78,460	74,913	36,977	49,671	125,527	14,058	31,663	31,037	129,021	1,399,350	17,727,772	1,362,700
1933	577,057	12,649	200,916	78,760	78,810	70,277	13,584	30,380	159,038	16,472	31,950	49,139	168,075	1,487,107	18,454,097	1,536,100
1934																
1935	1,126,000		361,200	345,300	140,600	111,100	33,000	48,200	359,300	19,100	36,400	66,300	198,800	2,370,700	23,166,700	1,909,900
1936		133,300												2,978,600	26,744,700	2,375,000
1937	1,883,700	223,700	673,800	668,500	204,900	176,800	119,100	128,600	496,600	48,400	49,800	95,300	269,900	4,085,300	30,258,100	3,331,500
1938														5,039,100	33,667,800	3,945,800
1939														3,835,100	28,156,700	3,159,000
														4,740,500	31,277,700	3,701,600

25a Industrial machinery & equipment.
25b Tractors.
26 Electrical equipment, industrial & commercial.
27 Farm equipment.
28 Office & store machinery & equipment.
29 Office & store furniture & fixtures.
30 Locomotives & railroad cars.

31 Ships & boats.
32a Business vehicles, motor.
33 Aircraft.
34 Professional & scientific equipment.
35 Carpenters' & mechanics' tools.
36 Misc. subsidiary durable equipment.

* Finished commodities.   † Construction materials.

TABLE I 3

Value of Finished Commodities and Construction Materials Destined
for Domestic Consumption, 1869, 1879, 1889–1939, 1913 Prices
(thousands of dollars)
Major and Minor Commodity Groups

	1a	1b	2	3	*PERISHABLE* 4	5a	5b	RESIDUAL*	TOTAL
1869	468,081	486,149	77,234	...	...	11,164	38,116	48,320	1,129,064
1879	1,134,199	843,942	127,723	...	...	25,698	73,157	98,972	2,303,691
1889	1,602,530	1,068,870	245,191	101,782	...	99,042	107,415	65,823	3,290,653
1890	1,337,366	1,147,501	246,990	102,820	70,125	126,564	111,996	...	3,143,362
1891	1,534,019	1,265,208	260,702	112,015	77,053	126,097	121,866	...	3,496,960
1892	1,576,130	1,337,866	273,738	127,720	84,577	118,493	127,326	...	3,645,850
1893	1,827,613	1,389,788	252,592	111,566	76,938	124,152	129,454	...	3,912,103
1894	1,781,447	1,347,891	251,578	118,406	71,812	127,897	122,496	...	3,821,527
1895	1,961,573	1,466,054	236,424	146,252	74,134	139,176	134,128	...	4,157,741
1896	2,090,520	1,350,128	233,676	134,957	74,222	140,136	126,967	...	4,150,606
1897	2,307,456	1,457,774	242,409	147,199	76,821	120,893	123,259	...	4,475,811
1898	2,298,662	1,509,273	260,763	163,215	108,167	115,417	125,841	...	4,581,338
1899	2,631,904	1,562,436	300,755	183,573	124,072	125,148	141,496	...	5,069,384
1900	2,637,829	1,581,180	334,775	178,736	112,090	131,669	137,955	...	5,114,234
1901	3,008,849	1,807,723	357,613	213,465	132,384	122,764	159,321	...	5,802,119
1902	2,895,340	1,830,495	351,457	204,004	145,305	129,630	111,824	...	5,668,055
1903	3,106,990	1,875,237	368,880	216,444	140,547	131,512	181,253	...	6,020,863
1904	3,097,013	1,922,517	356,711	221,994	141,729	128,068	174,047	...	6,042,079
1905	3,329,456	1,794,929	365,227	253,230	160,295	125,559	187,384	...	6,216,080
1906	3,751,246	2,066,873	405,841	258,144	183,580	125,305	176,971	...	6,967,960
1907	3,821,536	2,127,309	416,833	283,292	184,651	146,808	209,709	...	7,190,138
1908	3,254,577	2,095,951	407,497	246,190	148,449	140,390	195,258	...	6,488,312
1909	3,714,225	2,168,914	437,062	253,330	222,100	149,039	196,387	...	7,141,057
1910	3,781,856	2,281,011	471,031	255,833	212,912	168,721	209,717	...	7,389,081
1911	4,124,429	2,316,831	462,221	268,068	217,636	177,179	218,662	...	7,785,026
1912	4,175,283	2,317,818	468,913	284,592	237,402	178,621	216,573	...	7,879,202
1913	4,441,948	2,315,912	506,812	294,939	243,945	191,304	235,320	...	8,230,180

SUMMARY

	1a	1b	2	3	4	5a	5b	RESIDUAL*	TOTAL
1914	4,405,514	2,338,012	499,391	283,873	254,153	177,974	225,171	...	8,184,088
1915	4,155,099	2,210,837	469,228	309,029	256,095	171,132	221,232	...	7,792,652
1916	4,439,066	2,222,459	512,151	334,674	235,598	231,484	228,147	...	8,203,579
1917	4,142,150	2,336,864	580,718	329,590	215,397	334,420	239,807	...	8,178,946
1918	4,556,051	2,272,188	588,943	373,298	228,928	394,755	235,323	...	8,649,486
1919	4,507,442	2,279,291	566,919	381,578	206,894	448,874	221,219	...	8,612,217
1919	4,694,191	2,340,205	576,243	334,067	198,728	492,951	213,501	...	8,849,886
1920	4,813,721	2,194,536	639,622	359,761	227,590	563,820	214,785	...	9,013,835
1921	4,641,164	2,964,121	575,103	336,445	229,913	622,158	205,181	...	9,574,085
1922	5,012,879	2,817,415	549,087	425,208	277,557	729,364	147,716	...	9,959,226
1923	5,231,704	2,778,988	575,500	467,231	288,911	704,158	227,193	...	10,273,685
1924	5,632,538	2,786,195	665,327	483,881	278,588	790,744	216,409	...	10,853,682
1925	5,563,119	2,777,587	686,132	505,904	287,453	941,155	174,508	...	10,935,858
1926	5,802,202	2,867,366	706,697	502,729	313,715	1,116,873	218,313	...	11,527,895
1927	5,861,452	2,895,192	730,072	574,024	368,180	1,125,489	200,582	...	11,754,991
1928	5,792,570	2,839,764	744,399	665,004	378,499	1,330,251	193,667	...	11,944,154
1929	6,082,172	2,800,949	794,660	709,607	391,244	1,496,787	196,867	...	12,472,286
1930	6,026,599	2,834,629	725,396	665,922	368,894	1,479,914	177,503	...	12,278,857
1931	5,791,925	2,696,598	752,842	671,924	348,653	1,365,673	146,766	...	11,774,381
1932	5,455,839	2,534,824	682,920	588,497	311,400	1,429,582	120,763	...	11,123,825
1933	5,848,753	2,601,982	688,843	618,616	314,647	1,251,759	119,923	...	11,444,523
1934							143,755		
1935	6,046,702	2,441,411	797,962	626,248	355,735	1,506,646	128,131	11,903,000	12,046,755
1936							131,669		11,902,835
1937	7,058,784	2,765,015	923,261	602,208	399,403	1,849,030	86,819	13,113,700	13,245,369
1938	...	...	...	...	...	...	113,237	13,553,100	13,684,520
1939	...	...	...	...	...	...	125,100	14,345,200	13,666,337
									14,470,300

Estimates in 1913 prices for the residual minor groups (3 & 4 in 1869 and 1879; 4 in 1889). Residual minor groups were derived by using the movement of the implicit price indexes for the totals of those groups within each apposite major group for which price indexes were available. For these calculations the consumer durable group was treated in two segments.

* Residual minor groups (3 & 4 in 1869 and 1879; 4 in 1889).
1a Food & kindred products, mfd.
1b Food & kindred products, nonmfd.
2 Cigars, cigarettes & tobacco
3 Drug, toilet, & household preparations
4 Magazines, newspapers, stationery & supplies, & misc. paper products
5a Fuel & lighting products, mfd.
5b Fuel & lighting products, nonmfd.

Table I 3 cont.

SEMIDURABLE

	6	7	8	9	11	RESIDUAL†	TOTAL
1869	99,371	129,756	175,776	6,700	...	8,208	419,813
1879	245,917	335,739	194,061	17,726	...	16,595	810,038
1889	260,326	553,616	312,658	35,097	...	23,291	1,184,988
1890	298,958	578,993	319,458	37,851	...	24,538	1,259,798
1891	314,407	593,166	317,505	39,942	...	26,832	1,291,852
1892	309,869	629,057	345,750	43,888	...	27,018	1,355,582
1893	273,879	586,290	309,748	41,476	...	31,429	1,242,822
1894	265,975	567,849	304,056	41,033	...	27,861	1,206,774
1895	345,129	696,010	312,954	47,555	...	44,533	1,446,181
1896	293,662	722,042	303,140	44,879	...	46,642	1,410,365
1897	313,463	773,088	338,324	46,066	...	56,823	1,527,764
1898	297,589	755,512	365,307	47,754	...	54,875	1,521,037
1899	299,858	883,196	412,479	53,078	...	48,973	1,697,584
1900	296,234	898,202	400,290	55,777	6,132	33,464	1,690,099
1901	323,100	977,770	455,969	59,081	4,877	44,600	1,865,397
1902	341,773	1,025,000	453,204	63,153	4,349	45,305	1,932,784
1903	330,867	1,092,097	482,888	60,461	3,393	46,677	2,016,383
1904	313,949	1,106,561	499,238	57,780	4,997	48,078	2,030,603
1905	335,420	1,163,739	507,606	64,891	5,381	51,238	2,128,275
1906	338,696	1,287,660	527,528	74,342	6,192	51,458	2,285,876
1907	329,975	1,261,011	528,340	65,302	6,748	59,588	2,250,964
1908	300,867	1,286,987	538,914	66,802	7,557	45,293	2,246,420
1909	362,953	1,422,730	528,105	80,691	16,708	53,463	2,464,650
1910	337,055	1,345,126	551,057	80,500	27,818	54,079	2,395,635
1911	331,309	1,558,486	570,421	81,284	37,012	60,476	2,638,988
1912	362,790	1,648,426	573,235	92,567	57,018	60,220	2,794,256
1913	348,647	1,721,595	583,800	95,519	86,635	63,989	2,900,185
1914	356,313	1,659,502	523,801	87,115	111,075	69,098	2,806,904
1915	334,048	1,581,355	508,437	92,896	139,988	75,290	2,732,014
1916	356,692	1,664,210	630,500	92,853	201,643	93,892	3,039,790
1917	335,292	1,526,603	569,871	82,507	344,270	117,023	2,975,566
1918	326,003	1,440,680	606,504	73,489	444,203	56,395	2,947,274
1919	349,905	1,681,906	501,928	80,835	510,307	62,691	3,187,572
1919	327,711	1,644,186	507,371	121,579	541,145	64,124	3,206,116
1920	289,723	1,401,151	493,573	125,929	605,067	48,792	2,964,235
1921	356,274	1,831,030	466,021	144,648	374,822	66,990	3,239,785
1922	380,092	2,101,890	551,678	159,705	602,847	71,573	3,867,785
1923	425,651	2,113,456	620,564	169,437	659,752	82,846	4,071,706
1924	352,117	1,856,168	587,875	153,499	854,691	77,761	3,882,111
1925	412,550	2,044,958	566,578	186,012	1,166,134	82,166	4,458,398
1926	449,914	2,219,810	585,257	224,529	1,275,994	94,802	4,850,306
1927	457,884	2,435,861	572,900	216,660	1,592,449	101,334	5,377,088
1928	429,211	2,511,826	532,925	218,114	1,800,745	111,871	5,604,692
1929	466,680	2,669,247	554,832	227,858	1,664,719	123,572	5,706,908
1930	384,243	2,445,051	459,576	211,409	1,358,395	114,878	4,973,552
1931	371,345	2,207,184	410,168	191,794	1,231,613	105,142	4,517,246
1932	302,643	1,888,788	345,780	164,918	982,167	80,947	3,765,243
1933	301,915	1,734,997	360,881	156,863	968,734	70,318	3,593,708

SUMMARY

	6	7	8	9	11	RESIDUAL†	TOTAL
1934	...	...	...	...	...	...	3,732,700
1935	404,494	2,106,098	385,651	179,240	973,303	94,161	4,142,947
1936	...	...	...	...	...	...	3,960,000
1937	472,119	2,071,583	429,839	156,440	971,004	115,834	4,216,819
1938	...	...	...	...	...	...	3,859,300
1939	...	...	...	...	...	...	4,205,300

† Residual minor groups (10 in all years; 11 in 1895–33).

6 Dry goods & notions
7 Clothing & personal furnishings
8 Shoes & other footwear
9 Housefurnishings
10 Toys, games, & sporting goods
11 Tires & tubes

CONSUMER DURABLE

	12	13a	14a	14b	15	RESIDUAL‡	16
1869	71,463	...	15,327	7,706	9,877	22,116	...
1879	120,739	...	30,073	26,320	24,235	30,253	...
1889	167,077	...	56,443	59,316	36,881	52,476	31,463
1890	173,545	...	61,041	62,888	39,747	51,457	37,698
1891	183,011	...	69,049	64,907	41,797	52,583	38,557
1892	209,457	...	69,258	68,326	43,863	54,234	37,131
1893	196,864	...	56,650	63,702	36,156	51,154	25,568
1894	164,862	...	52,593	62,096	33,310	46,018	23,700
1895	205,164	...	71,196	74,259	40,354	57,231	37,197
1896	220,020	...	57,364	71,182	45,867	77,570	30,375
1897	217,248	...	61,398	74,925	50,375	87,021	32,318
1898	196,481	...	56,726	76,542	51,256	74,503	37,259
1899	221,455	...	71,709	90,049	58,319	96,206	42,475
1900	201,777	...	70,593	89,877	63,127	90,180	48,633
1901	227,000	...	75,531	93,762	58,420	103,721	55,318
1902	237,394	...	90,432	98,896	62,270	112,808	59,114
1903	246,895	...	91,223	94,409	72,780	109,090	66,702
1904	251,597	...	83,262	87,042	76,978	100,853	60,389
1905	281,643	...	87,321	97,121	96,911	119,560	69,329
1906	316,118	...	100,982	102,936	109,563	140,667	79,248
1907	275,006	...	98,120	91,908	106,786	130,478	80,258
1908	231,158	...	77,825	91,427	84,743	113,452	59,899
1909	296,307	...	103,844	105,128	96,233	132,677	73,716
1910	287,863	...	108,562	104,425	109,330	135,435	75,177
1911	255,076	...	103,617	97,811	118,752	135,602	77,009
1912	250,044	...	105,827	103,008	123,986	162,492	97,523
1913	236,725	124,900	102,214	107,134	130,242	22,229	104,361
1914	222,960	110,470	94,216	100,658	120,815	18,753	97,323
1915	212,317	119,647	84,560	104,294	120,597	23,813	90,082
1916	265,057	138,045	89,922	101,451	134,626	37,115	121,346
1917	265,056	167,564	82,997	78,537	134,212	42,604	138,597
1918	250,175	153,208	62,484	70,344	94,674	40,058	123,274
1919	294,125	170,079	68,735	85,028	102,330	44,651	176,072
1919	302,602	156,550	193,440		93,197	42,776	168,022
1920	245,948	187,002	197,104		105,361	40,607	155,036
1921	238,926	104,775	164,301		68,035	36,346	104,069
1922	289,317	135,925	235,808		79,740	45,965	130,334
1923	324,142	161,670	275,375		94,188	62,273	133,845

TABLE I 3 cont.

	12	13a	14a	14b	15	RESIDUAL‡	16
1924	372,107	165,834		265,067	71,102	116,883	107,196
1925	392,471	181,603		282,229	101,428	144,982	111,804
1926	415,289	194,261		281,967	119,404	186,421	119,190
1927	417,854	182,469		283,536	102,063	181,725	108,373
1928	422,600	176,490		312,524	123,282	253,040	90,946
1929	408,126	192,961		329,239	124,447	306,963	69,092
1930	301,533	142,960		205,999	87,112	222,556	62,176
1931	242,159	122,373		233,498	82,493	185,218	35,173
1932	172,166	78,890		172,018	61,992	118,999	23,775
1933	190,337	104,366		205,974	65,274	141,010	19,328
1934	...	...		...	...	...	...
1935	273,858	157,181		277,923	78,168	245,663	30,000
1936	...	...		...	...	...	...
1937	362,377	206,667		318,539	84,742	314,449	45,815
1938	...	...		...	...	...	...
1939	...	...		...	...	...	...

‡ Residual household durable groups (13a in 1869–1913; 13b in 1899–1939; 13c in 1919–1939).

12 Household furniture
13a Heating & cooking apparatus and household appliances except electrical
13b Electrical household appliances & supplies
13c Radios
14a Floor coverings
14b Misc. housefurnishings
15 China and household utensils
16 Musical instruments

	17	19	20a	20b	20c	22	RESIDUAL§	TOTAL
1869	...	...	...	...	...	...	93,527	220,016
1879	...	...	...	...	...	...	133,881	365,501
1889	...	...	...	...	...	1,894	203,195	608,745
1890	70,881	...	...	...	...	1,886	155,112	654,255
1891	68,097	...	...	...	...	2,099	157,587	677,687
1892	38,008	...	...	...	...	1,955	168,678	730,910
1893	68,894	...	...	...	...	1,906	161,763	662,657
1894	59,129	...	...	...	...	1,445	150,095	593,248
1895	70,200	...	...	...	...	1,887	179,803	737,291
1896	59,327	...	...	...	...	1,736	180,547	743,988
1897	70,285	...	...	...	...	1,702	208,035	803,307
1898	70,285	...	...	...	...	1,898	211,234	782,357
1899	97,086	...	3,234	...	...	2,671	221,556	904,760
1900	99,974	...	4,633	...	...	3,441	182,006	854,241
1901	94,643	...	6,038	...	...	4,654	207,356	926,443
1902	106,814	...	7,293	...	...	4,353	203,783	983,157
1903	110,068	...	8,867	...	...	4,408	193,426	997,868
1904	108,221	...	18,369	2,106	...	3,822	196,578	989,217
1905	128,625	...	20,254	2,433	...	4,504	210,163	1,117,864
1906	164,758	...	30,714	3,833	...	5,017	212,586	1,266,422
1907	165,389	...	38,105	4,790	66,563	6,936	141,928	1,206,267
1908	134,396	...	56,242	7,360	48,894	3,782	137,299	1,046,477
1909	194,329	...	108,515	14,867	49,383	4,774	161,353	1,341,126
1910	205,690	...	155,203	20,502	52,594	4,844	164,314	1,423,939
1911	205,627	...	167,883	21,126	45,936	4,547	164,815	1,397,801
1912	202,817	...	299,935	37,890	41,557	4,003	169,532	1,598,614
1913	196,019	34,023	372,803	46,112	40,137	4,090	154,089	1,675,078

SUMMARY

	17	19	20a	20b	20c	22	RESIDUAL§	TOTAL
1914	152,499	26,451	471,763	58,888	36,184	3,552	149,065	1,663,597
1915	144,051	24,428	686,875	77,904	31,853	3,134	159,810	1,883,365
1916	187,532	28,705	1,198,446	142,621	31,614	3,179	171,228	2,650,887
1917	132,517	20,230	1,332,509	161,066	35,564	2,019	183,794	2,777,266
1918	98,357	23,554	930,118	104,655	23,501	659	196,299	2,171,360
1919	191,557	24,377	1,332,159	173,872	15,422	2,091	194,091	2,874,589
1919	200,015	26,729	1,338,052	292,520	...	5,673	210,939	3,030,515
1920	157,707	29,693	1,495,202	287,790	...	6,143	197,049	3,104,642
1921	114,334	20,787	1,147,582	174,352	...	4,672	161,413	2,339,592
1922	165,919	22,516	1,957,082	308,152	...	3,520	202,847	3,577,125
1923	163,257	36,541	2,969,833	482,758	...	7,121	250,512	4,961,515
1924	151,121	30,491	2,637,197	462,616	...	8,213	251,582	4,639,409
1925	174,214	35,400	3,277,563	622,225	...	8,802	265,664	5,598,385
1926	192,318	38,128	3,693,696	649,249	...	13,113	281,082	6,184,118
1927	186,906	35,693	2,831,424	604,049	...	10,428	282,588	5,227,108
1928	191,067	34,857	3,165,426	567,807	...	10,192	285,879	5,634,110
1929	194,165	37,030	3,413,497	542,000	...	15,389	299,426	5,932,335
1930	127,177	23,640	2,172,338	460,547	...	14,888	274,946	4,095,872
1931	86,203	18,029	1,600,761	406,979	...	10,576	233,550	3,257,012
1932	53,997	12,664	903,046	317,281	...	6,277	168,576	2,089,681
1933	59,894	13,918	1,087,388	342,199	...	3,249	164,763	2,397,700
1934	...	...	...	...	...	...	...	3,357,600
1935	97,832	21,117	2,450,363	672,859	...	8,785	234,295	4,548,044
1936	...	...	...	...	...	...	...	5,680,600
1937	137,538	22,112	3,490,379	937,855	...	14,810	314,799	6,250,082
1938	...	...	...	...	...	...	...	4,185,300
1939	...	...	...	...	...	...	...	5,414,800

§ Residual nonhousehold durable groups (16 in 1869 and 1879; 17 in 1869, 1879, 1889; 20c in 1879–1907; 19 in 1879–1913; 18, 21, 23, 24 in all years).

17 Jewelry, silverware, clocks & watches
18 Printing & publishing: books
19 Luggage
20a Motor vehicles
20b Motor vehicle accessories
20c Carriages and wagons
21 Motorcycles & bicycles
22 Pleasure craft
23 Ophthalmic products & artificial limbs
24 Monuments & tombstones

PRODUCER DURABLE

	25a	25b	26	27	28	29	30	31
1869	...	...	...	...	...	...	...	...
1879	...	...	...	...	...	...	...	...
1889	211,321	...	17,044	71,947	9,418	41,602	105,561	32,042
1890	209,442	...	28,081	75,173	9,816	42,704	98,582	31,847
1891	230,090	...	33,514	66,138	11,203	44,343	107,839	35,594
1892	246,199	...	32,359	67,142	12,305	49,897	113,359	33,282
1893	231,368	...	23,611	64,382	11,949	46,568	132,578	32,604
1894	185,778	...	21,208	54,948	10,130	38,600	61,683	24,826
1895	276,282	...	32,547	57,094	15,298	47,024	71,893	32,512
1896	338,381	...	37,653	46,244	18,732	49,982	101,360	30,030
1897	214,446	...	32,668	59,665	11,420	48,627	89,958	29,554
1898	213,031	...	42,741	90,661	11,580	43,105	103,876	33,064
1899	272,703	...	65,116	102,121	14,582	48,159	137,592	46,665
1900	358,735	...	80,148	99,565	20,381	48,159	154,774	59,800
1901	344,376	...	81,366	108,542	19,742	54,719	147,780	80,415
1902	395,379	...	97,791	148,992	23,316	58,675	180,945	74,828
1903	460,223	...	118,779	116,583	27,059	63,993	223,111	75,375

Table I 3 cont.

	25a	25b	26	27	28	29	30	31
1904	345,455	...	91,381	122,759	21,413	64,790	184,304	65,028
1905	428,716	...	102,421	127,650	29,631	72,194	237,862	66,219
1906	542,581	...	146,968	161,110	41,690	80,425	324,386	63,699
1907	525,105	...	149,328	162,240	43,856	70,511	375,168	75,922
1908	368,021	...	105,277	133,528	31,024	59,349	144,294	38,826
1909	444,221	...	125,918	162,267	39,852	72,716	131,510	42,361
1910	508,884	...	163,390	169,893	48,020	69,551	288,443	44,590
1911	427,819	...	136,490	168,163	39,274	59,510	177,904	45,380
1912	496,215	8,359	177,190	187,287	48,181	60,413	321,432	45,907
1913	543,391	4,418	177,149	202,447	55,395	54,321	422,545	47,577
1914	431,311	17,266	146,697	187,423	47,659	50,675	221,352	42,724
1915	446,185	24,543	151,717	208,472	52,406	43,105	152,412	62,244
1916	687,383	28,381	203,642	241,232	74,939	49,906	286,380	82,707
1917	837,827	68,078	213,098	257,423	86,666	53,781	375,283	148,184
1918	784,780	153,141	196,229	234,522	78,590	49,825	343,459	353,682
1919	688,552	175,248	200,358	269,435	59,959	50,710	196,060	565,531
1919	685,591	196,982	252,510	309,284	74,764	59,683	238,505	562,172
1920	744,578	253,097	283,209	222,143	73,089	55,702	216,811	337,142
1921	445,592	55,757	224,283	183,497	55,041	60,744	173,350	135,939
1922	599,580	65,092	246,044	153,923	73,122	81,480	166,909	53,360
1923	789,400	96,286	330,236	301,365	95,099	117,651	327,426	42,866
1924	673,778	82,621	367,152	243,683	92,592	145,228	270,255	39,528
1925	768,158	107,837	379,801	285,375	101,515	153,889	208,947	32,669
1926	825,677	131,560	433,786	328,172	102,828	165,423	234,187	50,706
1927	754,615	137,650	426,456	314,280	102,840	169,937	177,720	41,539
1928	831,591	158,405	516,715	332,259	108,054	167,913	144,434	35,417
1929	1,009,586	186,482	575,403	363,959	109,001	197,984	190,991	45,842
1930	791,874	147,896	440,127	324,213	89,791	139,755	194,775	57,323
1931	540,460	32,486	332,119	161,306	67,109	110,503	46,921	51,710
1932	324,345	27,748	153,087	72,835	48,402	58,848	24,668	33,471
1933	355,988	22,309	137,425	82,905	48,618	60,272	9,098	20,472
1934	...	...	...	...	...	...	...	...
1935	601,496	222,538	242,416	348,085	75,107	94,232	18,634	30,031
1936	...	...	...	...	...	...	...	...
1937	909,561	357,348	428,081	645,270	98,938	137,054	62,291	74,985
1938	...	...	...	...	...	...	...	...
1939	...	...	...	...	...	...	...	...

25a Industrial machinery & equipment
25b Tractors
26 Electrical equipment, industrial & commercial
27 Farm equipment
28 Office & store machinery & equipment
29 Office & store furniture & fixtures
30 Locomotives & railroad cars
31 Ships & boats

	32a	32b	35	36	RE-SIDUAL‖	TOTAL PRODUCER DURABLE	TOTAL FINISHED COMMODITIES	CONSTRUCTION MATERIALS
1869	...	...	5,149	24,197	148,272	177,618	1,946,511	351,389
1879	...	...	10,132	46,448	271,538	328,118	3,807,348	545,742
1889	...	...	21,406	69,541	35,482	615,364	5,699,750	986,891
1890	...	...	25,367	79,701	40,082	640,795	5,698,210	1,443,095
1891	...	...	27,306	96,162	45,227	697,416	6,163,915	1,341,613
1892	...	...	27,263	105,254	47,038	734,098	6,466,440	1,759,617
1893	...	...	25,097	108,514	44,716	721,387	6,538,969	1,424,857

SUMMARY

	32a	32b	35	36	RE-SIDUAL‖	TOTAL PRODUCER DURABLE	TOTAL FINISHED COMMODITIES	CON-STRUCTION MATERIALS
1894	...	...	18,906	101,321	39,514	556,914	6,178,463	1,402,353
1895	...	...	22,216	92,115	39,697	686,678	7,027,891	1,461,338
1896	...	...	21,659	102,967	39,548	786,556	7,091,515	1,226,032
1897	...	...	19,525	107,855	35,453	649,171	7,456,053	1,435,814
1898	...	...	23,067	96,516	35,325	692,966	7,577,698	1,341,569
1899	...	...	26,834	103,226	41,519	858,517	8,530,245	1,246,964
1900	...	...	27,497	105,159	40,698	994,916	8,653,490	1,425,045
1901	...	...	29,656	110,933	50,871	1,028,400	9,622,359	1,618,673
1902	...	...	35,938	118,017	50,625	1,184,506	9,768,502	1,810,440
1903	...	...	37,736	134,830	52,608	1,310,297	10,345,411	1,712,873
1904	1,391	...	35,719	135,046	50,989	1,118,275	10,180,174	1,706,553
1905	1,601	...	38,631	138,668	57,263	1,300,856	10,763,075	1,813,889
1906	1,825	...	43,444	148,590	62,877	1,617,595	12,137,853	1,978,363
1907	2,428	51,718	51,317	171,063	12,603	1,691,259	12,338,628	2,090,592
1908	3,861	40,210	35,227	192,366	8,974	1,160,957	10,942,166	1,950,846
1909	8,480	42,588	47,432	187,793	13,165	1,318,303	12,265,136	2,101,797
1910	14,547	47,655	48,820	182,654	13,273	1,599,720	12,808,375	2,100,132
1911	24,680	44,153	41,276	181,134	13,487	1,359,270	13,181,085	2,002,890
1912	47,770	41,913	48,256	176,396	14,858	1,674,177	13,946,249	2,200,307
1913	47,065	39,854	53,632	161,675	17,873	1,827,342	14,632,785	2,384,390
1914	38,123	37,496	50,147	178,901	23,786	1,473,560	14,128,149	2,195,323
1915	75,554	35,473	57,773	137,200	28,250	1,475,334	13,883,365	2,125,457
1916	119,608	38,052	83,144	172,787	28,107	2,096,268	15,990,524	2,208,197
1917	205,309	46,802	82,867	170,397	53,837	2,599,552	16,531,330	1,974,536
1918	408,815	33,707	109,794	187,879	167,249	3,101,672	16,869,792	1,843,811
1919	389,596	24,850	87,227	143,790	44,830	2,896,146	17,570,524	1,826,917
1919	389,924	...	60,553	143,085	39,111	3,012,164	18,098,681	1,730,686
1920	474,205	...	58,157	151,968	46,139	2,916,240	17,998,952	1,823,321
1921	284,554	...	32,510	102,027	33,367	1,786,661	16,940,123	1,717,015
1922	530,611	...	50,704	126,597	44,736	2,192,158	19,596,294	2,090,217
1923	798,533	...	61,941	153,817	54,947	3,169,567	22,476,473	2,440,809
1924	792,757	...	56,423	107,732	56,989	2,928,738	22,303,940	2,487,632
1925	845,160	...	58,430	147,249	63,288	3,152,318	24,144,959	2,773,333
1926	807,788	...	58,043	160,128	75,217	3,373,515	25,935,834	2,910,877
1927	706,388	...	55,574	154,623	77,276	3,118,898	25,478,085	2,908,283
1928	801,730	...	70,255	144,855	104,908	3,416,536	26,599,492	2,894,807
1929	1,242,893	...	66,370	178,866	126,283	4,293,660	28,405,189	2,984,207
1930	973,820	...	53,943	153,107	96,302	3,462,926	24,811,207	2,386,237
1931	691,832	...	30,001	110,147	67,055	2,241,649	21,790,288	1,820,328
1932	361,749	...	17,685	75,717	40,497	1,239,052	18,217,801	1,074,685
1933	506,490	...	29,460	101,740	46,293	1,421,070	18,857,001	1,129,485
1934	...	...	...	...	...	2,203,300	21,340,355	1,261,493
1935	1,144,268	...	38,191	120,998	55,723	2,991,719	23,585,545	1,585,447
1936	...	...	...	...	...	4,005,200	26,891,169	2,188,896
1937	1,500,302	...	51,099	141,161	87,600	4,493,690	28,645,111	2,358,518
1938	...	...	...	...	...	3,345,400	25,056,337	1,986,792
1939	...	...	...	...	...	4,167,400	28,257,800	2,328,050

‖ Residual minor groups (34 in all years; 33 in 1912–29; 32b in 1879–1907; 25a, 26, 27, 28, 29, 30, 31 in 1869 and 1879).

32a Business vehicles, motor
32b Business vehicles, wagons
33 Aircraft
34 Professional & scientific equipment
35 Carpenters' & mechanics' tools
36 Misc. subsidiary durable equipment

PART II

Estimates of the Value of Output

IN PART II the sources and derivation of the estimates of the value of output are described in such a way that each step in the estimating procedure and the reliability of the final estimates can be appraised. Section A discusses the *Census of Manufactures* and the problem of setting up detailed and comparable series for the different census years. It concludes with two comparisons: the detailed estimates for 1919 with those of Kuznets, and the grand total of finished commodities and construction materials for 1899 with the census estimate of the net value of manufactured products. Section B reviews the intercensal estimates for manufactured commodities in terms of the interpolating series and the criteria of selection and evaluation; Section C the estimates of nonmanufactured commodities. Section D describes the estimates for the years since 1919.

A CENSUS OF MANUFACTURES

The primary source of information on the production of manufactured commodities in the United States is the *Census of Manufactures,* taken decennially 1869–99 and quinquennially 1899–1919.[1] The successive

[1] Census volumes consulted include:
Ninth Census, 1870: Statistics of the Wealth and Industry of the United States; Compendium of the Ninth Census
Tenth Census, 1880: II, Manufactures of the United States; VIII, The Newspaper and Periodical Press; Alaska; Seal Islands; Shipbuilding; X, Petroleum, Coke, and Building Stones; XXII, Power and Machinery Employed in Manufactures, and the Ice Industry of the United States
Eleventh Census, 1890: Manufacturing Industries, Part I, Totals for State and Industries; Part III, Selected Industries
Twelfth Census, 1900: VII, Manufactures, Part I, United States by Industries; IX and X, Manufactures, Parts III and IV, Special Reports on Selected Industries
Census of Manufactures, 1905: Part I, United States by Industries; Parts III and IV, Selected Industries
Thirteenth Census, 1910: VIII, Manufactures, General Report and Analysis; X, Manufactures, Reports for Principal Industries
Census of Manufactures, 1914: II, Reports for Selected Industries and Detail Statistics for Industries, by States; Abstract of the Census of Manufactures, 1914
Fourteenth Census, 1920: VIII, Manufactures, General Report and Analytical Tables; X, Manufactures, Reports for Selected Industries; Abstract of the Census of Manufactures, 1919

censuses are fairly comparable in scope, coverage, and detail, and when not, pose no insuperable difficulties. Several hundred industries are reported separately in each census; and their products are consistently valued at selling prices, f.o.b. factory. All nongovernment manufacturing establishments with a value of product of $500 or more a year are included.[2]

A few imperfections in comparability are: First, some slight errors may be present in the data for 1909 as the census schedules were not edited, and those for the other census years were.[3] Second, the extent of manufacturers' cooperation in filing returns varied, particularly in the censuses prior to 1899. For example, the canvass for 1889 was closed before reports from all establishments had been obtained. However, for the most part, the missing returns were unimportant, and their omission affected the industry totals only slightly.[4]

Third, in 1899 and prior years the products of hand trades and custom establishments were included together with those of manufacturing establishments. But the 1904 census listed values for 1899 excluding such establishments; and it was possible to make similar adjustments for the earlier years on the basis of individual industry comparisons. The adjustments amounted to less than 3 percent of the total value of finished commodities. Though the corrections for 1889, 1879, and 1869 are almost certainly too small, based as they are on 1899 relationships, comparability is probably not affected appreciably.

Finally, the scope of the 1869 census was somewhat more restricted than those for later years and several smaller industries were not covered.[5] Moreover, it did not use special schedules or employ 'expert special agents', and the later censuses did. This lack of specialized approach suggests that the data for 1869 were less carefully compiled and are probably less comprehensive in coverage. Although it cannot be measured precisely, the undercoverage may have been as much as 5 percent. It may be

---

[2] The approximate importance of establishments with a value of product of less than $500 is suggested by the $30 million aggregate reported in 1899 for all such establishments, including some engaged in hand trades (Census Reports, VII, Twelfth Census of U. S. Manufactures, Part I, p. xlviii). Our estimate for all finished commodities and construction materials in 1899 is $6,372 million. Thus even the assumption that the entire $30 million belonged to these categories would imply an understatement of less than .5 percent.
[3] See Thirteenth Census, by H. Parker Willis (*Journal of Political Economy*, XXI, 7, pp. 577–92).
[4] *Abstract of the Eleventh Census: 1890*, 2d ed., p. 140.
[5] These can be identified by examining the detailed commodity data in Table II 1 and noting the entries of 'not reported'. There were few major omissions.

offset in part by our undercorrection for the removal of hand trades and custom establishments in 1869.

1 Census Commodity Data

We turn now to the commodity values derived from the census industry reports. Every effort was expended to make the values for each of the several thousand commodities in Table II 1 comparable from census year to census year. To achieve this, two types of adjustment often had to be applied.

The first involved the translation of industry output into commodity output. Industry output includes *all* products manufactured by plants assigned to an industry, whether or not these products ordinarily belong to the industry; whereas commodity output includes products produced by and belonging ordinarily to an industry as well as similar products manufactured by plants classified under other industries. The total value of products for the shoe industry, for example, would include such commodities as handbags and leather novelties produced in the industry, but would exclude shoes made in industries other than the shoe industry. The commodity total for shoes would include all shoes, no matter in which industry they were produced. Thus to pass from an industry to a commodity basis required a correction for products not normally belonging to an industry—'other' products; or for products similar to those manufactured in the industry but produced as incidental products in other industries—'secondary' products; or for both 'other' and 'secondary' products.

For most years and most products, commodity values could be obtained directly. When a particular census reported data on an industry basis alone, percentage adjustments were made on the basis of the closest census year for which 'other' or 'secondary' products were reported separately.

Since most of the adjustments were small, they are not itemized. However, for some industries they had to be based on data outside the period 1869–1919, i.e., for census years after 1919. Note A to Table II 1 shows the percentage effects of this procedure on the commodity group estimates for 1919. Only 8 of the 37 minor group totals were changed by as much as 3 percent. The major group totals—consumer perishable, semidurable, and durable, producer durable, and construction materials—were changed only 0.5, 1.2, 1.7, 1.0, and 1.8 percent respectively.

As an over-all check on the adequacy of the adjustments for 'other' and 'secondary' products, the grand commodity totals for each census year

(Table II 1) are compared with appropriate grand industry totals.[6] In view of the roughness of the adjustments for 'other' and 'secondary' products, the agreement is amazingly close. The largest dollar difference, $102 million in 1919, is less than .2 percent. The largest percentage difference, in 1869, is only 1 percent.

The second type of adjustment was occasioned by the failure of the census, particularly in the earlier years, to report commodity values in the same detail each year. Many commodities combined in some census reports we assigned to various commodity groups; and to establish comparability with the details for later years, such combinations had to be split. Usually the percentage apportionments for the closest census year for which the more detailed values were shown separately were applied to the combinations; occasionally more intricate computations had to be made.

Note B to Table II 1 lists the various combinations together with the corresponding percentage apportionments and the commodity groups to which each commodity was assigned. Unless otherwise specified, the percentages are based on data for the census year succeeding the final year noted in the column 'Census years in which estimated'. From the Note, in conjunction with Table II 1, the importance within each commodity group of the commodity values so estimated can be appraised. For example, for Group 8, shoes and other footwear, of the $541 million total for 1914, $51 million was estimated by apportioning various commodity combinations.

2 Mixed Commodities

With the detailed census data set up in comparable array, commodities could be assigned to appropriate groups.[7] Most could be assigned directly; but of many the uses were so diverse as to require further division before the group assignments could be made. A large number of food and

[6] The derivation of the comparable industry totals is shown in Table II 3. Besides itemizing the adjustments made in the census figures to establish comparability, this table distributes the Census industry data by major industrial groups.

	1869	1879	1889	1899	1904	1909	1914	1919
				(millions of dollars)				
Grand commodity total	3,845	5,091	8,059	11,391	14,793	20,633	24,268	62,520
Comparable grand industry total	3,882	5,096	8,108	11,407	14,794	20,672	24,246	62,418

[7] Our system of classification and the component commodity groups are described in Part I, Sec. A. The 37 groups are designated in Tables I 1 and II 1, and in all other tables presenting details by minor commodity groups.

textile products, for example, are in part further fabricated and in part destined for sale to consumers without additional fabrication. The allocations of these mixed commodities are shown in detail in Table II 2. Notes A, B, and C describe the techniques employed and make clear their limitations. Because of these inherent limitations Table II 1 was constructed so as to show separately the values for mixed commodities assigned to each group and their relative importance in each census year.

The accompanying tabulation gives the percentages that the commodities classified as mixed, and consequently specifically allocated, constituted of the major group totals in 1879, 1904, and 1919. From it or from

	1879	1904	1919
Consumer perishable	45.2	33.2	32.7
Consumer semidurable	30.8	18.4	25.6
Consumer durable	18.1	15.1	13.3
Producer durable	30.4	32.8	6.2
Construction materials	19.0	10.8	12.2

the percentages in Table II 1 for each minor group the importance of even a fairly sizable error in allocation can be gauged.[8] Thus for the major groups in the tabulation an assumed net error of 20 percent, very much larger than is likely, would change the perishable group by about 6 percent in 1904 and 1919, and 9 percent in 1879; and the other groups somewhat less.

3 Comparisons with Other Estimates

In this Section we compare our estimates with two other sets of data. The first comparison, with Kuznets' original estimates for 1919, can be pursued in as much detail as desired; the second, with the census estimate of 'net value of product for 1899', can be made only for the over-all total of finished commodities and construction materials for that year.

a Kuznets' estimates for 1919

At first glance, comparison with Kuznets' original estimates would seem to be somewhat spurious since the two sets were based on similar procedures and compiled essentially by the same investigators. However, five years elapsed between the two compilations, and no figures in our set—except for a few percentages applied to commodity combinations and mixed commodities—were taken directly from *Commodity Flow and*

---

[8] However, the high percentages for some of the minor groups do not necessarily imply a likelihood of substantial error. To gauge the error, Notes A, B, and C to Table II 2 must be consulted.

Capital Formation, Volume One. All transcriptions and the attendant decisions were made as independently as possible under the circumstances.

Differences between Kuznets' figures and ours may stem from a variety of causes. First, the degree of census detail was usually less (though occasionally the reverse was true) in 1919 and in earlier years than since. In Kuznets' volume 1929 was the base year. Consequently the data for 1929, or even for a later year if more detail was provided, were used to derive approximations for the years prior to 1929. Kuznets' 1919 commodity estimates were accordingly based in part on the greater detail available for later years.

In our study 1919 is both the base and the end year. Since the estimates extend back to 1869 it was thought preferable to make 1919 as comparable as possible with earlier years rather than to try to make 1919 alone more accurate. This decision precluded, except in the few instances described above, the use of data available solely for years more recent than 1919. However, careful comparisons show that neither the accuracy of our classification nor the adequacy of our estimates was appreciably reduced by the decision.[9]

A second source, quantitatively more important, of differences between the two sets of estimates is changes in the apportionment of mixed commodities. For the most part these reflect improvements made possible by additional information, such as the materials consumed data reported in the censuses for 1914 and 1919, or from reconsideration of the classification of the commodities in question. In small part they are due to our classification as completely finished of some mixed commodities that Kuznets allocated 90 percent or more to finished by applying approximate percentages derived from the *Distribution of Sales of Manufacturing Plants in 1929.*

Third, either for one or both reasons mentioned in the preceding paragraphs or because the new classification seemed more appropriate, we put some commodities in different groups from those to which Kuznets assigned them.

Finally, differences may arise because we include all manufacturing establishments with a gross value of product of more than $500. Kuznets excluded establishments with a value of product between $500 and

[9] For checking purposes a commodity by commodity comparison with Kuznets' estimates was made. Lack of space prevents the inclusion of the long note prepared as a result of this comparison. All statements made here concerning the relations between Kuznets' estimates and ours are based on this note.

ESTIMATES OF THE VALUE OF OUTPUT

$5,000 in 13 industries (see *Commodity Flow and Capital Formation,* Volume One, p. 17). As he says, however, the total deduction for the 13 industries amounted to less than $60 million, an exceedingly minor correction.

Although properly to appraise the quantitative differences between our estimates and Kuznets' requires comparison of specific commodities, approximate judgments as to relative reliability can be made by comparing minor groups. The following tabulation, which gives gross and net differences as well as brief explanations for them, provides a basis for such judgments. The gross difference is the absolute sum of all changes without regard to sign; the net difference is the actual difference between our group total and the comparable group total of Kuznets.[10]

MINOR GROUP*	VALUE OF TOTAL OUTPUT 1919	GROSS DIFFERENCE	NET DIFFERENCE	EXPLANATION
	(millions of dollars)			
1a Food & kindred products (1)	10,841	530	−220	Chiefly better classification & allocation. Only some $30 million added to our total owing to less precise allocation.
2 Cigars, cigarettes, & tobacco (2 & part of 8)	1,024	15	+9	Inclusion of establishments with products of $500–5,000 value, & better classification.
3 Drug, toilet, & household preparations (3 & part of 8)	691	150	−83	Net decrease of some $70 million due to improvements; thus the changes stemming from less precise classification almost canceled.
4 Magazines, newspapers, stationery & supplies & misc. paper products (4 & part of 6b)	480	175	−160	Chiefly better classification & allocation.
5a Fuel & lighting products, mfd. (5a)	632	165	−100	Chiefly improvements. Only about $10 million added to our total owing to less precise allocation.

[10] In the basic commodity comparisons upon which the table is based, identity was assumed whenever a specific commodity, commodities, or aggregates of two or more commodities in the same minor group differed by less than 3 percent. Exceptions were made only when the absolute difference exceeded $5 million. Consequently the net differences in the table may not agree exactly with those obtained by a direct comparison of the group totals in Table II 1 with those in Tables I-4 and 5 of *Commodity Flow and Capital Formation,* Volume One.

MINOR GROUP*	VALUE OF TOTAL OUTPUT 1919	GROSS DIFFERENCE	NET DIFFERENCE	EXPLANATION
Caskets & coffins (6a)	...	64	−64	Now classified as unfinished since they constitute a part of the value of undertakers' services.
6 Dry goods & notions (7 & part of 8)	986	570	−100	Less precise estimates made our total about $200 million higher; remaining shifts of $370 million due to improvements.
7 Clothing & personal furnishings (9, 10, & part of 8)	3,866	145	−2	Improvements & added crudities about equal; &, as indicated by the small net difference, practically canceled.
8 Shoes & other footwear (11)	1,259	4	−4	A commodity omitted before 1919 because of difficulty of estimate.
9 Housefurnishings (semidurable) (12 & part of 8)	213	210	−155	Decrease of about $60 million due to added crudities of estimate; other changes due to improvements.
10 Toys, games, & sporting goods (13 & part of 6b)	161	225	−185	Net difference due to better classification; added crudities of about $40 million canceled.
11 Tires & tubes (14)	546	44	−44	Lack of data on 1 commodity, $11 million; remaining $33 million due to better classification.
12 Household furniture (15)	498	29	−29	Chiefly better allocation & classification.
13a Heating & cooking apparatus & household appliances, except electrical (16, parts of 17 & 20) 13b Electrical household appliances & supplies (part of 20)	351	95	+25	Improvements & added crudities about equal. Of the net difference, about $10 million due to poorer & about $15 million to better estimates.
14a Floor coverings (18) 14b Misc. housefurnishings (durable) (18)	370	180	+45	Except for $38 million decrease due to less precise classification, all changes due to improvements.

ESTIMATES OF THE VALUE OF OUTPUT

MINOR GROUP*	VALUE OF TOTAL OUTPUT 1919	GROSS DIFFERENCE	NET DIFFERENCE	EXPLANATION
15 China & household utensils (19)	236	125	+60	Improvements & added crudities about equal. Of the net difference, about $50 million due to poorer and about $10 million to better estimates.
16 Musical instruments (22)	256	2	−2	Better classification.
17 Jewelry, silverware, clocks & watches (23)	305	5	+1	Chiefly better allocation & classification.
18 Printing & publishing: books (24)	133	...	...	Identical.
19 Luggage (25)	65	...	...	Identical.
20a Motor vehicles (26)	1,364	...	...	Identical.
20b Motor vehicle accessories (27)	211	−70	−70	Better estimate.
20c Carriages & wagons (6 & 34a)	27	27	+27	New group; better classification.
21 Motorcycles & bicycles (28)	29	−11	−11	Chiefly better classification.
22 Pleasure craft (29)	5	−9	−9	Less complete estimate due to omission of pleasure craft of more than 5 gross tons.
23 Ophthalmic products & artificial limbs (30)	45	−14	−14	Probably better classification.
24 Monuments & tombstones (31)	73	31	+30	Better estimate.
25 Industrial machinery & equipment (32 & 34b)	1,918	510	+250	Chiefly less precise classification. Increase of $85 million & decrease of $125 million due to better classification. Increase of about $290 million due to poorer.
26 Electrical equipment, industrial & commercial (33)	457	150	+10	Chiefly better allocation & classification.
27 Farm equipment (34a)	395	335	−270	Increase of $17 million & decrease of $116 million due to improvements. Increase of $15 million & decrease of $187 million due to added crudities.

88   PART II

MINOR GROUP*	VALUE OF TOTAL OUTPUT 1919	GROSS DIFFERENCE	NET DIFFERENCE	EXPLANATION
28 Office & store machinery & equipment (35)	153	70	−70	Chiefly better allocation & classification.
29 Office & store furniture & fixtures (36)	91	26	−12	Decrease of $6 million due to improvements. Increase of $7 million & decrease of $13 million due to crudities.
30 Locomotives & rr. cars (37)	550	52	−52	Parts excluded from present total.
31 Ships & boats (38)	1,390	387	+387	Our total includes all work done; original total included work done on completed vessels only.
32a Business vehicles, motor (39)	380	...	...	Identical.
32b Wagons (part of 34)	43	43	+43	New group.
33 Aircraft (40)	9	4	−4	Parts excluded from our total.
34 Professional & scientific equipment (41)	80	39	−3	Increase of $2 million & decrease of $20 million due to improvements. Increase of $16 million & decrease of $1 million due to added crudities.
35 Carpenters' & mechanics' tools (42)	208	118	+65	Chiefly better classification.
36 Misc. subsidiary durable equipment (43, 44)	360	400	65	Increase of about $206 million & decrease of $126 million due to improvements. Increase of $27 million & decrease of $42 million due to added crudities.
Construction materials	3,366	960	−340	Increase of $200 million & decrease of $555 million due to improvements. Increase of $110 million & decrease of $95 million due to added crudities.

* The number in parentheses is Kuznets' group number corresponding to our grouping.

Several conclusions can be drawn from the tabulation. First, the gross differences are fairly large. Moreover, they usually reflect not a single large change but an aggregate of small ones. Second, the fact that for many groups the net differences are considerably less than the gross indicates a tendency for the various changes to cancel one another and accounts for the similarity between our totals and Kuznets', especially when major commodity group totals are compared. For consumer perishables the *net* difference is $618 million, or 4.5 percent of our total; for consumer semidurables, $490 million, or 7.0 percent; for consumer durables, $53 million, or 1.3 percent; and for producer durables, $409 million, or 6.8 percent.

Finally, the tabulation reveals that changes due to improvements in the technique of measurement and in classification far exceed those due to less accurate allocation. With few exceptions, our group totals are at least as reliable as, and in many instances probably preferable to the original estimates. This does not mean, however, that they are devoid of crudities due to methods of estimating. Before the reliability of any group can be judged, the commodities included as well as the derivation of the specific commodity estimates must be examined carefully.

b *Census net value of manufactured products, 1899*

Although only our total of finished commodities and construction materials can be compared with the census net value of products, the comparison is in one respect more of a check than that with Kuznets' data: it is with an estimate made by a completely different approach.[11]

By the census definition the *net* value of manufactured products includes the value of all raw materials consumed in manufacturing and the entire value added to them by manufacturing. The sum of these two values is roughly equal to the difference between the gross value of products and the value of all partly manufactured materials consumed in the manufacturing process.[12] To get the required data, the census schedules for 1899 called for a classification of the two types of materials consumed: raw and partly manufactured. Raw was defined to include products of mines, forests, farms, and fisheries; partly manufactured, to include all manufactured or semimanufactured products used as materials by manufacturing establishments.

The tabulation of returns from the schedules made possible a first approximation of net value: $8,371 million. The census added $98 million to this approximation to allow for imported partly manufactured mate-

---

[11] For a similar comparison between Kuznets' estimates and the net values of manufactures for the census years 1919–33 see *Commodity Flow and Capital Formation*, Vol. One, pp. 19–26.

[12] Minor adjustments for mark-ups and for changes in inventories are needed to assure exact equality.

rials. Since these materials were not reported as products by any domestic establishment, this addition did not constitute duplication.

The difference between the final census estimate, $8,469 million, and our estimate, $6,372 million, of the value of finished commodities and construction materials (Table II 1) seems, at first glance, unduly large and indicative of errors in one estimate or both. But the two estimates are not really comparable. Our estimate excludes the value of repairs and servicing done in manufacturing establishments, and also several industries, the most important of which is manufactured gas. Moreover, the census estimate is based on the 1899 census data as originally reported: i.e., including custom establishments, mechanical and hand trades, some agricultural industries, and some construction industries; ours is based upon census data that exclude all these items. To make the two estimates comparable we have either to subtract items from the census or add to ours. The limitations of the data available for the adjustments necessitated a combination of the two methods.

Reconciliation of NBER Estimate of the Value of Output of
Finished Commodities and Construction Materials
with Census Estimate of *Net* Value of Manufactured Products for 1899
(millions of dollars)

NBER			GROSS VALUE OF MFD. PRODUCTS	CENSUS MATERIALS PURCHASED IN PARTLY MFD. FORM	NET VALUE OF MFD. PRODUCTS
Value of output of finished commodities & construction materials	6,372	Original census totals*	13,004	4,634	8,371
Add:					
Repairs & servicing done in mfg. establishments	260	*Subtract:* Mechanical & hand trades	1,184	463	721
		Agric. industries (cotton compressing, cotton ginning, & tobacco stemming)	36	3	33
Custom establishments	304	Industries omitted in NBER estimates (gas, illuminating industry, & ordnance)	78	12	66
Construction industries (roofing, street constr. work)	59	*Add:* Imports of partly mfd. products*			98
Adj. totals	6,995		11,706	4,156	7,649

* *Twelfth Census*, VII, Manufactures, Part I, pp. cxxxvii, cxli.

ESTIMATES OF THE VALUE OF OUTPUT

The shortcomings of the reconciliation arise from crudities of certain figures in the table itself and from the impossibility of allowing quantitatively for other known incomparabilities. The deficiencies under the first head are minor. Additions to the NBER estimates are slightly too large because the value of roofing and street construction includes some construction materials already in the construction materials total. Moreover, the construction materials estimate itself contains some internal duplication. The adjustments to the basic census figures are inadequate because values for two very small agricultural industries, cotton cleaning and rehandling and hay and straw baling, were not subtracted, and because the addition to take care of imports should have been smaller by the amount of imports entering into all the classifications that were subtracted from the original census estimate.

Large differences arise from the incomparabilities that still remain. First, and most important, the census net value of products excludes only partly manufactured materials used in the manufacturing process; our value of output figure excludes also all unfinished products consumed in all other industries except construction, i.e., mining, trade, finance, etc. For this reason alone, we should expect the census *net* value estimate to be considerably higher than our value of output figure.

Second, the census stresses certain imperfections in its technique, particularly with respect to differentiating between raw and partly manufactured materials.[13] Its policy of classification yielded a conservative estimate of net value. This conservative bias is accentuated because the cost of partly manufactured materials to manufacturers is higher than their production values by the amount of transportation and other distributive charges. Consequently, the value of partly manufactured materials that the census deducted from the gross value of products was too large and the resulting net value too small.

Finally, the census estimate of net value includes the value of exported partly manufactured materials; our estimate of finished commodities and construction materials excludes them.

When all these factors are taken into consideration, it is apparent that the two sets of estimates roughly corroborate each other. Despite possible offsets arising from its conservative approach, the census net value ought to be several hundred million dollars higher than our value of output

[13] *Twelfth Census,* VII, Manufactures, Part I, p. cxli. Of course, there are similar difficulties involved in our classification of products. These are elaborated in Sec. 2 above.

total because of differences in definition. The actual difference, approximately $650 million, less than 10 percent, seems entirely reasonable.

B Intercensal Estimates

To make annual estimates that are as reliable as census year figures is of course impossible. But by the careful selection and combination of annual series, fairly reliable interpolators for most minor groups can be provided. Because the basic sources and materials, as well as their inherent limitations vary widely, the derivation of these interpolators is described in considerable detail.

1 The Data

Sources of annual data for the years prior to 1919 can be divided into two main classes: state materials and a heterogeneous classification including a wide variety of miscellaneous series. The relative homogeneity of the state materials, together with their direct relation to the state figures collected in the federal censuses, make it desirable to discuss them as a unit.

a *State materials*

To uncover the state data, annual reports of all states manufacturing 1 percent or more of the national total value of product in 1914 were examined. The reports for 23 states manufacturing 89.1 percent of the nation's output were supplemented by a finding list published in *Synopsis of Federal and State Statistical Laws and Reports*, by W. A. Countryman (19th Convention of Commissioners of State Labor Bureaus, Washington, D. C., April 28, 1903). Table 1 of this paper, a digest of laws and reports on manufactures, lists 31 states, 26 of which are said to have published figures on value of product. Since 7 of these were not among the 23 largest manufacturing states, the number of states included in our investigation was raised to 30 and the percentage coverage to 93.7.

Some of the states whose publications were examined did not collect data on value of product. Of the 10 largest states no annual figures were found for New York and California, while for Illinois, Michigan, Indiana, and Wisconsin, figures were given for a few scattered years alone, for too few industries, or were too scant in coverage to be of use. Nine of the remaining 13 states manufacturing 1 percent or more of the total value of product likewise provided few or no usable data. Moreover, several of the states tabulated by Countryman did little more than republish federal census data and over a dozen failed to provide sufficient continuous data.

ESTIMATES OF THE VALUE OF OUTPUT 93

Consequently, of the original 30 states—New York, Pennsylvania, Illinois, Ohio, Massachusetts, New Jersey, Michigan, Indiana, California, Wisconsin, Missouri, Connecticut, Minnesota, Maryland, Texas, Kansas, Iowa, North Carolina, Rhode Island, Virginia, Louisiana, Georgia, Washington, Nebraska, Tennessee, Maine, West Virginia, New Hampshire, Montana, and North Dakota—only 8 apparently collected annual statistics on manufactures for a period long enough to interpolate for at least one quinquennium. Table II 4 is designed to show not only the relative importance of these 8 states in total manufacturing but also the extent to which the figure for each state differs from that reported for the state by the federal census. Note A describes the nature and contents of the reports issued by each state.

The importance in total manufacturing is indicated roughly by the rank of the states in the federal census for 1914 and more precisely by the percentages in the last line of the table, ranging from 7 in 1889 to 26 in 1909. The fluctuations from 1909 to 1914 to 1919 are due to the absence of data for Pennsylvania in 1914, and for Ohio and New Jersey in 1919. The declines evidenced from 1909 to 1904 to 1899, although due partly to the changing composition of the sample, are due chiefly to less complete state censuses in the earlier years.

The variations in the coverage of the state data from census year to census year stand out conspicuously: that for Pennsylvania ranges from 13 to 100 percent, for Ohio from 42 to 77, and for Virginia from 21 to 100.[14] These variations can result from a change in the extensiveness of coverage, more or fewer industries being reported, or from a change in the intensiveness of coverage, more or fewer establishments within identical industries being reported. The accompanying tabulation is an attempt to separate the effects of these two causes of variation. Changes in extensiveness are eliminated, the percentages for each year referring solely to industries covered by *both* state and federal authorities. Since the percentages in this tabulation are much more stable than those in Table II 4, the state reports are apparently reasonably consistent with respect to intensity of coverage. Consequently, much of the variation in the percentages in Table II 4 arises from coverage of fewer industries by the states in the early years.

[14] Although 100 percent usually means that the state has accepted the reports of the federal census, comparison of years proximate to census years indicates that several states did achieve practically complete coverage.

Coverage in 8 States by State Agencies and by the United States Census of
Manufactures, Comparable Industries, Census Years

	PERCENTAGE THAT STATE TOTAL IS OF FEDERAL					
	1889	1899	1904	1909	1914	1919
Pennsylvania		50	60	75		100
Ohio	*	70	85	85		
Massachusetts	75	85	95	100†	100†	100†
New Jersey		85	90	90	90	
Missouri		75	85	100†	100†	100
Connecticut			75			
Rhode Island		90‡	85‡	60‡		
Virginia		75‡	80	80	80	90

To measure the intensiveness of coverage by the various state agencies, the state totals are here compared with totals for comparable industries reported for the different states by the *Census of Manufactures*. The totals reported by the state agencies are the same as those in Table II 4. The figures with which they are compared, i.e., totals reported by the census for the industries reported by the state bureaus, are the same as those in Table II 4 only when the extensive coverage is identical. Otherwise, the percentages given here must be higher than those in it, because the totals reported by the census have been reduced for the purposes of this comparison. Percentages were rounded to the nearest number divisible by five.

* Scattered data, insufficient for meaningful comparison, were collected by the Ohio agency in 1889.

† Reflects state acceptance of the reports of the *Census of Manufactures*.

‡ Very few industries were reported. Since the comparison is confined to these industries, the ratios are not as meaningful as for states in which a great number of industries are reported. For Rhode Island, 10 industries were included in 1899 and 1904, 8 in 1909; and for Virginia, 10 in 1899.

The description thus far provides a synthetic picture of the state data that suggests important deficiencies. At best 8 states, covering only about one-fourth of total manufacturing, are included; geographically the sample contains no state in the lower south, middle west, or far west. Moreover, the picture lacks detail. Neither finished nor construction material industries were analyzed separately from all industries.

Although an industry by industry comparison of state and United States data would reveal the adequacy of the state figures for each minor group directly, such an appraisal would be incomplete, because for many industries either state and federal classifications are not strictly comparable or else at least one of the requisite figures is not reported at all.

It is possible, however, to make some industry comparisons and thus further to assay the state figures. Since the comparisons are inadequate for analyses by minor groups, they are made for a single year, 1909, and show only the extensiveness and intensiveness of state coverage of specified finished product and construction material industries (Table II 5). An outline of the derivation of the table will best indicate both its meaning and limitations.

First, the census year 1909 was chosen because data for 7 of the 8 states in the sample were available for that year. Other census years would have been less satisfactory both because one or more of the large states are absent, and, in the earlier years, because of the lack of detail.

Second, all essentially finished or construction material industries were listed; i.e., those in which finished commodities or construction materials are produced, with a value of products of $5 million or more. The $5 million limit meant excluding 26 of a possible 166 industries, but most of these would subsequently have been eliminated anyhow because comparable state classifications were lacking.

Third, the census figures for the specific industries in each of the 7 states in the sample were listed only if the state ranked fifth or better in the industry or produced at least 10 percent of total output. These criteria reduced the 140 industries originally selected to 110 and provided 249 entries. Unimportance of an industry in the 7 states was not the sole reason for this reduction; for 11 industries little or no detail by states was given in the federal census.

Fourth, all comparable industry figures that could be obtained from the state reports were listed. Since comparable figures were often lacking, because the states either did not collect any appropriate data at all, defined their industries differently, or grouped several similar industries together, the usable entries were reduced still further. Only the 85 industries and 134 state entries in Table II 5 remained. However, the value of product for these 85 industries constituted 84 percent of the total value for the original 166 industries.

The reductions resulting from steps (2), (3), and (4) indicate the difficulty of complete comparisons of federal and state data. But since the entries are much more important when considered in terms of value rather than number, Table II 5 is useful as evidence of both the extensiveness and intensiveness of the state coverage for finished and construction material industries.

The extensiveness is indicated by the number of industries included, approximately one-half of the possible total, and by their distribution among the major and minor commodity groups. They are well distributed: 15 are classifiable as perishable, 25 as semidurable, 18 as consumer durable, 17 as producer durable, and 10 as construction material industries. Moreover, all except one of the minor commodity groups are represented by at least one industry.

The intensiveness of coverage is suggested by the percentages that the state industry totals are of corresponding national totals. The range and concentration of these percentages, entered for each state in column 6 of Table II 5, are shown in the accompanying frequency distribution.

Percentages that the Combined State Industry Totals are of
Respective United States Industry Totals
Frequency Distribution

PERCENTAGE GROUP	NUMBER
0– 9.9	26
10–19.9	18
20–29.9	19
30–39.9	6
40–49.9	6
50 & over	6

Almost one-third of the state-national percentages are less than 10 percent; most of them, 63 out of a possible 81, are less than 30 percent. Although low percentages do not necessarily indicate nonrepresentativeness, they suggest a need for careful evaluation. This need is even more strongly suggested when the percentages are arranged by major groups. The combined state samples constitute 7.3 percent of the United States total for comparable industries making perishable commodities, 30.7 of semidurable, 16.8 of consumer durable, 22.5 of producer durable, and 17.9 of construction materials (Table II 5).

Thus it is obvious that neither singly nor collectively do the state samples provide ideal interpolating series. The lack of data from 2 of the 6 most important industrial states, the use of industries to represent commodities, the relative smallness of the samples, and to some extent their shifting coverage, and the impossibility of accurate tests of representativeness, all emphasize the need both for additional data and for some measure of the reliability of the sample for each minor group.

Since tests of reliability are important only for the series finally selected as interpolators, discussion is deferred to Section 2, which lists the series selected and attempts to evaluate their adequacy.

b *Miscellaneous sources*

Among the more important sources consulted were reports and special studies of the United States Departments of Agriculture, Commerce, Labor, and Interior, the Bureaus of Railway Economics, of Corporations, and of Internal Revenue, the Interstate Commerce Commission, the Federal Trade Commission, and the War Industries Board. Private sources included industrial and commodity monographs, trade association releases, trade periodicals, and corporate reports. Since these sources are cited in Table II 6, Note B, detailed description would be superfluous. It suffices to mention that series were developed for 22 of the 44 commodity groups, and that several of the better series were for minor groups for which the state samples were especially poor.

Many of the miscellaneous series reflect modifications of data as reported. Quantities were multiplied by average prices; fiscal year figures were transformed into calendar year; and numerous minor adjustments were made to ensure consistency and comparability. Naturally these adjustments affect the adequacy of the resulting series; in fact, for some groups it is doubtful that the samples should be used for other than purely checking purposes. Yet, as will be brought out in Section 2, the movements of the miscellaneous series and those derived from state data were usually enough alike to inspire a fair degree of confidence in using them.

2 Selection and Evaluation

Table II 6 shows for each minor group the series finally selected as well as the complementary ones.[15] The notes to the table describe the components of each series briefly. Our first criterion of evaluation, the extensiveness and intensiveness of coverage, is likewise based on the information in Table II 6 and its notes, supplemented by the general comments in Section 1. Since it would be repetitive to describe the application of this criterion to every minor group, we take one group as an example. By adopting a similar procedure for any group in which he is especially interested, the reader can determine whether he agrees with our rating of a particular series. Minor Group 1a, Manufactured food and kindred products, is selected because almost every problem of evaluation is encountered.

Examination of Table II 6 reveals that there was a choice between the series based on state data and that compiled from data for various commodities. Inspection of the first series shows that at least four states are included in every census period except 1889–99, when only one is. This implies fair geographic extensiveness of coverage after 1899, and poor before. Note A to Table II 6 lists the industries included for each state. The immediate impression is one of good industrial extensiveness. Moreover, comparison of the industries included with the commodities that constitute the food group, listed for census years in Table II 1, reveals that every *important* commodity is included in the sample for 1914–19; sugar

[15] The term 'complementary' is applied to all series used for purposes of checking or corroborating the movements of the series finally selected.

alone is missing from 1899 to 1914; while before 1899 the sample is unsatisfactory. In short, industrial extensiveness of coverage was good after 1899, and poor before. Our over-all rating of the series based on state data, taking both geographic and industrial extensiveness into consideration, is fair for 1899–1919 and poor for 1889–99.[16]

The intensiveness of coverage of state data is much more difficult to appraise, since, as pointed out in Section 1, comparisons with federal census data cannot be accurate. A rough approximation, however, can be computed from Table II 5, which shows that the combined state coverage in 1909 for the 10 food industries there listed was only 6.3 percent. The lowness of this percentage suggests relatively poor intensiveness of coverage.

Extensiveness and intensiveness of coverage for the aggregate of miscellaneous commodity series can be determined from the descriptions of the individual series in Note B to Table II 6. For the food group both types of coverage seem good. Beverages and chocolate and confectionery products are the only important commodities not included directly or indirectly; and most of the series cover the entire United States. However, an additional element, the degree of artificiality, must be considered, because Note B indicates that most of the series are based on computations: either quantities are multiplied by not too comparable prices or fiscal year figures are roughly translated into calendar year figures. Moreover, such series as the Interstate Commerce Commission tonnage data and farm income from livestock represent manufacturers' output of finished foods only indirectly. Consequently, the rating of the aggregate for the miscellaneous food series must be reduced to fair, and should perhaps even be poor.

The above evidence indicates a slight margin of superiority for the state series 1899–1919, and a similar slight margin for the miscellaneous series 1889–99. This conclusion is confirmed by a second criterion: the stability of the census year ratios to the commodity group totals, measured by expressing each ratio as a percentage of the comparable ratio for the preceding census year (Table II 7). The period 1889–99 is not included in the averages because the interpolating data are relatively poor, and because it is ten years in length while the later periods are five.

In interpreting the entries in Table II 7 it must be kept in mind that although stable ratios suggest adequate interpolating series, they do not

[16] Since arithmetically accurate ratings are not feasible, we evaluate each aspect of the sample as good, fair, or poor. Similar designations are used for composite ratings.

necessarily prove their adequacy. Stability may be due to chance and intercensal movements of the sample completely at odds with the true movements. Instability, however, does imply inadequacy; for if the various series truly represented the census trend there would be no change whatsoever in the successive census-year ratios. Moreover, since our method of interpolation distributes differences in the ratios evenly over the intercensal period, the greater the instability of the ratios the greater the effect on the intercensal estimates.

The known inadequacies of most of the sample series make it reasonable to expect at least moderate changes in ratios computed at five and ten year intervals. Consequently, changes of less than 10 percent in five years were deemed small, and of less than 25 percent moderate. Only when the changes exceeded 25 percent was it thought necessary to review critically the rating of a series.

For the food group the percentage changes in the ratios of the series selected as the interpolator are small for 1904–09 and 1914–19, and moderate for 1899–1904 and 1909–14. Those in the ratios of the complementary series are small for 1904–09 and 1909–14, and moderate for 1899–1904 and 1914–19. These differences, however, were not believed sufficient to warrant modifying the earlier ratings of either series. For 1889–99 the smallness of the change in the ratios of the complementary series did suggest a reappraisal; but the evidence on coverage was so decisive as to outweigh the high degree of stability. Nor was the relative stability of the ratios of either series considered significant enough to justify raising either rating for 1889–99 from poor to fair.

As stated above, the degree of stability is of negative rather than positive assistance in evaluating a series. We sometimes lowered a rating because of great instability in the ratios, notably the series for Minor Groups 11 and 30; but we never raised a rating because of high stability.

The third criterion of evaluation is the correspondence between the annual movements of the various series. Since each series is directly related to the commodity group for which it was compiled, it is reasonable to assume that the correspondence between two or more provides some evidence upon which to appraise the reliability of each. But the evidence is crude if only because every series is usually defective in some way, implying distortion of some of the year to year movements. Moreover, since the series are rarely of equal merit they can hardly be expected to move identically.

We measured correspondence by computing the percentage changes from year to year in the movement of each series. The difference in each year between the percentage changes in the interpolating and complementary series was then taken to indicate the degree of corroboration. For example, if one series showed a percentage increase of 2.2 and the other a percentage decrease of 1.1, the difference in movement is 3.3. The smaller this difference the better the correspondence.

After due consideration of the probable deficiencies in most of the samples it was arbitrarily assumed that differences between the interpolating and the complementary series of less than 10.0 were small enough to warrant classing the series as corresponding. But it is obvious that even so defined they will not correspond in all years, especially if they had previously been rated poor or fair. Consequently, it was decided to rate the correspondence satisfactory if six out of ten years were classifiable as corresponding. Standards may be more or less rigorous, but no matter how rigorous, Table II 8 provides merely a crude test of reliability and can be used only in conjunction with the other criteria of evaluation.

The data for the food group in Table II 8 are split into two periods, 1889–99 and 1899–1919, because a different interpolating series was selected for each period (see Table II 6). The correspondence from 1889 to 1899 is fair, the movements in six of the ten years being classifiable as corresponding; while that from 1899 to 1919 is good, 17 of a possible 20 annual movements corresponding. Thus application of the third criterion strengthens slightly our belief in the adequacy of the food group samples. The correspondence, however, is not considered sufficient to justify raising the earlier ratings.

The above procedure does not eliminate subjective evaluation. In fact, even its more mechanical phases were tempered by the knowledge and experience gained during the compilation of each series. The most significant criterion for rating a series obviously remains the relatively imprecise one of extensiveness and intensiveness of coverage.

The accompanying tabulation gives the final rating of the series used for interpolating each commodity group.[18] Since the ratings for 1889–99 are in most instances lower than the corresponding ones in later years, they are shown separately. Those for 1899–1919 are sufficiently uniform for each census period to make it unnecessary to provide separate ratings for the four periods included.

[18] The ratings refer to the probable reliability of each series as a measure of year-to-year changes.

ESTIMATES OF THE VALUE OF OUTPUT

FINAL RATING OF SERIES USED FOR INTERPOLATION*
1899–1919

Good (G) 2, 5b, 6, 8, 14a, 20a, 32a, CM
Fair (F) 1a, 3, 5a, 7, 9, 11, 12, 13a, 13b, 15, 17, 19, 20b, 20c, 24, 25a, 25b, 26, 28, 29, 30, 31, 32b, 35, 36
Poor (P) 1b, 4, 10, 14b, 16, 18, 21, 22, 23, 27, 33, 34

* Ratings were assigned also to Minor Groups 1b and 5b, both composed of nonmanufactured commodities. For the detailed steps in making the estimates for these groups see Section C.

1889–1899†

Good (G) None
Fair (F) 2, 5b, 6, 7, 8, 14a, 30, CM
Poor (P) 1a, 1b, 3, 4, 5a, 9, 10, 11, 12, 13a, 14b, 15, 16, 17, 18, 19, 20c, 21, 22, 23, 24, 25, 26, 27, 28, 29, 31, 32b, 33, 34, 35, 36

† No rating is shown for Minor Groups 13b, 20a, 20b, 32a because few or no commodities in these groups were manufactured before 1899.

C NONMANUFACTURED COMMODITIES

Important in three groups—foods, fuels, and construction materials—nonmanufactured commodities include products of farms, fisheries, mines, and forests. Most of the estimates are based on data from the Department of Agriculture, and the Bureaus of Fisheries and Mines. The detailed figures together with descriptions of sources and methods are shown in Tables II 9, 10, and 11 and the notes to them.

1 Nonmanufactured Foods

a *Products of farms*

For agricultural foods *Gross Farm Income, Indexes of Farm Production and of Farm Prices in the United States, 1869–1937*, by Frederick Strauss and L. H. Bean (Department of Agriculture, Technical Bulletin 703, Dec. 1940) was especially helpful. From this monograph, hereafter referred to as Strauss and Bean, the decennial *Census of Agriculture*, and special crop reports of the Department of Agriculture farm income estimates could be compiled for almost every relevant crop and livestock product.[19]

[19] Lack of appropriate data prevented the computation of continuous estimates for several commodities; e.g., natural ice, honey, and maple sugar and sirup. For natural ice there were no satisfactory data; the combined values of honey and maple sugar and sirup amounted to $11 million in 1909 and $27 million in 1919 (14th Census, V, *Agriculture*, pp. 649, 849). Since the latter values constitute only .5 or .6 percent of the totals in Table II 9 and less than .2 percent of the estimates for all foods, their omission has little effect on the level of our estimates and probably even less on their fluctuations. It is likely that the omission of natural ice is also relatively unimportant.

The apportionment of the various agricultural foods between finished and unfinished presented problems similar to those involved in apportioning mixed manufactured commodities. Reliance was placed chiefly on the materials consumed method. The implications of this method are indicated in Note A to Table II 2; its application to specific groups of farm products is described in Note A to Table II 9.

The final estimates of finished farm products show long term movements fairly well, but may not measure year to year changes quite accurately, especially before 1900.[20] However, as these less reliable product estimates constitute at most only one-eighth of the perishable group total, the effect of even rather large errors would not be very great.

b *Products of fisheries*
Total values for edible fish for 1869, 1879, 1889, and 1908 (United States Censuses of the Fishery Industries) were interpolated and extrapolated on the basis of annual estimates of the catch in four important regions—New England, Middle Atlantic, Lake, and Pacific—and from occasional figures for other regions reported by the Bureau of Fisheries. The estimate of total catch was then allocated between finished and unfinished by means of the materials consumed method.

Because it was impossible to allow satisfactorily for wastage and because of the probable use of some edible fish as fertilizer, the level of the

---

[20] Since the compilation of our estimates, the Department of Agriculture has substantially completed its Income Parity Studies. Making use of these reports, many of which contain revised data back to 1909, as well as of many special sources, Harold Barger and Hans Landsberg of the National Bureau have refined and improved the production data for several crop and livestock series back to 1899 (*American Agriculture, 1899–1939: A Study of Output, Employment and Productivity,* National Bureau of Economic Research, 1942).

A review of the Barger-Landsberg series indicates that the ultimate effects of substituting their improved data would be relatively small. The revisions for the crops and products for which comparison was possible amounted to less than 10 percent in all except one instance; and even these differences showed a tendency to cancel when the values for the different commodities were totaled.

Despite the one exception, fluid milk, in which the revision gave values almost double those on which our estimate was based, the over-all effect of incorporating the Barger-Landsberg series would be to raise our total of finished nonmanufactured agricultural foods less than 10 percent. The effect on the total food group would be considerably smaller; while that on the perishable commodity group as a whole would average less than 2 percent. Year to year changes would hardly be influenced.

Because to incorporate the revised series would have occasioned laborious recalculations disproportionate to the improvements effected, we decided not to. But we advise the user of our estimates of nonmanufactured agricultural foods to bear in mind that they slightly understate the level of output.

ESTIMATES OF THE VALUE OF OUTPUT

final estimates for fresh fish destined for sale to ultimate consumers may be slightly too high. This slight exaggeration may be compensated in part by the possible failure of the various censuses of fisheries to achieve complete coverage. The year to year movements are believed to be fairly reliable.

c *Products of mines*

Annual values for the one food product here included, natural mineral waters, are from *Mineral Resources of the United States.*

2 Nonmanufactured Fuels

a *Products of mines*

Estimates were made for three products: anthracite coal, bituminous coal, and fuel briquets. Most of the data basic to these estimates were taken from *Mineral Resources of the United States.* The final estimates are believed to be tolerably good, except possibly those for bituminous coal, for which the apportionment between industrial (unfinished) and household (finished) was especially crude. The allocation for all years prior to 1915 was based upon that for 1915.

b *Products of forests*

Lack of data prevented the preparation of continuous estimates for firewood; but the few figures available give some idea of its importance. In 1880 consumption for domestic purposes amounted to about 141 million cords valued at close to $310 million; in 1908 it was apparently about 76 million cords with a value of about $225 million (*Consumption of Firewood in the United States,* Forest Service Circular 181, and *American Forests and Forest Products,* Department of Agriculture, Statistical Bulletin 21, Washington, D. C., 1928; issued Oct. 1927, revised March 1928, Table 213). These figures suggest a value approaching or, in prewar years, even exceeding that of coal destined for ultimate consumers.[21] Our failure to include firewood thus means a fairly serious deficiency in the fuel estimates, which the user should not forget.

[21] A recent Department of Agriculture publication, *Fuel Wood Used in the United States, 1630–1930* (Circular 641, Washington, D. C., Feb. 1942), provides additional evidence of the importance of firewood. The estimated total consumption by decades, in millions of cords, is: 1870–79, 1,407; 1880–89, 1,304; 1890–99, 1,087; 1900–09, 916; 1909–19, 913; and 1919–29, 746 (Table 2).

3 Construction Materials

a Products of forests

Estimates for lumber used in construction were pieced together by means of data from a wide variety of sources. Their reliability can be judged by consulting Note A to Table II 11. For reasons mentioned in the Note, the level of the final estimates is probably somewhat too high; there were no data on which satisfactorily to compute a downward adjustment. Our inability to make continuous estimates for certain miscellaneous lumber products, such as round timbers, poles, and the construction products of farms—the combined value of which runs to $25–100 million—compensates somewhat for the probable excess in the lumber estimates. The estimates for railroad cross ties are believed to be fairly reliable.

b Products of mines

Sand (building, paving, railroad ballast, and gravel) and crushed stone are the two major construction materials produced in mines. As indicated in Note A to Table II 11, values for the different types of sand and for crushed stone are reported in *Mineral Resources of the United States*. Since the values were small, no effort was made to extend any series beyond the earliest year for which each was reported. The year to year comparability of the totals is therefore reduced slightly.

D DERIVATION OF THE ESTIMATES SINCE 1919

1 Adjustments to Kuznets' Estimates for 1919–1933

Several shifts were made in the original commodity group classification in *Commodity Flow and Capital Formation* in order to make it more comparable with our estimates for the years before 1919. The adjustments were approximate. When differences in 1919 amounted to less than $5 million for any minor commodity group or when, by changing Kuznets' estimate we would have reduced its accuracy, no corrections were made. Only when our estimate for 1919 was an improvement over the corresponding one in *Commodity Flow* was the latter adjusted. For example, Kuznets' estimates for Minor Group 3, Drugs and household preparations, included a sizable amount of products of the chemicals, n.e.c., industry. Careful examination of the industry indicated that practically all the commodities there included should be classified as unfinished. Consequently, Kuznets' totals for the drug group were adjusted to exclude chemicals, n.e.c.

The corrections of Kuznets' modified estimates for exports and im-

ESTIMATES OF THE VALUE OF OUTPUT 105

ports were also rough.[22] Except those for three groups—food products, tractors, and construction materials—they were based on the 1929 relationships alone. Ratios of Kuznets' unadjusted value of domestic consumption to his unadjusted value of domestic output, computed for each minor group in 1929, were applied to his adjusted output values in every year, with the exception of the three groups already noted. For foods and tractors ratios were computed for every year; for construction materials they were computed for 1919 and 1929 and interpolated for the intervening years.

2 Estimates for Years since 1933

The 1935 and 1937 estimates of the value of the domestic consumption of manufactured commodities were based on the movement 1933–35 and 1935–37 of the value reported in the *Census of Manufactures* for 1935 and 1937. Separate estimates were made for each minor group. The sources for nonmanufactured commodities were *Agricultural Statistics, 1939*, p. 482 (for gross farm income from the sale of fruits, vegetables, nuts, dairy products, eggs, and chickens and the value of farm products retained for home consumption); and *Minerals Yearbook, seriatim* (for anthracite coal, coke, and fuel oil used for domestic purposes, also for nonmanufactured construction materials, crushed stone, sand and gravel).

The 1934, 1936, 1938, and tentative 1939 estimates were made only for the four major groups and construction materials.

a Perishable

The 1934 and 1936 estimates for perishable commodities consumed in the United States were based on the movement of the gross income of corporations manufacturing foods and kindred products, liquors and beverages, tobacco products, paper and pulp products, printing, publishing and allied products, petroleum and other mineral oil products, and chemicals and allied products (*Statistics of Income*); of gross farm income from the sale of fruits, vegetables, nuts, dairy products, eggs, and chickens; of the value of farm products retained for home consumption, and the value of anthracite coal and of coke used for domestic purposes. The estimate for 1938 was based on the sales of foods, paper and paper products (except boxes), newspapers and periodicals, newspapers (small),

---

[22] The procedure was based on the one Kuznets used in *Commodity Flow* to derive the original estimates. For most groups, exports and imports were compiled for 1929 alone; corrections for other years were based on the 1929 relationships.

chemicals, drugs, and petroleum and tobacco products (*Dun's Review,* May 1939), and on the farm income, coal, and coke totals.

For 1939 the tentative estimate was made from the movement of wholesale sales of beer, wine and liquors, drugs and drug sundries, groceries and foods, paper and products, and tobacco and its products (*Domestic Commerce,* Jan. 20, 1940); retail sales of filling stations (*ibid.,* Feb. 20, 1940); farm income (excluding the value of products retained for home consumption) and the wholesale value of all anthracite coal shipments (*Survey of Current Business,* Feb. 1939 and 1940).

b *Semidurable*

The 1934 and 1936 estimates for this major group were based on the movement of the gross income of corporations manufacturing textile mill products excluding woolen and worsted yarns, pulling, etc., leather and its manufactures, and rubber products (*Statistics of Income*). The 1938 sales of cotton textiles, silk and rayon goods, clothing, hosiery, shoes, and tires and other rubber goods (*Dun's Review,* May 1939) were used to extrapolate the 1937 estimate.

The preliminary 1939 estimate was based on the wholesale sales of amusement and sporting goods, dry goods, and clothing and furnishings (*Domestic Commerce,* Jan. 20, 1940).

c *Consumer durable*

The 1934 and 1936 estimates were based on the movement of the gross income of establishments manufacturing other wood products, household machinery and equipment; radios; musical, professional, and scientific instruments, and precious metal products and jewelry (*Statistics of Income*). The wholesale value of passenger cars sold in the United States (*Automobile Facts and Figures, 1939,* pp. 4, 9) was combined with the gross income totals to interpolate between the 1935 and 1937 estimates. For 1938 the passenger car value and the sales of furniture, electrical apparatus and appliances, and jewelry, watches, silverware, and findings (*Dun's Review,* May 1939) were used as an extrapolator. The 1939 estimate was based on the sales in the United States and Canada of passenger cars (Automobile Manufacturers' Association) and on wholesale sales of furniture and housefurnishings, jewelry and optical goods, and electrical goods (*Domestic Commerce,* Jan. 20, 1940).

d *Producer durable*

The value of producer durable commodities destined for domestic con-

ESTIMATES OF THE VALUE OF OUTPUT

sumption in 1934 and 1936 was estimated by means of the wholesale value of motor trucks sold in the United States (*Automobile Facts and Figures, 1939,* pp. 4, 9) and the gross income of corporations making locomotives and railroad equipment, factory machinery, agricultural machinery, electric machinery, miscellaneous machinery, office equipment and hardware, tools, etc. (*Statistics of Income*). The estimate for 1938 was based on the sales of motor trucks and of machinery, engines, and transportation equipment except automobiles and automotive accessories (*Dun's Review,* May 1939).

The tentative 1939 estimate was based upon the movement of wholesale sales of electrical goods and machinery equipment and supplies (*Domestic Commerce,* Jan. 20, 1940) and of the sales of trucks in the United States and Canada.

e *Construction materials*

The value of construction materials destined for domestic consumption in 1934 and 1936 was based on the gross income of sawmills; stone, clay and glass; paint and metal building materials corporations (*Statistics of Income*). The estimate for 1938 was based on sales of lumber and planing mill products, stone and stone products, clay and glass products, structural steel, heating, plumbing and air conditioning equipment, and paints, varnishes and lacquers (*Dun's Review,* May 1939). The estimate for 1939 of hardware, lumber and construction materials, metals and metal work, and plumbing and heating equipment was based on wholesale sales (*Domestic Commerce,* Jan. 20, 1940).

For all groups the tentative estimates for 1938 and 1939 were made before the 1939 *Census of Manufactures* and other detailed statistics had become available. Since the figures for all recent years will be superseded when the final report of the Department of Commerce (see Preface) is published, it was not thought worth while to attempt to improve the present estimates at this time. Inspection of the more detailed statistics suggests that there would be no changes sufficient to modify the conclusions reached in the analysis of movements over time (Part I, Sec. C).

TABLE II 1

Value of Manufactured Commodities, Census Years, 1869–1919
(thousands of dollars)

Major and Minor Commodity Groups

INDUSTRY NUMBER	COMMODITY	1869	1879	1889	1899	1904	1909	1914	1919
	Minor Group 1 Food and Kindred Products								
		FINISHED COMMODITIES							
		PERISHABLE							
I 36	Bread & other bakery products	36,797	65,628	128,037	174,843	268,774	395,594	491,616	1,150,940
I 44, 46	Canned fish & oysters, smoked fish, & salted & pickled fish	3,006	Not cov. by census	10,039	19,053	22,482	27,850	33,333	76,762
I 45	Canned & dried fruits & vegetables	4,514	14,643	24,845	46,947	75,227	92,641	151,960	392,425
I 61	Cheese	16,717	17,290	19,803	26,520	28,612	43,246	50,533	137,281
I 63	Chewing gum			(Included with I 80—Confectionery & Ice Cream)				17,243	53,430
I 65	Chocolate in cakes, sweetened or with nuts Milk chocolate Cocoa, powdered Other chocolate & cocoa products, except confectionery	423	607	1,969	4,508	6,711	10,438	16,761	43,052 9,058 9,423 3,115
	Finished chocolate & cocoa products made in other industries								647
I 74	Coffee, roasting & grinding Spice, roasting & grinding	10,039	19,887	65,100	60,315	79,305	104,122	137,546 4,442	279,734 11,146
I 80	Confectionery & ice cream	11,820	19,029	41,565	60,341	86,652	134,161	215,880	649,086
I 84	Cordials & flavoring sirups	198	317	1,821	2,016	3,359	9,250	14,701	44,970
I 122	Hominy and grits				2,567	8,455	12,509	15,036	9,249
	Oatmeal, breakfast food & all other cereal products	2,765	3,139	2,991	1,818	1,771	4,720	6,330	15,484
I 123	Breakfast foods made in Food preparations, n.e.s. industry			5,509	15,560	23,905	36,979	59,985	159,223
	Other food preparations for human consumption	1,544	974	2,908	8,212	12,611	23,999	36,210	86,103
	Macaroni, vermicelli & noodles		514	1,067	3,015	4,630	8,821	13,285	38,860
	Peanut butter		189	218	615	944	1,791	2,698	10,503
	Sweetening sirups other than cane		39	(Included with I 300—Sweetening sirup)				10,164	56,277

108

Minor Group 1 Food and Kindred Products

VII	188	Rum, whiskey & other distilled liquors	12,013	13,630	34,585	32,120	43,571	109,190	110,545	1,730
VII	189	Liquors, malt	55,261	99,845	180,539	234,048	294,766	370,233	436,637	376,563
VII	190	Liquors, vinous	2,165	2,110	2,769	6,371	10,798	12,079	15,462	16,218
VII	205	Mineral & soda waters	4,079	4,581	13,869	23,060	29,979	43,123	58,218	134,696
I	226	Oleomargarine	not reported	6,776	2,938	12,287	9,559	13,975	23,651	120,692
I	246	Pickles, preserves & sauces	1,658	3,211	13,061	31,329	30,933	41,557	60,137	155,961
I	263	Clean rice, fancy—head	not reported	2,281	4,873	6,355	12,157	17,400	16,435	70,649
I	272, 286	Sausage (incl. canned)			12,353	25,983	33,179	59,565	90,392	221,208
I	286	Fresh meat	75,286	249,941	252,169	342,970	398,163	578,485	769,384	1,642,462
I	287	Cured meat			194,453	246,197	256,945	340,289	408,001	1,245,950
		Canned goods			18,734	19,187	16,115	15,346	26,418	96,904
		Meat puddings, scrapple, head cheese, etc.		39	220	621	953	2,510	4,488	10,050
		Edible meat products not made in slaughtering & meat packing industries		66	372	1,050	1,612	4,245	7,611	37,126
I	309	Sweetening sirup	3,050	3,886	3,077	5,991	6,804	(Included with I 123, sweetening sirups other than cane)	10,235	29,695
I	331	Vinegar & cider	3,874	3,813	7,418	7,201	8,820	10,255		
		Total, Commodities Classified Directly	245,749	532,435	1,047,302	1,421,100	1,777,792	2,534,537	3,320,508	7,396,622
VIII	17	Baking powders & yeast	275	3,956	5,949	13,269	16,300	15,547	16,208	25,019
I	40	Butter	not reported	5,622	34,721	81,623	109,226	173,361	212,587	508,293
I	79	Condensed & evaporated milk	not reported	597	1,969	9,768	16,671	28,282	52,784	282,968
I	120	Flavoring extracts	451	825	1,920	5,945	7,372	6,548	5,674	14,776

109

INDUSTRY NUMBER		COMMODITY	1869	1879	1889	1899	1904	1909	1914	1919
I	122	Flour: wheat, corn, rye, buckwheat & barley	332,135	370,125	364,454	354,636	482,643	529,141	498,182	1,255,226
I	123, 180	Lard, incl. lard compounds & substitutes	not reported	24,040	52,658	70,618	90,718	168,935	181,096	633,367
XIV	159	Ice, mfd.	125	266	2,384	6,706	12,175	22,070	31,096	69,398
I	235	Peanuts, grading, roasting, cleaning, shelling	829	1,642	5,373	4,979	6,567	8,804	13,509	32,842
VIII	269	Salt	1,117	1,107	1,170	1,696	1,613	2,240	3,221	7,570
I	308, 309, 310	Sugar, granulated, refined & brown	100,939	126,993	90,013	190,191	229,092	239,461	267,107	614,500
		Total, Minor Group 1	681,620	1,067,608	1,607,913	2,160,531	2,750,169	3,728,926	4,601,972	10,840,581
		% that Commodities Classified Directly form of Group Total	36.1	49.9	65.1	65.8	64.6	68.0	72.2	68.2
		Minor Group 2 Cigars, Cigarettes and Tobacco								
XIV	247	Pipes, tobacco	446	628	1,877	2,467	2,828	5,300	4,210	11,525
XI	319, 320	Cigars, cigarettes & tobacco: chewing, smoking, snuff & all other	71,762	116,773	195,537	263,713	331,112	416,695	490,165	1,012,933
		Total, Minor Group 2	72,208	117,401	197,414	266,180	333,940	421,995	494,375	1,024,458
		% that Commodities Classified Directly form of Group Total	100.0	100.0	100.0	100.0	100.0	100.0	100.0	100.0
		Minor Group 3 Drug, Toilet and Household Preparations								
VIII	25	Bluing	107	401	531	669	789	1,248	1,258	2,847
VIII	95	Pharmaceutical metals & their salts							732	421
		Pills, tablets, powders, etc.	2,763	not reported	3,653	12,727	17,806	24,628	10,903	37,804
		Synthetic preparations							1,385	405
		Tinctures, fluid extracts, medicinal sirups, etc.							13,900	38,679
VIII	233	Patent medicines	13,104	11,834	26,292	48,073	60,731	68,290	83,455	162,474
VIII	240	Perfumes, cosmetics & toilet preparations	2,763	2,998	6,301	9,647	15,151	21,475	25,965	82,084
XIV	265	Druggists' & stationers' sundries	724	1,257	1,620	2,982	4,594	7,783	7,512	15,802

XIV	312	Surgical appliances	367	916	1,668	3,976	6,455	11,200	14,928	44,316
		Total, Commodities Classified Directly	17,065	17,406	40,065	78,074	105,526	134,624	160,038	384,832
VIII	24	Blacking, stains & dressings	583	1,062	2,067	3,210	4,233	5,998	7,042	18,020
VIII	66	Cleansing & polishing preparations	305	473	818	2,072	2,560	5,913	8,648	22,615
VIII	95	Alkaloids & derivatives	not reported		1,532	5,339	7,471	10,333	11,281	10,716
		Biological products	not reported		339	1,180	1,651	2,283	2,495	6,366
VIII	219	Castor oil	667	775	646	436	736	998	1,008	4,384
VIII	233	Patent compounds	1,618	1,461	3,247	5,937	7,501	8,434	10,321	28,969
VIII	294	Soap	17,628	20,530	34,201	41,464	56,024	87,783	99,255	215,405
		Total, Minor Group 3	37,866	41,707	82,915	137,712	185,702	256,366	300,088	691,307
		% that Commodities Classified Directly form of Group Total	45.1	41.7	48.3	56.7	56.8	52.5	53.3	55.7

Minor Group 4 Magazines, Newspapers, Stationery and Supplies and Miscellaneous Paper Products

XIV	8	Artists' materials	116	not reported separately	654	611	1,400	2,875	3,874	6,420
VIII	161	Ink, writing	301	432	927	1,063	1,546	2,059	2,290	6,172
VI	231	Playing cards	765	not reported	350	1,406	1,856	3,179	4,104	10,810
XIV	236	Pencils, lead	139	214	1,293	1,702	3,390	5,652	6,379	18,497
XIV	237	Pens, fountain & stylographic	not reported separately		333	856	1,967	3,347	6,504	15,633
III	239	Pens, steel	207	189	308	338	545	664	590	1,648
XIV	242	Phonograph needles	not reported separately			31	170	87	36	1,688
VI	254	Sheet music & books of music: published or printed & published		2,277	2,808	3,650	4,674	5,511	6,803	12,510

111

INDUSTRY NUMBER		COMMODITY	1869	1879	1889	1899	1904	1909	1914	1919
VI	255	Newspapers: subscriptions & sales	18,233	49,873	72,343	79,928	111,299	{84,439	99,542	192,820
		Periodicals: subscriptions & sales						50,624	64,035	85,187
IV	266	Rules, ivory & wood	not reported	74	172	232	278	161	708	1,294
		Total, Commodities Classified Directly	19,761	53,059	79,188	89,817	127,125	158,598	194,865	352,679
VI	108	Envelopes	1,206	1,589	2,571	3,334	5,411	7,122	9,786	20,154
XIV	210	Mucilage, paste & other adhesives, n.e.s.	72	10	735	1,471	2,046	2,831	3,323	6,406
VI	230	Fine paper: writing	6,240	4,620	6,372	8,483	13,409	17,326	19,874	51,210
VI	231	All other paper goods, n.e.s.	1,528	795	2,172	8,116	10,715	18,353	23,689	49,388
		Total, Minor Group 4	28,807	60,073	91,038	111,221	158,706	204,230	251,537	479,837
		% that Commodities Classified Directly form of Group Total	68.6	88.3	87.0	80.8	80.1	77.7	77.5	73.5

Minor Group 5 Fuel and Lighting Products
(a) Manufactured Fuel and Lighting Products

VIII	43	Candles	2,279	2,502	4,108	5,015	6,786	5,462	3,473	7,997
VIII	133	Gas-house coke, for sale	1,247	not reported	2,203	2,703	5,198	5,726	8,729	17,829
IV	200	Matches	3,535	4,661	2,191	5,998	5,639	11,337	12,538	18,470
		Total, Commodities Classified Directly	7,063	7,163	8,502	13,716	17,623	22,525	24,740	44,296
VIII	76	Coke	58	277	852	1,776	2,515	4,498	4,417	15,677
VIII	194, 241	Illuminating oils	22,580	32,447	50,298	72,453	88,625	91,711	89,062	188,530
		Lubricating oils		not reported		{3	82	453	3,800	37,008
		Gasoline				{105	1,025	5,877	37,562	346,314
		Total, Minor Group 5a	29,699	39,887	59,652	88,053	109,870	125,064	159,581	631,825

			23.8	18.0	14.3	15.6	16.0	18.0	15.5	7.0
% that Commodities Classified Directly form of Group Total										
Total, Major Group Perishables			850,200	1,326,676	2,038,932	2,763,697	3,538,387	4,736,581	5,807,553	13,668,008
Total, Perishables Classified Directly			361,844	727,464	1,372,471	1,868,887	2,362,006	3,272,279	4,194,526	9,202,887
% that Perishables Classified Directly form of Major Group Total			42.6	54.8	67.3	67.6	66.8	69.1	72.2	67.3

SEMIDURABLE

Minor Group 6 Dry Goods and Notions

XIV	78	Combs & hairpins, not made from metal or rubber	689	1,269	1,472	1,976	2,769	8,376	5,181	6,211
II	119	Flags & banners	not reported	134	510	1,160	956	2,218	3,792	5,454
XIV	146	Hairwork	1,396	1,039	1,762	1,382	1,752	11,025	3,277	6,909
II	203	Lacework, crocheted goods, handmade curtains of muslin & lace, ladies' & children's belts other than leather, & handkerchiefs	1,234	1,815	3,420	5,585	9,623	16,279	21,692	43,679
X	215	Pins, common or toilet	640	923		570	1,412	1,269	1,517	3,110
		Hairpins, metal				95	136	(Incl. with XIV 78)	641	1,650
		Safety pins			1,113	434	1,036	956	1,138	3,318
		Needles, other than knitting machine needles				611	751	670	798	2,040
VI	232	Paper patterns	not reported	691	508	757	3,051	3,518	4,514	7,090
V	250	Pocketbooks, purses & cardcases	1,141	1,821	2,229	2,569	3,879	3,736	3,835	13,823
II	284	Silk embroideries	13	45	81	58	112	485	34	128
		Silk laces, nets, veils, veiling	140	437	262	803	745	1,351	1,329	5,825
		Total, Commodities Classified Directly	5,253	8,174	11,357	16,000	26,222	49,883	47,748	99,237
XIV	5	Artificial flowers	712	1,333	2,472	1,713	1,429	6,530	5,500	12,264

INDUSTRY NUMBER		COMMODITY	1869	1879	1889	1899	1904	1909	1914	1919
XIV	42	Buttons	135	337	320	584	905	1,683	1,494	3,213
II	87, 88, 89	Lace goods & nets Cotton thread All other cotton woven goods	231 4,904 50,280	274 4,641 51,993	323 6,742 60,211	945 5,008 41,438	2,115 5,559 45,359	2,637 6,810 52,497	3,551 8,459 39,368	9,058 20,851 248,082
II	97	Dyeing & finishing textiles	5,608	12,314	8,455	8,225	3,782	7,121	12,573	47,905
XIV	110	Fancy articles, n.e.s.	252	3,371	6,216	8,108	10,722	11,106	15,825	55,112
XIV	111	Feathers & plumes	318	1,125	2,092	1,450	1,209	5,526	4,237	5,432
V	184	Leather goods, n.e.s.	no data	2,322	5,339	10,002	14,981	15,988	16,339	43,475
II	203	Embroideries	296	435	819	1,338	2,305	3,900	5,197	12,209
II	284	Silk ribbons Broadsilks Silk velvets & plushes Sewing & embroidery silks	843 1,720 none 157	4,094 6,109 504	14,475 14,639 2,359 1,855	13,700 30,896 3,724 2,130	13,857 33,807 3,381 2,553	18,962 54,792 5,161 2,456	20,399 76,435 14,032 3,335	25,152 215,598 31,915 4,629
IX	300	Statuary & art goods		(Incl. with XIV 110)			837	1,192	1,357	1,772
II	355, 356	Woolen & worsted woven goods, except shawls, blankets & carriage equipment	100,122	88,126	85,621	73,683	86,114	82,670	44,445	149,738
II	357	Mixed textiles	not reported	42,382			not reported separately			
		Total, Minor Group 6	170,831	227,534	223,295	218,944	255,137	328,914	320,294	985,642
		% that Commodities Classified Directly form of Group Total	3.1	3.6	5.1	7.3	10.3	15.2	14.9	10.1

Minor Group 7 Clothing and Personal Furnishings

II	70	Clothing, men's, regular factories	133,053	187,538	224,653	247,651	318,424	434,538	422,842	1,074,293
II	72	Clothing, women's, regular factories	12,653	31,389	66,851	156,272	242,894	377,205	468,029	1,151,611
II	77	Collars & cuffs	(Included with II 128)			9,078	7,250	9,924	12,566	35,452
II	86	Corsets	4,454	6,080	11,608	13,931	14,327	32,060	39,085	72,646
II	128	Furnishing goods, men's	(Incl. with II 70)	13,129	34,083	32,811	41,584	48,054	57,555	116,083
II	137x	Gloves & mittens, cloth								28,220

	No.	Commodity								
V	137	Gloves & mittens, leather, men's & boys'	3,803	7,018	9,609	{12,588	14,657	18,349	16,850	36,944
		Gloves & mittens, leather, women's & children's				3,517	2,632	4,442	4,088	11,063
II	152	Hats & caps, other than felt, straw & wool	4,368	5,255	9,205	12,132	13,228	13,973	19,060	43,390
II	153	Hats, fur-felt	9,345	11,203	19,624	25,868	34,647	44,249	34,080	71,743
II	154	Hats, straw	3,509	4,222	7,394	9,746	10,606	21,946	27,028	32,650
II	155	Hats, wool-felt	7,672	9,195	5,756	3,945	2,858	4,551	2,082	5,486
II	176	Bathing suits		9	32	869	1,225	1,268	2,034	6,645
		Hosiery		10,893	19,162	27,420	44,113	69,382	98,099	308,662
		Gloves & mittens, knitted		530	1,935	4,244	5,556	7,310	10,520	19,530
		Knitted headwear (except infants')		785	1,476	1,002	1,775	3,373	3,456	3,996
		Leggings		286	85	249	620	521	314	63
		Scarfs & shawls		246	115	329	1,293	916	714	4,055
		Shirts & drawers	17,194	12,692	32,962	45,676	56,644	70,738	57,523	98,286
		Sweaters, sweater coats, jerseys, cardigan jackets, etc.		1,724	3,576	3,499	8,345	22,524	26,195	61,094
		Union suits		(None)		3,692	6,794	14,874	35,596	105,244
		All other fancy knit goods		113	760	951	2,119	2,428	3,197	16,322
		Undistributed knit goods made as secondary products in other industries		37	84	32	1,580	none	5,088	8,375
II	203	Women's neckwear	832	1,223	2,305	3,764	6,486	10,973	14,621	20,800
II	262	Regalia & society badges & emblems	613	800	3,140	3,015	4,701	6,060	5,101	8,933
XIV	265	Rubber clothing	651	1,130	1,456	2,680	4,129	6,996	6,800	8,824
II	281	Shirts	(Incl. with II 70)	1,796	33,082	48,222	52,161	84,335	93,366	199,166
II	355, 356	Shawls, all-wool woven	1,770	1,971	2,099	501	557	405	66	854
	—	Military goods	283			(Presumably included elsewhere)				
		Total, Commodities Classified Directly	200,200	327,264	491,052	673,684	901,205	1,311,394	1,465,955	3,550,430

INDUSTRY NUMBER		COMMODITY	1869	1879	1889	1899	1904	1909	1914	1919
XIV	127	Fur goods	7,183	6,648	15,997	21,609	30,971	46,650	36,739	145,070
II	203	Trimmed hats	2,741	4,031	7,595	12,402	21,370	36,151	48,173	118,309
II	313	Suspenders, garters & elastic woven goods	(Included with II 128, II 203, Millinery goods; and XIV 265, rubber goods, n.e.s.)					14,175	12,564	31,396
XIV	327	Umbrellas & canes	3,948	5,664	11,277	11,340	11,031	13,159	11,436	20,981
		Total, Minor Group 7	214,072	343,607	525,921	719,035	964,577	1,421,529	1,574,867	3,866,186
		% that Commodities Classified Directly form of Group Total	93.5	95.2	93.4	93.7	93.4	92.3	93.1	91.8
		Minor Group 8 Shoes and Other Footwear								
V	30	Boots & shoes, other than rubber	180,372	{ 163,892	217,780	255,798	316,076	434,213	489,909	1,129,181
		Miscellaneous footwear		996	1,324	1,628	2,064	4,431	6,366	13,404
XIV	31	Boots & shoes, rubber	5,272	9,172	17,607	38,830	58,663	41,639	44,752	{90,780
		Shoes, canvas, with rubber soles								25,177
		Total, Minor Group 8	185,644	174,060	236,711	296,256	376,803	480,283	541,027	1,258,542
		% that Commodities Classified Directly form of Group Total	100.0	100.0	100.0	100.0	100.0	100.0	100.0	100.0
		Minor Group 9 House Furnishings (semidurable)								
XIV	38	Brooms, made from broom corn	6,340	5,015	6,722	8,777	10,023	13,818	13,486	28,977
XIV	39	Brushes, toilet	471	930	1,247	1,628	1,859	2,568	3,128	7,671
II 87, 88, 89		Bedspreads & quilts	4,385	5,200	6,686	7,833	10,604	15,331	16,575	{10,245 32,736 9,544
		Cotton blankets								
		Cotton table damask								
		Sheets & pillow cases								3,369
		Lace curtains & bedspreads	336	398	469	1,373	3,075	3,834	5,163	9,125
II	158	Comforts & quilts	not reported	318	1,994	3,411	3,586	4,420	6,573	11,984
		Mops & dusters	50	192	1,206	2,062	2,168	2,673	3,991	5,217
		All other house-furnishing goods	no data	631	3,951	6,758	7,104	8,758	13,035	37,964

116

II	187	Linen woven goods	298	246	612	796	1,690	1,575	1,766	3,799
		Total, Commodities Classified Directly	11,880	12,930	22,887	32,638	40,109	52,977	63,717	160,631
II 87, 88, 89		Towels, towelling, wash cloths, turkish towels & terry weave	1,086	1,287	1,627	2,171	3,859	5,362	8,668	27,671
XIV	344	Window shades & fixtures	not reported	2,092	6,835	6,561	7,260	15,092	14,465	24,604
		Total, Minor Group 9	12,966	16,309	31,349	41,370	51,228	73,431	86,850	212,906
		% that Commodities Classified Directly form of Group Total	91.6	79.3	73.0	78.9	78.3	72.1	73.4	75.4
		Minor Group 10 Toys, Games and Sporting Goods								
IV	23	Billiard tables, bowling alleys & accessories	1,744	2,359	2,909	1,698	2,290	6,055	5,202	15,355
XII	52	Carriages & sleds, children's	1,523	1,784	4,352	4,560	6,772	9,358	12,355	24,672
III	91	Pocketknives	1,688	1,773	1,689	2,261	2,847	3,498	3,845	9,926
III	116	Firearms	5,460	5,611	2,859	5,326	8,095	7,881	10,316	29,212
XIV	118	Fireworks	880	1,391	593	1,785	1,987	2,269	2,296	4,630
XIV	243	Cameras	305	38	229	743	1,276	435	1,567	10,565
XIV	296	Sporting & athletic goods	811	1,346	2,343	3,138	6,083	9,556	11,996	21,592
XIV	322	Toys & games	617	1,663	3,990	4,267	5,935	8,792	14,321	45,337
		Total, Minor Group 10	13,028	15,965	18,964	23,778	35,285	47,844	61,898	161,292
		% that Commodities Classified Directly form of Group Total	100.0	100.0	100.0	100.0	100.0	100.0	100.0	100.0
		Minor Group 11 Tires and Tubes								
XIV	265	Pneumatic tires & tubes, automobile	(Included with XIV 265, all other manufactures of rubber)				3,830	21,780	91,819	534,463
		Pneumatic tires & tubes, motorcycle & bicycle	(Included with XIV 265, all other manufactures of rubber)		13,309	13,309	2,847	3,402	5,193	11,876
		Total, Minor Group 11				13,309	6,677	25,182	97,012	546,339

117

INDUSTRY NUMBER	COMMODITY	1869	1879	1889	1899	1904	1909	1914	1919
	% that Commodities Classified Directly form of Group Total				0.0	0.0	0.0	0.0	0.0
	Total, Major Group Semidurables	596,541	777,475	1,036,240	1,312,692	1,689,707	2,377,183	2,681,948	7,030,907
	Total, Semidurables Classified Directly	461,005	538,393	780,971	1,042,356	1,379,624	1,942,381	2,180,345	5,230,132
	% that Semidurables Classified Directly form of Major Group Total	69.7	69.2	75.4	79.4	81.6	81.7	81.3	74.4

CONSUMER DURABLE

INDUSTRY NUMBER	COMMODITY	1869	1879	1889	1899	1904	1909	1914	1919
IV 129	*Minor Group 12 Household Furniture*								
	Household furniture	58,365	66,306	95,179	106,740	145,181	195,231	225,430	498,005
	% that Commodities Classified Directly form of Group Total	100.0	100.0	100.0	100.0	100.0	100.0	100.0	100.0
	Minor Group 13a Heating and Cooking Apparatus and Household Appliances except Electrical								
IV 261	Refrigerators	561	1,715	4,473	5,270	7,282	10,593	14,775	25,431
III 278	Sewing machines, household	9,234	8,716	8,063	11,512	13,122	14,154	14,143	29,827
III 305	Stoves, ranges & fireless cookers	15,333	11,460	21,972	34,477	42,178	51,159	53,198	112,307
III 306	Stoves, gas & oil	not reported		2,221	4,759	8,025	13,357	22,281	57,519
XIV 334	Washing machines & clothes wringers	1,381	1,184	2,491	3,739	3,843	5,832	7,736	41,492
	Total, Minor Group 13a	26,509	23,075	39,220	59,757	74,450	95,095	112,133	266,576
	% that Commodities Classified Directly form of Group Total	100.0	100.0	100.0	100.0	100.0	100.0	100.0	100.0
	Minor Group 13b Electrical Household Appliances and Supplies								
XIV 99	Dry primary batteries, including flashlight batteries	none			316	513	4,583	8,719	25,320
	Electrical household apparatus & appliances	none			312	351	1,733	3,465	38,748
	Total, Commodities Classified Directly		628	864	6,316	12,184	64,068

118

XIV	99	Incandescent lamps	none reported		1,230	2,434	3,500	6,072	20,176
		Total, Minor Group 13b		1,858	3,298	11,816	18,256	84,244
		% that Commodities Classified Directly form of Group Total			33.8	26.2	53.5	66.7	76.1

Minor Group 14   House Furnishings (durable)

(a) Floor Coverings

II	49	Rugs	63	106	2,629	7,138	10,593	17,881	23,551	51,989
II	50	Carpets, rag	1,202	1,031	2,050	2,099	2,294	3,071	3,333	6,138
II	175	Jute carpets & rugs	not reported	108	268	358	1,365	1,286	1,172	1,601
II	201	Mats & matting, from cocoa fiber, grass & coir	287	488	677	1,295	1,382	2,704	2,486	5,335
II	224	Oilcloth & linoleum, floor	3,896	4,397	3,587	7,221	9,606	15,331	16,972	41,366
		Total, Commodities Classified Directly	5,448	6,130	9,211	18,111	25,240	40,273	47,514	106,429
II	49	Carpets	16,676	24,207	34,756	28,876	36,747	38,719	32,628	44,968
		Total, Minor Group 14a	22,124	30,337	43,967	46,987	61,987	78,992	80,142	151,397
		% that Commodities Classified Directly form of Group Total	24.6	20.2	20.9	38.5	40.7	51.0	59.3	70.3

(b) Miscellaneous House Furnishings

X	19	Bells	1,301	1,356	1,047	1,587	1,272	1,222	1,234	1,060
III	91	Scissors, shears & clippers	1,008	1,059	1,009	1,351	1,700	2,090	2,307	10,160
IX	135	Lamps Chimneys	1,556	1,570	2,794	{1,499 2,719	{1,248 3,061	3,523	3,583	4,959
II	147	Hammocks	not reported	{193	105	840	783	1,012	812	1,103
II	158	Feather pillows & beds		212	1,326	2,268	2,385	2,940	4,359	8,129
X	178	Lamps, other than automobile lamps	799	2,696	3,242	6,657	6,984	10,599	8,472	18,090
XIV	202	Mattresses & spring beds, n.e.s.	not reported	5,047	14,971	17,633	27,255	35,152	39,852	90,703

119

INDUSTRY NUMBER		COMMODITY	1869	1879	1889	1899	1904	1909	1914	1919
II	225	Table, wall, shelf & stair oilcloth	not reported	855	1,289	2,893	3,540	5,639	6,025	12,530
II	355, 356	Blankets: All-wool woven, cotton-warp woven, & cotton-mixed woven	5,133	5,513	7,154	5,201	6,242	6,858	9,701	24,028
		Total, Commodities Classified Directly	9,798	18,501	32,937	42,648	54,470	69,035	76,345	170,762
II	87, 88, 89	Cotton tapestries	316	375	430	2,633	2,706	2,897	3,515	12,092
VIII	133	Receipts from sales of lamps & appliances by gas companies			none			790	2,478	5,050
IV	193	Looking-glass & picture frames	3,962	6,375	10,880	10,340	12,650	12,846	10,472	17,176
IX	207	Mirrors, framed & unframed	280	174	3,432	4,578	4,349	5,476	5,673	11,689
II	284	Silk upholstery & tapestries		none	3,601	980	1,513	372	815	2,092
		Total, Minor Group 14b	14,356	25,425	51,280	61,179	75,688	91,416	99,298	218,861
		% that Commodities Classified Directly form of Group Total	68.3	72.8	64.2	69.7	72.0	75.5	76.9	78.0
		Minor Group 15 China and Household Utensils								
X	3	Aluminum ware			not reported				20,058	53,375
II	91	Razors, plain & safety	4,308	4,523	4,310	5,770	7,265	8,927	{4,627	23,109
		Table cutlery							5,198	7,546
X	102	Enameled ware	846	690	1,061	5,981	9,206	14,093	17,749	36,324
IX	135	Blown tumblers, stemware & bar goods				1,599	2,928			
		Jellies, tumblers & goblets				2,007	1,639			
		Tableware	3,354	3,383	6,021	2,618	4,898	11,165	12,069	15,861
		Fruit jars				2,935	3,436			
IX	251	China, bone china, delft & beleek ware				1,298	3,479	3,741	3,538	10,022
		Cooking ware & other pottery products				3,973	3,424	1,767	2,385	7,709
		Red earthenware	4,009	4,600	4,339	762	822	1,718	1,632	3,992
		Stoneware & yellow & Rockingham ware			1,942	1,657	2,709	805	1,060	1,298
		White ware			3,572	6,376	9,196	3,107	2,606	4,603
								13,728	14,968	29,847

120

IV	351	Wooden goods, n.e.s.	5,535	5,591	3,843	3,830	9,111	11,350	10,853	23,645
		Total, Commodities Classified Directly	18,052	18,787	25,088	38,806	58,113	70,401	96,743	217,331
IX	136	Glass, cutting, staining & ornamenting	389	1,283	3,082	4,428	6,648	8,150	8,415	14,631
X	318	Tinware, n.e.s.	179	221	294	442	678	952	1,299	3,667
		Total, Minor Group 15	18,620	20,291	28,464	43,676	65,439	79,503	106,457	235,629
		% that Commodities Classified Directly form of Group Total	96.9	92.6	88.1	88.8	88.8	88.6	90.9	92.2
		Minor Group 16 Musical Instruments								
XIV	211	Percussion instruments String instruments, including harps Wind instruments Other band & orchestral instruments	1,393	589	1,303	2,343	2,403	2,228	2,691	{1,295 3,062 4,286 153
XIV	212, 213, 214	Pianos & organs Piano & organ parts—perforated music rolls	8,702	13,471	25,608	30,033	{48,272 128	64,483 216	63,441 834	101,898 3,104
XIV	242	Phonographs (including dictating machines) Records & blanks	none none	(Incl. with all other industries)	1,241 539	{2,966 4,703	5,407 5,034	15,290 11,176	95,888 46,799
		Total, Minor Group 16	10,095	14,060	26,911	34,156	58,472	77,368	93,432	256,485
		% that Commodities Classified Directly form of Group Total	100.0	100.0	100.0	100.0	100.0	100.0	100.0	100.0
		Minor Group 17 Jewelry, Silverware, Clocks and Watches								
X	67	Clocks	2,206	3,613	3,717	6,292	7,795	10,755	9,697	22,144
X	248	Plated ware	8,020	8,467	11,330	12,420	11,957	18,248	18,212	40,635
X	285	Silversmithing & silverware	2,257	2,425	6,197	13,006	19,935	22,825	19,046	26,668
X	338	Watches & watch movements	2,957	3,431	6,347	7,158	12,447	10,947	13,280	31,506
		Total, Commodities Classified Directly	15,440	17,936	27,591	38,876	52,134	62,775	60,235	120,953

INDUSTRY NUMBER		COMMODITY	1869	1879	1889	1899	1904	1909	1914	1919
X	173	Jewelry	19,956	20,044	31,383	41,983	48,442	73,161	72,846	183,857
		Total, Minor Group 17	35,396	37,980	58,974	80,859	100,576	135,936	133,081	304,810
		% that Commodities Classified Directly form of Group Total	43.6	47.2	46.8	48.1	51.8	46.2	45.3	39.7
		Minor Group 18 Printing and Publishing: Books								
VI	253	Books & pamphlets: published or printed & published	8,341	19,145	34,409	44,516	53,312	62,930	68,588	132,699
		% that Commodities Classified Directly form of Group Total	100.0	100.0	100.0	100.0	100.0	100.0	100.0	100.0
		Minor Group 19 Luggage								
V	323	Trunks & valises	7,445	7,270	10,849	12,727	19,091	28,703	26,768	64,864
		% that Commodities Classified Directly form of Group Total	100.0	100.0	100.0	100.0	100.0	100.0	100.0	100.0
		Minor Group 20a Motor Vehicles								
XII	11	Passenger vehicles, excl. omnibuses, sight-seeing wagons, etc.		none		4,390	23,279	157,345	419,903	1,363,521
		Total, Minor Group 20a				4,390	23,279	157,345	419,903	1,363,521
		% that Commodities Classified Directly form of Group Total				100.0	100.0	100.0	100.0	100.0
		Minor Group 20b Motor Vehicle Accessories								
XII	10	Motor vehicle bodies & parts		none			2,451	20,930	54,525	210,834
		Total, Minor Group 20b					2,451	20,930	54,525	210,834
		% that Commodities Classified Directly form of Group Total					0.0	0.0	0.0	0.0

XII 53	**Minor Group 20c** *Carriages and Wagons*							
	Carriages, buggies & light pleasure vehicles	33,550	33,339	52,675	51,485	55,958	48,835	34,194	22,682
	Sleighs & sleds	1,322	1,314	2,094	2,474	2,911	2,232	1,232	1,268
II 355, 356	Carriage cloths & robes	1,239	1,313	1,274	1,681	2,211	2,624	1,677	3,280
	Total, Minor Group 20c	36,111	35,966	56,043	55,640	61,080	53,691	37,103	27,230
	% that Commodities Classified Directly form of Group Total	100.0	100.0	100.0	100.0	100.0	100.0	100.0	100.0
XII 209	**Minor Group 21** *Motorcycles and Bicycles*								
	Bicycles	not reported	1,907	1,907	23,656	3,741	3,228	5,361	12,691
	Motorcycles		none		34	359	3,052	12,307	16,196
	Total, Minor Group 21		1,907	1,907	23,690	4,100	6,280	17,668	28,887
	% that Commodities Classified Directly form of Group Total		100.0	100.0	100.0	100.0	100.0	100.0	100.0
XIV 279, 280	**Minor Group 22** *Pleasure-Craft*								
	Work on boats of less than 5 gross tons	550	920	1,460	2,065	3,149	4,738	4,121	5,496
	% that Commodities Classified Directly form of Group Total	100.0	100.0	100.0	100.0	100.0	100.0	100.0	100.0
	Minor Group 23 *Ophthalmic Products and Artificial Limbs*								
XIV 6	Artificial limbs	158	131	454	715	842	1,262	1,414	3,106
XIV 227	Ophthalmic products	228	621	1,842	4,091	4,802	9,215	14,062	41,935
	Total, Minor Group 23	386	752	2,296	4,806	5,644	10,477	15,476	45,041
	% that Commodities Classified Directly form of Group Total	100.0	100.0	100.0	100.0	100.0	100.0	100.0	100.0

INDUSTRY NUMBER	COMMODITY	1869	1879	1889	1899	1904	1909	1914	1919
IX 199	*Minor Group 24 Monuments and Tombstones* Monuments & tombstones	6,581	7,543	15,247	20,323	25,689	38,405	40,977	73,361
	% that Commodities Classified Directly form of Group Total	100.0	100.0	100.0	100.0	100.0	100.0	100.0	100.0
	Total, Major Group Consumer Durable	245,179	289,070	466,206	603,369	782,886	1,148,856	1,553,358	3,967,940
	Total, Consumer Durable Classified Directly	203,421	236,391	378,348	507,879	664,268	979,063	1,354,620	3,441,708
	% that Consumer Durables Classified Directly form of Major Group Total	83.0	81.9	82.2	84.2	84.9	85.3	87.2	86.7

PRODUCER DURABLE

III 103, 124, 169x, 197, 260, 302x, 314	*Minor Group 25 Industrial Machinery and Equipment* Stationary & portable steam engines & turbines (except marine) Stationary and portable internal-combustion engines (not automobile, aviation, or marine) Water wheels, motors & turbines Traction engines, not locomotive Other engines & parts Steam & other power pumps Boiler shop products Air-compressing machinery Ammunition machinery							20,484 26,121 3,633 17,651 9,453 19,085 27,140 5,158 (Incl. with III 124)	27,900 58,987 4,136 172,667 52,294 56,227 143,666 18,650 570
				(Included with III 124, Miscellaneous machinery)						
	Bakers' machinery Bottling machinery Blowers & fans							2,555 1,359 (Incl. with III 124)	9,359 10,468 12,141
	Brick, pottery & other clay-working machinery Concrete mixers Condensers							2,439 2,956 (Incl. with III 124)	3,187 10,450 24,216

Cotton gins	4,902	10,176
Confectioners' machinery	(Incl. with III 124)	9,341
Cranes	4,194	52,534
Dredging machinery, excavating machinery & steam shovels	2,969	21,562
Elevators & elevator machinery	17,228	70,187
Firearms & ordnance machinery	(Incl. with III 124)	2,284
Flour-mill & grist-mill machinery	5,018	19,981
Glass-making machinery	1,091	3,316
Hydraulic rams	(Incl. with III 124)	3,597
Laundry machinery	7,565	13,891
Lawn mowers	2,848	3,777
Leather-working machinery, other than shoe machinery	1,067	4,691
Machine tools	31,447	184,632
Metal-working machinery, other than machine tools	17,420	57,541
Mining machinery	13,254	51,243
Oil-well machinery	10,569	28,351
Oil-mill machinery, cottonseed & other	1,878	11,306
Ore crushers	(Incl. with III 124)	2,367
Paper & pulp mill machinery	8,588	27,421
Photo-engraving machinery	(Incl. with III 124)	733
Printing machinery	19,228	53,325
Refrigerating machinery	10,522	30,667
Road-making machinery	3,545	15,778
Rubber-working machinery	2,726	17,002
Sand blast machines	(Incl. with III 124)	1,320
Shoe machinery	5,949	16,261

(Included with III 124, Miscellaneous machinery)

INDUSTRY NUMBER	COMMODITY	1869	1879	1889	1899	1904	1909	1914	1919
	Slot-vending machinery							(Incl. with III 124)	1,646
	Stokers, mechanical								4,280
	Sugar-mill machinery							1,972	14,847
	Well-drilling machinery other than oil-well							(Incl. with III 124)	2,567
	Wire-drawing machinery							13,393	1,402
	Woodworking machinery							3,882	36,763
	Brewers' machinery							1,306	(Incl. with III 124)
	Cannery machinery							8,768	21,343
	Steel barrels, drums & tanks							30,438	86,894
	Textile machinery								
	Parts, attachments & accessories for textile machinery							(Incl. with III 124)	34,788
III 134	Gas meters & water meters; gas machines; all other meters & appliances	1,294	1,189	1,639	3,912	5,017	11,857	13,525	23,804
III 278	Sewing machines, industrial types	4,405	4,153	3,841	5,485	6,252	6,743	6,747	14,231
	Total, Commodities Classified Directly	5,699	5,342	5,480	9,397	11,269	18,600	390,073	1,560,767
III 124	Misc. machinery & other machine shop products	106,986	97,404	186,749	293,031	355,875	473,796	160,428	357,840
	Total, Minor Group 25	112,685	102,746	192,229	302,428	367,144	492,396	550,501	1,918,607
	% that Commodities Classified Directly form of Group Total	5.1	5.2	2.9	3.1	3.1	3.8	70.9	81.3

Minor Group 26 Electrical Equipment, Industrial and Commercial

XIV	99	Generators (other than small dynamos under 10 k.w.)			5,905	6,027	9,940	10,405	19,308
		Transformers, over 50 k.w.			779	1,176	4,616	5,803	14,948
		Stationary motors			12,368	14,782	20,127	26,403	76,172
		Liquid primary batteries, incl. testing batteries			571	516	730	803	3,509
		Arc lamps			1,828	1,574	1,707	742	607
		Searchlights, projectors & focusing lamps			226	115	936	2,082	4,342
		Radio & wireless apparatus			none reported	114	448	673	7,835
XIV	99	Telegraph apparatus, excl. radio & wireless			1,642	997	1,509	1,576	4,982
		Telephone apparatus	none	1,767	9,188	13,792	10,507	18,755	23,155
		Measuring instruments, excl. testing & scientific		12,717	1,474	4,004	7,253	7,713	15,986
		Switchboards, panel boards, cutout cabinets for light & power			1,847	3,766	5,972	8,989	17,736
		Railway switches, signals & attachments			1,130	1,451	5,378	6,394	4,467
		Lightning arrestors & other protective devices			240	587	940	1,189	2,353
		Insulated cables, rubber & paper insulation			10,114	16,397	24,522	33,015	61,104
		All other electrical machinery & apparatus			6,813	14,340	18,995	27,424	151,759
		Industrial apparatus & appliances			40	45	221	584	16,045
		Converting apparatus: frequency changers, etc.			380	1,741	3,155	5,368	4,851
		Electric fans, incl. fan motors			1,055	1,168	2,451	4,836	9,908
		Motors for misc. uses			3,138	2,979	1,943	1,191	4,920
IX	251	Porcelain electrical supplies	none	339	470	1,500	3,047	4,130	12,615
		Total, Minor Group 26	1,935	13,056	59,208	87,071	124,397	168,075	456,602
		% that Commodities Classified Directly form of Group Total	100.0	100.0	100.0	100.0	100.0	100.0	100.0

127

INDUSTRY NUMBER		COMMODITY	1869	1879	1889	1899	1904	1909	1914	1919
XIV	2	*Minor Group 27 Farm Equipment*								
		Plows & cultivators	45,173	57,435	68,004	84,674	30,608	36,784	38,662	65,329
		Planters & seeders					11,225	12,141	12,189	17,490
		Harvesting implements					30,862	34,568	39,581	54,225
		Seed separators					6,640	11,030	13,096	22,365
		All other implements, incl. parts					14,462	22,933	27,844	64,105
		Agricultural implements made in other industries					1,350	2,989	4,034	14,938
XIV	92	Dairymen's, poultrymen's, & apiarists' supplies	21	not reported separately			7,108	16,789	18,983	36,801
III	259	Pumps, not incl. power pumps	3,514	4,545	5,116	1,673	3,558	6,963	7,928	34,052
XIV	342	Windmills	not reported	712	1,742	3,065	3,376	4,700	3,134	5,983
III	345	Barbed wire	1,264	3,923	7,969	19,139	28,720	13,882	13,764	30,896
		Woven-wire fence & poultry netting						19,835	19,796	30,527
III	346	Woven-wire fencing	1,092	3,315	5,648	7,205	11,998	15,223	15,628	18,263
		Total, Minor Group 27	51,064	69,930	88,479	115,756	149,907	197,837	214,639	394,974
		% that Commodities Classified Directly form of Group Total	100.0	100.0	100.0	100.0	100.0	100.0	100.0	100.0
III	58	*Minor Group 28 Office and Store Machinery and Equipment*								
		Adding machines, cash registers & parts & all other calculating machines	none	7	1,349	5,380	9,362	22,466	28,789	79,451
III	274	Scales & balances	2,505	2,885	2,061	4,648	5,325	7,797	8,834	18,826
XIV	295	Soda water apparatus	702	930	2,343	2,605	4,004	5,664	7,163	13,852
III	326	Typewriters & parts		none	2,804	5,356	8,220	15,221	18,918	41,277
		Total, Minor Group 28	3,207	3,822	8,557	17,989	26,911	51,148	63,704	153,406
		% that Commodities Classified Directly form of Group Total	100.0	100.0	100.0	100.0	100.0	100.0	100.0	100.0

Minor Group 29   Office and Store Furniture and Fixtures

IV	129	Store & office furniture & fixtures	9,876	{8,571	12,303	13,797	18,766	25,236	29,024	50,878
		Furniture for public buildings & seats for public conveyances		2,649	3,803	4,265	5,800	7,800	8,966	15,719
III	268	Safes & vaults	2,861	3,402	6,742	3,987	7,979	8,618	7,365	15,641
IV	282	Show cases	894	1,248	2,737	2,628	6,094	7,636	6,476	8,685
		Total, Minor Group 29	13,631	15,870	25,585	24,677	38,639	49,290	51,831	90,923
		% that Commodities Classified Directly form of Group Total	100.0	100.0	100.0	100.0	100.0	100.0	100.0	100.0

Minor Group 30   Locomotives and Railroad Cars

XII	56, 57	Electric rr. cars, passenger service				{6,687	{8,809	6,249	8,076	11,496
		Electric rr. cars, freight service					488	377	714	2,007
		Steam rr. cars, passenger service	24,380	21,823	57,511	7,368	18,140	13,830	44,012	4,855
		Steam rr. cars, freight service				62,161	69,209	61,804	96,218	369,090
		Cars made in other industries	4,744	4,246	11,191	14,801	18,464	19,888	15,941	15,590
XIV	99	Electric locomotives: mining, industrial, & railway							3,721	8,160
III	192	Steam locomotives	12,521	11,479	22,142	30,397	55,451	31,713	42,637	139,226
		Total, Minor Group 30	41,645	37,548	90,844	121,414	170,561	133,861	211,319	550,424
		% that Commodities Classified Directly form of Group Total	100.0	100.0	100.0	100.0	100.0	100.0	100.0	100.0

Minor Group 31   Ships and Boats

| XIV | 279, 280 | Work on vessels of 5 gross tons & over | 11,524 | 19,399 | 24,704 | 36,072 | 53,583 | 38,167 | 43,493 | 1,389,509 |
| | | % that Commodities Classified Directly form of Group Total | 100.0 | 100.0 | 100.0 | 100.0 | 100.0 | 100.0 | 100.0 | 100.0 |

INDUSTRY NUMBER		COMMODITY	1869	1879	1889	1899	1904	1909	1914	1919
		Minor Group 32 Business Vehicles								
		(a) Motor								
XII	11	Business vehicles	....	none	....	(Incl. with 20a, passenger motor vehicles)	982	5,267	40,832	354,522
		Gov. & municipal vehicles	....	none	....		15	104	3,998	13,619
		Omnibuses, sightseeing wagons, etc.	....	none	....		354	2,393	335	5,156
		Trailers	....	none	....					6,634
		Total, Minor Group 32a	....	....	....	....	1,351	7,754	45,165	379,931
		% that Commodities Classified Directly form of Group Total	....	100.0	....	....	100.0	100.0	100.0	100.0
		(b) Wagons								
XII	53	Business, farm, gov. & municipal wagons	17,247	17,138	27,082	31,423	37,599	42,026	36,533	42,413
		Public conveyances	818	813	1,311	1,121	1,323	945	326	105
		Total, Minor Group 32b	18,065	17,951	28,393	32,544	38,922	42,971	36,859	42,518
		% that Commodities Classified Directly form of Group Total	100.0	100.0	100.0	100.0	100.0	100.0	100.0	100.0
		Minor Group 33 Aircraft								
XIV	1	Aeroplanes & seaplanes				none			{ 355	8,046
		All other aeronautical products							82	564
		Total, Minor Group 33	....	....	....	....	....	....	437	8,610
		% that Commodities Classified Directly form of Group Total	....	....	....	....	....	....	100.0	100.0
		Minor Group 34 Professional and Scientific Equipment								
XIV	99	Electrical testing & scientific instruments	....	none	....	{ 368	1,001	547	1,073	3,336
		Therapeutic apparatus, incl. X-ray tubes				492	1,037	1,108	2,653	8,895
XIV	162	Instruments, professional & scientific	1,571	1,493	2,981	4,421	4,899	9,574	17,390	56,663
XIV	227	Optical goods & instruments	61	166	492	1,094	1,284	2,464	3,761	11,214
		Total, Minor Group 34	1,632	1,659	3,473	6,375	8,221	13,693	24,877	80,108
		% that Commodities Classified Directly form of Group Total	100.0	100.0	100.0	100.0	100.0	100.0	100.0	100.0

Minor Group 35 *Carpenters' and Mechanics' Tools*									
III	91	Augurs, bits, planes, & chisels	3,957	4,155	3,959	5,301	6,673	8,200	1,273	3,021
		Axes & hatchets							4,738	10,047
		All other cutlery & edge tools							3,018	4,693
III	115	Files	1,606	2,422	3,097	3,315	4,278	5,542	5,507	17,239
III	273	Saws	2,743	3,407	4,815	5,568	8,484	9,966	10,278	26,913
III	321	Carpenters' tools, n.e.s.	2,550	4,339	10,781	13,679	20,897	31,109	3,580	7,255
		Machinists' tools							9,078	69,925
		Shovels, spades, hoes & scoops							4,900	15,939
		Tools, other than specified							16,138	52,975
		Total, Minor Group 35	10,856	14,323	22,652	27,863	40,332	54,817	58,510	208,007
		% that Commodities Classified Directly form of Group Total	100.0	100.0	100.0	100.0	100.0	100.0	100.0	100.0
Minor Group 36 *Miscellaneous Subsidiary Durable Equipment*									
II	13	Awnings, tents, sails & canvas covers	2,219	1,516	6,034	9,034	11,134	14,329	18,138	45,433
XIV	20	Hose, rubber	450	779	3,958	4,429	10,737	13,811	16,854	26,998
XIV	38	Brooms made from materials other than broom corn	176	139	187	244	278	383	372	611
XIV	39	All other brushes	1,242	2,454	3,289	4,294	4,902	6,773	8,238	19,355
II	69	Clothing, horse	not reported	678	1,533	1,272	2,086	4,030	4,955	6,338
IX	90	Crucibles	1,530	1,981	996	3,572	1,840	2,533	2,502	6,674
IX	101	Emery & other abrasive wheels	154	317	716	1,363	2,033	6,616	7,144	31,127
IX	117	Fire extinguishers, chemical	not reported	203	194	216	576	746	1,590	5,249
IX	144	Grindstones	246	278	183	1,634	1,182	2,532	1,026	1,327
XIV	148, 303	Hand stamps & stencils & brands	42	780	2,284	2,574	2,772	3,622	4,421	9,049
IX	156	Hones & whetstones	326	282	68	246	387	337	327	879
III	157, 164	Horseshoes	(Incl. with III 124, Foundry products)		1,110	3,918	6,286	8,223	8,917	12,186

INDUSTRY NUMBER		COMMODITY	1869	1879	1889	1899	1904	1909	1914	1919
IV	181	Lasts	688	790	1,280	1,942	2,603	4,296	4,740	12,658
IX	204	Millstones	819	356	47	76	83	(Incl. with all other industries)		67
XIV	208	Models & patterns, except paper patterns	1,242	1,048	2,805	3,935	4,663	9,102	8,793	25,925
II	216	Nets & seines	159	296	1,017	1,498	1,751	1,926	3,135	5,191
XIV	243	Motion-picture machines	661	83	495	1,609	2,763	940	{1,894 1,498	{3,606 10,398
		All other photographic apparatus & parts								
IX	251	Chemical stoneware	219	260	554	473	773	887	743	805
VI	256	Printing materials	124	441	1,529	1,140	1,265	2,077	2,212	5,005
V	267	Saddlery & harness	17,809	20,734	28,840	34,107	42,560	54,879	54,588	85,727
XIV	283	Signs		not reported separately				8,036	14,489	19,344
XIV	315	Theatrical scenery, incl. stage equipment				not covered by census			327	1,067
XII	340	Wheelbarrows	426	204	1,067	409	1,060	1,462	998	3,219
XIV	341	Whips	1,231	1,682	2,132	2,707	3,116	3,909	3,182	3,090
II	355, 356	Horse blankets	1,239	1,327	1,722	1,741	1,724	2,049	2,018	1,606
		Total, Commodities Classified Directly	31,002	36,628	62,040	82,433	106,574	153,498	173,101	342,934
II	21	Hose, woven	454	not reported			392	758	613	8,544
II	83	Rope, cable & cordage		632	1,573	2,008	3,333	3,131	3,341	8,565
		Total, Minor Group 36	31,456	37,260	63,613	84,441	110,299	157,387	177,055	360,043
		% that Commodities Classified Directly form of Group Total	98.6	98.3	97.6	97.7	96.8	97.6	97.9	95.5
		Total, Major Group Producer Durables	295,265	322,443	561,585	828,767	1,092,941	1,363,718	1,646,465	6,033,662
		Total, Producer Durables Classified Directly	188,325	224,407	373,263	533,728	733,341	886,033	1,482,083	5,658,713
		% that Producer Durables Classified Directly form of Major Group Total	63.7	69.6	66.5	64.4	67.1	65.0	90.0	93.8

RECAPITULATION

Perishable	850,200	1,326,676	2,038,932	2,763,697	3,538,387	4,736,581	5,807,553	13,668,008
Semidurable	596,541	777,475	1,036,240	1,312,692	1,689,707	2,377,183	2,681,948	7,030,907
Consumer Durable	245,179	289,070	466,206	603,369	782,886	1,148,856	1,553,358	3,967,940
Producer Durable	295,765	322,443	561,585	828,767	1,092,941	1,363,718	1,646,465	6,033,662
All Finished Mfd. Commodities	1,987,685	2,715,664	4,102,963	5,508,525	7,103,921	9,626,338	11,689,324	30,700,517
% Each Major Group forms of Total Finished Mfd.								
Perishable	42.8	48.9	49.7	50.2	49.8	49.2	49.7	44.5
Semidurable	30.0	28.6	25.3	23.8	23.8	24.7	22.9	22.9
Consumer Durable	12.3	10.6	11.4	11.0	11.0	11.9	13.3	12.9
Producer Durable	14.9	11.9	13.7	15.0	15.4	14.2	14.1	19.7
Total, All Finished Mfd.	1,987,685	2,715,664	4,102,963	5,508,525	7,103,921	9,626,338	11,689,324	30,700,517
Total, All Commodities Classified Directly	1,169,595	1,726,655	2,905,053	3,952,850	5,139,239	7,079,756	9,211,574	23,533,440
% All Commodities Classified Directly form of All Finished Mfd.	58.8	63.6	70.8	71.8	72.3	73.5	78.8	76.7

CONSTRUCTION MATERIALS

XIV	4	Blasting & detonating caps & fuses	230	176	605	1,205	1,844	2,411	3,126	6,470
IX	7, 199	Artificial stone products Marble & stone work, incl. roofing slate & other slate products	16,353	16,402	33,257	43,344	{4,157 59,155	18,726 74,688	21,959 66,078	33,640 55,804
XIV	9	Asbestos building materials			Included with XIV 264 and XIV 302				1,943	5,038
IX	37, 251, 271	Brick, except fire brick & silica brick Tile (not drain tile) Architectural terra-cotta	28,570	32,846	{55,954 796 1,431	50,004 1,276 2,028	66,975 2,726 3,793	80,517 5,292 6,251	67,812 5,706 6,088	93,862 8,137 3,988
		Fireproofing, terra-cotta lumber, & hollow building tile or blocks Drain tile Sewer pipe Sanitary ware			403 5,010 5,395 1,593	1,665 3,662 4,560 2,212	4,317 5,522 8,416 3,933	4,667 9,799 10,322 5,989	8,385 8,522 14,015 7,874	17,965 10,946 16,755 14,872
XIV	39	Brushes, paint & varnish	1,041	2,056	2,756	3,599	4,109	5,676	6,917	10,673

133

INDUSTRY NUMBER		COMMODITY	1869	1879	1889	1899	1904	1909	1914	1919
IX	59	Cement	1,772	2,740	7,472	13,612	26,032	53,611	82,204	138,714
VIII	76	Tar	not reported			249	613	1,409	2,867	6,919
X	82	Copper, tin & sheet-iron work	14,768	18,238	24,224	36,464	56,026	89,288	94,335	157,092
XIV	99	Interior and underground conduits		none		1,066	2,416	5,098	4,875	19,267
III	132	Gas & electric fixtures	5,142	5,482	9,908	14,538	19,794	30,240	30,211	43,062
VIII	133	Tar	480	not reported	876	1,075	2,064	1,877	3,255	4,663
IX	135	Window glass	3,811	5,047	9,037	10,879	11,611	11,743	17,496	41,101
		Obscured glass, incl. cathedral & sky light glass	26	63	360	732	972	1,359	2,417	4,300
		Wire glass, polished, and all other building glass	(Incl. with window glass)		10	125	565	481	1,054	2,522
IX	135	Shades, globes & other gas goods	920	927	1,651	2,498	1,949	3,239	3,542	33,534
III	149	Builders' hardware	7,024	7,065	8,335	11,180	14,274	20,244	22,877	48,947
III	164	Rails, incl. rerolled or renewed rails, rail joints & fastenings	47,999	58,691	60,895	46,533	66,400	98,300	66,975	125,184
		Bars for reinforced concrete			none			5,589	7,752	18,429
III	164, 307	Structural ironwork	1,315	3,533	39,104	69,336	94,219	138,038	165,070	305,660
III	166	Cast-iron pipe & fittings	6,437	5,851	11,219	17,603	21,378	28,396	25,979	48,515
III	167	Iron & steel, doors & shutters	not reported	427	77	276	1,275	2,595	4,503	9,144
IV	196, 343	Lumber, planing mill products, incl. window & door screens & weather strips	100,297	91,735	229,500	261,427	384,210	520,965	511,631	889,513
VIII	229, 329	Paints, colors, putty & fillers	16,885	20,513	38,214	49,027	59,781	81,501	94,039	254,443
VI	230	Building papers	not reported	1,265	1,753	3,026	4,846	9,251	9,476	17,737
XIV	234	Paving materials	405	928	2,247	3,566	4,560	5,644	34,530	41,290
VIII	241	Liquid asphaltic road oils & tars	296	{298	1,971	688	3,138	2,216	4,018	6,014
		Asphalt, other than liquid asphalt		142	641	741	2,982	2,725	4,867	12,500

		Item								
III	249	Plumbers' supplies	not reported separately	{11,613	14,343	20,917	42,420	42,116	57,896
IV	258	Wall board			118	425	492	594	1,496	8,117
XIV	264	Roofing materials	1,501	2,869	13,552	13,773	19,990	19,324	28,964	81,341
III	276	Screws, wood	1,774	1,132	1,817	2,031	1,667	4,843	4,770	12,411
X	298	Bathtubs, lavatories & sinks	none	29	45	262	394	594	720	6,515
III	301	Steam fittings & steam & hot-water heating apparatus	3,507	5,251	23,703	22,615	25,509	55,382	65,458	164,069
III	305	Hot-air furnaces	4,150	3,102	5,947	9,331	11,415	13,846	14,379	32,114
III	330	Vault lights & ventilators	45	303	505	375	537	1,061	2,275	2,256
VI	332	Wall paper, not made in paper mills	2,155	6,236	7,395	10,610	12,574	14,377	15,808	22,933
IX	333	Wall plaster & composition flooring	2,730	1,088	2,969	5,408	10,306	12,979	16,604	27,551
IV	349	Wood preserving	not reported	102	145	2,427	3,412	14,282	21,332	33,482
		Total, Construction Materials Classified Directly	269,633	294,537	622,503	739,796	1,051,265	1,517,849	1,626,320	2,955,385
IX	135	Plate glass, polished	299	731	4,172	5,159	7,978	11,569	13,656	23,344
IX	136	Glass, cutting, staining & ornamenting	156	516	1,240	1,782	2,675	3,280	3,386	5,887
III	164, 165	Bolts, nuts, washers & rivets	4,698	6,581	8,084	9,133	9,595	15,483	11,644	42,623
III	164, 169	Cut nails & spikes, wire nails & spikes, forged nails & spikes & all other, incl. tacks	8,465	3,964	11,672	10,405	11,195	13,095	12,477	27,023
III	164, 170	Wrought pipe, iron & steel	24,078	43,431	33,851	69,571	56,864	90,838	83,772	250,484
IX	186	Lime	4,882	850	2,318	4,222	8,075	9,468	6,799	11,372
IV	195	Lath	1,601	2,431	3,520	4,699	5,436	9,963	6,267	8,293
		Shingles	6,080	10,388	17,138	18,870	24,010	30,262	20,134	38,517
IX	300	Statuary & art goods	(Partly incl. with XIV 110, Fancy articles, n.e.s.)				1,619	2,305	2,623	3,424
		Total, Construction Materials	319,892	363,429	704,498	863,637	1,178,712	1,704,112	1,787,078	3,366,352
		% Construction Materials Classified Directly form of Total	84.3	81.0	88.4	85.7	89.2	89.1	91.0	87.8

INDUSTRY NUMBER		COMMODITY	1869	1879	1889	1899	1904	1909	1914	1919
		REPAIRS AND SERVICING CONSUMER DURABLE								
XII	12	Automobile repairing			not reported				30,531	224,885
IV	23	Billiard tables, bowling alleys & accessories: custom work	30	41	50	29	40	106	88	283
XII	53	Carriages & wagons: repair work & parts	10,008	9,945	15,670	21,227	21,862	26,489	28,837	25,664
IV	129	Furniture: custom work & repairing	274	312	447	502	682	918	1,020	2,194
XIV	211	Musical instruments & materials, not specified: custom work & repairing	52	22	49	87	89	83	100	324
XIV	212, 213, 214	Musical instruments, organs & pianos: repairs	83	128	243	285	440	740	622	1,252
XIV	242	Phonographs & graphophones: custom work & repairing		none		1	6	3	2	269
V	250	Pocketbooks, purses & card-cases: custom work & repairing	2	4	5	5	8	8	8	28
		Total, Repairs and Servicing of Consumer Durable	10,449	10,452	16,464	22,136	23,127	28,347	61,208	254,899
		PRODUCER DURABLE								
XIV	1	Aeroplanes, seaplanes, & airships & parts: repair work				none			210	1,232
XIV	2	Agricultural implements: amount received for repair work	1,687	2,145	2,540	3,197	1,968	3,115	1,437	12,947
X	35	Brass, bronze, & copper products: custom work & repairs	115	240	440	779	899	1,318	1,467	7,208
XIII	54	Cars & general shop construction & repairs by electric rr. companies: motive power & machinery department: repairs to motors		not reported		258	3	4,004	4,933	7,082
		work for other corporations		not reported			508	88	57	75

136

Car department:								
repairs to cars of all kinds		not reported		7,848	11,255	22,870	27,629	60,060
work for other corporations				27	37	625	441	1,174
all other products or work				474	685	1,714	2,205	2,241
Bridge & building department:								
repairs & renewals			not reported	179	253	274	200	262
all other products or work				54	75	235	57	75
All other products & work, not classified				9	17	1,676	1,286	2,778
XIII 55 Cars & general shop construction & repairs by steam-rr. companies: motive power & machinery department:								
repairs to locomotives, motors, etc.				57,383	101,327	127,929	169,058	463,953
work for other corporations				3,339	5,681	4,735	7,053	16,889
all other products or work				30,449	40,782	49,019	57,018	135,813
Car department:								
repairs to cars of all kinds			not reported	74,666	105,319	147,194	183,754	479,229
work for other corporations			117,810	7,085	6,947	8,784	14,820	31,101
all other products or work				20,105	24,493	30,464	32,403	58,246
Bridge & building department:								
repairs & renewals				3,937	4,351	1,907	2,450	7,288
work for other corporations				242	41	46	37	23
all other products or work				1,236	704	847	641	1,224
All other products or work, not classified			not reported		5,286	18,060	31,213	74,510
XIV 99 Electrical machinery, apparatus & supplies: custom work & repairing		none		2,064	2,799	5,693	5,677	27,106
III 164 Iron & steel—steel works & rolling mills: custom work & repairing		290	794	1,122	1,172	1,325	1,710	6,307
XIV 279, 280 Shipbuilding, steel & wooden, incl. boat building: repair work	9,918	16,713	10,021	23,155	22,850	26,759	33,021	183,922
III 345 Wire: custom work & repairing	11	21	44	106	158	233	327	236
(a) Work done in rr. repair shops	not reported		120,643	207,391	307,764	420,889	535,645	1,342,792
(b) All other servicing of producer durables	11,731	19,409	13,839	30,423	29,846	38,443	43,849	238,958
Total, Repairs & Servicing of Producer Durables	11,731	19,409	134,482	237,814	337,610	459,332	579,494	1,581,750
Total, All Repairs & Servicing	22,180	29,861	150,946	259,950	360,737	487,679	640,702	1,836,649

UNFINISHED COMMODITIES

INDUSTRY NUMBER	COMMODITY	1869	1879	1889	1899	1904	1909	1914	1919
	Census Industry Group 1 Food and Kindred Products								
40,	Powdered milk	not reported		none	384	554	796	{1,968	12,182
61,	Sugar of milk				29	45	54	401	2,633
79	Buttermilk sold							{1,279	4,027
	Casein			{220	4,435	2,364	9,829	991	2,200
	Whey sold		73		2,531	1,369	629	73	3,424
	Cream			{309	3,107	10,681	12,048	13,802	26,174
	Skimmed milk sold		not reported					786	2,454
41	Butter, processed							7,703	2,872
65	Chocolate in cakes, unsweetened								8,135
	Chocolate coatings								33,051
	Chocolate liquor								2,790
	Cocoa, other than powdered	472	677	2,194	5,023	7,478	11,629	18,675	14,181
	Cocoa butter								13,897
	Unfinished chocolate & cocoa products made in other industries								721
122	Bran & middlings, & feed & offal	50,959	57,853	58,965	99,691	152,202	231,279	245,073	505,521
123	Other food preparations for animals & fowls	2,329	501	2,830	7,994	12,276	23,343	46,531	152,841
138	Starch, glucose, corn oil, grape sugar, dextrine, corn-oil cake & meal	4,951	9,936	13,788	25,554	27,594	42,486	45,137	158,388
263	Clean rice, second-head, screenings & brewers'	not reported	839	1,793	{1,725	3,302	3,287	5,220	12,813
	Polish & bran				552	774	1,098	1,125	3,465
	Hulls & waste				62	117	166	74	880
272,	Oleo oil			{12,202	11,483	10,202	16,476	11,926	31,213
286,	Oleo stock			23	320	632	1,332	1,362	7,685
287	Stearin			120	1,650	3,259	6,872	2,752	8,999
	Sausage casings			1,384	2,910	3,716	6,671	10,146	26,355
	Hoofs, horns, & horn tips, strips, etc.	743	21,983	18	246	486	1,056	945	2,181
	Hides & pelts			26,166	41,329	53,171	79,827	87,484	243,561
	Hair, hog & cattle			52	714	1,411	3,169	2,957	4,059
	Wool			2,009	3,334	5,230	8,327	7,938	20,071
	Custom & contract work			23	141	199	1,330	1,255	1,746
308	Molasses				{25	221	292	1,536	2,365
	Sugar, raw	464	283	340	1,642	431	796	239	247
	Pulp, beet				22	202		2,095	5,799
	All other products				54	46	259	384	2,893

138

309	Sugar, raw	10,383		11,447	22,287	25,958	{7,615 {6,742	9,899 26,563
	Sugar, clarified		14,456				2,632	9,058
	Molasses & sirup					2,735	3,284	15,317
310	Molasses & sirup		(Included with 309)			6,814	8,751	25,037
40	Butter	not reported	{1,237	2,101	2,793	5,305	6,087	15,691
79	Condensed & evaporated milk		951	1,618	2,121	5,848	9,544	25,309
120	Flavoring extracts	599	854	1,751	2,911	100,164	116,274	308,137
122	Flour: wheat, corn, rye, buckwheat & barley	9,173	17,358	29,852	39,829	65,179		
123, 180	Lard, incl. lard compounds & substitutes	not reported	5,939	7,318	11,461	16,843	31,193	107,599
235	Peanuts, grading, roasting, cleaning, shelling	68	135	442	409	724	1,111	2,701
308, 309, 310	Sugar, granulated, refined & brown	4,953	10,103	18,544	26,751	58,539	81,909	248,744
	Total, Census Industry Group 1	85,094	143,178	195,519	323,519	456,754	693,933	794,999	2,113,878

Census Industry Group 2 Textiles and their Products

15	Bags, other than paper	12,578	13,039	19,905	19,357	36,838	55,234	77,865	212,184
49	Contract work	not reported	none		20		none		
68	Cloth, sponging & refinishing		223	400	566	1,053	1,544	1,531	3,691
70	Clothing, men's, contract shops	14,130	19,915	23,857	26,299	33,815	46,141	33,671	81,988
71	Clothing, men's, buttonholes	not reported		817	710	729	814	665	1,136
72	Clothing, women's, contract shops	364	904	1,926	4,502	6,997	10,988	12,597	63,609
83,	Linen thread				2,332		3,407	3,409	6,609
175,	Binder twine				14,186		14,080	24,095	46,256
187	Twine, other than binder twine	6,449	10,771	26,810	5,888	41,024	11,351	16,789	36,265
	Yarns for sale				4,456		5,434	8,320	13,288
	Jute woven goods, except carpets & rugs, & all other woven goods				7,307				
87,	Cotton bags & bagging			2,192	2,554	3,954	5,346	9,100	14,911
88,	Cotton waste for sale			5,680	5,564	10,062	4,862	9,706	18,769
89	Yarns for sale			34,031	56,165	80,936	10,874	14,422	39,399
	Ducks			8,664	14,263	17,006	109,400	132,913	463,710
	Tape & webbing	105,949	125,630	1,887	2,521	4,060	27,590	9,180	237,215
	Batting, wadding & mattress felts			2,094	864	1,173	5,559	45,189	16,665
	Other unfinished cotton products			6,422	{7,653	7,047	16,977	437	9,037
	Contract work				916	1,216	1,697	21,594 1,894	37,067 6,082
	Unbleached & bleached sheetings, shirtings & muslin			98,744	113,294	141,565	200,013	196,521	477,408

139

INDUSTRY NUMBER	COMMODITY	1869	1879	1889	1899	1904	1909	1914	1919
112	Felt goods	(Incl. with 355, 356)	2,389	3,071	5,364	8,332	11,459	13,277	38,908
121	Flax & hemp, dressed						467	283	2,369
145,	Haircloth	815	1,310	981	159	347	2,230	2,395	3,315
328	Excelsior						1,763	2,547	4,979
	Imitation leather & leatheroid	2,138	1,952	6,088	10,671	13,464	3,179	6,192	26,301
	Curled hair & all other upholstering materials, n.e.s.						9,061	8,283	9,930
151	Hat & cap materials	2,991	2,055	3,213	3,568	5,970	7,636	6,492	24,432
152, 154	Contract work	80	96	168	221	246	260	353	846
153	Fur-felt hat bodies & hats in the rough	533	639	1,120	993	661	2,704	2,373	7,657
	Contract work				492	561	554	509	24
155	Wool-felt hat bodies & hats in the rough	237	284	176	120	100	309	13	165
	Contract work		none		24			none	
158	Cotton batting, not made in cotton mills	not reported	127	797	1,364	1,434	1,768	2,630	1,531
176	Fleece lining (shoe & glove)		65	1,089	2,205	1,249	1,314	670	2,521
	Eider down			122	723	1,019	442	517	1,175
	Jersey cloth & stockinette		1,221	2,158	1,305	1,145	784	4,379	28,691
	Tricolette				1,709	2,406	2,492	4,005	17,172
	All other knitted cloth	848	76	2,286	332	354	269	1,252	9,788
	Contract work		682		274	208	1,083	3,649	8,771
203	Dress & cloak trimmings, braids & fringes	464	not reported	1,285	2,098	3,615	6,116	8,150	13,000
217	Oakum			363	440	361	338	359	983
225	Enameled oilcloth		371	561	1,257	1,542	2,265	2,495	3,421
281	Neckbands for sale as such	not reported	148	247	360	389	659	767	1,643
	Contract work		1,161	1,940	2,828	3,059	4,944	5,749	12,320
284	All other silk mfrs.	6,967	21,748	35,905	23,759	28,023	33,432	35,255	119,876
	Contract work		697	1,106	2,337	3,716	8,364	8,401	38,335
335	Waste		not reported	1,968	4,932	8,708	11,705	18,379	31,401
352	Wool pulling		not reported		531	882	5,181	8,273	17,361
353	Wool scouring		separately		890	1,053	3,289	4,565	13,680
354	Shoddy	1,834	5,175	8,162	6,738	8,113	7,315	6,765	22,092
	Contract work			18	291	336	230	407	1,099

140

355,	Woolen, worsted, merino & other yarns		21,939						239,119
356	Woolen, worsted, mohair & other upholstering goods	26,372	{6,897	{3,634 3,177	3,709 5,231	2,564 8,083	3,785 20,506	3,077 15,340	9,356 41,542
	Worsted tops & slubbing, noils & wool waste			154	1,569	1,189	3,026	3,437	18,387
	Contract work	58,571				not reported			
21	Bleaching & dyeing	none	36	1,004	925	3,268	6,325	5,117	11,800
49	Belting & hose, woven	4,353	6,319	9,072	7,538	9,592	10,107	8,505	13,199
83	Carpets	2,591	3,609	8,983	11,466	19,033	17,885	19,081	49,012
87, 88, 89	Rope, cable & cordage Towels, towelling, wash cloths, turkish towels & terry weaves	142	169	214	285	506	704	1,137	3,631
	Lace goods & nets	310	368	433	1,267	2,838	3,539	4,766	12,154
	Cotton thread	2,814	4,511	4,896	6,901	9,484	13,841	14,458	38,554
	Cotton tapestries	210	249	286	1,748	1,799	1,924	2,334	8,027
	All other cotton woven goods	4,449	12,902	22,244	55,156	85,418	136,579	165,052	444,884
97	Dyeing & finishing textiles	8,383	19,983	20,446	36,738	47,068	76,435	96,719	276,063
203	Embroideries	1,102	1,621	3,054	4,987	8,594	14,538	19,372	45,510
	Trimmed hats & hat frames	150	221	417	680	1,172	1,983	2,642	6,489
284	Silk ribbons	1,026	1,929	2,667	4,842	8,126	13,912	17,810	41,038
	Silk upholstery & tapestries	none		111	30	47	11	25	65
	Broadsilks	1,764	5,116	8,820	21,873	33,869	54,154	65,444	176,399
	Silk velvets & plushes	none		786	1,241	1,127	1,720	4,678	10,638
	Sewing & embroidery silks	85	272	999	1,147	1,375	1,322	1,796	2,492
313	Suspenders, garters & elastic woven goods			not reported separately			14,175	12,563	31,395
355, 356	Woolen & worsted woven goods, except shawls, blankets & carriage equipment	41,121	65,906	71,539	100,831	137,572	202,225	211,238	563,301
357	Mixed textiles	not reported	23,840			not reported separately			
	Total, Census Industry Group 2	309,820	386,565	504,259	677,488	928,312	1,356,296	1,540,243	4,292,211

141

INDUSTRY NUMBER	COMMODITY	1869	1879	1889	1899	1904	1909	1914	1919
	Census Industry Group 3 Iron and Steel and Their Products								
103, 124, 169x, 197, 260, 302x, 314	Marine steam engines & turbines							1,300	74,053
	Automobile, aviation & marine internal-combustion engines	(Incl. with III 124, Misc. machinery and other machine shop products)						19,193	115,381
	Foundry products, n.e.s.							126,429	421,049
	Tempering & welding, iron & steel								11,357
113, 163	Pig iron	69,013	88,204	145,613	206,513	228,911	387,830	312,762	785,960
	Ferroalloys								49,327
	Slag		278	8	61	728	307	462	751
	Blast-furnace gas to other departments						593	2,341	5,261
116	Contract work	72	74	38	70	107	104	137	396
149	Locks & all other hardware, incl. vehicle, piano & organ hardware	12,930	13,006	15,344	20,580	26,278	37,268	42,081	99,957
150	Hardware, saddlery	3,043	3,443	3,883	3,913	4,546	4,886	3,808	13,237
164	Structural shapes		5,593	15,463	29,362	32,731	65,565	57,475	151,970
	Merchant bars, mill shafting, spike & chain rods, bolt & nut rods, horseshoe bars, & strips		56,697	68,567	100,597	84,069	121,488	102,729	375,854
	Wire rods & steel rods				35,530	52,995	61,948	61,578	149,188
	Nail & tack plate				3,117	2,462	2,540	2,008	2,548
	Armor plate, gun forgings & ordnance				7,526	10,550	10,649	19,948	55,700
	Car & locomotive wheels, rolled or forged, & all other rolled products, incl. all forged or other iron & steel products, n.o.e.	77,601	23,355	63,886	25,868	32,429	58,310	56,292	131,290
	Ingots				2,781	3,985	3,594	1,383	33,315
	Direct steel castings				14,610	20,600	38,862	44,734	134,644
	Scrap iron or steel				10,788	11,080	18,164	16,335	37,414
	Plates or sheets, other than for tinning		22,432	39,359	68,109	77,802	133,272	129,786	523,621
	Black plates for tinning		not reported		20,968	25,297	30,956	43,147	94,456
	Skelp		13,980	23,629	49,160	46,780	64,515	52,443	151,557
	Hoops, bands & cotton ties		1,779	3,063	4,483	12,760	10,430	19,945	69,865
	Axles, rolled or forged					2,876	3,831	3,407	9,753
	Blooms, billets & slabs, steel, incl. rolled blooms, etc., for forging purposes				96,322	109,611	110,762	82,334	260,985
	Sheet & tin plate bars		3,968	1,183			37,745	45,373	117,856
	Muck & scrap bar		2,441	7,412	5,941	3,941	4,986	2,968	10,756
	Iron & steel rolling mill products made in other industries		not reported			347	6,628	2,832	7,143

142

164, 297	Springs, steel, car & carriage	3,708	4,627	5,484	7,204	7,266	9,091	12,272	52,889
166	Castings, other than pipe & fittings	172	156	299	470	571	758	682	1,614
168	Iron and steel, forgings, not made in steel works or rolling mills	8,512	6,589	9,179	10,595	12,292	20,596	28,391	173,972
275	Screws, machine	1,466	935	1,502	2,615	3,444	3,829	7,767	45,004
277, 278	Sewing machine cases	1,750	{ 1,970	2,147	2,686	5,030	5,487	5,577	13,588
	Sewing machine attachments		398	368	526	599	646	644	1,158
317	Tin plate & terneplate	not reported		31,371	34,767	46,733	66,270	175,776
	All other products, incl. plates redipped, tin dross, scruff, scrap, etc.				521	516	1,634	2,073	4,549
326	Typewriter supplies	not reported		782	1,493	2,292	4,254	5,277	10,481
345	Wire brads, tacks & staples	not reported					1,324	1,325	3,161
	Plain wire, iron & steel						22,632	22,317	58,756
	Galvanized & other coated wire						16,213	15,950	37,641
	Wire rope, cable & strand	3,783	6,893	14,000	33,626	50,458	6,684	7,974	29,826
	Other woven-wire products						2,834	2,823	4,724
	Cold-rolled flat wire, washers & other fabricated iron & steel wire products						9,605	8,899	20,406
346	Wire rope & cable & other wirework products	1,984	6,023	10,263	13,091	21,800	27,659	28,426	78,235
124	Misc. machinery & other machine shop products	92,615	84,320	161,663	253,668	308,070	410,152	312,736	772,079
		9,080	12,719	15,623	17,649	18,544	29,923	22,504	82,372
164, 165	Bolts, nuts, washers & rivets	16,359	7,660	22,556	20,109	21,635	25,308	24,113	52,222
164,	Cut nails & spikes, wire nails & spikes, forged nails & spikes & all other, incl. tacks								
164, 170	Wrought pipe—iron & steel	2,885	5,204	4,056	8,336	6,813	15,157	16,076	77,374
	Total, Census Industry Group 3	304,973	372,744	635,370	1,110,259	1,284,982	1,875,752	1,845,326	5,590,471
	Census Industry Group 4 Lumber and Its Remanufactures								
18	Baskets & rattan & willow ware	1,101	1,984	3,619	3,836	5,472	6,008	6,768	12,383
32	Boxes, cigar	985	2,978	7,276	6,009	7,988	8,712	8,853	13,649
34	Boxes, wooden packing, except cigar boxes	12,303	16,020	33,462	53,346	79,305	106,487	118,532	238,542
60	Charcoal, not incl. production in the lumber & wood distillation industries	(Incl. with VIII 348)	1,371	1,340	1,593	1,404	996	459	673
75	Coffins, burial cases & other undertakers' goods	3,950	8,003	11,999	13,687	19,881	24,050	25,730	64,237
81	Cooperage	25,435	31,922	36,564	38,432	49,414	49,612	50,008	91,893
85	Cork, cutting	749	1,554	2,817	4,357	4,455	5,892	7,811	16,182

143

INDUSTRY NUMBER	COMMODITY	1869	1879	1889	1899	1904	1909	1914	1919
129	Contract work	69	78	112	125	171	229	351	754
195	Pulp wood	not reported		not reported separately				631	not reported separately
258	Pulp goods, except wall board	not reported separately		245	879	1,018	1,228	3,092	16,799
347	Wood carpet	not reported	102	512	1,057	801	490	557	(Incl. with all other industries)
350	Wood, turned & carved	5,103	8,671	11,257	14,733	20,754	22,840	19,676	36,694
193	Looking-glass & picture frames	248	400	682	648	793	805	657	1,077
195	Lumber and timber products	175,945	194,517	367,945	423,851	393,123	489,772	466,345	907,825
	Total, Census Industry Group 4	225,888	267,600	477,830	562,553	584,579	717,121	709,470	1,400,708
	Census Industry Group 5 Leather and Its Finished Products								
22	Belting, leather	3,888	5,567	7,365	9,061	12,130	20,210	20,157	39,073
28	Boot & shoe cut stock, not made in shoe factories	not reported	7,796	18,531	24,057	28,645	46,224	62,040	163,363
29	Boot & shoe findings, not made in boot & shoe factories	3,753	3,015	6,989	8,047	10,172	26,194	29,065	66,022
30	Cut stock & findings made in shoe factories								8,377
	Received for crimping, stitching, buttonhole making & contract work	1,272	1,162	1,545	1,621	2,056	4,430	6,340	876
	Other income from custom work, leather scraps, remnants, etc.								4,098
185	Leather: tanned, curried & finished	155,508	198,062	170,243	194,202	236,921	312,572	348,957	849,356
	Contract work				4,322	8,190	12,766	12,287	51,800
	Byproducts of tanning, currying & finishing				3,286	4,568	5,226	7,913	13,605
250	Contract work	9	15	18	21	31	30	31	112
184	Leather goods	258	694	1,595	2,988	4,475	4,775	4,881	12,986
	Total, Census Industry Group 5	164,688	216,311	206,286	247,605	307,188	432,427	491,671	1,209,668
	Census Industry Group 6 Paper and Printing								
16	Bags, paper, excl. those made in paper mills	1,726	4,783	5,843	7,907	11,731	18,258	21,140	55,077
27	Bookbinding & blank-book making	22,917	19,499	27,787	33,848	41,061	50,895	53,610	89,347
33	Boxes, paper & other, n.e.s.	4,292	8,164	20,027	29,092	39,263	57,989	78,162	212,425
47	Card cutting & designing		53	247	629	1,101	1,049	1,108	5,522
48	Cardboard, not made in paper mills	not reported	2,138	2,387	2,831	4,176	6,766	9,305	19,355

144

105	Engraving & diesinking		1,000	1,854	1,427	2,354	2,187	3,086	6,923
106	Engraving, steel & copper plate, incl. plate printing	2,603	3,086	3,445	5,249	6,115	9,706	14,185	24,307
107	Engraving, wood		731	1,546	610	644	707	733	1,126
177	Labels & tags	680	781	945	997	2,221	4,213	8,846	23,862
191	Lithographing	2,456	6,746	17,556	21,707	24,639	33,290	38,204	69,810
230	All other paper (except writing paper, building paper & cardboard, bristol board, etc.)	38,085	{41,922	57,699	92,214	138,602	197,739	250,866	571,481
	Wood pulp		5,171	7,081	18,498	23,145	30,177	31,678	80,095
245	Photo-engraving	not reported		2,294	4,638	8,046	13,342	17,282	32,754
253, 254,	Electrotyping, lithographing, engraving, etc., except photo-engraving		1,940	1,956	2,425	2,961	6,339	7,498	9,681
255	Newspapers & periodicals: advertising		39,136	71,243	95,861	145,518	202,533	255,633	528,299
	Newspapers & periodicals: printed for publication by others					⎧	9,020	8,577	22,913
	Sheet music & books of music: printed for publication by others					⎨ 151,439	1,001	823	3,767
	Job printing, incl. machine composition for others	38,082	54,736	77,029	97,437	⎩	198,076	249,650	460,613
	Books & pamphlets: printed for publication by others						10,210	19,050	32,861
	Ready prints (patent insides & outsides)						2,293	1,965	2,011
	All other products for sale & in execution of orders		6,240	6,558	8,511	12,602	11,885	13,801	30,805
304	Stereotyping & electrotyping	1,050	708	2,134	3,685	4,890	6,237	8,205	15,659
325	Type founding	2,234	2,388	4,015	2,913	2,796	2,789	2,379	2,137
108	Envelopes	1,159	1,526	2,470	3,204	5,199	6,843	9,402	19,364
230	Fine paper: writing	2,752	2,037	2,810	3,740	5,912	7,640	8,763	22,580
231	All other paper goods, n.e.s.	1,515	788	2,154	8,052	10,629	18,206	23,501	48,995
	Total, Census Industry Group 6	119,551	203,573	319,080	445,475	645,044	909,390	1,137,552	2,391,769
	Census Industry Group 7 Liquors and Beverages								
188	Alcohol & cologne spirits	23,527	26,695	67,737	62,959	85,336	91,897	93,207	30,300
198	Malt	12,197	18,547	23,795	19,665	30,743	38,835	48,494	39,053
	Total, Census Industry Group 7	35,724	45,242	91,532	82,624	116,079	130,732	141,701	69,353

145

INDUSTRY NUMBER	COMMODITY	1869	1879	1889	1899	1904	1909	1914	1919
	Census Industry Group 8 Chemicals and Allied Products								
26	Bone, carbon & lampblack	194	661	1,031	939	1,266	2,136	2,954	7,579
62, 73,	Chemicals	20,319	{37,732	57,990	55,216	81,485	133,497	180,365	574,674
311	Byproducts & residues of chemical operations		901	1,384	1,463	2,164	5,885	4,410	25,924
	Contract work		19	30	28	39	108	189	481
76	Byproducts of coke production, except gas & tar		not reported		658	1,693	4,095	8,652	40,113
94	Drug grinding		not reported	437	4,308	5,146	6,007	8,080	16,938
98	Dyestuffs & extracts	2,738	4,996	8,838	6,989	10,031	15,691	19,996	122,277
109	Explosives	4,116	5,636	11,031	17,009	27,793	38,120	39,778	82,362
	Contract work, shooting wells				not reported				3,435
114	Fertilizers	5,571	22,658	37,535	42,778	58,017	102,097	155,176	287,716
133	Byproducts of mfd. gas except coke & tar	96	not reported	178	218	423	5,898	9,669	4,091
139	Glue & gelatin	1,785	4,514	4,458	5,626	10,479	14,779	18,174	36,204
143	Grease & tallow, not incl. lubricating grease	9,585	21,803	11,870	18,981	29,874	37,197	41,499	95,606
160	Ink, printing	586	1,079	2,322	3,009	5,641	8,662	13,552	25,786
194	Lubricating greases, not made in petroleum refineries	not reported	476	1,102	936	1,145	1,930	6,537	9,817
218	Oil, cake & meal, cottonseed	2,237	7,799	19,607	59,549	97,758	149,885	214,765	588,220
220	Oils, essential	551	234	240	763	1,406	1,531	1,865	5,021
221	Other oils, n.e.s., incl. lard oil & oleo oil, not made in slaughtering establishments	17,568	10,966	14,172	23,618	27,446	39,821	44,573	184,703
222	Oil, linseed	7,353	14,886	22,757	26,287	26,667	34,717	42,973	114,045
229, 329	Varnishes, japans & shellac	4,987	8,017	14,935	19,123	22,534	32,531	37,949	92,771
241	Fuel oils		3,389	6,440	7,551	9,205	36,463	84,018	318,124
	Coke, petroleum		35	159	176	150	508	819	3,928
	Light products of distillation, except gasoline		382	1,179	2,063	2,750	5,131	15,779	86,139
	Lubricating & axle grease	3,368	52	640	1,591	903	1,016	2,293	8,147
	Petrolatum		28	1,347	864	491	552	1,243	3,750
	Paraffin wax		632	3,054	7,791	10,007	9,389	8,897	28,348
	Partly refined oils, acid oil, reclaimed acid & other special products		325	1,467	1,699	6,856	6,307	8,999	37,763
324	Turpentine & rosin	3,521	5,842	8,029	20,231	24,073	25,488	21,313	56,499
348	Wood distillation & charcoal mfr.	2,029	(Incl. with 62)		5,996	8,811	9,795	9,910	28,122
17	Baking powders & yeast	733	1,405	2,391	3,135	5,142	7,842	8,998	23,537
24	Blacking, stains & dressing	182	332	645	1,002	1,322	1,874	2,200	5,628
66	Cleansing & polishing preparations	69	107	186	470	581	1,342	1,963	5,134
76	Coke	1,111	5,259	16,190	33,743	47,790	85,467	83,917	242,663

146

95	Alkaloids & derivatives	not reported		2,343	3,278	4,534	4,951	4,700
133	Biological products			1,762	2,466	3,411	3,728	9,510
	Receipts from sales of lamps & appliances by gas companies		673					
			506				7,393	10,547
219	Castor oil	832	not reported	1,797	3,816	5,538	257	821
233	Patent compounds	24	43	58	68	133	6,193	17,382
241	Lubricating oils	971	877	1,948	3,562	4,500	52,012	159,234
	Illuminating oils	88	1,763	7,268	10,894	23,471	38,431	47,133
	Gasoline	698	1,004	1,556	2,241	2,836	7,744	333,553
269	Salt	none	2,580	7,963	13,824	17,540	28,764	29,025
294	Soap	4,077	4,043	4,271	6,206	7,722	68,578	20,394
		940	1,349	1,724	2,397	3,422	10,763	
							7,959	
	Total, Census Industry Group 8	96,329	171,824	279,085	418,894	598,116	929,102	1,271,083	3,797,844

Census Industry Group 9 Stone, Clay and Glass Products

37	Fire & silica brick & stove lining	3,644	4,021	{6,470	9,053	11,753	17,044	16,948	49,615
	Other brick & tile products			2,181	4,304	5,501	2,695	3,166	8,840
59	All other products of the cement industry	262	406	1,107	2,016	3,841	9,664	19,646	36,551
64	China decorating, not incl. that done in potteries	not reported	606	496	334	803	743	925
135	Milk jars	183	not reported	729	1,161	2,071	4,961	4,653
	Lantern globes	30	185	497	853	436	521	1,023
	Plate glass, rough	not reported	74	76	4	37	26	171
	Wire glass, rough	7,749	7,818	11	125	568	1,057	2,271
	All other bottles & jars			13,914	18,013	29,034	30,296	43,460	79,995
	All other products				691	2,323	2,370	4,023	12,752
	Opal ware				1,582	870			
	Cut glass	1,344	1,356	2,414	672	988	9,036	10,563	15,372
	All other pressed & blown glass				1,385	3,533			
186	Limestone	1,328	231	631	1,149	2,197	2,681	3,345	4,132
206	Minerals & earths, ground or otherwise treated	527	1,417	2,770	3,622	4,319	4,553	10,294	44,638
135	Plate glass, polished	229	756	not reported	2,611	3,920	636	1,118	10,004
136	Glass cutting, staining & ornamenting	2,092	365	1,817	1,810	3,461	4,806	4,962	8,627
186	Lime	176	110	994	2,890	2,746	4,558	7,248	16,846
207	Mirrors, framed & unframed	18,386		2,167		not reported	3,457	3,582	7,380
	Quartz milled								
	Total, Census Industry Group 9	54,336	16,739	35,748	51,721	77,406	95,626	135,663	303,795

147

INDUSTRY NUMBER	COMMODITY	1869	1879	1889	1899	1904	1909	1914	1919
	Census Industry Group 10 Metals and Metal Products, Other than Iron and Steel								
3	All other aluminum manufactures, incl. ingots, plates & sheets				not reported			22,718	26,220
14	Babbitt metal & solder	324	275	3,036	9,605	13,690	20,652	62,220	67,500
35	Castings & machinery fittings							8,820	137,260
	Ingots & bars							43,020	44,250
	Plates & sheets							14,570	103,409
	Rods	14,302	29,771	54,521	96,563	111,544	163,370	13,935	43,598
	Tubing							34,062	43,366
	Wire, plain								74,148
100	Electroplating	not reported	1,849	2,921	2,812	3,066	4,663	4,820	10,354
102, 172,	Enameling	225	183	182	1,287	1,980	3,033	2,185	2,693
298	Stamped ware	not reported	3,125	9,327	14,297	21,958	34,763	43,671	99,331
	Japanning	216	190	351	216	607	331	381	771
131	Galvanizing	3,620	8,565	13,437	11,228	29,168	33,345	51,723	85,551
140	Gold & silver, leaf & foil	1,411	1,614	2,978	2,666	2,695	2,631	2,432	4,461
141	Gold & silver, reducing & refining, not from the ore	792	8,908	29,890	11,021	17,469	22,030	26,685	52,307
178	Automobile lamps		none		41	259	1,736	4,901	14,864
	Reflectors	62	209	252	517	542	822	656	1,032
183	Lead, bar, pipe & sheet	12,453	5,125	7,642	6,842	8,488	8,370	9,431	16,396
215	Hooks & eyes				575	691		1,694	928
	Knitting machine needles	571	799	964	648	677	2,694	755	4,665
	Snap fasteners & clasps				258	303		768	7,996
238	Pens, gold	389	443	597	665	576	996	534	1,498
288, 291, 292x	Smelting & refining, metals, n.e.s.			not reported separately					20,074
289	Smelting & refining, copper	11,684	not reported		165,132	240,780	378,806	444,022	651,102
290	Smelting & refining, lead	3,499	2,725	2,977	175,466	185,827	167,406	171,579	196,795
292	Smelting & refining, zinc	1,224	8,411	28,189	18,188	24,791	34,206	53,538	104,123
293	Smelting & refining, not from the ore	1,094	417	(Incl. with 'all other industries')	7,832	17,507	28,249	40,539	51,050
316	Tin & other foils, n.e.s.	not reported			1,593	2,795	3,419	5,070	19,438
336	Watch & clock materials, except watch cases	1,349	829	1,959	812	1,010	1,589	2,389	3,159
337	Watch cases	2,151	4,231	7,946	7,175	7,954	9,695	6,633	16,617
173	Jewelry	2,168	2,178	3,410	4,561	5,263	7,949	7,914	19,976
318	Tinware, n.e.s.	11,016	13,604	18,068	27,198	41,718	58,563	79,874	225,510
	Total, Census Industry Group 10	68,550	93,451	188,647	567,198	741,358	989,318	1,161,539	2,150,442

148

Census Industry Group 12   Vehicles for Land Transportation

10	Contract & custom work		none		37	609	1,426	7,614
11	Automobile chassis			515	2,885	29,465	44,336	650,565
	All other products of motor vehicle industry, incl. bodies & parts & repair work done in factories		none					
51	Carriage & wagon materials	5,582	9,608	15,449	23,776	29,009	32,800	23,606	27,413
56, 57	All other products, incl. parts & repair work	6,888	6,166	16,249	21,599	25,373	49,280	56,251	169,217
	Parts & repair work done in other industries	53	47	124	165	205	210	980	3,290
209	Motorcycle & bicycle parts		522	6,503	1,083	3,874	5,352	18,171
10	Motor vehicle bodies & parts	none	none		1,076	36,704	81,066	471,885
	Total, Census Industry Group 12	12,523	15,821	32,344	52,558	59,668	152,942	213,017	1,348,155

Census Industry Group 14   Miscellaneous Industries

1	Aircraft under construction at close of year			none			126	1,659
	Engines and parts		none					2,855
4	Ammunition							92,967
	Safety fuses, other fuses, naval & rr. torpedoes	2,023	1,552	5,326	10,611	16,233	21,224	27,516	17,259
	Contract settlements			none					3,354
9	Textile-mill products & all other asbestos products		not reported					
20	Belting, rubber	213	370	1,880	2,104	5,099	6,559	1,073	16,398
31	Heels, rubber		none			7,548	5,358	7,989	22,436
42	Button parts							5,754	16,104
	Blanks or molds	157	394	373	{ 24	{ 22	2,769	{ 111	1,070
					656	916		2,349	3,092
93	Dental goods	540	803	2,421	3,472	7,287	10,106	15,025	27,281

149

INDUSTRY NUMBER	COMMODITY	1869	1879	1889	1899	1904	1909	1914	1919
99	Fuses, cut-outs & fuse plugs				355	868	1,002	1,757	7,895
	Small dynamos (under 10 k.w.), starting motors & generators, automotive				3,466	3,837	3,142	5,933	36,663
	Sockets, receptacles, bases & attachment plugs				594	2,011	4,522	5,513	15,008
	Annunciators & push buttons				225	186	236	264	710
	Transformers, under 50 k.w.				2,184	3,292	4,185	7,317	10,613
	Rheostats, resistances, controllers, motor starters, regulators, etc.				831	933	2,675	9,788	23,083
	Generator parts & supplies	none	1,037	7,468	1,102	1,220	996	1,527	6,217
	Vehicle & railway motors				2,944	3,442	4,772	7,234	7,171
	Motor parts & supplies				none		2,795	4,512	18,722
	Storage batteries				2,792	{1,569	4,244	10,615	56,648
	Battery parts & supplies					1,646	1,056	3,266	6,986
	Carbons				1,731	2,711	1,935	3,603	13,292
	Telephone parts & supplies				1,325	2,072	3,752	4,061	23,059
	Insulated wire				11,178	18,123	27,103	36,491	67,579
	Circuit fittings, not elsewhere provided for				1,679	3,525	1,080	2,068	5,053
	Magneto ignition apparatus, generators, spark plugs & coils	not reported			328	678	6,092	22,261	51,287
104	Engravers' materials	(Incl. in 'other industries')	82	193	267	162	873	684	2,009
125	Foundry supplies		211	655	1,101	1,033	2,241	1,963	9,528
130	Furs, dressed	294	272	652	1,401	3,219	2,393	2,878	21,551
142	Graphite, ground & refined	not reported	293	77	598	476	1,588	2,401	2,754
159	Receipts from cold storage	7	15	137	380	892	2,041	3,415	7,143
171	Ivory, shell & bone work, excl. combs & hairpins	1,223	1,647	2,172	2,120	3,242	2,111	2,147	2,910
174	Jewelry & instrument cases	224	136	1,501	1,194	2,365	3,218	3,602	8,551
179	Lapidary work	106	540	313	5,740	7,586	9,100	5,317	29,741
211	Musical instruments, n.e.s., parts & materials	554	234	518	931	955	886	1,070	3,502
214	Piano & organ parts, except perforated music rolls	3,007	4,655	8,849	10,378	16,733	22,557	23,786	39,906
242	Phonograph cabinets & parts & accessories	none	(Incl. with all other industries')		269	1,503	763	323	14,836

Code	Commodity								
244	Motion picture films, not exposed, & all other photographic materials	not reported	140	2,087	5,681	9,392	21,036	34,197	69,072
	Motion picture projection films			none			4,206	not reported separately	32,092
257	Pulp, from fiber other than wood	not reported		524	103	(Incl. with 'all other industries')			524
265	Tires, solid							13,736	52,922
	Rubber packing							3,508	7,317
	Rubber reclaimed	6,760	11,740	15,128	27,841	42,894	72,666	11,135	20,173
	All other manufactures of rubber							42,137	151,101
270	Sand & emery paper & cloth	436	327	1,560	1,468	1,843	5,439	5,401	11,612
283	Advertising novelties		not reported separately				5,916	10,684	25,404
299	Stationery goods, n.e.s.	35	6,152	9,863	5,284	9,248	17,371	23,887	61,565
302	Steam packing	not reported		963	3,354	8,594	11,674	13,940	39,377
306X	Straw goods	7,390	9,346	330	37				
339	Whalebone cutting	262	527	683	135	186	(Incl. with 'all other industries')		
358	Teasels	not reported		85			not reported		
5	Artificial flowers	238	444	824	571	476	2,176	1,834	4,088
42	Buttons	1,364	3,412	3,233	5,902	9,148	17,016	15,110	32,491
99	Incandescent lamps		not reported		2,285	4,519	10,215	11,278	37,471
110	Fancy articles, n.e.s.	44	586	1,080	1,408	1,862	1,929	2,749	9,574
111	Feathers & plumes	581	2,052	3,819	2,647	2,207	10,085	7,733	9,913
127	Fur goods	961	889	2,140	2,891	4,144	6,241	4,915	19,408
159	Ice, manufactured	126	265	2,385	6,706	12,175	22,069	31,096	69,397
210	Mucilage, paste, & other adhesives, n.e.s.	68	9	686	1,374	1,912	2,644	3,105	5,985
265	Pneumatic tires & tubes, automobile			none	4,389	2,062	11,220	33,961	150,746
	Pneumatic tires & tubes, motorcycle and bicycle			none	1,755	939	1,122	1,713	2,920
327	Umbrellas & canes	611	876	1,745	1,755	1,707	2,036	1,770	3,246
344	Window shades & fixtures	not reported	157	514	494	546	1,136	1,089	1,852
	Total, Census Industry Group 14	27,224	49,163	80,184	146,305	235,238	389,571	508,717	1,515,142
	Total, All Unfinished Commodities	1,486,314	1,982,211	3,045,874	4,686,199	6,034,724	8,672,210	9,950,881	26,183,436

INDUSTRY NUMBER		COMMODITY	1869	1879	1889	1899	1904	1909	1914	1919
		INDUSTRIES AND COMMODITIES NOT ELSEWHERE CLASSIFIED								
VIII	76	Coke, excl. gas-house coke: gas	no reports	not reported		333	844	2,609	6,010	16,685
XIV	126	Fuel, mfd.		102	(Incl. with 'all other industries')			453	1,155	2,359
VIII	133	Gas, mfd., illuminating & heating: gas	29,330		15,971	69,572	112,888	138,869	175,198	282,401
		Gas, mfd., illuminating & heating: receipts from rent of lamps & appliances			166	204	434	718	1,122	1,763
III	228	Ordnance & accessories		not reported	2,425	2,240	558	(Incl. with 'all other industries')		77,508
I	252	Poultry, killing & dressing, not done in slaughtering & meat packing establishments		not reported					16,902	52,133
		Total, Industries & Commodities, n.c.c.	29,330	102	54,562	72,349	114,724	142,649	200,387	432,849

RECAPITULATION

	1869	1879	1889	1899	1904	1909	1914	1919
All Commodities	3,845,401	5,091,267	8,058,843	11,390,660	14,792,818	20,632,988	24,268,372	62,519,803
Finished	1,987,685	2,715,664	4,102,963	5,508,525	7,103,921	9,626,338	11,689,324	30,700,517
Construction materials	319,892	363,429	704,498	863,637	1,178,712	1,704,112	1,787,078	3,366,352
Repairs and servicing	22,180	29,861	150,946	259,950	360,737	487,679	640,702	1,836,649
Unfinished	1,486,314	1,982,211	3,045,874	4,686,199	6,034,724	8,672,210	9,950,881	26,183,436
Commodities, n.e.c.	29,330	102	54,562	72,349	114,724	142,649	200,387	432,849

PERCENTAGES

	1869	1879	1889	1899	1904	1909	1914	1919
All Commodities	100.0	100.0	100.0	100.0	100.0	100.0	100.0	100.0
Finished	51.7	53.3	50.9	48.4	48.0	46.7	48.2	49.1
Construction materials	8.3	7.1	8.7	7.6	8.0	8.3	7.4	5.4
Repairs and servicing	.6	.6	1.9	2.3	2.4	2.4	2.6	2.9
Unfinished	38.6	38.9	37.8	41.1	40.8	42.0	41.0	41.9
Commodities, n.e.c.	.8	*	.7	.6	.8	.7	.8	.7

*Less than one-half of one-tenth percent.
n.e.c.: not elsewhere classified.
n.e.s.: not elsewhere specified.

n.o.c.: not otherwise classified.
n.o.e.: not otherwise enumerated.

NOTE A TO TABLE II 1

Estimates from Data Later than 1919 for Products not Belonging to an Industry (*o*) and Products Made in Other Industries (*s*)
(thousands of dollars)

Major and Minor Commodity Groups

	Value 1919	Estimated Correction for *o*	Estimated Correction for *s*	Difference between *o* & *s*	Difference as % of Total Values
Consumer Perishable, Total	13,668,008	68,919		68,919	0.5
1 Food & kindred products	10,840,581	54,964		54,964	0.5
2 Cigars, cigarettes & tobacco	1,024,458		35	35	
3 Drug, toilet & household preparations	691,307	3,247		3,247	0.5
4 Magazines, newspapers, stationery & supplies, & misc. paper products	479,837	10,557		10,557	2.2
5 Fuel & lighting products, mfd.	631,825	116		116	
Consumer Semidurable, Total	7,030,907	88,144	965	87,179	1.2
6 Dry goods & notions	985,642	6,839	262	6,577	0.7
7 Clothing & personal furnishings	3,866,186	63,774	703	63,071	1.6
8 Shoes & other footwear	1,258,542				
9 House furnishings (semidurable)	212,906	5,892		5,892	2.8
10 Toys, games & sporting goods	161,292	11,639		11,639	7.2
11 Tires & tubes	546,339				
Consumer Durable, Total	3,967,940	65,825		65,825	1.7
12 Household furniture	498,005	17,557		17,557	3.5
13a Heating & cooking apparatus, & household appliances, except electrical	266,576	4,374		4,374	1.6
13b Electrical household appliances & supplies	84,244				
14a Floor coverings	151,397				
14b Misc. house furnishings (durable)	218,861	11,979		11,979	5.5
15 China & household utensils	235,629	5,894		5,894	2.5
16 Musical instruments	256,485				
17 Jewelry, silverware, clocks & watches	304,810	18,509		18,509	6.1
18 Printing & publishing books	132,699				
19 Luggage	64,864				
20a & b Motor vehicles & accessories	1,574,355	5,989		5,989	0.4

	Value 1919	Estimated Correction for o	Estimated Correction for s	Difference between o & s	Difference as % of Total Values
20c Carriages & wagons	27,230				
21 Motorcycles & bicycles	28,887				
22 Pleasure-craft	5,496				
23 Ophthalmic products & artificial limbs	45,041	1,523		1,523	3.4
24 Monuments & tombstones	73,361				
Producer Durable, Total	6,033,662	67,761	5,112	62,649	1.0
25 Industrial machinery & equipment	1,918,607	8,929	4,885	4,044	0.2
26 Electrical equipment, industrial & commercial	456,602				
27 Farm equipment	394,974	6,350		6,350	1.6
28 Office & store machinery & equipment	153,406	11,584		11,584	7.6
29 Office & store furniture & fixtures	90,923	2,349		2,349	2.6
30 Locomotives & railroad cars	550,424				
31 Ships & boats	1,389,509				
32a Business vehicles, motor	379,931				
32b Business vehicles, wagons	42,518				
33 Aircraft	8,610				
34 Professional & scientific equipment	80,108	7,153		7,153	8.9
35 Carpenters' & mechanics' tools	208,007	23,881		23,881	11.5
36 Misc. subsidiary durable equipment	360,043	7,515	227	7,288	2.0
All Finished Commodities, Total	30,700,517	290,649	6,077	284,572	0.9
Construction Materials	3,366,252	61,386		61,386	1.8

NOTE B TO TABLE II 1

Commodity Values Estimated from Combined Totals, and Other Commodity Apportionments

INDUSTRY NUMBER	CENSUS YEARS IN WHICH ESTIMATED	COMMODITIES BY CENSUS GROUPS	GROUP CLASSIFICATION	% OF COMBINED TOTAL ACCOUNTED FOR BY EACH COMMODITY
		1 FOOD AND KINDRED PRODUCTS		
40, 61	1889	Cascin; whey sold; cream Products not belonging to the industry	Un	
	1879	Butter[a] Cheese[a]	1, Un 1	84.1 15.9

154

65	1919	Finished chocolate & cocoa products made in other industries	1	47.3
	1869–1914	Unfinished chocolate & cocoa products made in other industries	Un	52.7
		Chocolate in cakes, sweetened or with nuts; milk chocolate; cocoa, powdered; other chocolate & cocoa products, except confectionery; finished chocolate & cocoa products made in other industries	1	47.3
		Chocolate in cakes, unsweetened; chocolate coatings; chocolate liquors; cocoa, other than powdered; cocoa butter; unfinished chocolate & cocoa products made in other industries	Un	52.7
74, 235	1869–1899	Coffee & spice, roasting & grinding	1	91.8
122	1869, 1879	Peanuts, grading, roasting, cleaning, shelling	1, Un	8.2
		Hominy & grits; oatmeal, breakfast foods & all other cereal products	1, Un	86.4
		Flour: wheat, corn, rye, buckwheat & barley	Un	.7
		Bran & middlings, & feed & offal	Un	12.9
122, 123, 286	1914	Food preparations for human consumption remaining in Food preparations, n.e.s. industry	1	34.8
		Food preparations for human consumption transferred to other industries	1, Un	65.2
	1879–1909	Food preparations for human consumption remaining in Food preparations, n.e.s., industry	1	41.7
		Food preparations for human consumption transferred to other industries	1, Un	58.3
122	1904–1909	Meat products made in Food preparations industry (industry total)	1, Un	33.0
		Breakfast foods made in Food preparations, n.e.s., industry[b]	1	67.0
	1879–1899	Meat products made in the Food preparations industry (industry total)	1, Un	4.0
123	1909	Breakfast foods made in Food preparations, n.e.s. industry	1	22.7
		Peanut butter	1	19.7
		Sweetening sirups, other than cane	1	53.6
		Macaroni, vermicelli & noodles	1	3.1
	1879–1904	Other food preparations for human consumption	1	15.2
		Peanut butter	1	41.4
		Macaroni, vermicelli & noodles	1	40.3
		Other food preparations for human consumption	Un	
		Other food preparations for animals & fowls	1	
263	1914–1919	Clean rice, fancy-head[c]	Un	28.3
	1914–1919	Clean rice, second-head, screenings & brewers'[c]	Un	71.7
		Hulls & waste	1	
	1899	Products not belonging to the industry	Un	67.8
	1899	Clean rice, fancy-head[d]	Un	32.2
		Clean rice, second-head, screenings & brewers'[d]		
		Hulls & waste		
	1879–1889	Products not belonging to the industry	1	73.1
		Clean rice, fancy-head	Un	26.9
		Clean rice, second-head, screenings & brewers'; polish & bran; hulls & waste		

155

INDUSTRY NUMBER	CENSUS YEARS IN WHICH ESTIMATED	COMMODITIES BY CENSUS GROUPS	GROUP CLASSIFICATION	% OF COMBINED TOTAL ACCOUNTED FOR BY EACH COMMODITY
286, 287	1879–1909	Meat puddings, scrapple, head cheese, etc.[e]	1	
		Edible meat products made in other industries	1	
		Lard compound & substitutes	1	
	1889–1899	Canned goods[f]	1	9.9
	1909	Oleo stock	Un	90.1
		Tallow		
	1889–1909	Sausage casings[g]	1	1.4
	1889	Fresh meat[h]	Un	98.6
	1914–1919	Custom & contract work		3.3
		Other products[i]	Un	96.7
	1909–1914	Hair, hog & cattle		1.1
		Other products[i]	Un	98.9
	1909	Hoofs, horns & horn tips, strips, etc.		1.3
		Other products[i]	Un	6.7
	1889–1904	Oleo stock	Un	1.0
		Stearin	Un	2.9
		Hoofs, horns & horn tips, strips, etc.	Un	88.1
		Hair, hog & cattle	Un	1.3
	1889	Custom & contract work	Un	98.7
		Other products[i]		
	1889–1899	Hides & pelts[i]	Un	83.0
	1879	Fresh meat; cured meat; canned goods; sausage	1	9.7
		Stearin; sausage casings; hoofs, horns & horn tips, strips, etc.; hides & pelts; hair, hog & cattle; wool; custom & contract work	1, Un	7.3
308	1889	Sugar, beet (industry total)[k]	Un	
309	1909	Sugar, refined & brown	1, Un	22.8
	1904	Sugar, raw & clarified	1, Un	77.2
		Sugar, refined & brown	1, Un	90.4
	1879–1899	Molasses & sirup; sugar, raw; sugar, clarified		9.6
		Sweetening sirup	1	2.5
		Sugar, refined & brown	1, Un	88.2
		Molasses & sirup; sugar, raw & sugar, clarified	Un	9.3
	1869	Sweetening sirup	1	2.8
310	1909	Sugar, refined & brown	1, Un	97.2
		Sugar, refined	1, Un	98.9
		Molasses and sirup	Un	1.1

156

II TEXTILES AND THEIR PRODUCTS

49	1879	Rugs[1]	14a	.3
	1869	Carpets[1]	14a, Un	99.7
		Rugs	14a, Un	90.4
70	1869–1904	Clothing, men's, regular factories	7	9.6
	1869–1904	Clothing, men's, contract shops	Un	97.2
72	1869–1904	Clothing, women's, regular factories	7	2.8
	1869–1904	Clothing, women's, contract shops	Un	2.1
83, 175, 187	1904	Jute carpets & rugs	14a	2.6
		Linen woven goods	9	34.4
		Rope, cable & cordage	36, Un	5.6
		Linen thread	6, Un	
		Binder twine; twine, other than binder twine; yarns for sale; jute woven goods, except carpets & rugs & all other woven goods	Un	55.3
	1879–1889	Jute carpets & rugs	14a	.7
		Linen woven goods	9	1.6
		Rope, cable & cordage	36, Un	27.6
		Linen thread	6, Un	4.8
		Binder twine; twine, other than binder twine; yarns for sale; jute woven goods, except carpets & rugs & all other woven goods	Un	65.3
	1869	Linen woven goods	9	25.0
		Linen thread	Un	75.0
		Rope, cable & cordage	36, Un	35.4
		Other cordage & twine manufactures	7	64.6
87, 88, 89	1889–1914	Cotton blankets; cotton table damask; sheets & pillow cases, bedspreads & quilts	6, Un	7.5
		All other cotton woven goods	9	92.5
	1869–1909	Lace curtains & bedspreads	6, Un	38.3
	1889	Lace goods & nets	9, Un	61.7
		Towels, toweling, wash cloths, turkish towels & terry weave	6, Un	12.1
		Tape & webbing	Un	12.4
		Other unfinished cotton products & contract work		42.2
		All other products not belonging to the industry		33.3
	1869, 1879	Cotton blankets; cotton table damask; sheets & pillow cases; bedspreads & quilts	7	2.5
		Towels, toweling, wash cloths, turkish towels & terry weaves	9, Un	.7
		Lace & lace curtains	9, Un	.5
		Threads	6, Un	4.4
		Tape & webbing	6, Un	.7
		Tapestries	14b, Un	.3
		All other cotton woven goods	6, Un	31.2
		All unfinished cotton goods products	Un	59.7

157

INDUSTRY NUMBER	CENSUS YEARS IN WHICH ESTIMATED	COMMODITIES BY CENSUS GROUPS	GROUP CLASSIFICATION	% OF COMBINED TOTAL ACCOUNTED FOR BY EACH COMMODITY
152, 153, 154, 155	1869	Hats & caps, other than felt and wool, & hats, straw	7, Un	31.0
		Hats, fur-felt	7, Un	40.4
		Hats, wool-felt	7, Un	28.6
152, 153, 154	1879–1889	Hats & caps, other than felt & wool	7, Un	43.5
		Hats, fur-felt	7, Un	56.5
152, 154	1869–1899	Hats, straw	7	44.1
		Hats & caps, except felt, straw & wool	7	54.9
		Contract work	Un	1.0
153	1869–1889	Fur-felt hats	7	94.6
		Fur-felt hat bodies & hats in the rough; contract work	Un	5.4
155	1869, 1879	Hats, wool-felt	7	97.0
		Hats in the rough & hat bodies	Un	3.0
158	1879–1909	Comforts & quilts	9	21.5
		Feather pillows & beds	14b	14.3
		Mops & dusters	9	13.0
		All other house-furnishing goods	9	42.6
		Cotton batting, not made in cotton mills	Un	8.6
176	1914	Tricolette	Un	66.6
		Products not belonging to the industry	Un	33.4
	1904–1909	Bathing suits	7	25.3
		Tricolette	Un	49.7
		Products not belonging to the industry	Un	25.0
	1899	Bathing suits	7	20.9
		Eider down	Un	17.4
		Tricolette	Un	41.1
	1889	Products not belonging to the industry	Un	20.6
		Tricolette; all other knitted cloth; contract work	Un	73.0
		Products not belonging to the industry	Un	27.0
	1879	Bathing suits	7	.6
		Jersey cloth & stockinette; eider down; tricolette; all other knitted cloth; contract work	Un	83.8
		Products not belonging to the industry	Un	15.6
	1879	Hosiery; shirts & drawers; leggings; gloves & mittens, knitted; knitted headwear (except infants'); sweaters, sweater coats, jerseys, cardigan jackets, etc.; scarfs & shawls & all other fancy knit goods^m	7, Un	95.3
		Fleece lining (shoe & glove)^m	7	
	1869	All finished knit goods	7	95.3
		All unfinished knit goods	Un	4.7

158

203	1869-1909	Women's neckwear	7	12.2
		Lace work, crocheted goods, hand-made curtains of muslin & lace, lace, ladies' & children's belts other than leather, & handkerchiefs	6	18.1
		Embroideries	6, Un	20.5
		Trimmed hats & hat frames	7, Un	42.4
		Dress & cloak trimmings, braids & fringes	Un	6.8
225	1879-1899	Table, wall, shelf & stair oilcloth	14b	69.7
		Enameled oilcloth	Un	30.3
281	1909-1919	Shirts	7	88.1
		Neckbands for sale as such	Un	.8
		Contract work	Un	6.0
		Products not belonging to the industry		5.1
	1879-1904	Shirts	7	93.8
		Contract work	Un	5.5
		Neckbands for sale as such	Un	.7
284	1889	Sewing & embroidery silks[a]	6, Un	32.0
	1889	Machine twist, fringe & floss silks[n]	Un	68.0
	1889	Silk embroideries	6	4.6
		All other products		95.4
	1889	Contract work	Un	65.9
		All other products[o]		34.1
	1889-1904	All other silk manufactures		63.6
		Products not belonging to the industry[p]		36.4
	1879	Silk embroideries	6	.2
		Contract work	Un	3.1
		All other silk manufactures	Un	96.7
	1869	Silk embroideries	6	.1
		Silk ribbons	6, Un	14.7
		Silk laces, nets, veils, veiling, etc.	6, Un	1.2
		Broad silks	6, Un	27.4
		Sewing & embroidery silks	6, Un	1.8
		All other silk manufactures; contract work	Un	54.8
355, 356	1879	Blankets: all-wool woven, cotton-warp woven, & cotton-mixed woven	14b	30.6
		Horse blankets	36	19.4
	1879	Woolen, worsted, merino & other yarns[q]	Un	
	1879	Shawls: all-wool woven	7	1.2
		Carriage cloths & carriage robes	20	.8
		Woolen & worsted woven goods, except shawls, blankets & carriage equipment	6, Un	93.8
		Woolen, worsted, mohair & other upholstering goods; worsted slubbing, noils & wool waste; contract work	Un	4.2

159

INDUSTRY NUMBER	CENSUS YEARS IN WHICH ESTIMATED	COMMODITIES BY CENSUS GROUPS	GROUP CLASSIFICATION	% OF COMBINED TOTAL ACCOUNTED FOR BY EACH COMMODITY
	1869	Blankets, etc.	14	2.9
		Shawls: all-wool woven	7	1.0
		Horse blankets	36	.7
		Carriage cloths & carriage robes	20	.7
		Woolen & worsted woven goods, except, etc.	6, Un	79.8
		All other woolen manufactures	Un	14.9

III IRON AND STEEL AND THEIR PRODUCTS

INDUSTRY NUMBER	CENSUS YEARS IN WHICH ESTIMATED	COMMODITIES BY CENSUS GROUPS	GROUP CLASSIFICATION	% OF COMBINED TOTAL ACCOUNTED FOR BY EACH COMMODITY
91	1869-1909	Pocket-knives	10	15.4
		Scissors, shears & clippers	14b	9.2
		Table cutlery; razors, plain & safety	15	39.3
		Axes & hatchets; augurs, bits, planes & chisels; all other cutlery & edge tools	35	36.1
113, 163	1879-1904	Slag; blast furnace gas to other departments	Un	25.0
		Products not belonging to the industry		75.0
116	1869-1909	Firearms	10	98.7
		Contract work	Un	1.3
124, 302X	1914	Steel barrels, drums & tanks	25	1.8
		Misc. machinery (incl. machinery not reported separately for both 1919 & 1914) & other machine shop products	25, Un	98.2
124, 166	1869-1904	Foundry & machine shop products, excl. locomotives & stoves & hot-air furnaces	25, Un	96.8
		Iron and steel—cast-iron pipe	C, Un	3.2
124, 305	1869-1899	Foundry & machine shop products, incl. cast-iron pipe & excl. locomotives	25, C, Un	92.7
		Stoves & hot-air furnaces	13, C	7.3
124, 192	1869-1879	Foundry & machine shop products, incl. cast-iron pipe & stoves & hot-air furnaces	13, 25, C, Un	94.0
		Locomotives not made by rr. companies	30	6.0
149	1869-1909	Locks & all other hardware, incl. vehicle, piano & organ hardware	Un	64.8
		Builders' hardware	C	35.2
164	1904	Scrap iron or steel	Un	12.5
		Custom work & repairing	S	1.3
		All other iron or steel products, not rolled		69.9
		Products not belonging to the industry		16.3
	1879-1889	Wire rods & steel rods; nail & tack plate; armor plate, gun forgings & ordnance; car & locomotive wheels, rolled or forged, etc.; ingots; direct steel castings; scrap iron or steel	Un	56.3
		Custom work & repairing	S	34.9
		All other iron or steel products, not rolled		.7
		Products not belonging to the industry		8.1

160

166	1869	Rails, incl. rerolled or renewed rails, rail joints & fastenings 17q	C	97.4
	1869–1909	Cast-iron pipe & fittings	Un	2.6
275, 276	1869, 1879	Castings, other than pipe & fittings	Un	33.7
		Screws, machine	C	66.3
278	1879–1909	Screws, wood	13a	65.7
		Sewing machines, household types	25	31.3
		Sewing machines, industrial types	Un	3.0
	1869	Sewing machine attachments	13a	67.7
		Sewing machines, household types	25	32.3
		Sewing machines, industrial types	13a	78.7
305	1869–1909	Stoves, ranges & fireless cookers	C	21.3
		Hot-air furnaces	Un	78.2
326	1889–1904	Typewriters & parts	27	21.8
		Typewriter supplies	Un	87.5
345	1909	Woven-wire fence & poultry netting	27	12.5
		Other woven-wire products	27	36.2
	1879–1904	Barbed wire; woven-wire fence & poultry netting	27	25.0
	1869	Woven-wire fence & poultry netting		
		Wire brads, tacks & staples; plain wire, iron & steel; galvanized & other coated wire; wire rope, cable & strand; other woven-wire products; cold-rolled flat wire, etc.	Un	74.8
		Custom work & repairing	S	.2
346	1869–1909	Woven-wire fencing	27	35.5
		Wire rope & cable & other wirework products	Un	64.5

IV LUMBER AND ITS REMANUFACTURES

23	1869–1904	Billiard tables, bowling alleys & accessories	10	98.3
		Custom work	S	1.7
129	1914–1919	Store & office furniture & fixtures	29	76.4
		Furniture for public buildings, incl. public conveyance seats	36, Un	23.6
	1869–1909	Household furniture	12	85.1
		Store & office furniture & fixtures	29	11.0
		Furniture for public buildings, incl. public conveyance seats	29	3.4
		Contract work	Un	.1
		Custom work & repairing	S	.4
258	1889–1914	Pulp goods, except wall board	Un	67.4
		Wall board	C	32.6

161

INDUSTRY NUMBER	CENSUS YEARS IN WHICH ESTIMATED	COMMODITIES BY CENSUS GROUPS	GROUP CLASSIFICATION	% OF COMBINED TOTAL ACCOUNTED FOR BY EACH COMMODITY
		V LEATHER AND ITS FINISHED PRODUCTS		
30	1899, 1904, 1914	Misc. footwear	8	50.1
		Cut stock & findings made in shoe factories; amount received for crimping, stitching, buttonhole making & contract work; other income, custom work, leather scraps, remnants, etc.	Un	49.9
	1909	Boots & shoes, other than rubber	8	98.0
		Misc. footwear	8	1.0
		Cut stock & findings, etc.; amount received, etc.	Un	1.0
	1869–1889	Boots & shoes, other than rubber	8	98.7
		Misc. footwear	8	.6
		Cut stock, etc.	Un	.7
250	1869–1919	Pocketbooks, purses & cardcases	7	99.0
		Contract work	Un	.8
		Custom work & repairing	S	.2
		VI PAPER AND PRINTING		
230	1919	Fine paper: writing	4, Un	84.1
		All other paper	Un	15.9
	1889	Fine paper: writing	4, Un	76.9
		All other paper	Un	23.1
	1889	Building papers	C	24.9
		All other paper	Un	75.1
	1879	Fine paper; writing	4, Un	12.1
		Building papers	C	2.3
		All other paper	Un	76.2
		Wood pulp	Un	9.4
	1869	Fine paper: writing(r)	4, Un	19.1
		All other paper(r)	Un	80.9
231	1889–1909	Playing cards	4	8.0
		All other paper goods, n.e.s. (excl. collars & cuffs, paper)	4, Un	92.0
253, 254, 255	1879–1899	Books & pamphlets: published or printed & published	4	22.7
		Sheet music & books of music: published or printed & published	Un	2.7
		Electrotyping, engraving, lithographing, etc., except photo-engraving	4	2.3
		Newspapers & periodicals: printed for publication by others; sheet music & books of music: printed for publication by others; job printing; books & pamphlets: printed for publication by others	Un	64.9
		All other products for sale & in execution of orders	Un	7.4

VII LIQUORS AND BEVERAGES

188	1909	Whisky, brandy, gin, & rum	1	54.3
		Alcohol & cologne spirits	Un	45.7
	1869–1899	Whisky, brandy, gin, & rum	1	33.8
		Alcohol & cologne spirits	Un	66.2

VIII CHEMICALS AND ALLIED PRODUCTS

43, 294	1869–1899	Candles	5a	5.4
		Soap	3, Un	94.6
62, 73, 311	1909	Contract work	Un	4.9
		Byproducts, not chemical		95.1
	1904	Chemicals	Un	72.7
	1904	Byproducts, chemical	Un	1.3
		Contract work	Un	26.0
	1899	Byproducts, not chemical		97.3
		Chemicals	Un	2.6
		Byproducts & residues of chemical operations	Un	.1
	1879, 1889	Contract work	Un	97.6
		Chemicals	Un	2.3
	1889–1909	Byproducts & residues of chemical operations	Un	.1
		Contract work		
95		Pharmaceutical metals & their salts; pills, tablets, powders, etc.; synthetic preparations; tinctures, fluid extracts, medicinal sirups, etc.	3	54.5
		Alkaloids & derivatives	3, Un	32.9
		Biological products	3, Un	12.6
133	1914	Byproducts (except coke & tar)†	Un	39.7
		Products not belonging to the industry		50.3
	1869, 1889–	Receipts from sales of lamps & appliances	13, Un	89.8
	1914	Receipts from rents of lamps & appliances	N.C.	0.2
	1909	Byproducts (except coke & tar)†	Un	40.1
		Products not belonging to the industry		59.9
	1904	Byproducts (except coke & tar)	Un	43.5
		Products not belonging to the industry		55.5
	1889–1899	Coke, for sale	3, Un	63.1
		Tar	C	25.1
		Byproducts (except coke & tar)	Un	5.1
		Products not belonging to the industry		6.7

163

INDUSTRY NUMBER	CENSUS YEARS IN WHICH ESTIMATED	COMMODITIES BY CENSUS GROUPS	GROUP CLASSIFICATION	% OF COMBINED TOTAL ACCOUNTED FOR BY EACH COMMODITY
160, 161	1879	Ink, printing	Un	67.8
		Ink, writing	4, Un	32.2
219, 221, 223	1914–1919	Castor oil	3, Un	2.7
	1879–1889	Other oils, incl. lard oil & oleo oil, not made in the slaughtering industry	Un	97.3
229, 239	1879–1889	Paints, colors, putty & fillers	C	71.9
		Varnishes, japans & shellac	Un	28.1
233	1869–1909	Patent medicines	3	83.5
		Patent compounds	3, Un	16.5
241	1879–1909	Lubricating & axle grease	5a, Un	64.8
		Petrolatum	Un	35.2
	1879–1909	Gasoline	5a, Un	87.1
		Other light products of distillation	Un	12.9
	1909	Partly refined oils, acid oil & other special products	Un	56.1
		Products not belonging to the industry	Un	43.9
	1904	Asphalt, other than liquid asphalt	C	20.6
		Partly refined oils, acid oil & other special products	Un	44.6
		Products not belonging to the industry		34.8
	1899	Asphalt, other than liquid asphalt	C	20.1
		Partly refined oils, acid oil, reclaimed acids sold, & other special products	Un	46.1
		Products not belonging to the industry		33.8
	1879–1889	Illuminating oils	5a	90.8
		Fuel oils	Un	9.2
	1879, 1889	Lubricating oils	5a, Un	65.5
		Lubricating greases & petrolatum	5a, Un	34.5
	1879, 1889	Coke, petroleum	C	12.5
	1879, 1889	Asphalt, other than liquid asphalt	C	38.8
		Lubricating oils	5a, Un	28.6
		Partly refined oils, acid oil, reclaimed acids sold, & other special products	Un	20.1
		Products not belonging to the industry		
	1889	Illuminating oils; liquid asphaltic road oils & tar; lubricating oils; lubricating & axle grease; gasoline; fuel oils; light products of distillation except gasoline; petrolatum; paraffin wax	5a, C, Un	86.4
		Illuminating oils	5a, Un	1.1
	1869	Liquid asphaltic road oils & tar; asphalt other than liquid asphalt	C	
		Fuel oils; coke, petroleum; light products of distillation; petrolatum; paraffin wax; partly refined oils, acid oil, reclaimed acid, & other special products	Un	12.5

164

IX STONE, CLAY AND GLASS PRODUCTS

7, 199	1879–1889	Artificial stone products; marble & stone work	C	68.5
		Monuments & tombstones	24	31.5
37, 251, 271	1889	China, bone china, delft & belleek ware; red earthenware; cooking ware & other pottery products	15	69.2
		Porcelain electrical supplies	26	5.4
		Sanitary ware	C	25.4
	1889–1914	Stoneware & yellow & Rockingham ware	15	77.8
		Chemical stoneware	36	22.2
	1869, 1879	Stoneware & yellow & Rockingham ware; china, bone china, delft & belleek ware; red earthenware; cooking ware & other pottery products; white ware	15	73.4
		Porcelain electrical supplies	26	.4
		Chemical stoneware	36	.4
		Brick, excp. fire brick & silica brick; tile (not drain); architectrural terra-cotta; fireproofing, terra-cotta lumber, & hollow building tile or blocks; sanitary ware; draintile; sewer pipe	C	16.2
		Fire & silica brick & stove lining; other brick & tile products	Un	9.6
59, 186, 333	1879–1899	Cement	C, Un	54.5
		Lime	C, Un	26.9
59	1869–1899	Wall plaster & composition flooring	C	18.6
		Cement	C	87.1
135	1909–1919	All other products	Un	12.9
		Fruit jars; table ware; jellies, tumblers & goblets; blown tumblers, stem ware & bar goodsw	15	50.1
		Lamps & chimneysw	14b	49.9
	1889–1909	Shades, globes & other gas goods & lantern globesw	Un	92.1
		Wire glass, rough	C	7.9
	1879	Wire glass, polished & all other building glass	C, Un	22.2
		Plate glass, polished	C	10.3
	1869–1889	Obscured glass, incl. cathedral skylight glass	15	7.3
		Fruit jars; tableware, jellies & blown tumblers	14b	51.3
		Lamps & chimneys	15, Un	8.9
		Shades, globes & other gas goods, etc.	Un	83.4
		All other bottles & jars; all other products	Un	16.6
	1869–1889	Opal ware, cut glass & all other pressed glass	C	84.2
		Shades, globes & other glass goods	Un	8.5
	1869	Lantern globes	C	7.3
		Plate glass, polished		
		Plate glass, rough		
		Obscured glass, incl. cathedral & skylight glass		

165

INDUSTRY NUMBER	CENSUS YEARS IN WHICH ESTIMATED	COMMODITIES BY CENSUS GROUPS	GROUP CLASSIFICATION	% OF COMBINED TOTAL ACCOUNTED FOR BY EACH COMMODITY
186	1909–1919	Limestone	C	65.3
		Products not belonging to the industry		34.7
	1869–1904	Lime	C, Un	84.0
		Limestone	C	16.0

X METALS AND METAL PRODUCTS OTHER THAN IRON AND STEEL

INDUSTRY NUMBER	CENSUS YEARS IN WHICH ESTIMATED	COMMODITIES BY CENSUS GROUPS	GROUP CLASSIFICATION	% OF COMBINED TOTAL ACCOUNTED FOR BY EACH COMMODITY
35	1869–1909	Wire, plain; tubing; ingots & bars; plates & sheets; rods; castings & machinery fittings	Un	99.2
		Custom work & repairs	S	.8
82, 318	1869–1899	Copper, tin & sheet-iron work	C, Un	57.2
		Tinware, n.e.s.	15, Un	42.8
102, 172, 298	1909	Enameled ware	15	28.5
		Stamped ware	Un	70.3
		Bathtubs, lavatories & sinks	C	1.2
	1899, 1904	Enameled ware	15	27.4
		Stamped ware	Un	65.5
		Bathtubs, lavatories & sinks	C	1.2
		Enameling	Un	5.9
	1879, 1889	Enameled ware	Un	95.9
		Bathtubs, lavatories & sinks	C	4.1
	1869	Enameled ware	15	88.3
		Enameling	Un	11.7
178	1899–1909	Automobile lamps[x]	Un	92.8
		Lamps, other than automobile lamps & reflectors[x]	14b, Un	7.2
	1869–1909	Lamps, other than automobile lamps	14b	22.7
		Reflectors	Un	17.1
215	1909	Pins, common or toilet	6	12.0
		Safety pins	6	48.2
		All other needles, incl. sewing machine needles	6, Un	35.8
		Knitting needles; hooks & eyes; snap fasteners & clasps	Un	18.3
	1899, 1904	Hooks & eyes	Un	45.9
		Snap fasteners & clasps	Un	34.5
		Products not belonging to the industry		19.1
	1879, 1889	Pins, common or toilet; hairpins, made of metal; safety pins	6	46.4
		All other needles, incl. sewing-machine needles	6, Un	72.5
		Knitting-machine needles; hooks & eyes; snap fasteners & clasps	Un	27.5
	1869	Pins; hairpins; safety pins	6	
		Knitting-machine needles	Un	

XII VEHICLES FOR LAND TRANSPORTATION

10, 11	1899	Automobile bodies & parts	20b, Un	11.3
		Automobiles	20a, 32, Un, S	88.7
11	1919	Passenger vehicles[y]	20a	22.6
		Business vehicles[y]	20a	77.4
	1904	Omnibuses, sightseeing wagons, etc.	32a	15.6
		Government & municipal vehicles	32a	.7
		Passenger vehicles excl. omnibuses, etc.	20a	83.7
	1899	Passenger vehicles	20a	89.5
		All other products of motor-vehicle industry	Un	10.5
53	1889–1919	Repair work & parts	S	74.2
		Products not belonging to the industry		25.8
	1869, 1879	Carriages, buggies, & light pleasure vehicles	20c	53.3
		Sleighs & sleds	20c	2.1
		Business, farm, government, & municipal wagons	32b	27.4
		Public conveyances	32b	1.3
		Repair work & parts	S	15.9
56, 57	1869–1904	Cars made in other industries	30	98.9
		Parts made in other industries	Un	1.1
	1869–1889	Steam- & electric-rr. cars: passenger & freight service	30	67.6
		Parts & cars made in other industries	30, Un	13.3
		All other products, incl. parts & repair work	Un	19.1
209	1899–1914	Motorcycle & bicycle parts, incl. side cars & delivery cars	21, Un	66.5
		Products not belonging to the industry		33.5
	1889	Bicycles	21	78.5
		Bicycle parts	21, Un	21.5

XIV MISCELLANEOUS INDUSTRIES

1	1914–1919	All other aeronautical products[z]	33	73.8
		Repair work[z]	S	26.2
	1914	Aeroplanes & seaplanes	33	47.1
		Engines & parts	Un	52.9
2	1904–1909	All other implements, incl. parts	27	
	1869–1889	Products not belonging to the industry		
		Plows & cultivators; planters & seeders; harvesting implements; seed separators; all other implements, incl. parts; agricultural implements made in other industries	27	96.4
		Amount received for repair work	S	3.6
4	1869–1914	Ammunition; safety fuses, other fuses, naval torpedoes & railroad torpedoes	Un	89.8
		Blasting & detonating caps & fuses	C	10.2
111	1879–1904	Artificial flowers	6, Un	37.7

167

INDUSTRY NUMBER	CENSUS YEARS IN WHICH ESTIMATED	COMMODITIES BY CENSUS GROUPS	GROUP CLASSIFICATION	% OF COMBINED TOTAL ACCOUNTED FOR BY EACH COMMODITY
20	1869–1909	Feathers & plumes	6, Un	62.3
		Hose, rubber	36	67.8
20, 31, 265	1869	Belting, rubber	Un	32.2
		Belting & hose, rubber	36, Un	4.3
		Boots & shoes, rubber & canvas	8	38.3
31	1914	Rubber goods, n.e.s.	3, 7, Un	57.4
		Boots & shoes, rubber & canvas	8	84.8
		Heels, rubber	Un	15.2
	1904, 1909	Boots & shoes, rubber & canvas	8	88.6
		Heels, rubber	Un	11.4
38	1869–1909	Brooms, made from broom corn	9	97.3
		Brooms, made from materials other than broom corn	36	2.7
38, 39	1879–1904	Brooms	9, 36	49.6
		Brushes	9, 36, C	50.4
39	1869–1909	Brushes, toilet	9	17.1
		All other brushes	36	45.1
		Brushes, paint & varnish	C	37.8
42	1909	Buttons	6, Un	87.1
		Button parts; blanks or molds	Un	12.9
	1899–1904	Button parts^a	Un	90.5
	1869–1889	Buttons	6, Un	9.5
78, 110	1879–1889	Button parts; blanks or molds	6	
		Combs & hairpins, except those made from metal or rubber^{bb}	6, Un	88.7
		Fancy articles, n.c.s.^{bb}	13b	11.3
99	1909	Household apparatus & appliances^{cc}	26	70.2
	1904	Industrial apparatus & appliances^{cc}	13b	26.4
		Household apparatus & appliances	26	3.4
	1899	Rheostats, resistances, controllers, motor starters, regulators, etc.	Un	
		Household apparatus & appliances	13b	
		Industrial apparatus & appliances	26	
	1899–1909	Generators (other than small dynamos under 10 k.w.)^{dd}	Un	
		Small dynamos (under 10 k.w.), starting motors & generators, automotive^{dd}	Un	26.3
		Generator parts & supplies^{dd}	26	73.7
	1899	Transformers, over 50 k.w.	Un	
		Transformers, under 50 k.w.	Un	

168

	1899	Measuring instruments, excl. testing & scientific	26	80.0
		Electrical testing & scientific instruments	34	20.0
		Lightning arrestors & other protective devices	26	40.3
	1899–1914	Fuses, cut-outs & fuse plugs	Un	59.7
		Insulated cables, rubber & paper insulation	26	47.5
	1899–1909	Insulated wire	Un	52.5
		Stationary motorse	26	61.1
	1904	Vehicle & railway motorse	Un	38.9
		All other electrical machinery & apparatus	26	49.9
	1899	Products not belonging to the industry	26	3.6
		All other electrical machinery & apparatus	34	2.4
		Therapeutic apparatus, incl. X-ray tubes	20, Un	12.3
		Magneto-ignition apparatus, generators, spark plugs & coils	Un	31.8
		Circuit fittings, not elsewhere provided for	26	63.0
	1879, 1889	Products not belonging to the industry	Un	37.0
		Finished electrical machinery & suppliesff	7, Un	96.7
127, 130	1869, 1879	Unfinished electrical apparatusff	Un	3.3
159	1899–1919	Fur goods	26	66.6
	1869–1889	Furs, dressed	34	33.4
		Receipts from cold storage	1, Un	97.2
211	1869–1914	Products not belonging to the industry	Un	2.8
		Ice, manufactured		
		Receipts from cold storage		
		Wind instruments; string instruments, incl. harps; other band & orchestral instruments; percussion instruments	16	69.7
		Parts & materials	Un	27.7
212, 213,	1909	Custom work & repairing	S	2.6
214		Repairs	S	34.9
	1904	Products not belonging to the industry	16	65.1
		Piano & organ parts—perforated music rollsgg	Un	
		Piano & organ parts excl. perforated music rollsgg	S	
	1869–1899	Repairsgg	16	73.8
		Pianos & organs; perforated music rolls	Un	25.5
		Piano & organ parts, excl. perforated music rolls	S	.7
227	1869–1919	Repairs	23	78.9
234	1889	Ophthalmic products	34	21.1
		Optical goods & instruments	C	
		Paving materialshh		

169

INDUSTRY NUMBER	CENSUS YEARS IN WHICH ESTIMATED	COMMODITIES BY CENSUS GROUPS	GROUP CLASSIFICATION	% OF COMBINED TOTAL ACCOUNTED FOR BY EACH COMMODITY
242	1899–1914	Phonograph needles	4	10.2
		Cabinets & other parts & accessories	Un	89.8
	1899–1909	Custom work & repairing	S	.6
		Products not belonging to the industry		99.4
	1899–1904	Phonograph parts & accessories	4, Un	64.4
		All other products	Un	35.6
243	1869–1909	Cameras	10	31.6
		All other photographic apparatus & parts; motion-picture machines	36	68.4
264	1869–1889	Roofing materials[i]	C	8.9
265	1869–1909	Druggists' & stationers' sundries[i]	3	8.0
		Rubber clothing[i]	7	83.1
		All other manufactures of rubber[i]	Un	
279, 280	1869	Work on vessels of 5 gross tons & over	31	52.4
		Work on boats of less than 5 gross tons	22	2.5
		Repair work	S	45.1
283	1909	Signs	36	57.6
		Advertising novelties	Un	42.4

[a] The products of combined butter and skim cheese factories in 1879 were apportioned between butter and cheese. The value to be apportioned to butter was determined by multiplying the per pound price, $.232, of butter made in butter factories to the amount produced in the combined butter and cheese factories. Because no price per pound for cheese made in the combined factories could be obtained, the value of cheese made in the combined factories was estimated by subtracting the estimate for butter and the value of skimmed milk from the total value of products of the combined cheese and skim cheese factories.
[b] The amount of food preparations transferred to the slaughtering industry is the difference between the total transferred to other industries in 1904 and 1909 and the amount transferred to the flour and gristmill industry (taken directly from the Census).

[c] The 1919 values for clean rice, fancy-head and clean rice, second-head, screenings and brewers' were estimated on the basis of quantity and value data for 1923 and 1921. For 1919 as for 1921 the total quantity of clean rice was apportioned between fancy- and second-head. The 1923 values per pound were then multiplied by the quantity figures, the resulting values totaled and equated to the 1919 total value for clean rice. The 1914 values were estimated on the basis of 1909 data. The 1914 quantities were multiplied by 1909 prices, then equated to the 1914 total value for clean rice.
[d] The total quantity figure for clean rice was divided between fancy- and second-head rice as in 1904, then multiplied by 1904 prices per pound for each grade of rice. The resulting values were totaled, then equated to an estimated 1899 commodity total excluding hulls and waste.

e These products were estimated on the basis of their relation in 1914 to the value of meat products made in the Food preparations industry: meat puddings, scrapple, head cheese, etc., 8.1 percent; edible meat products made in other industries, 13.7 percent; lard compounds and substitutes, 160.6 percent.

f Estimated from the 1904 percentage of canned goods to canned beef, 209.3 percent.

g Estimated from the relation in 1914 of sausage casings to sausages, 11.2 percent.

h An estimate was made for veal and 'all other' meat on the basis of the percentage, 104.5, fresh meat including veal and 'all other' was, in 1899, of fresh meat, excluding veal and 'all other'.

i 'Other products' is the difference between the industry total and the commodity total for products already estimated. In 1914 it covered hair, hog and cattle and all other products not belonging to the industry, including custom work; in 1909, hoofs, horns, and horn tips, strips, etc., hair, hog and cattle and all other products, including custom work; in 1904, 1899, and 1889, stearin and oleo stock as well as the commodities listed for 1909.

j Sheep, lamb, goat and kid pelts were estimated on the basis of the percentage, 20.2, that their cost was, in 1904, of the total cost of sheep, lambs, goats and kids.

k Sugar, beet, was included with 'all other industries' in 1889. However, the estimate of Guilford L. Spencer, Expert Special Agent of the Bureau of the Census, was used (see *Census of Manufactures*, IX, 1900, Part III, p. 545).

l For 1879 quantities alone were reported. They were multiplied by 1889 per unit prices for carpets and for rugs, the resulting values were totaled, then equated to the 1879 commodity total derived for carpets and rugs.

m For 1879 quantities alone were reported. They were multiplied by 1889 per unit prices for each item reported separately. The resulting values were totaled, then equated to the 1879 commodity total for the items here estimated, this commodity total being the total census value reported for the items. All commodities were estimated separately and later combined.

n The estimate for machine twist and fringe and floss silks was added to other silk manufactures, which include fringes and gimps, braids and bindings, trimmings, organzine and tram, hard crepe twist, spun silk, artificial silk, raw silk and miscellaneous unclassified silk fabrics as well as machine twist and fringe and floss silks as here estimated.

o 'All other products' is the difference between all other products as reported by the Census and an estimate for silk embroideries. It includes contract work, millinery trimmings, ladies' dress trimmings, and cloak trimmings.

p Before this allocation was made all other products not belonging to the industry were estimated by subtracting millinery trimmings, ladies' dress trimmings, and cloak trimmings from 'all other products'.

q The quantity of yarn produced in 1879 and the cost per pound of purchased yarn were reported in the Census of Manufactures. The 1879 cost per pound of purchased yarn was multiplied by the ratio of the sales price per pound of yarn to the cost per pound of yarn purchased in 1889. The number of pounds of yarn produced in 1879 was then multiplied by the estimated sales price per pound in that year.

r The value for 1869 was estimated by multiplying the quantity produced by a price based upon the 1879 price as extrapolated by a price index of iron rails (Aldrich Report).

s The 1869 percentage allocation was based upon the proportion that each paper industry constituted of the combined industry total.

t The 1904 value for chemicals was rendered comparable to those for 1909 and later years by excluding an estimate for all byproducts and contract work, based upon the percentage, 30.2, that byproducts and contract work were, in 1909, of the sum of other specified chemicals, unclassified chemicals, chemical byproducts and residues, byproducts, not chemical and contract work.

u The estimate did not include all byproducts (except coke and tar). The values for the byproducts reported separately were added to the estimates of the byproducts included with products not belonging to the industry.

v In 1879 and 1889 all other products included coke, petroleum, as well as asphalt, other than liquid asphalt; partly refined oils, acid oil and other special products; and products not belonging to the industry. From this total, coke was deducted in 1879 and 1889 on the basis of the percentage, 310, that it was in 1899 of a total for coke and all other products as defined above. The resulting 1879 and 1889 values for all other products were then probably closely comparable with those reported for 1899 and 1904.

w In all years except 1889 the values for the various commodities included the cost of containers. The total cost of barrels was reported for 1889 as well as the number of barrels used in measuring the production of each commodity listed in the table.

Total cost, reduced 6.2 percent to allow for containers used for products not belonging to the industry, was divided by the number of barrels to get the average cost per barrel. The average cost per barrel was then multiplied by the number of barrels used for each commodity. Since the sum of these estimates differed from the total cost of barrels as previously calculated, the ratio of the latter to the former was employed to correct the estimated values of barrels used for each commodity. The final estimates were added to the respective 1889 commodity values for which barrel data were available.

x Quantity data were available in 1909, 1914, and 1919 for pressed and blown glass and bottles and jars. The 1919 values were estimated on the basis of 1925 prices per unit; the price per unit of each type of pressed and blown glass and for each type of bottle and jar was first calculated for 1925. From the total value of bottles and jars in 1919 all other bottles and jars not reported separately were estimated on the basis of the percentage, 10.0, that the value of a comparable 'all other bottles and jars' figure was of the 1925 total for bottles and jars. The resulting values 'were added and equated quantity figures for each type of bottle or jar were then multiplied by the 1925 per unit value. The resulting values 'were added and equated to the 1919 total value for bottles and jars excluding the estimate for all other bottles and jars. The values for the pressed and blown glass items in 1919 were calculated similarly. For pressed and blown glass the value of all other pressed and blown glass was estimated to be 7.13 percent of the total value.

The 1914 and 1909 values were estimated similarly except that 1904 price data were used instead of 1925. The 1904 values were believed more satisfactory because the relative weights to be assigned to each commodity differed less from 1904 to 1914 than from 1914 to 1925. Furthermore, the marked postwar price changes were avoided.

All other bottles and jars were estimated to be 5.5 percent of the total in 1909 and 1914; all other pressed and blown glass to be 16.04 percent.

The values for each item were estimated separately for each year. After the separate estimates had been made, commodities in the same minor commodity groups were combined.

y The values for automobile lamps were estimated in 1889, 1904, and 1909 according to the percentage, 1.05, that automobile lamps were in 1914 of the value of finished automobiles, including trucks and trailers. The remainder of the commodity total for each year was apportioned between lamps, other than automobile, and reflectors on the basis of the percentage each was of the 1914 total for lamps, other than automobile lamps and reflectors.

z Complete chassis was apportioned between passenger vehicles and business vehicles on the basis of the 1921 ratios.

aa All other products in 1919 included repair work, all other aeronautical products, and products not belonging to the industry. Repair work was estimated in 1919 on the basis of the percentage, 68.0, that it was in 1914 of the total for all other products including repair work. All other aeronautical products were estimated in 1919 and 1914 on the basis of the percentage, 83.0, that airships, balloons, parachutes, etc. were in 1925 of the value for all other products, including all other aeronautical products and products not belonging to the industry, but excluding repair work. The residual included only commodities not belonging to the industry.

bb The values for button parts were estimated in 1899 and 1904 on the basis of the percentage, 3.4, that button parts constituted in 1914 of the total reported for all other buttons. This estimate was deducted from the total value of buttons in both years.

ᵉᵉ The census industry totals for celluloid and celluloid goods in 1879 and 1889 were apportioned between fancy articles, n.e.s., and combs and hairpins, except those made from metal or rubber, on the basis of the division in each year of the combined industry total for fancy articles and combs. In 1889 the apportionment was 17.5 percent to combs and 82.5 to fancy articles; in 1879, 25.2 percent to combs and 74.8 to fancy articles.

ᵈᵈ The 1909 total for electric heaters, stoves, ranges, and cooking devices was apportioned between household and industrial appliances on the basis of the 1914 division of a similar group of commodities. Of the total, 85.0 percent was included with household appliances and 15.0 with industrial. The value for industrial appliances includes also welding apparatus; the household figure includes flatirons.

ᵉᵉ For 1909 the total value of direct current generators and small dynamos . . . was apportioned 33.3 percent to the former and 66.7 to the latter. To the estimate for the former was added the value of alternating current generators.

Before the total of direct current generators and small dynamos . . . could be apportioned in 1904 and 1889, the generator parts and supplies included in the total were estimated on the basis of the percentage, 17.5, they were of the 1909 total for direct current generators, dynamos, and generator parts and supplies. As in 1909, the residual was then apportioned between generators and small dynamos.

ᶠᶠ Railway motors were included with stationary motors 1899–1914. Railway motors were estimated on the basis of the percentage, 18.2, they were of the combined 1919 total of railway motors and stationary motors. This estimate was then added to the total of other vehicle motors.

ᵍᵍ The commodity total was allocated on the basis of the division of the 1899 total between finished and unfinished.

ʰʰ Perforated music rolls, piano and organ parts made in establishments whose principal products are pianos and organs, and repairs were estimated in 1904 from the total of all other products reported by the Census. As in 1909, music rolls were estimated to be 4.5 percent of this total.

Of the total of all other products including repairs, parts, and music rolls, 44.4 percent was apportioned to repairs and products not belonging to the industry—on the basis of the apportionment of a similar total in 1914. Of this estimate, 34.9 percent represented repairs, also based on 1914 data.

The remainder of the total of all other products including parts, rolls, and repairs, 51.1 percent, was taken to represent the total value of parts and materials made in establishments whose principal products were finished pianos and organs. The balance of the total for parts and materials, except perforated music rolls, was reported by establishments whose chief products were parts.

ⁱⁱ The 1889 industry total for paving materials was derived by straight line interpolation between 1879 and 1899. The residual of the total the Census reported for paving materials and street construction work in 1889 was classed as street construction work.

ʲʲ The industry totals reported by the Census included roofing work as well as materials in 1879 and 1889. Construction work was eliminated on the basis of the 1899 allocation of an industry total including both materials and work, 45.8 percent remaining as roofing materials alone.

ᵏᵏ Estimated from a total excluding pneumatic automobile, bicycle and motorcycle tires. For the tire estimates, see Note B to Table II 2, Minor Group 11.

TABLE II 2

Mixed Commodities and their Allocation, Census Years, 1869–1919
(thousands of dollars)

Major and Minor Groups

INDUSTRY NUMBER		COMMODITY	1869	1879	1889	1899	1904	1909	1914	1919
			PERISHABLE							
VIII	17	*1 Food and Kindred Products*								
		Baking powders & yeast								
		Total	1,008	5,361	8,340	16,404	21,442	23,389	25,206	48,556
		Finished	275	3,956	5,949	13,269	16,300	15,547	16,208	25,019
		Unfinished	733	1,405	2,391	3,135	5,142	7,842	8,998	23,537
I	40	Butter								
		Total	not reported	6,859	36,822	84,416	113,638	180,175	221,338	533,330
		Finished		5,622	34,721	81,623	109,226	173,361	212,587	508,293
		Unfinished		1,237	2,101	2,793	4,412	6,814	8,751	25,037
I	79	Condensed & evaporated milk								
		Total	not reported	1,548	3,587	11,889	20,149	33,587	58,871	298,659
		Finished		597	1,969	9,768	16,671	28,282	52,784	282,968
		Unfinished		951	1,618	2,121	3,478	5,305	6,087	15,691
I	120	Flavoring extracts								
		Total	1,050	1,679	3,671	8,856	10,912	12,396	15,218	40,085
		Finished	451	825	1,920	5,945	7,372	6,548	5,674	14,776
		Unfinished	599	854	1,751	2,911	3,540	5,848	9,544	25,309
I	122	Flour: wheat, corn, rye, buckwheat & barley								
		Total	341,308	387,483	394,306	394,465	547,822	629,305	614,456	1,563,363
		Finished	332,135	370,125	364,454	354,636	482,643	529,141	498,182	1,255,226
		Unfinished	9,173	17,358	29,852	39,829	65,179	100,164	116,274	308,137
I	123, 180	Lard, incl. lard compounds & substitutes								
		Total	not reported	29,979	59,976	82,079	107,561	194,490	212,289	740,966
		Finished		24,040	52,658	70,618	90,718	168,935	181,096	633,367
		Unfinished		5,939	7,318	11,461	16,843	25,555	31,193	107,599

XIV	159	Ice, manufactured								
		Total	251		4,769	13,412	24,350	44,139	62,192	138,795
		Finished	125		2,384	6,706	12,175	22,070	31,096	69,398
		Unfinished	126		2,385	6,706	12,175	22,069	31,096	69,397
I	235	Peanuts, grading, roasting, cleaning, shelling								
		Total	897	1,777	5,815	5,388	7,107	9,528	14,620	35,543
		Finished	829	1,642	5,373	4,979	6,567	8,804	13,509	32,842
		Unfinished	68	135	442	409	540	724	1,111	2,701
VIII	269	Salt								
		Total	5,194	5,150	5,441	7,902	9,335	11,398	13,984	36,595
		Finished	1,117	1,107	1,170	1,696	1,613	2,240	3,221	7,570
		Unfinished	4,077	4,043	4,271	6,206	7,722	9,158	10,763	29,025
I	308, 309, 310	Sugar, granulated, refined & brown								
		Total	105,892	137,096	108,557	216,942	267,934	298,000	349,016	863,244
		Finished	100,939	126,993	90,013	190,191	229,092	239,461	267,107	614,500
		Unfinished	4,953	10,103	18,544	26,751	38,842	58,539	81,909	248,744
	3	*Drug, Toilet and Household Preparations*								
VIII	24	Blacking, stains & dressing								
		Total	765	1,394	2,712	4,212	5,555	7,872	9,242	23,648
		Finished	583	1,062	2,067	3,210	4,233	5,998	7,042	18,020
		Unfinished	182	332	645	1,002	1,322	1,874	2,200	5,628
VIII	66	Cleansing & polishing preparations								
		Total	374	580	1,004	2,542	3,141	7,255	10,611	27,749
		Finished	305	473	818	2,072	2,560	5,913	8,648	22,615
		Unfinished	69	107	186	470	581	1,342	1,963	5,134
VIII	95	Alkaloids & derivatives								
		Total		not reported	2,205	7,682	10,749	14,867	16,232	15,416
		Finished			1,532	5,339	7,471	10,333	11,281	10,716
		Unfinished			673	2,343	3,278	4,534	4,951	4,700
		Biological products								
		Total		not reported	845	2,942	4,117	5,694	6,223	15,876
		Finished			339	1,180	1,651	2,283	2,495	6,366
		Unfinished			506	1,762	2,466	3,411	3,728	9,510

175

INDUSTRY NUMBER		COMMODITY	1869	1879	1889	1899	1904	1909	1914	1919
VIII	219	Castor oil								
		Total	691	818	716	494	804	1,131	1,265	5,205
		Finished	667	775	646	436	736	998	1,008	4,384
		Unfinished	24	43	70	58	68	133	257	821
VIII	233	Patent compounds								
		Total	2,589	2,338	5,195	9,499	12,001	13,495	16,514	46,351
		Finished	1,618	1,461	3,247	5,927	7,501	8,434	10,321	28,969
		Unfinished	971	877	1,948	3,562	4,500	5,061	6,193	17,382
VIII	294	Soap								
		Total	18,568	21,879	35,925	43,861	59,446	93,258	107,214	235,799
		Finished	17,628	20,530	34,201	41,464	56,024	87,783	99,255	215,405
		Unfinished	940	1,349	1,724	2,397	3,422	5,475	7,959	20,394

4 Magazines, Newspapers, Stationery and Supplies, and Miscellaneous Paper Products

VI	108	Envelopes								
		Total	2,365	3,115	5,041	6,538	10,610	13,965	19,188	39,518
		Finished	1,206	1,589	2,571	3,334	5,411	7,122	9,786	20,154
		Unfinished	1,159	1,526	2,470	3,204	5,199	6,843	9,402	19,364
XIV	210	Mucilage, paste & other adhesives, n.e.s.								
		Total	140	19	1,421	2,845	3,958	5,475	6,428	12,391
		Finished	72	10	735	1,471	2,046	2,831	3,323	6,406
		Unfinished	68	9	686	1,374	1,912	2,644	3,105	5,985
VI	230	Fine paper: writing								
		Total	8,992	6,657	9,182	12,223	19,321	24,966	28,637	73,790
		Finished	6,240	4,620	6,372	8,483	13,409	17,326	19,874	51,210
		Unfinished	2,752	2,037	2,810	3,740	5,912	7,640	8,763	22,580
VI	231	All other paper goods, n.e.s.								
		Total	3,043	1,583	4,326	16,168	21,344	36,559	47,190	98,383
		Finished	1,528	795	2,172	8,116	10,715	18,353	23,689	49,388
		Unfinished	1,515	788	2,154	8,052	10,629	18,206	23,501	48,995

VIII	76	*5a Fuel and Lighting Products, Manufactured* Coke Total Finished Unfinished	1,169 58 1,111	5,536 277 5,259	17,042 852 16,190	35,519 1,776 33,743	50,305 2,515 47,790	89,965 4,498 85,467	88,334 4,417 83,917	258,340 15,677 242,663
VIII	194, 241	Illuminating oils Total Finished Unfinished	23,278 22,580 698	33,451 32,447 1,004	51,854 50,298 1,556	74,694 72,453 2,241	91,366 88,625 2,741	94,547 91,711 2,836	96,806 89,062 7,744	235,663 188,530 47,133
		Lubricating oils Total Finished Unfinished	88 88	1,763 none 1,763	7,268 7,268	10,897 3 10,894	23,553 82 23,471	38,884 453 38,431	55,812 3,800 52,012	196,242 37,008 159,234
		Gasoline Total Finished Unfinished	none none	2,580 none 2,580	7,963 7,963	13,929 105 13,824	18,565 1,025 17,540	34,641 5,877 28,764	106,140 37,562 68,578	679,867 346,314 333,553
		Perishable, Totals Total Finished Unfinished	517,662 488,356 29,306	659,176 599,212 59,964	783,983 666,461 117,522	1,085,798 894,810 190,988	1,465,085 1,176,381 288,704	1,918,981 1,464,302 454,679	2,203,026 1,613,027 589,999	6,263,374 4,465,121 1,798,253

SEMIDURABLE

XIV	5	*6 Dry Goods and Notions* Artificial flowers Total Finished Unfinished	950 712 238	1,777 1,333 444	3,296 2,472 824	2,284 1,713 571	1,905 1,429 476	8,706 6,530 2,176	7,334 5,500 1,834	16,352 12,264 4,088
XIV	42	Buttons Total Finished Unfinished	1,499 135 1,364	3,749 337 3,412	3,553 320 3,233	6,486 584 5,902	10,053 905 9,148	18,699 1,683 17,016	16,604 1,494 15,110	35,704 3,213 32,491
II	87, 88, 89	Lace goods & nets Total Finished Unfinished	541 231 310	642 274 368	756 323 433	2,212 945 1,267	4,953 2,115 2,838	6,176 2,637 3,539	8,317 3,551 4,766	21,212 9,058 12,154

INDUSTRY NUMBER	COMMODITY	1869	1879	1889	1899	1904	1909	1914	1919
	Cotton thread								
	Total	7,718	9,152	11,638	11,909	15,043	20,651	22,917	59,405
	Finished	4,904	4,641	6,742	5,008	5,559	6,810	8,459	20,851
	Unfinished	2,814	4,511	4,896	6,901	9,484	13,841	14,458	38,554
	All other cotton woven goods								
	Total	54,729	64,895	82,455	96,604	130,777	189,076	204,420	692,966
	Finished	50,280	51,993	60,211	41,438	45,359	52,497	39,368	248,082
	Unfinished	4,449	12,902	22,244	55,166	85,418	136,579	165,052	444,884
II 97	Dyeing & finishing textiles								
	Total	13,991	32,297	28,901	44,963	50,850	83,556	109,292	323,968
	Finished	5,608	12,314	8,455	8,225	3,782	7,121	12,573	47,905
	Unfinished	8,383	19,983	20,446	36,738	47,068	76,435	96,719	276,063
XIV 110	Fancy articles, n.e.s.								
	Total	296	3,957	7,296	9,516	12,584	13,035	18,574	64,686
	Finished	252	3,371	6,216	8,108	10,722	11,106	15,825	55,112
	Unfinished	44	586	1,080	1,408	1,862	1,929	2,749	9,574
XIV 111	Feathers & plumes								
	Total	899	3,177	5,911	4,097	3,416	15,611	11,970	15,345
	Finished	318	1,125	2,092	1,450	1,209	5,526	4,237	5,432
	Unfinished	581	2,052	3,819	2,647	2,207	10,085	7,733	9,913
V 184	Leather goods, n.e.s.								
	Total	258	3,016	6,934	12,990	19,456	20,763	21,220	56,461
	Finished	none	2,322	5,339	10,002	14,981	15,988	16,339	43,475
	Unfinished	258	694	1,595	2,988	4,475	4,775	4,881	12,986
II 203	Embroideries								
	Total	1,398	2,056	3,873	6,325	10,899	18,438	24,569	57,719
	Finished	296	435	819	1,338	2,305	3,900	5,197	12,209
	Unfinished	1,102	1,621	3,054	4,987	8,594	14,538	19,372	45,510
II 284	Silk ribbons								
	Total	1,869	6,023	17,142	18,542	21,983	32,874	38,209	66,190
	Finished	843	4,094	14,475	13,700	13,857	18,962	20,399	25,152
	Unfinished	1,026	1,929	2,667	4,842	8,126	13,912	17,810	41,038

	Broadsilks									
	Total	3,484	11,225	23,459	52,769	67,676	108,946	141,879	391,997
	Finished	1,720	6,109	14,639	30,896	33,807	54,792	76,435	215,598
	Unfinished	1,764	5,116	8,820	21,873	33,869	54,154	65,444	176,399
	Silk velvets & plushes								
	Total	not reported		3,145	4,965	4,508	6,881	18,710	42,553
	Finished			2,359	3,724	3,381	5,161	14,032	31,915
	Unfinished			786	1,241	1,127	1,720	4,678	10,638
	Sewing & embroidery silks								
	Total	242	776	2,854	3,277	3,928	3,778	5,131	7,121
	Finished	157	504	1,855	2,130	2,553	2,456	3,335	4,629
	Unfinished	85	272	999	1,147	1,375	1,322	1,796	2,492
IX	300	Statuary & art goods								
	Total		not reported			2,456	3,497	3,980	5,196
	Finished					837	1,192	1,357	1,772
	Construction material					1,619	2,305	2,623	3,424
II	355, 356	Woolen & worsted woven goods, except shawls, blankets & carriage equipment								
	Total	141,243	154,032	157,160	174,514	223,686	284,895	255,683	713,039
	Finished	100,122	88,126	85,621	73,683	86,114	82,670	44,445	149,738
	Unfinished	41,121	65,906	71,539	100,831	137,572	202,225	211,238	563,301
II	357	Mixed textiles								
	Total	not reported	66,222			(Presumably included with other industries)			
	Finished		42,382						
	Unfinished		23,840						
XIV	127	7. *Clothing and Personal Furnishings* Fur Goods								
	Total	8,144	7,537	18,137	24,500	35,115	52,891	41,654	164,478
	Finished	7,183	6,648	15,997	21,609	30,971	46,650	36,739	145,070
	Unfinished	961	889	2,140	2,891	4,144	6,241	4,915	19,408
II	203	Trimmed hats & hat frames								
	Total	2,891	4,252	8,012	13,082	22,542	38,134	50,815	124,798
	Finished	2,741	4,031	7,595	12,402	21,370	36,151	48,173	118,309
	Unfinished	150	221	417	680	1,172	1,983	2,642	6,489

INDUSTRY NUMBER		COMMODITY	1869	1879	1889	1899	1904	1909	1914	1919
II	313	Suspenders, garters & elastic woven goods			(Included elsewhere)					
		Total						28,350	25,127	62,791
		Finished						14,175	12,564	31,396
		Unfinished						14,175	12,563	31,395
XIV	327	Umbrellas & canes								
		Total	4,559	6,540	13,022	13,095	12,738	15,195	13,206	24,227
		Finished	3,948	5,664	11,277	11,340	11,031	13,159	11,436	20,981
		Unfinished	611	876	1,745	1,755	1,707	2,036	1,770	3,246
II 87, 88, 89	9	*House Furnishings (semidurable)* Towels, towelling, wash cloths, turkish towels & terry weave								
		Total	1,228	1,456	1,841	2,456	4,365	6,066	9,805	31,302
		Finished	1,086	1,287	1,627	2,171	3,859	5,362	8,668	27,671
		Unfinished	142	169	214	285	506	704	1,137	3,631
XIV	344	Window shades & fixtures								
		Total	not reported	2,249	7,349	7,055	7,806	16,228	15,554	26,456
		Finished		2,092	6,835	6,561	7,260	15,092	14,465	24,604
		Unfinished		157	514	494	546	1,136	1,089	1,852
XIV	265	*Tires and Tubes* Tires & tubes, automobile								
		Total		none			5,892	33,000	125,780	685,209
		Finished					3,830	21,780	91,819	534,463
		Unfinished					2,062	11,220	33,961	150,746
		Tires & tubes, motorcycle & bicycle								
		Total		none		17,698	3,786	4,524	6,906	14,796
		Finished				13,309	2,847	3,402	5,193	11,876
		Unfinished				4,389	939	1,122	1,713	2,920
		Semidurable, Totals								
		Total	245,939	385,030	406,734	529,339	676,417	1,029,970	1,197,656	3,703,971
		Finished	180,536	239,082	255,269	270,336	310,083	434,802	501,603	1,800,775
		Construction materials					1,619	2,305	2,623	3,424
		Unfinished	65,403	145,948	151,465	259,003	364,715	592,863	693,430	1,899,772

CONSUMER DURABLE

XIV	99	**13b Electrical Household Appliances and Supplies** Incandescent lamps Total Finished Unfinished		none		3,515 1,230 2,285	6,953 2,434 4,519	15,715 5,500 10,215	17,350 6,072 11,278	57,647 20,176 37,471
II	49	**14a Floor coverings** Carpets Total Finished Unfinished	21,029 16,676 4,353	30,526 24,207 6,319	43,828 34,756 9,072	36,414 28,876 7,538	46,339 36,747 9,592	48,826 38,719 10,107	41,133 32,628 8,505	58,167 44,968 13,199
II	87, 88, 89	**14b Miscellaneous house furnishings (durable)** Tapestries Total Finished Unfinished	526 316 210	624 375 249	716 430 286	4,381 2,633 1,748	4,505 2,706 1,799	4,821 2,897 1,924	5,849 3,515 2,334	20,119 12,092 8,027
VIII	130	Receipts from sales of lamps & appliances by gas companies Total Finished Unfinished	832 832	not reported not reported	1,462 none 1,462	1,797 1,797	3,816 3,816	6,328 790 5,538	9,871 2,478 7,393	15,597 5,050 10,547
IV	193	**Looking-glass & picture frames** Total Finished Unfinished	4,210 3,962 248	6,775 6,375 400	11,562 10,880 682	10,988 10,340 648	13,443 12,650 793	13,651 12,846 805	11,129 10,472 657	18,253 17,176 1,077
IX	207	**Mirrors, framed & unframed** Total Finished Unfinished	456 280 176	284 174 110	5,599 3,432 2,167	7,468 4,578 2,890	7,095 4,349 2,746	8,933 5,476 3,457	9,255 5,673 3,582	19,069 11,689 7,380
II	284	**Silk upholstery & tapestries** Total Finished Unfinished		not reported	3,712 3,601 111	1,010 980 30	1,560 1,513 47	383 372 11	840 815 25	2,157 2,092 65

INDUSTRY NUMBER	COMMODITY	1869	1879	1889	1899	1904	1909	1914	1919
IX 136	*15 China and Household Utensils*								
	Glass, cutting, staining & ornamenting								
	Total	774	2,555	6,139	8,821	13,243	16,236	16,763	29,145
	Finished	389	1,283	3,082	4,428	6,648	8,150	8,415	14,631
	Construction materials	156	516	1,240	1,782	2,675	3,280	3,386	5,887
	Unfinished	229	756	1,817	2,611	3,920	4,806	4,962	8,627
X 318	Tinware, n.e.s.								
	Total	11,195	13,825	18,362	27,640	42,396	59,515	81,173	229,177
	Finished	179	221	294	442	678	952	1,299	3,667
	Unfinished	11,016	13,604	18,068	27,198	41,718	58,563	79,874	225,510
X 173	*17 Jewelry, Silverware, Clocks and Watches*								
	Jewelry								
	Total	22,124	22,222	34,793	46,544	53,705	81,110	80,760	203,833
	Finished	19,956	20,044	31,383	41,983	48,442	73,161	72,846	183,857
	Unfinished	2,168	2,178	3,410	4,561	5,263	7,949	7,914	19,976
XII 10	*20b Motor Vehicle Accessories*								
	Motor vehicle bodies & parts								
	Total			none		3,527	57,634	135,591	682,719
	Finished					2,451	20,930	54,525	210,834
	Unfinished					1,076	36,704	81,066	471,885
	Consumer Durable, Totals								
	Total	61,146	76,811	126,173	148,578	196,582	313,152	409,714	1,335,883
	Finished	41,758	52,679	87,858	95,490	118,618	169,793	198,738	526,232
	Construction materials	156	516	1,240	1,782	2,675	3,280	3,386	5,887
	Unfinished	19,232	23,616	37,075	51,306	75,289	140,079	207,590	803,764
	PRODUCER DURABLE								
III	*25 Industrial Machinery and Equipment*								
	103, 124, 169X, 197, 260, 302X, 314								
	Foundry and machine shop products, n.e.s.								
	Total	199,601	181,724	348,412	546,699	663,945	883,948	(See III 124)	
	Finished	106,986	97,404	186,749	293,031	355,875	473,796		
	Unfinished	92,615	84,320	161,663	253,668	308,070	410,152		

		shop products								
		Total							473,164	1,129,919
		Finished							160,428	357,840
		Unfinished						(Included with III 103, etc.)	312,736	772,079
II	21	*Miscellaneous Subsidiary Durable Equipment*								
		36 Belting & hose, woven								
		Total	none	36	1,004	925	3,660	7,083	5,730	20,344
		Finished		none			392	758	613	8,544
		Unfinished	none	36	1,004	925	3,268	6,325	5,117	11,800
II	83	Rope, cable & cordage								
		Total	3,045	4,241	10,556	13,474	22,356	21,016	22,422	57,577
		Finished	454	632	1,573	2,008	3,333	3,131	3,341	8,565
		Unfinished	2,591	3,609	8,983	11,466	19,033	17,885	19,081	49,012
		Producer Durable, Totals								
		Total	202,646	186,001	359,972	561,098	689,971	912,047	501,316	1,207,840
		Finished	107,440	98,036	188,322	295,039	359,600	477,685	164,382	374,949
		Unfinished	95,206	87,965	171,650	266,059	330,371	434,362	336,934	832,891

CONSTRUCTION MATERIALS

IX	135	Plate glass, polished								
		Total	299	731	4,172	5,159	7,978	12,205	14,774	33,348
		Construction materials	299	731	4,172	5,159	7,978	11,569	13,656	23,344
		Unfinished			none			636	1,118	10,004
IX	136	Glass, cutting, staining & ornamenting*								
		Total	774	2,555	6,139	8,821	15,243	16,236	16,763	29,145
		Finished	389	1,283	3,082	4,428	6,648	8,150	8,415	14,631
		Construction materials	156	516	1,240	1,782	2,675	3,280	3,386	5,887
		Unfinished	229	756	1,817	2,611	5,920	4,806	4,962	8,627
III	164, 165	Bolts, nuts, washers & rivets								
		Total	13,778	19,300	23,707	26,782	23,139	45,406	34,148	124,995
		Construction materials	4,698	6,581	8,084	9,133	3,595	15,483	11,644	42,623
		Unfinished	9,080	12,719	15,623	17,649	18,544	29,923	22,504	82,372

INDUSTRY NUMBER	COMMODITY	1869	1879	1889	1899	1904	1909	1914	1919
III 164, 169	Cut nails & spikes, wire nails & spikes, forged nails & spikes & all other, incl. tacks								
	Total	24,824	11,624	34,228	30,514	32,830	38,403	36,590	79,245
	Construction materials	8,465	3,964	11,672	10,405	11,195	13,095	12,477	27,023
	Unfinished	16,359	7,660	22,556	20,109	21,635	25,308	24,113	52,222
III 164, 170	Wrought pipe, iron & steel								
	Total	26,963	48,635	37,907	77,907	63,677	105,995	99,848	327,858
	Construction materials	24,078	43,431	33,851	69,571	56,864	90,838	83,772	250,484
	Unfinished	2,885	5,204	4,056	8,336	6,813	15,157	16,076	77,374
IX 186	Lime								
	Total	6,974	1,215	3,312	6,032	11,536	14,026	14,047	28,218
	Construction materials	2,092	850	2,318	4,222	8,075	9,468	6,799	11,372
	Unfinished	4,882	365	994	1,810	3,461	4,558	7,248	16,846
IV 195	Lumber & timber products								
	Total	183,626	207,336	388,603	447,420	422,569	529,997	492,746	954,635
	Construction materials	7,681	12,819	20,658	23,569	29,446	40,225	26,401	46,810
	Unfinished	175,945	194,517	367,945	423,851	393,123	489,772	466,345	907,825
IX 300	Statuary & art goods*								
	Total		not reported			2,456	3,497	3,980	5,196
	Finished					837	1,192	1,357	1,772
	Construction materials					1,619	2,305	2,623	3,424
	Construction Materials, Totals								
	Total	257,238	291,396	498,068	602,635	582,428	765,765	712,896	1,582,640
	Construction materials	47,469	68,892	81,995	123,841	127,447	186,263	160,758	410,967
	Finished	389	1,283	3,082	4,428	7,485	9,342	9,772	16,403
	Unfinished	209,380	221,221	412,991	474,366	447,496	570,160	542,366	1,155,270

*This commodity is included in the totals for construction materials even though it has already been recorded under the minor group in which the finished portion is classified.

GRAND TOTALS

Total	1,283,857	1,595,859	2,168,791	2,918,627	3,594,784	4,920,182	5,003,865	14,059,367
Finished	818,090	989,009	1,197,910	1,555,675	1,964,682	2,546,582	2,477,750	7,167,077
Construction materials	47,469	68,892	81,995	123,841	127,447	186,263	160,758	410,967
Unfinished	418,298	537,958	888,886	1,239,111	1,502,655	2,187,337	2,365,357	6,481,323

PERCENTAGES

Total	100.0	100.0	100.0	100.0	100.0	100.0	100.0	100.0
Finished	63.7	62.0	55.2	53.3	54.7	51.8	49.5	51.0
Construction materials	3.7	4.3	3.8	4.2	3.5	3.8	3.2	2.9
Unfinished	32.6	33.7	41.0	42.5	41.8	44.5	47.3	46.1

Note A to Table II 2
Allocation Based on Census Reports of Materials Consumed in Manufacturing

For many of the more important industries the Census of Manufactures reports detailed data on materials consumed. Between 1899 and 1919 such data are usually reported for one or more census years.[a] Since *total* cost of materials is reported for all years, percentages for the closest year for which we have detailed data are applied to the total cost of materials (excluding fuel and rent for power when possible) for the years for which we have no detailed data.

Some discussion and comment on this method of apportioning mixed commodities appear in *Commodity Flow and Capital Formation,* Volume One, pp. 17, 18, and 68. In one respect the technique is more exact than Kuznets'; the detailed data, when available for 1919 or earlier years, cover an entire industry, not merely a part. But the principal defect of the method, that the estimates of unfinished are minima because some industries using specified materials do not report them separately in any year, still holds. It is possibly compensated in part by the inclusion of an indeterminate amount of transportation charges and distributive costs in the cost of materials as reported in the Census.

The mixed commodities to which the materials consumed method could be applied are listed below, by minor commodity groups, together with a description of the industries and years for which data were available.

1 Food and Kindred Products

Baking powder and yeast: Consumption in the bread and other bakery products industry was estimated from the 1923 percentage.

Butter: Consumption in the bread and other bakery products industry was estimated from the 1923 percentage; in the chocolate and cocoa products industry from the percentage the 1919 estimate in *Commodity Flow and Capital Formation,* Volume One, Note A to Table I 3, constituted of a residual of unidentified other materials consumed in the industry in 1919; in the confectionery and ice cream industry from the percentage the 1919 estimate in *ibid.* constituted of a residual of unidentified other materials consumed in the industry in 1919; in the oleomargarine industry from the 1899 percentage. In this last estimate, the figures for all years except 1914 and 1919 were adjusted to include oleomargarine made in the meatpacking industry. The estimates for 1914 and 1919, computed independently, were based upon the quantity of butter consumed as reported for the fiscal year 1915 and an average of the fiscal years

---

[a] In a few instances no detailed data are available except for years after 1919. We chose to use these 'remote' figures rather than omit the estimates. For example, it was considered better to apply percentages computed from data in the 1923 Census on materials consumed in the bread and other bakery products industry to total materials consumed by it in 1919 and prior years than not to use the materials consumed data for the industry. The crudity of this technique, however, should be kept in mind. Whenever such 'remote' figures are utilized, it is clearly indicated in the comprehensive commodity notes below.

1919 and 1920 (Katherine Snodgrass, *Margarine as a Butter Substitute;* Food Research Institute, Stanford University, Dec. 1930; Fats and Oils Studies 4, App. Table V A). These data were multiplied by appropriate butter prices calculated from data in the 1889, 1914, and 1919 Censuses.

Condensed and evaporated milk: Consumption in the bread and other bakery products industry was estimated from the 1923 percentage.

Flavoring extracts: Consumption in the chocolate and cocoa products industry was estimated from the 1919 percentage; in the mineral and soda waters industry from the percentage the 1919 figure (based on 1929 data) in *Commodity Flow and Capital Formation,* Volume One, Note A to Table I 3, constituted of the total cost of materials excluding fuel and rent for power; and in the confectionery (including chewing gum) and ice cream industry from the 1919 percentage (an additional figure in 1919 for flavors consumed in the chewing gum industry—*ibid.*—having first been included).

Flour: Consumption in the bread and other bakery products industry was estimated from the 1923 percentage. In the macaroni industry the 1919 figure (based on 1929 data) from *ibid.* was used; for 1914 the 1919 percentage of the total cost of materials, and for the earlier years the 1914 percentage of the commodity produced estimate was applied to the respective commodity estimates.

Lard including lard compounds and substitutes: Consumption in the bread and other bakery products industry was estimated from the 1923 percentage; in the oleomargarine industry, from the 1899 percentage. The 1919, 1914, 1909, and 1904 figures for the amount consumed in the oleomargarine industry were then raised to allow for oleomargarine made in the meat-packing industry.

Sugar: The amounts consumed in 8 industries were estimated. For the bread and other bakery products industry the 1923 percentage was used in all years. For the butter, cheese and condensed milk industry data were available for all years except 1879; for that year the 1889 percentage was applied. For the canning and preserving fruits and vegetables, and pickles, preserves, and sauces industry the 1919 figure (based on 1929 data) from *ibid.* was applied to the 1919 total cost of materials, excluding fuel and rent of power, and the resulting percentage used for all years. A similar procedure was followed for the flavoring extracts and cordials and sirups and the mineral and soda water industries. For the chocolate and cocoa products industry the 1919 percentage was used for all other years. For the confectionery and ice cream industry the 1919 percentage was similarly applied; in 1919, however, the amount consumed in the chewing gum industry (*ibid.*) was first added. For the oleomargarine industry the 1899 percentage was applied in all other years; the resulting estimates for the years after 1899 were further adjusted to allow for oleomargarine made in the meat-packing industry.

3 Drug, Toilet and Household Preparations

Castor oil: Consumption in the soap and natural dyestuffs and extracts industries was estimated from the 1919 percentages.

Soap: Consumption in 5 textile industries was estimated. Considerable soap is probably consumed also in other industries for which no data are available. The amount consumed in the silk manufactures industry was estimated from the 1889 percentage; in dyeing and finishing textiles, from the 1889 and 1899 percentages; in the knit goods industry, from the 1889 and 1904 percentages; in the wool manufactures industries, from the 1889 and 1904 percentages; and in the fur-felt hat industry, from the 1899 percentage.

NOTE B TO TABLE II 2

Allocation by Special Methods

1 FOOD AND KINDRED PRODUCTS

Ice, manufactured: An approximation, 50 percent to finished and 50 to unfinished, was based on data in *Commodity Flow and Capital Formation,* Volume One (see p. 73) which indicated that about 55 percent of manufactured ice was finished, and on data reported in the Tenth Census: 1880, Vol. XXII *Power and Machinery Employed in Manufactures* and *The Ice Industry of the United States.*

Of the total tonnage of natural ice sold in 20 principal cities during the season 1879–80, 42 percent went to private families, the remainder to brewers, butchers and meat packers, butter dealers, ships, and miscellaneous consumers.

Salt: The production of salt by type was reported in *Mineral Resources of the United States, seriatim,* Part II. As a rough approximation, table and dairy salt were considered finished and all other types (common fine, common coarse, packers', coarse solar, rock, and milling) unfinished. Values for 1919, 1914, and 1909 were taken from the 1920 volume, p. 19, the 1915 volume, p. 268, and the 1909 volume, p. 664. For 1904 and 1899 quantity data on the production of table and dairy salt were multiplied by prices, by applying, to the price of all salt in the two earlier years, the ratio of the price of table and dairy salt to the price of all salt in 1906. For years before 1899 the 1899 percentage apportionment, 21.5 to finished and 78.5 to unfinished, was used.

3 DRUG, TOILET AND HOUSEHOLD PREPARATIONS

Alkaloids and derivatives: For 1919 the value of alkaloids and their salts used as materials in the druggist's preparations and patent medicines and compounds industries was reported. Classified as unfinished, the percentage it constituted of the total production of alkaloids and derivatives for 1919, 30.5, was used in all the earlier years.

Biological products: Lack of more pertinent data compelled the use of the apportionment for 1927 when the Census reported that 40.1 percent of biological products were for human use and 59.9 percent for animal use. These percentages were used in all years, the estimates of products for animal use being classified as unfinished.

ESTIMATES OF THE VALUE OF OUTPUT 189

Patent compounds: A crude apportionment, based upon detailed data in 1921, put insecticides, boiler compounds, and fire-extinguishing compounds, comprising 37.5 percent of total patent compounds in 1921, under unfinished.

5a FUEL AND LIGHTING PRODUCTS, MANUFACTURED

Coke: From *Mineral Resources of the United States, 1920,* Part II, pp. 401–4, data were taken on the sales of coke to furnaces, foundries, and domestic and other consumers. Since the value of coke sold to domestic and other consumers in 1919, $16,383,219, probably included sales of screening and breeze, the value of screening and breeze sold was estimated from more detailed data reported for 1920, when 27.6 percent of total production was sold as screening and breeze. The total production figure for 1919 was multiplied by this percentage and the resulting estimate of screening and breeze subtracted from the domestic sales figure above. The residual, $15,676,551, was assumed to be the value of finished coke for 1919.

Few data are available on the distribution of coke prior to 1919. In *Mineral Resources of the United States, 1915,* Part II, p. 541, about 5 percent of coke consumed was reported to be used principally for domestic purposes. Lack of more exact data compelled the application of this approximate percentage to total production for 1914 and all earlier years.

Illuminating oils: A crude apportionment for 1919, 1914, and 1909 was based on estimates of J. E. Pogue in *Economics of Petroleum* (New York, 1921). A chart on page 140 of that volume showed that the following amounts (approximate) of illuminating oils were used for tractors, boats, and stationary engines, i.e., for power purposes: 1919, 475 million gallons; 1914, 150; 1909, 50. These amounts, constituting about 20, 8, and 3 percent of the corresponding annual outputs, were assumed to be the unfinished portion of illuminating oils. To years before 1909, the 1909 percentage was applied.

Lubricating oils: It was assumed that of the important uses of lubricating oils—railroad, industrial, tractor, exports and automotive, truck and passenger car—only that in passenger cars was finished in our terminology. To estimate it the following procedure was adopted. Beginning and end of the year registration figures for passenger cars were averaged to get an approximation of cars in use (see *Automobile Facts and Figures, 1938,* p. 16). These estimates of cars in use were then multiplied by a conversion factor of 25 gallons, the figure used by Pogue in his estimates (*op. cit.,* Table 78, p. 180). Finally, the consumption figure in gallons for each year was multiplied by a corresponding price per gallon derived from the quantity and value data reported in the Census of Manufactures for 1919, 1914, 1909, 1904, and 1899. The procedure was like that used for lubricating oils, except that the conversion factor was 300 gallons, based, according to Pogue, upon a War Industries Board investigation in 1918, modified by additional calculation and experience (*ibid.,* p. 123).

Since for both lubricating oils and gasoline, exports are included with the unfinished portion, the finished portion was not adjusted for exports or imports.

6 DRY GOODS AND NOTIONS

Cotton thread: Apportionment in 1919 was based upon sample data for 1924 on billings of silk thread (*Distribution of Textiles,* Bulletin 56, Harvard University, Bureau of Business Research). Table 24, p. 186, of that volume indicated that 64.9 percent of machine twist silk thread was sold to cutters-up and other manufacturers. No data on industrial sales by wholesalers were available. For years other than 1919, the estimated value of unfinished for 1919 was extrapolated by an index of the cost of materials in the men's and women's clothing industries.

All other cotton woven goods: The apportionment was based upon sample data on billings reported for 1924 in the *Distribution of Textiles.* From Tables 30, 32, 34, and 36 of that volume, billings of voiles, marquisettes, lawns, pique, twills, sateens, plushes, velvets, etc., dress corduroys, all-cotton fine goods, cotton, silk, and rayon mixtures, ginghams, drills, denims, outing flannels and dometts, canton flannels, etc., cottonades and cotton suitings, osnaburgs, and all other woven fabrics were added. Billings to converters, cutters-up, and other manufacturers were 72.0 percent of all billings. Supplementary data from Table 39 revealed that manufacturers who did their own converting billed 38 percent of their goods to cutters-up and other manufacturers. These two percentages, representing industrial billings by the two types of cotton goods manufacturers, were weighted and combined on the basis of data in Table 27, which showed that of total billings of all cotton woven fabrics, 77 percent were yarn-dyed and grey goods and 23 percent were converted for mills' own account. The final weighted percentage of industrial billings was thus 64.2 percent. Lack of data compelled the assumption that no other industrial sales were made by wholesalers. The final percentage was applied in 1919 and the resulting estimate of unfinished cotton woven goods extrapolated by an index of the cost of materials in the women's clothing industry.

Dyeing and finishing textiles: Contract work was first estimated from 1929 data in the *Distribution of Sales of Manufacturing Plants: 1929,* Table 3. The percentage that contract work (unfinished in our classification) constituted of the value of products for the industry, 52.3, was used for all years. The remainder of the industry was then apportioned for 1919 on the basis of sample data for 1924 (*Distribution of Textiles,* Table 42) which showed that 69 percent of billings of converters and finishers were to cutters-up and other manufacturers. For years before 1919 industrial use was estimated by applying an index of the cost of materials in the women's clothing industry to the value estimated for 1919.

Silk ribbons: Apportionment between finished and unfinished in 1919 was based upon sample data for 1924 (*Distribution of Textiles,* Table 24), which showed that 62 percent of billings of ribbons were to cutters-up and other manufacturers. Since it was impossible to ascertain other billings by wholesalers to manufacturers, the above percentage is a maximum estimate of finished ribbons. For years other than 1919, the estimated 1919 value for unfinished was ex-

ESTIMATES OF THE VALUE OF OUTPUT 191

trapolated by an index of the cost of materials in the millinery and lace goods industry.

Broadsilks: 45 percent of the billings of the 1924 sample were direct to cutters-up and other manufacturers (*Distribution of Textiles,* Table 22). Use of this percentage to estimate unfinished for 1919 yields a minimum estimate of unfinished because no adequate data on the billings of wholesalers are available. For years other than 1919 the estimated value of unfinished broadsilks for 1919 was extrapolated by an index of the cost of materials in the women's clothing industry.

Silk velvets and plushes: The percentage, 25, that sample billings in 1924 were direct to cutters-up and other manufacturers (*Distribution of Textiles,* Table 23) was used for all years to estimate the value of unfinished silk velvets and plushes.

Sewing and embroidery silk: The percentage, 35, that sample billings in 1924 of silk threads were direct to cutters-up and other manufacturers (*Distribution of Textiles,* Table 25) was used for all years to estimate the value of unfinished sewing and embroidery silks.

Woolen and worsted woven goods: An approximate apportionment was based upon data in the *Distribution of Textiles* for the distribution of billings in 1924. The percentage, 79, that billings of men's and women's wear woolen and worsted fabrics were direct to cutters-up (*ibid.,* Table 13) was used to estimate the value of unfinished woven goods for 1919, lack of adequate data preventing any adjustment for billings of wholesalers to cutters-up. For years other than 1919, the estimated 1919 value of unfinished was extrapolated by an index of the cost of materials in the men's and women's clothing industries.

Mixed textiles: Since the exact constitution of this industry is unknown, there is no accurate method of apportioning the commodity total between finished and unfinished. To approximate an allocation, the estimates for other cotton woven goods, broadsilks and silk ribbons and woolen and worsted woven goods were totaled. This mixed textile total was allocated by the percentage distribution of this aggregate: 64 to finished and 36 to unfinished.

7 CLOTHING AND PERSONAL FURNISHINGS

Fur goods: From the 1925 census it was estimated that 11.8 percent of the commodity total for that year was fur trimmings. Since trimmings were classified as unfinished, this computation indicated an apportionment of 88.2 percent to finished and 11.8 to unfinished.

Trimmed hats and hat frames: The value of unfinished for all years was estimated from the percentage that hat frames and linings constituted of total trimmed hats, hat frames, and hat linings, 5.2—a crude apportionment, based on 1927 data.

Suspenders, garters and elastic woven goods: According to the 1923 Census, the value of elastic webbing produced was about the same as the value of suspenders, garters, and elastic woven goods made from purchased webbing (in

1923 establishments making elastic webbing were transferred from the suspenders . . . industry to the cotton smallwares industry). On this basis a crude allocation was made, 50 percent to finished and 50 to unfinished.

9 House Furnishings (semidurable)

Towels, towelling, wash cloths, turkish towels and terry weave: Apportionment between finished and unfinished was based upon the distribution of billings in 1924 (*Distribution of Textiles*). 11.6 percent of these fabrics were sold to cutters-up and other manufactures (*ibid.*, Table 28). Lack of data compelled the assumption that no other industrial sales were made by wholesalers.

11 Tires and Tubes

Tires and tubes, automobile: For 1919 and 1914 total output was reported by the Census of Manufactures. Upon the assumption that tires and tubes used for original equipment were unfinished, casings required for original equipment (*Special Circular 3500,* Bureau of Foreign and Domestic Commerce, Rubber Section, Table III) were estimated to be 22 and 27 percent respectively of total output in 1919 and 1914. To get the estimated values of unfinished tires and tubes the total value of casings and tubes was multiplied by these percentages.

Prior to 1914 tire and tube data were not reported separately in the Census of Manufactures. Total production as well as its apportionment had to be estimated. For 1909 and 1904 the method used in *Special Circular 3500* for 1910 and later years was used. Tires required for original equipment were estimated on the basis of total cars and trucks produced, less an allowance for trucks equipped with solid tires. The conversion factor was four casings per unit. Renewals were estimated from registration figures for December 31 of the preceding year, a conversion factor of five casings per pneumatic tired car being used. A small allowance was then made for exports. Adding these estimates gave an estimated output of 1,500,000 casings in 1909 and 250,000 in 1904. It was assumed that an equal number of tubes was produced. Of total output 34 percent represented requirements for original equipment in 1909, and 35 percent in 1904.

To translate the above estimates into values, some sort of price index was required, since per unit prices for tires and tubes were available only for 1914. Approximations were based on two sources: price lists of the United States Rubber Products Corporation for 1911 and 1914 and quotations in the *India Rubber World,* December 1, 1910, for 1907 through 1910. The latter stated that prices did not change much between 1904 and 1907. On the basis of the above data, it was decided that, on 1914 as a base, the 1909 price was about 140 and the 1904 price about 150. This crude index, applied to the prices per casing and per tube in 1914, yielded prices that could be used to translate the quantities estimated above into values.

Prior to 1904 neither quantity nor value was estimated. Since only 800 cars

ESTIMATES OF THE VALUE OF OUTPUT

were registered in 1898 and 3,200 in 1899 the output of automobile tires must have been very small, and for the most part unfinished, i.e., original equipment.

Tires and tubes, motorcycle and bicycle: For 1919 and 1914 tires and tubes used for original equipment were estimated from the number of bicycles and motorcycles produced each year. Two tires were allowed for each bicycle and motorcycle and two tubes for each motorcycle in 1919. Since no tubes were reported for 1914 two tires were allowed for each vehicle. The above method gave 19.7 percent in 1919 and 24.8 percent in 1914 as the estimated requirement for original equipment. The 1914 estimate was extrapolated to 1909, 1904, and 1899 on the basis of a production index for bicycles and motorcycles.

From these estimates of original equipment for the earlier years the total output of tires was estimated by multiplying them by the 1914 ratio of total output to output required for original equipment. This somewhat unsatisfactory method was adopted because better data were lacking.

Prior to 1899 few if any pneumatic tires were made. The use of solid or cushion tires on bicycles cannot be estimated since all solid rubber tires are an indeterminate part of all other rubber manufactures, classified by us as unfinished.

13b   ELECTRICAL HOUSEHOLD APPLIANCES AND SUPPLIES

Incandescent lamps: Allocation of 35 percent to finished and 65 to unfinished, representative for 1929, was based on information supplied by the General Electric Company, Incandescent Lamp Department (see *Commodity Flow and Capital Formation,* Vol. One, p. 119).

14   HOUSE FURNISHINGS (DURABLE)

Carpets: Apportionment between finished and unfinished was based upon sample data, covering about one-fourth of the industry, on billings in 1924 (*Distribution of Textiles*). The percentage of billings direct to manufacturers and institutions, 56 (pp. 74, 77), was applied to the 1919 and 1914 census data on carpets excluding rugs made of sewed strips. For years before 1914 the percentage, 20.7, that unfinished carpets constituted in 1914 of total carpets, including rugs, made of sewed strips was used.

Silk upholstery and tapestries: The percentage, 3, that billings of the 1924 sample were direct to cutters-up and other manufacturers (*Distribution of Textiles,* Table 23) was used for all years to estimate the value of unfinished upholstery and tapestries.

Lamps and appliances sold by gas companies: Since most of these lamps and appliances were purchased from other manufacturers, duplication would result if the gross receipts from such sales were included as finished. Net receipts alone, the difference between gross sales and the amount reported paid for lamps and appliances purchased for resale, should be included. Cost data are available back to 1899 but exceed slightly the estimated sales values in 1899 and 1904. Thus before 1909 entire gross sales are classified as unfinished.

15 CHINA AND HOUSEHOLD UTENSILS

Tinware: Lack of better information compelled the use of census data for 1927, when stamped household tinware was 1.6 percent of the total production of tinware. The other 98.4 percent was considered unfinished.

17 JEWELRY, SILVERWARE, CLOCKS AND WATCHES

Jewelry: Apportionment between finished and unfinished was based upon census data for 1927, when 9.8 percent of the total output of jewelry was jewelry findings, classified as unfinished. The other 90.2 percent was considered finished.

20 MOTOR VEHICLE ACCESSORIES

Motor vehicle bodies and parts: Because direct information on replacement parts and parts used for original equipment was not available, an indirect method of apportionment was used. The wholesale or manufacturers' value of replacement parts, accessories, and tires was estimated to be $854,500,000 in 1921 (*Automotive Industries,* Feb. 22, 1923, p. 466). To get a per car basis this estimate was divided by the number of passenger cars registered (average of beginning and end of year registration); all automobile registration data are from *Automobile Facts and Figures, 1938.* Multiplication of the replacement per car figure by the average number of cars registered in 1919, 1914, 1909, and 1904 gave estimates of the total replacement bill for these years in 1921 prices. To express the estimates in current prices, a price index was needed. In its absence a crude substitute was calculated from the number and value of passenger cars produced each year. This per unit passenger car price was put in index form (1921:100) and used to extrapolate the estimates in 1921 prices.

The estimates in current prices obtained by the above procedure included tires as well as other parts and accessories. To get parts and accessories excluding tires the values of tires used for replacement (see Minor Group 11) were subtracted.

It was assumed that all parts produced in 1899 were for original equipment.

25 INDUSTRIAL MACHINERY AND EQUIPMENT

Miscellaneous machinery and machine-shop products: Of the total production of foundry and machine shop products in 1927, 40.1 percent was machinery and parts. This percentage, applied to the 1919 foundry and machine shop industry total excluding metal working machinery, gave a machinery and parts estimate of $894,916 thousand. From this estimate the known values for specified classes of machinery were subtracted. To the remainder, $273,259 thousand, was added the value of machinery made as secondary products in other industries, the sums being assumed to be miscellaneous machinery and parts or the finished portion of miscellaneous machinery and machine-shop products. A similar procedure followed for 1914 (after the subtraction of metal working

ESTIMATES OF THE VALUE OF OUTPUT

machinery, machine tools, textile machinery, and an estimated value for steel barrels, drums, and tanks from the 1914 industry total) yielded a miscellaneous machinery estimate of $160,428 thousand. For both years the values of unfinished estimated by the above method include an indeterminate amount of contract and repair work as well as miscellaneous machine shop products.

Foundry and machine-shop products: Prior to 1914 no commodity detail whatsoever was reported for this industry. Consequently, the commodity totals for the earlier years could be apportioned only crudely between finished and unfinished on the basis of the 1914 division. By this method 53.6 percent was classified as finished and 46.4 as unfinished.

36 Miscellaneous Subsidiary Durable Equipment

Belting and hose, woven, other than rubber: In 1919 and 1914 the apportionment between unfinished and finished was based upon the industry division between belting manufacturers and hose manufacturers, as reported by the census. The estimates for hose were treated as finished. Estimates for 1904 and 1909 were based upon the 1914 allocation. It was assumed that prior to 1904 no woven hose was produced, since the *Abstract of the Census of Manufactures: 1914,* p. 92, states that the increase in the industry from 1899 to 1904 was due largely to the replacement of leather hose by woven hose.

Rope, cable and cordage: A crude apportionment was based upon the detailed data reported in the 1919 Census. Manila drilling cable, transmission rope, and other commercial and bolt ropes, 14.9 percent of the total, were classified as finished; all other types of rope as unfinished.

Construction Materials

Plate glass, polished: The percentage classified as unfinished in 1919, 30, was based on the proportion of the total production of plate glass that was consumed in the automobile industry in 1921 (*Facts and Figures of the Automobile Industry, 1922,* p. 11). Estimates for 1914 and 1909 were made by using the percentage, 5, that the 1919 estimate constituted of the output of closed cars in that year. The use of plate glass in the automobile industry was assumed to be negligible prior to 1909.

Bolts, nuts, washers and rivets: For 1919 it was possible to get data on the values of railroad spikes, bolts and nuts, and of bolts, nuts, rivets and washers, other than railroad, made in rolling mills. The percentage that railroad spikes, bolts and nuts, classified as construction materials, constituted of the total, 34.1, was applied to the 1919 commodity total, and, because of lack of other data, to the commodity totals of all the other years as well.

Cut nails and spikes, wire nails and spikes, forged nails and spikes and all other including tacks: Lack of data compelled the use of a purely arbitrary procedure for the apportionment between construction materials and unfinished. The percentage derived for bolts, nuts, washers and rivets was applied to the nail totals.

Wrought pipe: For 1919, 1914, 1909, and 1904 the wrought pipe and tubing made in rolling mills was reported in sufficient detail for a crude apportionment between construction materials and unfinished. Boiler tubes, seamless, hot finished or cold drawn, and all other were classified as unfinished; casing, tubing drain and line pipe, other black pipe, and other galvanized pipe were classified as construction materials. Since boiler tubes were reported separately for 1919 alone, the amount made in rolling mills was estimated for the three earlier years by using the percentage that such tubes constituted in 1919 of all wrought welded pipe, 6.

It was assumed that establishments in the wrought pipe industry proper and in other industries manufactured pipe and tubing in the same proportion as the rolling mill establishments. Thus, wrought pipe and tubing used as construction materials were estimated through 1904; for preceding years the 1904 percentage allocation was used, 89.3 to construction materials and 10.7 to unfinished.

Lime: Values of lime sold, by uses, were reported for 1919, 1914, and 1909 in the respective volumes of *Mineral Resources of the United States,* Part II. Since they differ slightly from census data, they could not be used directly. Instead the amount sold as building lime in each year was expressed as a percentage of all lime, excluding that sold to dealers. Lime sold to dealers was assumed to be distributed in the same proportions as lime sold directly to the various types of ultimate user. Estimates of lime used for construction purposes were based upon the percentages thus derived: 40.3 for 1919, 48.4 for 1914, and 67.5 for 1909. Although a definite trend is revealed by the above percentages, the percentage in 1906, the earliest year for which comparable data were available, was only 69.7. Thus an approximation of 70 percent to construction materials was adopted for all years prior to 1909.

Lumber and timber products: The census data for this industry are not strictly comparable from year to year because of the varying treatment of logging camps. In some census years all logging camps were covered; in others only those connected with saw mills. Consequently it was impossible to apportion the commodity totals between construction materials and unfinished by using a fixed percentage. The values of lumber and timber intended for construction materials had to be estimated directly.

Although many construction materials (other than planing mill products) are composed of lumber and timber, the values for two alone, lath and shingles, are here estimated. The other principal products used in construction—railroad ties, mine timbers, and poles—are discussed in Note A to Table II 11.

The quantity and value data for lath and shingles for 1919, 1909, 1904, 1899, and 1889 in the respective census volumes were compiled by the Bureau of the Census in cooperation with the Department of Agriculture Forest Service. For 1879 quantity data alone are available and for 1914 no data whatsoever. For 1914 quantities of lath were estimated by straight line interpolation between 1912 and 1915, the nearest years for which quantities were reported; quantities of shingles were estimated from an interpolation index between 1912 and 1915 based upon the output of reporting mills of cypress, white pine, and

ESTIMATES OF THE VALUE OF OUTPUT

cedar, the principal woods from which shingles were manufactured. A 1914 price for lath was calculated by applying the Bureau of Labor Statistics wholesale price index for lath to the 1919 census price; a 1914 price for shingles was calculated by using an average of the BLS prices for cypress and red cedar shingles to interpolate between 1911 and 1919, two years for which Forest Service prices were available. Values of lath and shingles were then obtained by multiplying the quantity estimates by the appropriate price estimates.

Prices, needed for 1879 alone, were estimated by extrapolating the 1889 census prices of lath and shingles respectively by the prices of average quality, 1 inch softwoods, and of first quality, 1 inch softwoods (*American Forests and Forest Products,* Department of Agriculture, Statistical Bulletin 21, 1927, Table 76, p. 118). Values were then obtained by multiplying the 1879 quantities by the estimated prices.

NOTE C TO TABLE II 2

Allocation Based upon Percentage Sales to Industrial Consumers in 1929

The use of percentages derived from census reports for 1929[a] is difficult to defend, especially for the period before World War I. The few times they were used it was in the belief that almost any type of apportionment is preferable to none at all if the commodity is obviously mixed. Unless otherwise specified, the percentages below are from *Commodity Flow and Capital Formation,* Volume One, Table B-1, pp. 72, 73.

1 FOOD AND KINDRED PRODUCTS

Peanuts: 92.4 percent to finished, 7.6 to unfinished.

3 DRUG, TOILET AND HOUSEHOLD PREPARATIONS

Blacking, stains, and dressings: 76.2 percent to finished, 23.8 to unfinished.
Cleansing and polishing preparations: 81.5 percent to finished, 18.5 to unfinished.

4 MAGAZINES, NEWSPAPERS, STATIONERY AND SUPPLIES, AND MISCELLANEOUS PAPER PRODUCTS

Envelopes: 51.0 percent to finished, 49.0 to unfinished. In the envelopes industry, 49.0 percent of sales were direct to industrial consumers. No other data on industrial sales by wholesalers could be obtained from the wholesale census.
Mucilage, paste and other adhesives, n.e.s.: 51.7 percent to finished, 48.3 to unfinished.

[a] *Distribution of Sales of Manufacturing Plants* and *Wholesale Distribution: Summary for the United States.* The derivation of the basic 1929 percentages is explained in *Commodity Flow and Capital Formation,* Vol. One, Note B to Table I-3, pp. 71–3.

Fine paper, writing: 69.4 percent to finished, 30.6 to unfinished.

All other paper goods, n.e.s.: 50.2 percent to finished, 49.8 to unfinished. These percentages were derived from the figures for the paper goods, n.e.c. industry in *Distribution of Sales of Manufacturing Plants: 1929,* and from the sales of wholesale establishments selling other paper products reported in the *Census of Wholesale Distribution: United States Summary: 1929,* Table 2.

6 Dry Goods and Notions

Artificial flowers: 75.0 percent to finished, 25.0 to unfinished.

Buttons: 9.0 percent to finished, 91.0 to unfinished.

Lace goods and nets: 42.7 percent to finished, 57.3 to unfinished.

Fancy articles, n.e.s.: 85.2 percent to finished, 14.8 to unfinished, the percentages reported in *Distribution of Sales of Manufacturing Plants: 1929* for the fancy and miscellaneous articles industry. No other data on the sales distribution of wholesalers were available.

Feathers and plumes: 35.4 percent to finished, 64.6 to unfinished.

Leather goods, n.e.s.: 77.0 percent to finished, 23.0 to unfinished, the percentages calculated from the figures for the leather goods, n.e.c. industry reported in *Distribution of Sales of Manufacturing Plants: 1929,* and from the figures on the sales of wholesale establishments selling leather goods, n.e.c., in the *Census of Wholesale Distribution: United States Summary: 1929,* Table 2.

Embroideries: 52.1 percent to finished, 47.9 to unfinished. These percentages were applied after an estimated value for contract work, based upon data from the *Census of Manufactures: 1929,* had been subtracted. In 1929 the value of contract work was 59.4 percent of total embroidery production.

Statuary and art goods: 34.1 percent to finished, 65.9, the percentage of sales reported as sales to industrial consumers—assumed to be contractors—to construction materials.

7 Clothing and Personal Furnishings

Umbrellas and canes: 86.6 percent to finished, 13.4 to unfinished, the percentages reported in *Distribution of Sales of Manufacturing Plants* for the umbrella, parasol, and cane industry. No other data on the sales distribution of wholesalers were available.

9 House Furnishings (semidurable)

Window shades and fixtures: 93.0 percent to finished, 7.0 to unfinished.

14b Miscellaneous House Furnishings (durable)

Cotton tapestries: 60.1 percent to finished, 39.9 to unfinished.

Looking glass and picture frames: 94.1 percent to finished, 5.9 to unfinished.

Mirrors, framed and unframed: 61.3 percent to finished, 38.7 to unfinished.

15 CHINA AND HOUSEHOLD UTENSILS

Glass cutting, staining and ornamenting: 50.2 percent to finished, 20.2 to construction materials, and 29.6 to unfinished, the percentages reported for the glass products industry in *Distribution of Sales of Manufacturing Plants: 1929*. The percentage allocated to construction materials is that reported sold to contractors, institutions, churches, etc. No other data on the distribution of sales by wholesalers were available.

CONSTRUCTION MATERIALS

See the allocation of statuary and art goods under Minor Group 6 and that of glass, cutting, staining, and ornamenting under Minor Group 15.

TABLE II 3

Industrial Composition of the *Census of Manufactures*, 1869–1919

(thousands of dollars)

CENSUS INDUSTRY GROUPS	1869	1879	1889	1899	1904	1909	1914	1919
Food & kindred products	695,748	1,118,305	1,574,179	2,199,202	2,845,556	3,937,617	4,816,709	12,438,890
Textiles & their products	760,032	978,642	1,279,282	1,646,732	2,179,250	3,108,369	3,473,438	9,248,290
Iron & steel	589,548	664,579	1,209,305‡	1,824,532	2,205,607	3,170,228	3,228,989	9,417,880
Lumber & its remfrs.	418,580	471,328	852,316	1,004,719	1,214,475	1,582,522	1,593,862	3,055,829
Leather & its finished products	377,620	422,783	483,782	582,050	724,390	992,713	1,104,595	2,610,231
Paper & printing	153,041	289,503*	449,224	607,905	859,812	1,179,284	1,456,046	3,012,583
Liquors & beverages	110,481	167,187	327,214	382,899	501,254	674,310	772,080	603,895
Chemicals & allied products	205,420	266,366†	516,653	761,690	1,075,521	1,526,597	2,001,636	5,610,299
Stone, clay & glass products	114,917	99,511	212,332	270,726	391,231	531,737	614,162	1,085,531
Metals, other than iron & steel	123,160	152,688	275,588	701,170	912,291	1,243,726	1,419,589	2,763,710
Tobacco mfrs.	71,762	116,773	195,537	263,713	331,112	416,695	490,165	1,012,933
Vehicles for land transportation	104,424	104,969	200,176	277,485	320,624	561,764	1,034,497	4,058,912
Rr. repair shops			132,428	227,485	323,212	437,564	552,618	1,354,446
Misc. industries	157,424	243,521	399,179	656,564	909,339	1,308,539	1,686,941	6,144,291
All other industries			469	59	230	390	1,104	362
Subtotal comparable with commodity total (see Table II 1)	3,882,157	5,096,155	8,107,664	11,406,931	14,793,904	20,672,055	24,246,431	62,418,082
Custom establishments§	101,043	135,373	247,246	303,212				
Mechanical & hand trades§	249,115	261,754	993,701	1,183,616				
Agricultural industries		5,651	25,187	38,262				
Roofing work		3,376	15,942	16,226				
Street construction work			28,164	42,512				
Adjusted totals‖	4,232,315	5,502,309	9,417,904	12,990,759	14,793,904	20,672,055	24,246,431	62,418,082
Census grand totals¶	4,232,325	5,369,579	9,372,379	13,000,149	14,793,903	20,672,052	24,246,435	62,418,079
Add:								
Petroleum & printing values not reported in Census totals		132,904	47,733					
Iron & steel not reported in Census totals				9,887				
Subtract:								
U.S. Navy shipbuilding			9,420,181					
Products of gov. establishments in D.C.			2,277					
Adj. Census grand totals‖	4,232,325	5,502,483	9,417,835	12,990,262	14,793,903	20,672,052	24,246,435	62,418,079

* Includes newspaper and periodical printing valued at $89,199.
† Includes petroleum valued at $43,705 reported in a special survey of the petroleum industry.
‡ Includes iron and steel rolling mill products valued at $47,733 reported among detailed data for the industry but not included in the census totals for 1889.
§ The 1889, 1879, and 1869 values for custom establishments are entirely estimated. The values for the hand trades are only partly estimated in those years. Clothing, men's, custom work and repairing was estimated to be $126,219 in 1889; furniture, cabinet making, repairing and upholstering was estimated to be $23,884 in 1889 and $7,159 in 1879.
‖ The small discrepancies in 1869, 1879, and 1899 between the adjusted total—the sum of the data for separate industries—and the adjusted census grand totals are probably due to minute changes made in some of the individual figures by census authorities and not carried over to the grand totals.
¶ *Abstract of the Census of Manufactures: 1919*, p. 14, and *Twelfth Census*, Vol. VII, Manufactures, Part I, p. xlvii.

TABLE II 4

Value of Products Reported for Eight States by the United States Census of Manufactures and by State Agencies, Census Years, 1889–1919
(millions of dollars)

Rank of State in 1944 Census	Penn.* 2	Ohio† 4	Mass.‡ 5	N. J.§ 6	Mo.‖ 11	Conn.¶ 12	R. I.** 19	Va.†† 20	Total	% Total Is of Adj. Census Grand Total‡‡
1889 State Census % State is of Census	13	42	523 766 82	65		126 215 58			649 981 66	7 10
1899 State Census % State is of Census	210 1,598	305 732	737 903 68	355 544	153 306 50		82 165 50	21 102 21	1,863 4,350 43	14 33
1904 State Census % State is of Census	278 1,882 15	721 934 77	994 1,109 90	579 760 76	348 424 82	204 364 56	107 202 53	74 139 53	3,305 5,814 57	22 39
1909 State Census % State is of Census	1,234 2,532 49	1,057 1,404 75	1,491 1,491 100	824 1,125 73	574 574 100		66 280 24	117 208 56	5,363 7,614 70	26 37
1914 State Census % State is of Census			1,641 1,641 100	1,091 1,381 79	637 638 100			190 243 78	3,559 3,903 91	15 16
1919 State Census % State is of Census	7,041 7,044 100		4,011 4,011 100		1,576 1,558 101			608 610 100	13,236 13,223 100	21 21

202

General Note

The comparison is for census years and by states between the totals reported for all manufacturing industries in each state by the United States Census of Manufactures and the totals reported by the respective state agencies. A blank indicates that no data were reported by the state for the census year in question.

No attempt is made to render the totals exactly comparable in either extensiveness or intensiveness of coverage. Coverage by the Census of Manufactures is assumed to be complete, because reports for *all* manufacturing industries are included; therefore, in the Note to Table II 4, the extensiveness or range of industries covered by each state sample is compared with the *universe* or total reported by the Census of Manufacturers. Intensiveness refers to the relative coverage by the state of particular industries. Here again, the totals from the United States Census are assumed to be the universe, and the totals reported by the state bureaus are compared with them.

Certain major adjustments for differences in the content of state and federal totals have been made, however. For example, since the Census includes railroad repair shops and the illuminating gas industry, while the state bureaus usually exclude them, the totals for these industries were subtracted from the United States Census total for each census year. Custom and repair shops and hand trades, included in the United States Census in 1889, have been also subtracted whenever possible. The adjustment was crude; only industries classified completely as custom or repair shops or hand trades were subtracted; those in which custom or repair or hand work was combined with manufacturing could not be apportioned, for there was no satisfactory basis for dividing the reported census data. Since we have little direct information on the policies followed by the state agencies in 1889, it can be said merely that the coverage percentages may be slightly understated.

* In 1919 and 1909 the extensiveness of coverage by the state agency and the United States Census was approximately the same. Pennsylvania's intensiveness of coverage rose sharply from 1909 to 1919, however. In 1904 and 1899 coverage was considerably poorer than in the later years. Also, the state sample, emphasizing reports for identical establishments, does not adequately depict the steady growth in total manufactures.

† For Ohio the extensiveness of coverage by the two agencies was roughly similar; intensiveness of coverage by the state increased considerably from 1899 to 1904. In 1889 the state reported data for scattered establishments; no comparison was possible.

‡ As Massachusetts accepted the United States Census industry totals for 1919, 1914, and 1909, no correction was made in either total, since it could not affect the comparison in any way. In 1904, 1899, and 1889 the Massachusetts Bureau of Statistics covered fewer establishments but still covered all industries. Since totals for identical establishments for each two consecutive years were reported, the intensiveness of coverage changed once every two years.

§ The New Jersey reports failed to cover any food industries other than breweries, canning, confectionery, and 'food products.' Although the last-mentioned industry included several reported separately by the United States Census, its scope was not broad enough to cover all food products; this deficiency accounts for the major portion of the difference between the state and federal totals. Moreover, intensive coverage by the state agency is slightly narrower.

‖ Missouri accepted the United States Census totals for 1914 and 1909. Differences for

1914 are due to minor revisions of the data by the state agency. Before 1909 its reports were incomplete in all respects. The probability that it included small establishments not covered by the United States Census in 1919 accounts for the slight excess it reported.

¶ For Connecticut the United States Census reported more establishments in most industries and also covered more industries.

** Only 10 industries were reported for Rhode Island by the state agency: cotton goods; hosiery and knit goods; silk goods; woolen and worsted goods; jewelry and silversmithing; rubber and elastic goods; dyeing and finishing, textiles; jewelers' findings; refining, gold and silver; electroplating, enameling, engraving and die-sinking. In 1909, however, the last 2 were not included, and intensiveness of coverage in the remaining 8 was considerably reduced.

†† For Virginia coverage of industries was similar 1904–19. The United States Census reported more establishments in all years. In 1899 the state agency reported fewer industries.

‡‡ The comments in the General Note concerning custom and repair shops and the hand trades do not entirely apply here. Adjustments were made in 1889, separately for each industry affected, to remove all such work on the basis of the 1899 overlap. Such a procedure could not be followed for the individual states because detailed revised 1899 figures were lacking. If the figures collected by the state agencies are assumed to include some custom and repair work, the percentage given here for 1889 is a little too high. But the effect of this lack of comparability, if it exists, is so slight as not to modify the interpretation of the 1889 percentage in the text.

NOTE TO TABLE II 4

Description of the State Reports

The following descriptions include the title of the report in which the data are published,[a] the years for which the reports are available, and a summary of pertinent information concerning the reliability, continuity, and usability of the data.

PENNSYLVANIA

Calendar year figures were published in the *Annual Report of the Bureau of Statistics and Information,* Department of Labor and Industry, 1892–1912. No report was published for 1913, 1914, or 1915. In 1919 the first annual *Report on Productive Industries,* published by the Bureau of Statistics and Information, Department of Internal Affairs, contained data for 1916–19.

For 1892–94, 381 identical establishments in 51 industries were reported; 1896–1905, 710 identical establishments in 84 industries. For neither period was the coverage good, extensively or intensively. From 1906 to 1912 coverage improved decidedly, additional establishments and industries being canvassed each year. But even by 1912 not much more than half the manufactured products of the state were covered, and several important industries, including the entire food group, were still completely omitted. For 1916–19, however, coverage was almost complete and the 1919 state and federal nearly identical.

There are several major breaks in comparability. The first, in 1896, together with the inadequacies of many of the figures reported for the '90's, made the use of data before 1899 inadvisable except for a few minor groups mentioned specifically in Table 5. That in 1906 was marked enough to suggest the un-

[a] The titles of the state reports vary somewhat from year to year. To simplify the presentation we usually give the title of the 1909 report (for Connecticut, 1908).

desirability of using the 1905 data. Consequently 1899–1904 was treated as a unit, and new series were started in 1906. The final break, evidenced by non-publication of reports for three years, was naturally disastrous for the continuity of the sample. Moreover, the lack of comparability between the figures collected for 1912 and 1916 made it impossible to construct satisfactory estimates for the missing years.

OHIO

Calendar year figures were published in the *Annual Report of the Bureau of Labor Statistics* to the General Assembly of the State of Ohio, 1893–1912. The data for selected industries reported between 1885 and 1892 were too scattered to inspire any confidence.

One serious break, which caused the value of products reported to increase approximately 60 percent from 1900 to 1901, was discovered. The 1901 report, attributing this "to the amended law enacted by the Legislature at its last session", stated that in 1901 (and consequently later years) the Bureau sought statistics from large and small concerns alike whereas previously it had collected data from large concerns alone.[b] Owing to this break, it was necessary to study carefully the figures reported for 1900, 1901, and 1902, industry by industry.[c] Significant variations were discovered in examining wages paid and number of wage earners as well as number of establishments and value of product. For a few industries the data for all three years seemed comparable, but for most the 1900 figure had to be omitted, leaving two periods, 1893–99 and 1901–12. The data for the first period had to be examined further to remove industries reflecting obvious errors or inconsistencies.

Even after 1901 the coverage of the state agency was considerably less than that of the federal census, owing to the almost complete omission of most paper and printing industries and to the failure to include very small establishments.

MASSACHUSETTS

Calendar year figures were published, 1886–1919, in the *Annual Report on the Statistics of Manufactures* by the Director of the Bureau of Statistics. The annual reports were supplemented by complete state censuses of manufactures for 1885, 1895, and 1905.

For 1886–1906 figures were presented for identical establishments by pairs of years, giving two sets of figures for each year, the one comparable with the preceding year, the other with the following. The construction of a single series from the original data is described in Note A to Table 5. The intensity of coverage gradually increased so that by 1906 "the returns made each year had come to approximate 90 percent of completeness of the canvass made in census

---

[b] *Annual Report of Ohio Bureau of Labor Statistics, 1901*, pp. 7, 8.
[c] In several industries the full effect of the change in collection methods was not apparent until 1902. Consequently both 1901 and 1902 had to be omitted.

years (and for the leading industries were quite as complete in the non-census as in the census years)".[d] Because of this approach to completeness, all returns received were published beginning with 1907 instead of returns for identical establishment alone. However, there was a partial break between 1907 and 1908 owing to the adoption of the federal system of classification in the latter year. Until 1907 Massachusetts used its own system of industry classification, which was somewhat less detailed than that of the United States Census. For most industries the classifications could be matched well enough to set up continuous series. The few minor groups for which two distinct series, one for 1889–1907 and the other for 1909–19, had to be used are mentioned in the footnotes of Note A to Table 5. For 1909–19 the state agency achieved practically complete coverage and, in consequence, accepted the United States census data for 1909, 1914, and 1919 as fully comparable with and in place of the state canvas.

New Jersey

Calendar year figures were published, 1897–1916, in the *Annual Report of the Bureau of Statistics of Labor and Industry*. The scattered figures given in several reports between 1880 and 1896 were not reliable enough to justify their use for interpolation.

No important break was found in the figures, coverage remaining at about 75 percent of the federal census throughout the period. Comparison of state and federal data for census years revealed that the other 25 percent was probably composed of food industries, many of which were not included in the state totals at all, and numerous "petty" establishments not canvassed by the state. That the omission of "petty" establishments and of such industries as bread and bakery products was deliberate is suggested by the contention in the 1906 report that the presentation is a complete annual census of the "real" factories of the state, but does not include a vast number of "petty" concerns.[e]

Missouri

Calendar year figures were published, 1896–1910, and 1914–19, in the *Annual Report of the Bureau of Labor Statistics*.[f] Some reports between 1890 and 1895 contained scattered noncontinuous figures for fiscal years ending June 30. For 1911, 1912, and 1913 no state-wide data were published. The figures given for a few of the larger cities were not thought sufficiently dependable for use as an index of state output.

Two breaks occurred in the Missouri data. The first, evidenced by a sudden improvement in both extensive and intensive coverage between 1900 and 1901, necessitated the use of separate series for 1902–09 except for a few in-

[d] *Annual Report on the Statistics of Manufactures,* 1909, p. xxx.
[e] *Annual Report of the Bureau of Statistics of Labor and Industries of New Jersey,* 1907, pp. ix, x.
[f] Sometimes entitled the *Missouri Red Book*. The state agency was called the Missouri Bureau of Labor Statistics and Inspection in the earlier years.

dustries specified in the footnotes of Note A to Table 5. Coverage increased gradually, reaching 100 percent by 1909, when the federal figures were accepted by the state. The second and more important break, in 1911, compelled the abandonment of all the Missouri figures for the inter-censal period 1909–14 except those for the boot and shoe industry, for which special data were available. For 1914–19 the state coverage was apparently slightly higher than the federal, probably because some very small establishments were included.

CONNECTICUT

Fiscal year figures for years ending November 30 (1889–91, 1900–04, and 1906) were published in the *Annual Report of the Bureau of Labor Statistics.* Data for 1900–04 alone were usable for interpolation. Although state coverage was far from complete, it remained fairly constant throughout the period.

RHODE ISLAND

Calendar year figures 1893–1900 and 1904–10 for selected industries were published in the *Annual Report of the Commissioner of Industrial Statistics* to the General Assembly. Ten industries were reported in the earlier period, and such of these as fit into our minor group classifications were used 1893–99. In the later period only 8 industries were reported continuously. Moreover, a break occurred in 1906 when the state agency undertook to present figures for identical establishments alone. Although there was an overlap in 1906 that made it possible to splice the various series, the movement 1904–06 is for nonidentical establishments, while that for 1906–09 is for identical. Since the Rhode Island figures were applicable to only 3 minor groups, their influence on the interpolation samples is slight.

VIRGINIA

Calendar year figures 1897 and 1899–1919 were published in the *Annual Report of the Bureau of Labor and Industrial Statistics.* Before 1904 the data were for principal industries reported in alternate years and could not be used for interpolation.

No important breaks were noted in the data, and most of the industries could consequently be used for the entire period 1904–19. Coverage was extended, however, between 1909 and 1919 by the addition of several industries. Moreover, between 1914 and 1919 a gradual increase in intensive coverage was observed.

TABLE II 5

Value of Product, Selected Industries,
Reported by United States Census of Manufactures and by State Agencies, 1909
(thousands of dollars)

	CENSUS TOTAL (1)	STATE (2)	CENSUS TOTAL FOR STATE (3)	RANK OF STATE IN 1909 CENSUS (4)	TOTAL REPORTED BY STATE AGENCIES (5)	% STATE IS OF CENSUS (6)
Bread & other bakery products	396,865	Mass.	26,146	4	26,146	6.6
		Ohio	23,007	5	15,520	3.9
Confectionery	134,796	Mass.	15,266	2	15,266	11.3
		Ohio	7,307	5	6,697	5.0
Liquors, distilled	204,699	Ohio	12,011	5	9,642	4.7
Liquors, malt	374,730	Mo.	27,447	5	27,447	7.3
Mineral & soda waters	43,508	Mass.	2,193	4	2,193	5.0
Slaughtering & meat packing	1,370,568	Mo.	79,581	5	79,581	5.8
Flavoring extracts	8,114	Mass.	931	4	931	11.5
Flour-mill & grist-mill products	883,584	Ohio	48,093	5	32,081	3.6
Ice, mfd.	42,953	Ohio	2,270	5	1,471	3.4
Salt	11,328	Ohio	1,807	3	757	6.7
Pipes, tobacco	5,312	Mo.	396	3	396	7.5
Tobacco mfrs.	416,695	Mo.	30,951	4	30,951	7.4
		Ohio	28,907	5	21,720	5.2
Blacking & cleansing & polishing preparations	14,679	Mass.	3,713	2	3,713	25.3
Soap	111,358	Ohio	17,077	3	20,719[a]	18.6[a]
		N.J.	13,674	4	20,641[a]	18.5[a]
		Penn.	9,124	5	7,077	6.4
Printing & publishing	737,876	Ohio	41,657	5	22,224	3.0
Buttons	22,708	N.J.	2,750	3	3,440	15.1
Cotton goods, incl. cotton small wares	628,392	Mass.	186,462	1	186,462	29.7
		R.I.	50,313	4	15,650	2.5
Dyeing & finishing textiles	83,556	N.J.	15,796	2	18,343	22.0
		R.I.	13,956	3	4,459	5.3
Fancy articles, n.e.s.	22,632	Mass.	6,618	2	6,619	29.2
Leather goods[d]	18,838	Mass.	1,581	5	1,581	8.4
Silk & silk goods, incl. throwsters	196,912	N.J.	65,430	1	53,764	27.3
		Penn.	62,061	2	60,750	30.9
		Mass.	8,942	5	8,942	4.5

208

Woolen, worsted & felt goods, & wool hats	435,979	Mass.	141,967	1	32.6
		Penn.	77,447	2	11.5
		R. I.	74,600	3	10.6
		N. J.	33,939	4	7.6
Clothing, men's, incl. shirts	568,077	Ohio	24,869	5	3.7[b]
Clothing, women's	384,752	Ohio	19,493	3	[b]
		Mass.	11,728	5	3.0
Corsets	33,257	Mass.	3,752	4	11.3
		N. J.	3,336	5	10.8
Furnishing goods, men's	87,710	Ohio	4,623	4	3.9
Hats & caps, other than felt, straw, & wool	13,689	Penn.	1,097	2	[c]
		Mass.	659	5	[c]
Hats, fur-felt	47,865	Penn.	13,023	1	13,567[c]	22.0[c]
		N. J.	8,825	4	9,073	19.0
		Mass.	3,746	5	3,746	7.8
Hats, straw	21,424	Mass.	6,589	2	6,589	30.8
Hosiery & knit goods	200,144	Penn.	49,658	2	29,554	14.8
		Mass.	14,736	3	14,724	7.4
Millinery & lace goods	85,894	Mass.	3,977	5	3,977	4.6
Umbrellas & canes	15,864	Penn.	5,060	2	3,723	23.5
Boots & shoes	442,631	Mass.	187,046	1	187,046	42.3
		Mo.	35,410	3	35,410	8.0
		Ohio	28,771	5	28,870	6.5
Boots & shoes, rubber	49,721	Mass.	18,722	1	18,722	3.8
Brooms	14,432	Penn.	1,261	3	235	1.6
		Ohio	1,079	4	[e]	[e]
Brushes	14,694	Mass.	2,875	2	2,875	19.6
		N. J.	1,564	3	418	2.8
Window shades & fixtures	18,571	Ohio	1,219	4	1,670[e]	5.7[e]
Carriages & sleds, children's	8,805	N. J.	1,155	4	347	1.9
Sporting & athletic goods	11,052	Mass.	1,755	2	1,755	19.9
Toys & games	8,264	Mass.	2,510	2	2,510	22.7
Furniture & refrigerators	239,887	Penn.	1,751	2	1,751	21.2
Stoves & furnaces, incl. gas & oil stoves	78,853	Ohio	18,952	4	13,033	5.4
			15,358	1	11,316	14.4

209

	CENSUS TOTAL (1)	STATE (2)	CENSUS TOTAL FOR STATE (3)	RANK OF STATE IN 1909 CENSUS (4)	TOTAL REPORTED BY STATE AGENCIES (5)	% STATE IS OF CENSUS (6)
Carpets & rugs, other than rag	71,188	Penn.	24,879	2	26,065	36.6
		Mass.	12,812	3	12,812	18.0
		N. J.	1,945	4	1,945	2.7
Oilcloth & linoleum	23,339	N. J.	10,143	1	10,292	44.1
Looking glass & picture frames	13,475	Ohio	879	4	695	5.2
Mattresses & spring beds	35,783	Ohio	3,307	2	2,808	7.8
		Mass.	2,227	4	2,227	6.2
		Penn.	2,223	4	1,296	3.6
Cutlery & edge tools[d]	22,885	Mass.	4,391	5	4,391	19.2
		N. J.	2,014	4	1,198	5.2
Glass, cutting, staining, & ornamenting	92,095	N. J.	883	4	424	0.5
Pottery, terra cotta & fire clay products	76,119	Ohio	21,173	1	12,234	16.1
		N. J.	13,139	2	7,370	9.7
Musical instruments, pianos & organs & materials	89,790	Mass.	4,957	3	4,957	5.5
Clocks & watches, incl. cases & materials	35,197	N. J.	3,848	4	3,615	10.3
		Ohio	2,873	5	2,446	6.9
Silverware & plated ware	42,229	Mass.	6,539	3	6,539	15.5
		R. I.	6,198	4	5,983	14.2
		N. J.	3,035	5	2,725	6.5
Jewelry	80,350	R. I.	20,685	1	6,024	7.5
		Mass.	15,211	3	15,211	18.9
		N. J.	13,272	4	10,853	13.5
Trunks & valises[s]	28,028	Penn.	2,859	2	1,013	3.6
		Va.	2,551	4	2,265	8.1
Carriages & wagons & materials	159,893	Ohio	21,949	1	16,257	10.2
		Penn.	12,748	5	3,371	2.1
Bicycles, motorcycles & parts	10,699	Mass.	2,706	1	2,706	25.3
		Ohio	2,308	2	2,682	25.1
Optical goods	11,735	Mass.	3,058	2	3,058	26.1
Marble & stone work	113,093	Mass.	7,804	4	7,805	6.9
Foundry & machine shop products[d]	883,948	Ohio	125,521	2	125,729f	14.2
		Mass.	71,967	5	71,967	8.1
Electrical machinery, apparatus, & supplies	221,309	Penn.	31,351	2	17,215	7.8
		N. J.	28,365	3	15,650	7.1
		Mass.	28,143	4	28,143	12.7
Agri. implements	146,329	Ohio	14,440	3	10,464	7.2

210

Industry		State				
Pumps, excl. steam pumps	5,583	Ohio	2,747	1	1,890	33.9
Wirework, incl. wire rope & cable	41,938	Mo.	3,396	4	3,396	8.1
Safes & vaults	8,491	Ohio	5,488	1	3,782	44.5
		Penn.	1,338	2	2,913	34.3
Locomotives	31,582	Penn.	g		14,892	47.2
Cars, steam-rr., excl. operations of rr. companies	123,730	Penn.	27,510	1	31,417	25.4
		Ohio	6,451	4	2,100[h]	1.6 [h]
Cars, street-rr., excl. operations of rr. companies	7,810	Ohio	1,955	1		[h]
Shipbuilding, incl. boat building	73,360	N.J.	8,841	2	8,681	11.8
		Mass.	6,996	3	1,848[i]	2.5
		Penn.	6,178	4	5,581	7.6
Instruments, professional & scientific	10,504	Mass.	864	4	864	8.2
Tools, n.e.s.[d]	30,381	Mass.	7,219	1	7,219	23.8
		Ohio	4,648	2	7,772	25.6
		Penn.	3,798	3	3,246	10.7
Awnings, tents & sails	14,499	Mo.	1,784	2	1,784	12.3
		Ohio	1,387	3	1,465	10.1
		Mass.	886	3	886	6.1
Emery & other abrasive wheels	6,711	Mass.	1,982	5	1,982	29.5
		Ohio	670	4	341	3.8
Models & patterns, excl. paper patterns	8,868	Mass.	625	5	625	7.0
Signs & advertising novelties	13,546	Ohio	2,598	2	2,474	18.3
Saddlery & harness[d]	54,225	Ohio	4,934	1	4,186	7.7
Brick & tile	92,777	Ohio	9,358	2	12,886	13.9
Cement	63,205	Penn.	18,855	1	15,692	24.8
Gas & electric fixtures & lamps & reflectors	45,057	N.J.	5,771	3	7,359	16.3
Paint & varnish	124,889	Penn.	14,020	3	2,166	1.7
		Ohio	13,617	4	10,829	8.7
		N.J.	12,767	5	9,293	7.4
Roofing materials	19,204	Ohio	3,900	1	6,082	31.7
		N.J.	2,285	4	2,238	11.7
Iron & steel bolts, nuts, washers, & rivets, not made in steel works or rolling mills	24,485	Mass.	2,427	4	2,427	9.9
Iron & steel, nails & spikes, cut & wrought, incl. wire nails not made in steel works or rolling mills	8,192	Mass.	2,928	1	2,928	35.7
Structural iron work[a]	133,241	Penn.	29,846	1	20,133	15.1
		Ohio	18,920	2	6,862	5.2
Plumbers' supplies[a]	43,687	Ohio	5,155	3	4,226	9.7
Steam fittings & heating apparatus[a]	54,084	Mass.	5,948	5	5,948	11.0

Notes to Table II 5

aThe Ohio total includes candles and tallow; the New Jersey total, tallow; since the total United States production of candles and tallow is less than $5 million, the amount of both included in the totals must be negligible. The Ohio and New Jersey values are therefore expressed as percentages of the Census of Manufactures total for soap alone.

bThe Ohio total for clothing, men's, included women's clothing; the figure shown is the percentage that that total (35,056) is of the Census of Manufactures total for all clothing (952,829).

cPennsylvania combined fur-felt hats with hats and caps other than felt, straw and wool; the state total is therefore taken as a percentage of the combined Census of Manufactures total.

dThis is one of several industries for which the 1909 Census of Manufactures reported no totals for the separate states. State totals were available, however, for each of these industries combined with one or more related industries. E.g., leather goods, n.c.s., trunks and valises, and saddlery and harness were combined in the Census tables showing value of products by states; boots and shoes included cut stock and findings; cutlery and tools, n.c.s. were combined; and foundry and machine shop products included structural iron work, plumbers' supplies, and steam fittings and heating apparatus.

In 1914 all these industries were shown separately and were also reported by states. The rank in 1914 of the states in each industry was used for 1909, as was the percentage that each state constituted of the total value of products for the nation. The 1914 percentages were then applied to 1909 industry totals to derive approximate census values for five of the seven states in the sample. Since both Massachusetts and Missouri accepted the U. S. Census in 1909, and usually presented separate values for the industries combined by the federal agency, no estimates had to be made and figures from these two states were entered in both columns 3 and 5.

eOhio reported brooms and brushes as a single item. The state total is therefore expressed as a percentage of the federal total for brooms and brushes.

fThis total includes foundry products valued at $76,261,000. These unfinished commodities were included to make the state total comparable with the U. S. total for the state.

gThe U. S. Census did not give a division by states; this industry is used in the comparison because Pennsylvania produces a very substantial proportion of the nation's locomotives.

hThe Ohio total is for all cars and furnishings; it is expressed as a percentage of the Census of Manufactures total for steam and street railroad cars.

iThis total is for wooden shipbuilding only; the state includes steel shipbuilding with all other industries.

212

Table II 6
Composition of Interpolating Series by Minor Commodity Groups

MINOR COMMODITY GROUP	1889–1899	1899–1904	1904–1909	1909–1914	1914–1919
		PERISHABLE			
1 Food & kindred products Series used	Natural mineral waters; rice; peanuts; butter; cheese; condensed & evaporated milk; coffee imports; slaughtering; sugar meltings	Ohio; Mass.; N.J.; Mo.	Ohio; Mass.; N.J.; Mo.; Va.	Ohio; Mass.; N.J.; Va.	Pa.; Mass.; Mo.; Va.
Complementary series	Mass.	Natural mineral waters, rice, peanuts, butter, cheese, condensed & evaporated milk, coffee in all years together with ICC tonnage for sugar, dressed meat, other packing house products & flour 1899–1919 & production of canned tomatoes, peas & corn 1909–19, multiplied by appropriate prices			
2 Cigars, cigarettes & tobacco Series used	Quantity production of cigarettes, fine-cut tobacco, cigars weighing more than 3 lb. per M, little cigars, smoking tobacco, plug & twist tobacco, & snuff multiplied by appropriate prices				
	Ohio; Mass.	Pa.; Ohio; Mass.; N.J.; Mo.	Ohio; Mass.; N.J.; Mo.; Va.	Ohio; Mass.; N.J.; Va.	Pa.; Mass.; N.J.; Mo.
Complementary series					
3 Drug, toilet & household preparations Series used	Mass.	Ohio; Mass.; N.J.; Mo.	Pa.; Ohio; Mass.; N.J.; Mo.	Pa.; Ohio; Mass.; N.J.	Pa.; Mass.; Mo.
4 Magazines, newspapers, stationery & supplies & misc. paper products Series used	Mass.	Pa.; Ohio; Mass.; N.J.	Ohio; Mass.; N.J.; Va.	Pa.; Mass.; N.J.; Va.	Pa.; Mass.; N.J.; Mo.; Va.
5a Fuel & lighting products, mfd. Series used Complementary series		Coke sold for domestic purposes; production of crude petroleum Lubricating oil; kerosene; gasoline			
		SEMIDURABLE			
6 Dry goods & notions Series used	Pa.; Mass.; R.I.	Pa.; Mass.; N.J.; Conn.	Pa.; Mass.; N.J.; R.I.; Va.	Pa.; Mass.; N.J.; Va.	Pa.; Mass.; N.J.; Va.
7 Clothing & personal furnishings Series used	Pa.; Ohio; Mass.; R.I.	Pa.; Ohio; Mass.; N.J.; Conn.	Pa.; Ohio; Mass.; N.J.; Mo.; R.I.; Va.	Pa.; Ohio; Mass.; N.J.; Va.	Pa.; Mass.; N.J.; Mo.; Va.
8 Shoes & other footwear Series used	Ohio; Mass.; Mo.	Pa.; Ohio; Mass.; N.J.; Mo.	Pa.; Ohio; Mass.; N.J.; Mo.; Va.	Pa.; Ohio; Mass.; N.J.; Mo.; Va.	Pa.; Mass.; N.J.; Mo.

MINOR COMMODITY GROUP	1889–1899	1899–1904	1904–1909	1909–1914	1914–1919
9 House furnishings (semidurable) Series used	Pa.; Mass.	Pa.; Mass.; N.J.	Pa.; Ohio; Mass.; N.J.	Pa.; Ohio; Mass.; N.J.	Pa.; Mass.; N.J.
Complementary series			ICC tonnage for household goods & furniture		
10 Toys, games & sporting goods Series used	Mass.	Mass.	Mass.	Mass.	Pa.; Mass. Exports of firearms
11 Tires & tubes Series used	Movement of combined automobile & bicycle series	Ohio; N.J.	Ohio; Mass.; N.J.	Renewals of automobile casings multiplied by BLS rubber tire price relatives Mass.; N.J.
Complementary series					
		CONSUMER DURABLE			
12 Household furniture Series used	Ohio; Mass.	Ohio; Mass.; Mo.	Ohio; Mass.; Mo.; Va.	Ohio; Mass.; Va.	Pa.; Mass.; Mo.; Va.
Complementary series			ICC tonnage for household goods & furniture		
13a Heating and cooking apparatus & household appliances, except electrical Series used	Pa.; Ohio; Mass.	Pa.; Ohio; Mass.; N.J.; Mo.	Ohio; Mass.; N.J.; Mo.; Va.	Ohio; Mass.; N.J.; Va.	Pa.; Mass.; N.J.; Mo.; Va.
13b Electrical household appliances & supplies Series used		Pa.; Ohio; Mass.; N.J.; Mo.	Pa.; Ohio; Mass.; N.J.; Mo.	Pa.; Ohio; Mass.; N.J.	Pa.; Mass.; N.J.; Mo.
14a Floor coverings Series used	Pa.; Mass.	Pa.; Mass.; N.J.	Pa.; Mass.; N.J.	Pa.; Mass.; N.J.	Pa.; Mass.; N.J.
14b Misc. house furnishings (durable) Series used	Pa.; Mass.	Pa.; Ohio; Mass.; N.J.; Conn.	Pa.; Ohio; Mass.; N.J.	Pa.; Ohio; Mass.; N.J.	Pa.; Mass.; N.J.
Complementary series			ICC tonnage for household goods & furniture		
15 China & household utensils Series used	Pa.; Mass.	Pa.; Mass.; N.J.; Conn.	Pa.; Mass.; N.J.	Ohio; N.J.	Pa.; Mass.; N.J.
		Red earthenware; stoneware & yellow & Rockingham ware; white ware, incl. C. C. ware; china, bone china, delft & belleek ware; misc. pottery			
16 Musical instruments Series used	Pa.; Mass.	Pa.; Ohio; Mass.; N.J.; Conn.	Ohio; Mass.; N.J.	Ohio; Mass.; N.J.	Pa.; Mass.; N.J.; Mo.
Complementary series				Sales of two piano companies	
17 Jewelry, silverware, clocks & watches Series used	Mass.	Ohio; Mass.; N.J.; Conn.	Ohio; Mass.; N.J.; Mo.; R.I.	Ohio; Mass.; N.J.	Pa.; Mass.; N.J.; Mo.

18	Printing & publishing: books Series used	**Mass.**	Ohio; Mass.; N.J.; Mo.	Ohio; Mass.; N.J.; Mo.	Ohio; N.J.		Pa.; Mass.; N.J.; Mo.
19	Luggage Series used	Mass.	Ohio; Mass.; N.J.; Mo.			Pa.; Ohio; Mass.; N.J.; Mo.; Va.	Mass.; N.J.; Mo.; Va.
20a	Passenger motor vehicles Series used				Factory sales, passenger cars		
20b	Motor vehicles accessories Series used				Factory sales, passenger cars		
20c	Passenger vehicles, carriages & wagons Series used	Ohio; Mass.; Mo.	Ohio; Mass.; N.J.; Mo.; Conn.	Pa.; Ohio; Mass.; N.J.; Mo.; Va.	Pa.; Ohio; Mass.; N.J.; Va.	Pa.; Ohio; Mass.; N.J.; Va.	Pa.; Mass.; N.J.; Mo.; Va.
21	Motorcycles & bicycles Series used		Exports of bicycles & motorcycles		Ohio; Mass.		Exports of bicycles & production of Indian Motorcycle Co.
	Complementary series	Ohio; Mass.				Exports of bicycles & motorcycles	
22	Pleasure-craft Series used	Mass.	Mass.	Pa.; Mass.; N.J.	Pa.; Mass.; N.J.	Pa.; Mass.; N.J.	Pa.; Mass.; N.J.
23	Ophthalmic products & artificial limbs Series used			Movement of Minor Group 3		Mass.; N.J.	
24	Monuments and tombstones Series used				Granite monumental stone Mass.		Mass.
	Complementary series				Mass.		

PRODUCER DURABLE

25	Industrial machinery & equipment Series used	**Mass.**		Pa.; Ohio; Mass.; N.J.; Mo.; Conn.	Ohio; Mass.; N.J.; Mo.; Va.	Ohio; Mass.; N.J.; Va.	Pa.; Mass.; N.J.; Mo.
	Complementary series				Exports of machinery, n.e.s.		
26	Electrical equipment, industrial & commercial Series used	Mass.		Pa.; Ohio; Mass.; N.J.; Mo.	Pa.; Ohio; Mass.; Mo.	Pa.; Ohio; Mass.; N.J.	Pa.; Mass.; N.J.; Mo.
	Complementary series					Gross revenues of two companies	
27	Farm equipment Series used	**Pa.; Ohio; Mass.**		Pa.; Ohio; Mass.; N.J.; Mo.	Pa.; Ohio; Mass.; N.J.; Mo.; Va.	Pa.; Ohio; Mass.; N.J.; Va.	Pa.; N.J.; Mo.; Va.
	Complementary series						ICC tonnage of agricultural implements multiplied by BLS price relative

	MINOR COMMODITY GROUP	1889–1899	1899–1904	1904–1909	1909–1914	1914–1919
28	Office & store machinery & equipment Series used	Movement of Minor Group 25	Pa.; Ohio; Mass.; N.J.; Conn.	Ohio; Mass.; N.J.; Mo.; Va.	Ohio; Mass.; N.J.; Va.	Pa.; Mass.; N.J.; Mo.
29	Office & store furniture & fixtures Series used	Movement of Minor Group 12	Pa.; Ohio; Mass.; Mo.	Pa.; Ohio; Mass.; Mo.; Va.	Pa.; Ohio; Mass.; Va.	Pa.; Mass.; Mo.; Va.
30	Locomotive & rr. cars Series used Complementary series	Pa.; Mass.	Pa.; Ohio; Mass. Locomotives & cars built multiplied by available prices	Pa.; Ohio; Mass.	Pa.; Ohio	
31	Ships & boats Series used	Mass.	Mass.	Pa.; Mass.; N.J.	Pa.; Mass.; N.J.	Pa.; Mass.; N.J.
32a	Business motor vehicles Series used			Factory sales, motor trucks		
32b	Business wagons Series used	Ohio; Mass.; Mo.	Ohio; Mass.; N.J.; Mo.; Conn.	Pa.; Ohio; Mass.; N.J.; Mo.; Va.	Pa.; Ohio; Mass.; N.J.; Va.	Pa.; Mass.; N.J.; Mo.; Va.
33	Aircraft Series used Complementary series				Domestic consumption, incl. exports, multiplied by per unit prices of motor trucks Same series multiplied by export prices	
34	Professional & scientific equipment Series used	Movement of Minor Groups 25 & 26			Mass.; N.J.	Pa.; Mass.; N.J.
35	Carpenters' & mechanics' tools Series used	Pa.; Mass.	Pa.; Ohio; Mass.; N.J.	Pa.; Ohio; Mass.; N.J.	Ohio; Mass.; N.J.	Pa.; Mass.; N.J.
36	Misc. subsidiary durable equipment Series used	Mass.	Pa.; Ohio; Mass.; Mo.	Ohio; Mass.; Mo.	Ohio; Mass.	Pa.; Mass.; Mo.
	Construction materials Series used	Roofing slate; building lime; cement; structural stone; cut & wire nails; iron & steel rails; softwood production, lath and shingle.	Roofing slate; building lime; mfd. asphalt; building stone; paving stone; stone curbing; stone flagging; rubble; riprap; crushed railroad ballast, concrete and road metal; building sand; paving sand; sand railroad ballast; gravel; sand-lime brick; common brick; vitrified brick; face brick; fancy or ornamental brick; enameled brick; architectural terra cotta; hollow building tile and fireproofing; tile, not drain; drain-tile; sewer pipe; sanitary ware; softwood production, lath and shingles; structural shapes; concrete bars; cut & wire nails; iron & steel rails; pipe, butt & lap welded			
				Chemical stoneware, millstones, grindstones, oilstones		
	Complementary series	Ohio; Mass.	Pa.; Ohio; Mass.; N.J.; Mo.; Conn.	Pa.; Ohio; Mass.; N.J.; Mo.; Va.	Pa.; Ohio; Mass.; N.J.; Va.	Pa.; Mass.; N.J.; Mo.; Va.

Note A to Table II 6

Industrial Composition of the State Series

This note describes in tabular form the composition of the state series used either as interpolating or complementary series. It lists the industries included during each intercensal period for every state for which usable data were available. To designate complementary series, used for corroboration alone, the letter (c) follows the minor group number of a series so used.

The asterisk after some of the industry titles within the various minor groups denotes that figures for the industry were available for a majority of years during the intercensal period but not for the entire period. In such cases the series excluding the industry was spliced to the one including the industry at the year it was first included.

1889–1899	1899–1904	1904–1909	1909–1914	1914–1919
		Minor Group I (c for 1889–99) [a]		
		PENNSYLVANIA		
	Bread & other bakery products*; canned goods*; chewing gum*; confectionery and ice cream*; dairy products*; flouring mill products*; ice (artificial)*; liquors, distilled*; liquors, malt*; pickles, preserves & sauces*; salt*; slaughtering & meat packing*; soda & mineral water*			

OHIO

| | | Same | Same* | |

MASSACHUSETTS [b]

| Food preparations; liquors, malt, distilled & fermented; liquors & beverages, not spirituous | Same | Same; butter*; canning & preserving, fish*; coffee & spice, roasting & grinding*; confectionery*; flavoring extracts*; flour & grist mill products*; pickles, preserves & sauces*; sausages*; slaughtering & meat packing, wholesale*; vinegar & cider*; bread & other bakery products*; cordials & sirups* | Same | Same; ice, mfd.; ice cream; chocolate & cocoa products |

Baking powder; bread & other bakery products; butter, cheese, & condensed milk; pickles; canned & preserved goods; chocolate & cocoa products; coffee & spices, roasting & grinding; confectionery; ice cream; cordials & sirups; flour & gristmill products; ice; slaughtering & meat packing; sugar refining; vinegar & cider; flavoring preparations; liquors, distilled; liquors, malt; table waters; butterine & oleomargarine; peanut products, caramels

217

1889–1899	1899–1904	1904–1909	1909–1914	1914–1919
	Brewing (beer, ale & porter); confectionery; food products; canning	Same	Same	
		NEW JERSEY		
	Bakery products; canning, preserving, pickling; candy, confections, gum; flour, feed, meal, cereals; grocers' sundries, n.e.s.; liquors, malt; packing house products	Same; carbonated beverages, soda; creamery & dairy products; grocers' sundries, n.e.s.*		Carbonated beverages, soda; baking powder, yeast; butterine, oleomargarine; coffee, roasting, grinding; creamery & dairy products; grocers' sundries, n.e.s.
		MISSOURI		
		VIRGINIA		
		Canneries, fruits & vegetables; flour & gristmill products; ice, artificial; pickles, vinegar, & apple cider; breweries	Same	Candy, chewing gum, etc.; canneries, fruits & vegetables; crabs, oysters, clams-packing; flour & gristmill products; ice, artificial; peanut cleaning, coffee roasters; pickles, vinegar & apple cider
		Minor Group 2 (c)		
	Cigars			
		PENNSYLVANIA		
Cigars*; tobacco, chewing and smoking*	Same	Same	Same*	Cheroots & stogies; chewing tobacco; cigars; cigarettes; smoking tobacco; pipes, tobacco
		OHIO		
Tobacco, snuff and cigars	Same	MASSACHUSETTS[b] Tobacco, cigars & cigarettes*; tobacco, chewing & smoking & snuff*; tobacco, snuff & cigars*	Tobacco, cigars & cigarettes*; tobacco, chewing & snuff*; tobacco mfrs.*	Tobacco mfrs.
		NEW JERSEY		
	Cigars & tobacco	Same	Same	
		MISSOURI		
	Corncob & wooden pipes; cigars, cigarettes, cheroots; tobacco, chewing & smoking	Same	Same*	
		VIRGINIA		
		Tobacco & its products; cigars, cigarettes & cheroots	Same	Corncob & wooden pipes; cigars, cigarettes, cheroots; tobacco, chewing & smoking

Minor Group 3

PENNSYLVANIA

Drugs, chemicals & druggists' sundries*; extracts, toilet articles & perfumery*; soap, candles & tallow

Tallow, candles, soap & grease; drugs & medicines; perfumes, toilet articles, etc.; polishes & dressings

OHIO

Same

Same

MASSACHUSETTS[b]

Soap*

Same*

Druggists' preparations; cleansing & polishing preparations; soap; patent medicines & compounds; blacking; perfumes, toilet articles, etc.

NEW JERSEY

Soap*

Same, excl. perfumes

Same; stains & dressing

MISSOURI

Cleansing & polishing preparations; patent & proprietary medicines; soap; toilet preparations; surgical appliances

Same

Drugs, chemicals, patent compounds; cleansing & polishing preparations; liquid soap

Minor Group 4

PENNSYLVANIA[a]

Chemical products; soap & tallow

Drugs, chemicals, patent compounds; soap, candles, washing preparations

Paper mill goods, not specified

Inks

Paper & paper goods; crayons, pencils, crucibles, etc.; ink, mucilage & paste

Inks & mucilage; paper

OHIO

Same

Same

Glue and gelatin*; paper mill goods, not specified*

Inks

Same

Same

MASSACHUSETTS[b]

Same; ink, writing; mucilage & paste; stationery goods, not specified; pens & pencils

Same; stationery goods, n.e.s.*; bookbinding & blank-bookmaking*

NEW JERSEY

Paper goods, n.e.s.; bookbinding & blank-bookmaking; mucilage & paste; stationery goods, n.e.s.; envelopes; glue, isinglass

Same

Same

MISSOURI

Same*

Stationery supplies, paper goods, n.e.s.; envelopes

	1889–1899	1899–1904	1904–1909	1909–1914	1914–1919
VIRGINIA	Same		Paper & pulp mill products; stationery & printing	Same	Stationery & printing
PENNSYLVANIA[a] *Minor Group 6*	Woolen & worsted fabrics*; lace goods & embroideries*; silk ribbons*; silk broadgoods*		Silk & silk goods & throwsters; lace goods & embroideries	Same*, handkerchiefs & embroideries*	Handkerchiefs & embroideries; silk & silk goods; thread; woolen, worsted & felt goods; needles, pins, hooks & eyes; artificial flowers, feathers & plumes; buttons; fancy articles & specialties; flags, banners, regalia, emblems; hairwork; cotton goods
MASSACHUSETTS[b]	Linen*, mixed textiles*; silk & silk goods; cotton, woolen and other textiles*; woolen goods; straw and palm leaf goods; buttons & dress trimmings; fancy articles; hairwork; cotton goods; ivory, bone, shell & horn goods	Silk & silk goods; woolen goods; worsted goods; straw & palm leaf goods; buttons & dress trimmings; fancy articles; hairwork; cotton thread & yarn; woolen woven goods & yarn; ivory, bone, shell & horn goods; cotton goods	Same; cotton small wares*; linen goods*	Linen; silk & silk goods; woolen & worsted goods; fancy articles; buttons; cotton small wares; combs & hairpins; ivory, bone, shell & horn goods*	Same, excl. ivory, bone, shell & horn goods
NEW JERSEY	Buttons (ivory, metal & pearl*); silk (broad & ribbon goods); textile products; thread; cotton goods; woolen & worsted goods; cotton, finishing & dyeing; leather goods; silk dyeing		Same	Same; embroideries*	Same*
CONNECTICUT	Cotton goods*; silk goods*; dyeing & finishing textiles	Cotton goods*, cotton mills*; silk goods*			
RHODE ISLAND			Cotton goods*; silk goods*; dyeing & finishing textiles*		
VIRGINIA			Silk mill products; cotton goods	Same	Same

220

Minor Group 7

State					
Pennsylvania[a]	Hosiery; knit goods*; neckwear*; shirts*; suspenders*; underwear*; umbrellas; hats and caps*; wool hats*; fur & felt hats*	Same	Hats & caps, other than straw*; hosiery & knit goods*; underwear*; umbrellas and parasols*	Clothing, men's; clothing, women's & children's; corsets; fur goods; furnishing goods, not specified; gloves, other than leather; hats and caps, other than straw; hats, straw; hosiery & knit goods; ladies' shirts; millinery; neckwear; overalls; shirts; shirtwaists; suspenders; underwear; gloves, leather; umbrellas & parasols	
Ohio	Hats, caps and furnishings*; woolen goods*; clothing, men's*; clothing, ladies*; regalia*	Clothing*; cotton & woolen goods, knit & woven*; furs*; gloves & mittens*; hats, caps & furnishings*; regalia*	Same*		
Massachusetts[b]	Clothing; hosiery & knit goods; leather goods	Same	Hosiery & knit goods; clothing, men's; clothing, women's; corsets*; fur goods*; garters, suspenders, & hose supporters*; hats & caps, other than straw*; millinery*; neckwear*; shirts*; other clothing*; leather goods*; pocketbooks*	Same; hats, straw; furnishing goods, men's*	Same
New Jersey			Same; shirtwaists, women's; underwear, women's & children's	Same	Same, excl. clothing*	Clothing, men's & boys'; clothing, women's & children's; hats & caps, straw & felt; millinery & headwear, women's; furnishing goods, men's*
Missouri	Clothing; corsets & corset waists; hats (fur & felt); hats (straw); knit goods; shirts		Clothing, men's & boys'; clothing, women's & children's		
Connecticut	Corsets*; hosiery & knit goods*; hats & caps*; woolens & woolen mills*				
Rhode Island	Hosiery & knit goods*; woolen & worsted goods*	Same*			

1889–1899	1899–1904	1904–1909	1909–1914	1914–1919
		VIRGINIA		
		Knitting mill products; overalls, shirts & clothing; woolen mill products	Same	Same; hats & caps
		Minor Group 8		
		PENNSYLVANIA[a]		
Boots & shoes*	Boots & shoes	Same	Same*	Boots & shoes; boots & shoes, rubber
Same	Same	Same	Same*	
		OHIO		
Boots & shoes	Boots & shoes	Same	Boots & shoes; boots & shoes, rubber	Same
		MASSACHUSETTS[c]		
	Shoes	Shoes	Shoes	Shoes*
Boots & shoes, slippers & pumps	Same	Same	Same[d]	Same
		NEW JERSEY		
		MISSOURI[d]		
		VIRGINIA		
		Boots & shoes	Same	
		Minor Group 9		
		PENNSYLVANIA[a]		
Blankets, flannels, etc.*; cotton goods*; tapestry & table covers*	Blankets, flannels, etc.; cotton goods	Cotton goods; brooms*	Same*	Blankets, flannels, etc.; cotton goods; curtains; brooms; brushes; window shades & fixtures; towels
		OHIO		
		Brooms & brushes	Same*	
		MASSACHUSETTS[b]		
Cotton goods; brooms, brushes & mops	Same	Same; window shades & fixtures*	Same	Same
		NEW JERSEY		
Cotton goods; brushes	Cotton goods; brushes	Same	Same	Same*

222

Minor Group 10[e]

PENNSYLVANIA[a]	Sporting & athletic goods; toys & games (children's); firearms; fireworks	Same	Fireworks; billiard tables & supplies; children's carriages, sleds, etc.; sporting & athletic goods; toys & games
MASSACHUSETTS[b]		Same; billiard tables & materials*; carriages & sleds, children's*	Same, excl. firearms

Minor Group 11[f]

OHIO		Rubber goods	Rubber goods*
MASSACHUSETTS[b]		Rubber goods	Rubber goods, n.e.s.
NEW JERSEY		Rubber goods	Same	Same*

Minor Group 12

PENNSYLVANIA[a]	Furniture*	Furniture	Furniture*	Furniture
MASSACHUSETTS[b]	Furniture	Furniture	Furniture
MISSOURI	Furniture, rattan & willow goods	Same	Furniture, rattan & willow goods
VIRGINIA		Furniture, upholstering & caskets	Same	Same

Minor Group 13a

PENNSYLVANIA[a]	Stoves, heaters & ranges*; sewing machines*	Stoves, heaters & ranges		Washing machines & wringers; stoves, heaters & ranges; refrigerators

1889–1899	1899–1904	1904–1909	1909–1914	1914–1919
Stoves, ranges & furnaces*	Same	OHIO Same; clothes wringers, washboards, washing machines	Same*	
Cooking, lighting & heating apparatus	Same	MASSACHUSETTS[b] Same*; stoves & furnaces, excl. gas & oil stoves*	Stoves & furnaces, excl. gas & oil stoves; refrigerators	Same
	Furnaces, ranges & heaters	NEW JERSEY Same	Same	Same*
	Stoves, ranges, radiators, etc.	MISSOURI Same		Stoves, ranges, radiators, etc.
		VIRGINIA Stoves	Stoves	
	Supplies, electrical	*Minor Group 13bg* PENNSYLVANIA[a] Same	Same*	Same
	Electrical goods & supplies*	OHIO Same	Same*	
	Electrical apparatus & appliances	MASSACHUSETTS[h] Same*; electrical machinery, apparatus & supplies*	Electrical machinery, apparatus & supplies	Same
	Electrical appliances	NEW JERSEY Same	Same	Same*
	Electrical apparatus	MISSOURI Same		Electrical apparatus
Carpets*	Carpets; rugs, incl. yarns	*Minor Group 14a* PENNSYLVANIA[a] Carpets and rugs*; oilcloth and linoleum*	Same*	Same; mats & matting
Carpetings, textile & other	Same	MASSACHUSETTS[b] Same*; carpets & rugs, rag*; carpets & rugs, other than rag*	Same	Same

224

Carpets & rugs; oilcloth & linoleum	Same	NEW JERSEY Same	Same*	Lamps & chimneys; mirrors; beds & bed springs; awnings, tents & sails; mattresses & bedding; statuary & art goods

Minor Group 14b[1]
PENNSYLVANIA Mattresses & bedding*

Mouldings & frames*; mattresses & pillows*	Same	OHIO Same*	MASSACHUSETTS[b] House furnishing goods, n.e.s.; mattresses & spring beds; looking glass & picture frames; statuary & art goods; lamps & reflectors	Same; mirrors
Lamps; mattresses & bedding; window shades	Same; glass mirrors	NEW JERSEY Same	Same*	
Same, excl. pottery				

Minor Group 15[1]
PENNSYLVANIA

Glass, tableware*; pottery*; tinware*	Same	OHIO Cutlery & edge tools; glass & glassware; hollow ware	Same*	Cut glass; glass, tableware; aluminum & its products; cutlery; tin & stamped ware; enameled & galvanized ware
Glass; earthen, plaster & stone ware	Same	MASSACHUSETTS[k] Same*	NEW JERSEY Same; glass tableware	Woodenware, n.e.s.; glass, cutting, staining & ornamenting
Cutlery; wooden goods	Same	CONNECTICUT Same		Same*
Cutlery & tools*				

Minor Group 16
PENNSYLVANIA[a]

Pianos and organs*	Same	Musical instruments, not specified; pianos & organs

1889–1899	1899–1904	1904–1909	1909–1914	1914–1919
	Pianos & other musical instruments*	OHIO Same	Same*	
Musical instruments & materials	Same	MASSACHUSETTS[b] Same*; musical instruments & materials, n.e.s.*; musical instruments, organs*; musical instruments, pianos*	Musical instruments & materials, n.e.s.; musical instruments, pianos; musical instruments, organs	Same
	Musical instruments	NEW JERSEY Same	Same	Same*
	Musical instruments & parts*	MISSOURI CONNECTICUT		Musical instruments
		Minor Group 17 PENNSYLVANIA[a]		
	Jewelry & watches*	OHIO Same	Same*	
Clocks & watches; jewelry	Same	MASSACHUSETTS[b] Same*; jewelry*; silversmithing & silverware*; plated ware*	Jewelry; silversmithing & silverware; plated ware	Same
	Jewelry; silver goods; watches, cases & materials	NEW JERSEY Same	Same	Same*
		MISSOURI Jewelry, clocks & watches*	Jewelry, clocks & watches	Jewelry, clocks & watches
	Silver & plated ware*	CONNECTICUT RHODE ISLAND Jewelry*; silversmithing & silverware		Silverware & plated ware; watches & clocks; jewelry

226

Minor Group 18

PENNSYLVANIA[a]	OHIO	MASSACHUSETTS[k]	NEW JERSEY	MISSOURI		
Printing, publishing & bookbinding	Printing & binding*	Printing & binding	Printing & binding*	Same*	Same	Printing
	Same	Same*				publishing
	Printing & bookbinding	Same	Same			Printing and publishing, book & job*; printing & publishing*
	Printing, publishing, lithographing, bookbinding	Same*		Same*		Same*
						Printing, publishing, lithographing, bookbinding

Minor Group 19

PENNSYLVANIA[a]	OHIO	MASSACHUSETTS[b]	NEW JERSEY	MISSOURI	VIRGINIA	
Trunks & valises	Trunks & valises*	Trunks & suitcases*	Trunks & valises*			
	Same	Trunks & valises	Same			Same
	Trunks & traveling bags	Same	Same	Same*		Same*
	Trunks, valises, cases, etc.*	Same*			Trunks & bags	Trunks, valises, cases, etc.
					Same	Same

Minor Group 20c

PENNSYLVANIA[a]	OHIO	MASSACHUSETTS[b]	NEW JERSEY	MISSOURI		
Carriages & wagons*	Carriages & wagons*	Carriages, wagons & parts*	Carriages, wagons & wagons			Carriages, wagons & parts
Carriages & wagons	Same	Same*	Carriages & wagons			Same
Carriages & wagons	Carriages & wagons	Same	Same			Same*
Carriages, wagons & repairs	Same	Same*	Same	Same		Carriages, wagons & repairs*

1889–1899	1899–1904	1904–1909	1909–1914	1914–1919
	Carriages & carriage parts*	CONNECTICUT		
		Carriages, wagons, etc.	Same	
		Minor Group 21 (e)		
		OHIO		
Bicycles & bicycle sundries*		Bicycles & bicycle sundries	Same*	
Bicycles, tricycles, etc.*	Same	MASSACHUSETTS b		
		Same*	Bicycles, motorcycles & parts	
		Minor Group 22[1]		
		PENNSYLVANIA a		
		Steamship & boat building*	Same*	Same
Shipbuilding	Same	MASSACHUSETTS k		
		Same*; shipbuilding, wooden, incl. boat building*	Shipbuilding, wooden, incl. boat building	Same
		NEW JERSEY		
		Shipbuilding	Same	Same*
		Minor Group 23 m		
		MASSACHUSETTS	Surgical appliances	Surgical appliances; artificial limbs
	Stone, cut & monumental	*Minor Group 24* (e)		
		MASSACHUSETTS b		
		Stone, cut & monumental*	Monuments & tombstones	Monuments & tombstones
		Minor Group 25		
	Machinery & parts; steam pumps	PENNSYLVANIA a		Engines, gas & gasoline; engines, stationary; machinery & parts; gas meters; pumps & valves; elevators & hoists; machine tools
	Machinery; elevators	OHIO		
		Machinery; elevators	Machinery*; elevators*	
Machines & machinery	Same	MASSACHUSETTS b		
		Same*; foundry & machine shop products*	Foundry & machine shop products	Same; machine tools*; textile machinery & parts*

228

Machinery	Same	Same*
Foundry products: engines, etc.*	Same	Foundry products, engines, etc.
Machine shops*	**Connecticut**	
	Virginia	
	Iron & machinery	Same
Supplies, electrical	*Minor Group 26g*	
	Pennsylvania	
Electrical goods & supplies*	Same	Same*
	Ohio	
Same	Same	Same*
	Massachusetts[k]	
	Same*; electrical machinery, apparatus & supplies*	Electrical machinery, apparatus & supplies
Electrical appliances	**New Jersey**	
	Same	Same*
Electrical apparatus	**Missouri**	
	Same	Electrical apparatus
	Minor Group 27	
	Pennsylvania[a]	
Agricultural implements & machinery*; fences, railing & wire goods*	Same	Same*
	Ohio	
Agricultural implements*	Same	Same*
	Massachusetts[k]	
Agricultural implements	Same	Agricultural implements & machinery
	New Jersey	
Agricultural machinery & implements	Same	Same*
	Missouri	
Agricultural implements, silos, tractors, dairy apparatus	Same	Agricultural implements, silos, tractors, dairy apparatus
	Virginia	
	Agricultural implements	Same

229

1889–1899	1899–1904	1904–1909	1909–1914	1914–1919
		Minor Group 28[n]		
		PENNSYLVANIA[a]	Scales & balances	
	Scales	MASSACHUSETTS[b]		Scales, typewriters; soda water apparatus
		Typewriters & supplies	Same	Same*
		NEW JERSEY		
		Minor Group 29[o]		
		PENNSYLVANIA[a]		
	Safes & vault doors	Safes, vaults & locks	Same*	Same
		OHIO		
	Billiard tables, bars & store fixtures; safes, vaults & locks	Same	Same*	
		MASSACHUSETTS[b]		
		MISSOURI	Showcases	Showcases
		Bank, store & office fixtures*		
		Minor Group 30[p]		
		PENNSYLVANIA[a]		
Cars & car wheels*; locomotives, stationary engines, etc.*	Locomotives & cars, built & repaired; locomotives, stationery engines, etc.	Cars & car wheels; steam & electric locomotives	Same*	Cars & car wheels; engines, rr.
		OHIO		
	Cars & car furnishings*	Same	Same*	Same
Rr. construction & equipment	Same	MASSACHUSETTS[b]		
		Same*		
		Minor Group 31[q]		
		PENNSYLVANIA[a]		
		Steamship & boat building*	Same*	Same
		MASSACHUSETTS[k]		
Shipbuilding	Same	Same*; shipbuilding, wooden, incl. boat building*	Shipbuilding, wooden, incl. boat building	Same
		NEW JERSEY		
		Shipbuilding	Same	Same*

230

	Minor Group 32b		
	PENNSYLVANIA[a] Carriages, wagons & parts*	Carriages, wagons & parts*	Carriages, wagons & parts
Carriages & wagons*	Carriages & wagons*	OHIO Carriages & wagons	Same
Carriages & wagons	Same	MASSACHUSETTS[b] Same*	Same*
Carriages, wagons & repairs*	Carriages & wagons	NEW JERSEY Same	Carriages, wagons & repairs*
	Same	MISSOURI Same	
	Carriages & carriage parts*	CONNECTICUT Same	Same
		VIRGINIA Carriages, wagons, etc.	
		Minor Group 34[m] PENNSYLVANIA[a]	Instruments, professional & scientific
		MASSACHUSETTS Instruments, professional & scientific; optical goods	Instruments, professional & scientific
		NEW JERSEY Scientific instruments	Same*
		Minor Group 35 PENNSYLVANIA[a]	
Axes & edge tools; files*; saws*; shovels, scoops & spades*; wrenches, picks, etc.*	Same	Axes & edge tools; shovels, scoops & spades	Axes & edge tools; files; saws; shovels, scoops & spades
	Tools & implements	OHIO Same	Same*
Artisans' tools	Same	MASSACHUSETTS[b] Artisans' tools*; cutlery & edge tools*	Cutlery & edge tools; tools, n.e.s.; files*; saws*	Cutlery & tools, n.e.s.
	Artisans' tools	NEW JERSEY Same	Same*

231

1889–1899	1899–1904	1904–1909	1909–1914	1914–1919
		Minor Group 369 PENNSYLVANIA [a]		
	Cordage & twine, jute & linen goods			Crucibles; emery & other abrasive wheels; grindstones; belting, rubber; lasts; models & patterns, not paper; cordage & twine, jute & linen goods; handstamps, stencils & brands; photographic apparatus & supplies; enameled & electric signs; wheelbarrows; horse blankets; horse shoes
		OHIO		
	Advertising novelties & signs*; awnings, tents & sails; cordage & twine*; harness & saddlery*; patterns & models*; stencils, stamps & seals*; whips*	Same	Same*	
		MASSACHUSETTS [b]		
Cordage & twine; wooden goods; models, lasts & patterns; awnings, sails, tents, etc.; photographic materials & supplies; saddlery & harness; whips, lashes & stocks	Same	Same*	Cordage & twine; models & patterns, excl. paper patterns; emery wheels & other abrasive wheels; lasts; printing materials & type founding; awnings, sails, tents, etc.; saddlery & harness; hand stamps, stencils & brands; signs & adv. novelties; whips; photographic materials & supplies	Same, excl. emery wheels & other abrasive wheels
		MISSOURI		
	Awnings, tents, canvas; harness, saddlery, straps	Awnings, tents, canvas; harness, saddlery, straps*		Awnings, tents, canvas; patterns, models, lasts; photographic supplies
		Construction Materials [c] PENNSYLVANIA [a]		
	Iron and steel for bridges; plumbers' supplies; structural iron; wall paper; bath boilers and tanks	Cement*; glass, plate; glass, window; paints, white lead, etc.; structural iron	Same*	Cement; chandeliers & gas fixtures; glass, decorative; glass, plate; glass, window; mantels & tile; paints, white lead, etc.; planing mills & building material; plumbers' supplies; radiators & steam fitting; sky lights & cornices; structural iron; wall paper; granite & marble work; building paper & roofing material; tar; artificial stone; brick; lime; paving materials; pottery, terra cotta & fire-clay products; wall plaster; fire escapes; iron & steel work, ornamental

232

sand, cement, plaster*; paints & varnish*; roofing materials*; sash, doors, lumber*	cement*; lighting apparatus*; marble & granite*; paints & varnish*; plumbing, steam supplies*; roofing materials*; sash, doors, lumber*; stone, cut & sawed*	Same; copper, tin & sheet-iron products

MASSACHUSETTS[b]

Stone, quarried; brick, tile & sewer pipe; cement, kaolin, lime & plaster; building materials; paints & varnishes	Same	Iron & steel, bolts, nuts & rivets; iron & steel, spikes, nails, tacks, etc.; structural ironwork; lumber planing mill products, incl. sash, doors & blinds; brick & tile; lime; marble & stone work; plumbers' supplies; artificial stone; paints and varnishes; gas & electric fixtures; steam fittings & heating apparatus
	Same*	Same*

NEW JERSEY

	Boilers, tanks, etc.; brick & terra cotta; cornices & skylights; lime & cement; paints; quarrying stone; roofing; sash, blinds & doors; steel & iron, structural	Same; gas and electric light fixtures; art tile

MISSOURI

	Brick, tile, pottery, clay*; lime*; paint, varnish, supplies*; planing mill products*; stone, marble, granite, slate*; structural iron*; sheet metal goods*	Same*; asphalt and tar*

CONNECTICUT

Wood preserving*	Artificial stone, tile, plaster, cement; brick, pottery, clay; lime; paint, varnish & supplies; stone, marble, granite, slate; sheet metal goods

VIRGINIA

Brick & tile; lime, cement & limestone; sash, doors & blinds	Same	Lime, cement & limestone

[a] Though no asterisks appear after the names of industries recorded for 1914–19, all figures are for an incomplete period, since Pennsylvania reported no data for 1914 and 1915.
[b] The artificial adjustments applied to some of the figures reported for Massachusetts, mentioned in the brief commentaries on the state data in Note A to Table II 4, are now described more fully in order that their effects may be appraised.
For 1886–1906 the Massachusetts data were reported by pairs of years for identical establishments, yielding two figures for each industry for each year, the one comparable with that for the preceding year, the other with that for the following year. Adding the industries within a minor commodity group gave two totals for each year. To get a single series the pairs of totals were spliced, working backwards from 1905–06.[‡] Year to year movements.

[‡] Although splicing by separate industries would be more accurate, it is not believed that the use of minor group totals affects the results enough to justify such a laborious refinement.

233

ments were not changed by this procedure; all series were simply set at 1905–06 levels.

Also available for Massachusetts were decennial censuses for 1895 and 1904. Since the data reported covered all industrial establishments in the state, the industries were arranged by minor groups and the respective totals compared with those previously derived for the same years. Final estimates for 1886–1906 were based on the resulting ratios. For the years between 1895 and 1904 geometric interpolations of 1895 and 1904 ratios were applied to the series previously derived; for 1905 and 1906, the 1904 ratio was used; and for 1886–94, the 1895 ratio. Exceptions to this procedure, in Minor Groups 8, 13b, 15, 18, 22, 26, 27, and 31, are discussed in specific footnotes.

c The correction of the Massachusetts data for boots and shoes differed from the general adjustment described in footnote b. The continuous series derived for 1889–1906 was compared with 1889 and 1899 federal census totals for Massachusetts as well as with the 1895 and 1904 Massachusetts state census totals; ratios were computed for each of the four years, and five-year interpolations made instead of the usual ten-year. This modification was possible because of the homogeneity of the boot and shoe industry and the consequent comparability of state and federal census totals.

d Special reports comparable with the regular state totals for 1909, 1910, and 1914 were made for the Missouri boot and shoe industry in 1911 and 1913. Since 1912 alone had to be estimated, a departure was made from the general rule of excluding Missouri totals during the 1909–14 intercensal period. The 1912 estimate was based on the movement from 1911 to 1912 to 1913 of figures for boots and shoes manufactured in St. Louis, Kansas City, and St. Joseph (*Annual Report of the Missouri Bureau of Labor Statistics*).

e Firearms were estimated separately from other sporting goods 1914–19 because of their erratic output during the war (see Note B to Table 5, Minor Group 10). The state industries listed here were used to interpolate the Minor Group totals (excluding firearms).

f Before being used for interpolation the state data were modified in order to incorporate a crude adjustment for the growth of tire renewals. From Table III, *Special Circular 3500* (Bureau of Foreign and Domestic Commerce, Rubber Section), annual ratios of renewals to total output of tire casings were obtained for 1904–09. By the methods used in *Special Circular 3500* comparable ratios were calculated for 1910–19. These annual ratios, 1904–19, were applied to the total value of products for the rubber goods industries in Ohio, Massachusetts, and New Jersey, and the resulting estimates then selected as the interpolating series for 1904–14 and as a complementary one for 1914–19.

g Since household and industrial electrical appliances were not reported separately, the sample for all electrical appliances was apportioned according to the breakdown in census years of the combined total for Minor Groups 13b and 26. Apportionment for intercensal years was based on straight line interpolation of the census year percentages. The two series thus derived were then used to interpolate Minor Groups 13b and 26.

h The adjustment of the Massachusetts data for electrical equipment differed from the usual adjustment. The single series derived for 1889–1906 was compared with the 1899 federal census total as well as with the 1895 and 1904 Massachusetts state census totals, and five-year interpolations made instead of the usual ten-year.

i To get a more representative sample, the totals for Minor Groups 9, 14b, and 15 (excluding pottery) were combined and used for interpolation in place of the figures for 14b alone.

j Since the production of pottery products was reported in *Mineral Resources of the United States, seriatim* (see Note B to this table, Minor Group 15), no data for the pottery industries are included in the state samples 1899–1919.

k In this group the single Massachusetts series first derived for 1889–1906 was used instead of estimates based on the state decennial censuses. Also, because of apparent inconsistencies in the Massachusetts sample, the data for 1909–14 were omitted.

l A special shipbuilding census for 1916 made it possible to divide the intercensal period into two parts, 1914–16 and 1916–19. The state samples were used for the first part alone; for the second, the census figures were interpolated along a straight line. This procedure was considered preferable to the use of the state samples which showed a tremendous increase arising from extraordinary military demands.

m For interpolation from 1909 to 1919 the state samples for Minor Groups 23 and 34 were combined and the resulting totals used for both groups. For years before 1909 Minor Group 23; Minor Group 34 was estimated from the movement of the sample for Minor Group 3; Minor Group 34 was estimated from the combined state samples for Minor Groups 25 and 26.

n Since most state reports included office machinery with industrial machinery, the sample for this group was combined with that for Minor Group 25, and the interpolation based on the combined total.

o The state data for this group were used only to interpolate the census values for vaults and showcases. The totals of furniture for offices and public buildings were interpolated by the sample used for Minor Group 12. The two series were then added.

p The state data for the railroad car industry were used for direct interpolation only from 1889 to 1909. For 1909–14 railroad car figures for Ohio and Pennsylvania were first adjusted by data from special sources; and for 1914–19 the state figures were used only as a complementary series. Moreover, the state figures for the locomotive industry were used as a complementary series throughout. For details regarding the sources of the special data see Note B to Table II 6, Minor Group 30.

q Before being used for interpolation the state totals were combined with several series from *Mineral Resources of the United States* (see Note B to Table II 6, Minor Group 36).

Note B to Table II 6
Miscellaneous Interpolating Series
Minor Group 1

Data for natural mineral waters are from *Mineral Resources of the United States* (*seriatim*).

Data for rice, peanuts, cheese, butter, and condensed and evaporated milk were taken directly or derived from *Gross Farm Income, Indexes of Farm Prices in the United States, 1869–1937,* by Frederick Strauss and Louis Bean (Department of Agriculture, Washington, D.C., 1939). The figures for rice and peanuts were taken directly; those for cheese and butter were reduced to cover factory production alone on the basis of unpublished percentage estimates by E. E. Vial, Bureau of Agricultural Economics; production of condensed and evaporated milk was taken directly but the prices used for translation into values were first adjusted to conform with prices for census years reported in the *Census of Manufactures*.

Calendar year imports of coffee are from the *Monthly Summary of Foreign Commerce of the United States* (*seriatim*).

Annual data on 'tonnage originating on road', reported for the year ending June 30, 1916 and all earlier years on a fiscal year basis, and for calendar years, 1916–19, *Statistics of Railways,* Interstate Commerce Commission, were used to derive series for sugar, dressed meats, other packing-house products, and flour. The figures for each commodity were adjusted to a calendar year basis by means of the 1916 calendar-fiscal ratios.

Several adjustments for comparability had also to be made. The figures for 1917–19 were raised to include Class II railroads on the basis of 1916 ratio; those for 1913 and 1914 were raised to include Class III roads on the basis of the 1912 ratios of Class II and III to Class II alone. The data reported for 1910 and earlier years for all railroads were presumably comparable with the 1911 figures for Class I, II, and III roads. Consequently two ICC tonnage series were derived for each commodity: 1914–19, for Class I and II roads; 1899–1914, for all roads. Conversion into dollar values was based on various price series.

For sugar the average annual price per pound of granulated sugar *Wholesale Prices, 1890–1922* (Bureau of Labor Statistics, Bulletin 320) was used; for dressed meats a weighted average of three BLS price series: native sides, New York beef, weight 4, mutton: dressed, weight 1, and pork: cured short clear sides, weight 5.[a] For other packing-house products the BLS price for lard: prime contract, was used; for flour two BLS series were combined: wheat, spring patents, New York, average price per barrel, weight 9, and meal: corn, fine yellow, New York, average price per 100 pounds, weight 1.[a] The wheat series was extrapolated from 1913 to 1919 by an index of the price of wheat, standard patents, Minneapolis; and the corn meal from 1917 to 1919 by an index of the price of meal: corn, Philadelphia.

[a] Rough weights were determined from quantities reported for census years in the *Census of Manufactures*.

The pack of canned tomatoes, cases of 24 No. 3 cans (*Yearbook of Agriculture, 1923,* pp. 780–1), was multiplied by the BLS price per dozen No. 3 cans, Standard New Jersey. Lack of satisfactory price data prevented the extension of the series back of 1909.

The pack of canned corn and peas, cases of 24 No. 2 cans, was taken from *Canned Food Pack Statistics, 1937,* Part 1, Vegetables (pp. 9, 11), compiled by the National Canners Association, Division of Statistics. BLS prices for corn, per dozen No. 2 cans, and peas, per dozen No. 2 cans, Republic, sifted, were used for conversion into values.

Addition of the preceding foods series provided a complementary total series for the food group 1899–1919. For 1889–99, however, the series that extended through this decade were combined with sugar meltings (Willett and Gray, *Weekly Statistical Trade Journal*), multiplied by the BLS price per pound for granulated sugar, and with the gross income from the slaughter of animals adjusted for changes in inventories (Strauss, *op. cit.*). This aggregate was used for interpolation in preference to data from one state, Massachusetts.

Minor Group 2

Calendar year production of smoking tobacco, fine-cut tobacco, snuff, plug and twist tobacco, cigars not weighing more than 3 pounds per thousand, cigars weighing more than 3 pounds per thousand, and cigarettes (*Annual Report of the Commissioner of Internal Revenue, seriatim*) were multiplied by prices, then added to get the total used for interpolation.

The following prices were given in the Report of the Commissioner of Corporations on the *Tobacco Industry, 1915,* Part III, Prices, Costs and Profits:

Smoking tobacco	1893–1910, 1912, 1913	Snuff	1900–10, 1912, 1913
Fine-cut tobacco	same	Little cigars	1895–1910, 1912, 1913
Plug & twist tobacco	same	Big cigars	1901–10
Cigarettes	same		

Prices for 1910 and earlier years were for the tobacco trust; prices for 1912 and 1913 were for companies that succeeded the trust upon its dissolution by the courts. All prices include taxes, and the later are comparable with the earlier.

Prices for 1911 were derived by straight line interpolation of the figures for 1910 and 1912. The several series were then extrapolated from 1914 to 1918 on the basis of prices calculated from data in Lloyd L. Shaulis, *Prices of Tobacco and Tobacco Products* (War Industries Board, *Bulletin 19*). The Bulletin prices for six types of cigarette were weighted and combined on the basis of the relative quantities of leaf used in their manufacture in 1917. The weights taken from *Bulletin 19,* p. 8, were: Burley and Turkish, 16; Virginia, 6.5; Virginia and Turkish, 4.2; Turkish and Virginia, 2.5; Turkish, 2.2; and Burley, 0.4. Similarly, to derive a single price series for smoking tobacco a weighted average of the prices for scrap, long cut, and cut plug was constructed. The weights, 3, 2, and 4, respectively, were taken from *Bulletin 19,* p. 13.

The War Industries Board prices for little cigars and snuff were used for extrapolation without adjustment; those for long-cut tobacco were used to extrapolate the fine-cut series. Since no prices later than 1910 were available for big cigars, the prices of little cigars were used as an index for 1910–18.

Prices for 1919 were estimated from data in *Prices of Tobacco Products* (Federal Trade Commission, Jan. 1922, p. 32). Prices of cigarettes, smoking and plug tobacco in 1918 and 1919 were used to extrapolate the previously derived 1918 figures. Lack of detailed data for big and little cigars, snuff and fine-cut tobacco compelled the use of the average movement 1918–19 of the prices of smoking and plug tobaccos to extrapolate these series.

Since until 1897 production of little cigars was included with cigarettes, the prices of cigarettes had to be made comparable. For 1895 and 1896 prices of the two items were averaged with weights based on quantities produced in 1897. For earlier years cigarette prices were adjusted on the basis of the ratio of the average price derived for 1895 to the cigarette price in that year.

Prices for the years preceding 1893 were estimated from the BLS series and data in the Aldrich Report, *Wholesale Prices, Wages and Transportation* (Senate Document 1394, 52d Cong., 2d Sess.), Part 2, Table XI, pp. 116, 117. The BLS prices extended to 1890 and included plug tobacco and smoking tobacco; prices for earlier years in the Aldrich Report were for plug tobacco alone. Consequently, all extrapolations for the years preceding those covered in the Report of the Commissioner of Corporations were necessarily rough and based on much the same series.

Minor Group 5a

For the estimates of coke for census years see Note B to Table II 1. Intercensal estimates were made by methods similar to those described there. For 1918 the same method was used as for 1919; for 1915 and all earlier years 5 percent of total coke production was estimated to be destined for domestic consumption. Estimates for 1916 and 1917 were based on straight-line interpolation of the 1915 and 1918 ratios of domestic to total coke.

The annual value at well of crude petroleum was taken from *Mineral Resources of the United States, 1921,* Part II, p. 261. Ratios of census year totals for illuminating oils, lubricating oils and gasoline to the values for crude petroleum were calculated, and intercensal estimates based on straight line interpolation.

Intercensal estimates for the other commodities in Minor Group 5a were based on the movement of the previously derived series for coke and petroleum products.

Complementary series were derived also for the major petroleum products. Gasoline consumption was estimated by multiplying the average annual passenger car registration (*Automobile Facts and Figures, 1939,* p. 16) by a conversion factor of 300 gallons per car (J. E. Pogue, *Economics of Petroleum,* New York, 1921, p. 123). BLS prices were used for conversion into values 1913–19; for earlier years the BLS series was extrapolated by the value per barrel of crude petroleum (*Mineral Resources of the United States, 1923,* Part II, p. 379). A similar procedure was followed for lubricating oils. Here automobile registration was multiplied by a conversion factor of 25 gallons (Pogue, *op. cit.,* p. 180) ; prices were taken from the same sources, a BLS series being extrapolated by prices of crude petroleum for years before 1913. Kerosene output 1916–19 was taken from *Mineral Resources of the United States* (*seriatim*) ; for 1914, from the Census of Manufactures, and for 1915 it was estimated from the 1916 ratio to the total output of crude petroleum. Prices of tank-wagon kerosene (Pogue, *op. cit.,* p. 136) were used for conversion into values.

Minor Groups 9, 12, and 14b

The complementary series for semidurable and durable house furnishings and furniture is little more than a crude index of values. It consists of ICC tonnage data for household goods and furniture (for a description of the general adjustments made to ICC data see Minor Group 1 above) multiplied by BLS relatives for a composite price series of all housefurnishing goods (Bureau of Labor Statistics, *Bulletin 320*).

Minor Group 10

Because of the extraordinary output during the war firearms were estimated independently of other sporting goods 1914–19. Lack of state samples or other adequate data compelled the use of exports (*Monthly Summary of Foreign Commerce, seriatim*) for the interpolation. It is doubtful that exports are a good index of output but they are believed better than other sporting goods or straight line interpolation.

Minor Group 11

For 1899–1904 tires and tubes were estimated from the movement of the combined annual series for Minor Groups 20a and 21. For years before 1899, for lack of more adequate data, the movement of the bicycle series alone was used.

For 1914–19 tire renewals (see Note B to Table II 2, Minor Group 11) were multiplied by the BLS price series for automobile tires at factory, reported in *Rubber Industry of the United States, 1839–1939* (Bureau of Foreign and Domestic Commerce, Trade Promotion Series 197, Table 10).

Minor Group 15

The interpolating series used for this group was a combination of china and household utensils, excluding pottery, reported in the state samples (see Note A to Table II 6, Minor Group 15, for states included) and the following products reported under clay-working industries in *Mineral Resources of the United States:* red earthenware; stoneware and yellow and Rockingham ware; white ware, including C. C. ware; china, bone china, delft and belleek ware; and miscellaneous pottery, the greater part of which consists of red and brown white-lined cooking ware.

Minor Group 16

Sales of the Baldwin and American Piano companies, 1909–19, were taken from annual reports in *Moody's Industrials*. Because of their narrow scope, the data serve merely as rough corroboratory totals.

ESTIMATES OF THE VALUE OF OUTPUT

Minor Group 20a, 20b

Factory sales of passenger cars (*Automobile Facts and Figures, 1939*, p. 4) were used to interpolate the census year figures for both passenger cars and parts and accessories. Since no figure was given for 1900 (the 1900 figure there being the census value for 1899) straight line interpolation was applied to our estimates for 1899 and 1901.

A complementary series for parts was developed by using automobile registration figures, based on averages of end of year figures (*ibid.,* p. 16).

Minor Group 21

The sum of bicycle and motorcycle export was used to interpolate from 1899 to 1914. For bicycles exports were used to interpolate between 1914 and 1919; for motorcycles, the output of the Indian Motorcycle Company (annual reports in *Moody's Industrials*) multiplied by per unit export prices was used.

Minor Group 24

Intercensal estimates 1899–1919 were based on the values of monumental stone (*Mineral Resources of the United States, seriatim*). For 1889–99 the values for total granite were used.

Minor Group 25

Exports of machinery, n.e.s. were used as a complementary series. Calendar year data for the machinery category, excluding adding and calculating machines, cash registers and parts, sewing machines, and typewriters, are from *Monthly Summary of Foreign Commerce of the United States* (*seriatim*).

Minor Group 26

Combining gross revenues of the General Electric and the Westinghouse Electric and Manufacturing companies 1909–19 (annual reports in *Moody's Industrials*) gave a rough complementary series.

Minor Group 27

For 1914–19 ICC tonnage for agricultural implements (for adjustments to ICC figures see Minor Group 1 above) was converted to values by the price index of farm machinery (*Monthly Labor Review*, Aug. 1935, p. 528). Lack of satisfactory price data prevented the use of the ICC data before 1914.

Minor Group 30

Intercensal estimates for railroad cars, 1889–1909, were based on state data (for states included see Note A to Table II 6, Minor Group 30). For later years better series were available. For 1911–14 the number of cars produced (*Railway Age*, Jan. 3, 1931, p. 84) was multiplied by the average domestic price (*Final Report of the Chairman of the United States War Industries Board to the President of the United States,* Senate Committee Print No. 3, 74th

Cong., 1st Sess., p. 978). This series was extrapolated from 1911 to 1909 by the combined totals for Ohio and Pennsylvania.

For 1914–19 production of passenger and freight cars (*Railway Age, loc. cit.*) was converted into values by the use of average selling prices per car, based on those of six large companies, ascertained by correspondence with Julius Parmelee, Statistician of the Bureau of Railway Economics. Passenger car prices were available for the entire period; but all-steel and wood and steel freight car prices were given only through 1918, and all wood ones only through 1917. Freight car prices for the missing years were estimated from the movement of per pound prices from the same source.

Intercensal estimates for locomotives were based on the number of locomotives built as given in A. F. Burns, *Production Trends in the United States Since 1870*, p. 300 (compiled from various issues of *Railway Age* and *Railroad Gazette*). For 1889–1914 per unit export prices calculated from data in *Monthly Summary of Foreign Commerce of the United States* (*seriatim*) were used for conversion into values; for 1914–19 average selling prices (Bureau of Railway Economics) were used.

As indicated in the preceding description, census year values for cars and locomotives were interpolated separately; the estimates were then combined to get a group total.

Minor Group 32a

Intercensal estimates were based on the annual sales of motor trucks 1904–19 (*Automobile Facts and Figures, 1939*, p. 4). Since no significant number of trucks was produced before 1904, all motor vehicle production was classified as passenger cars in the early years.

Minor Group 33

From *Air Commerce Bulletin*, Vol. 1, No. 5 (Washington, D.C., Sept. 2, 1929, p. 6), the annual consumption of aeroplanes by the Army and Navy 1912–19 was taken; no data were reported for civil consumption. To these totals were added calendar year exports (*Monthly Summary of Foreign Commerce, seriatim*). Since no good price series was available and per unit export prices were not comparable from one year to the next, per unit motor truck prices (*Automobile Facts and Figures, 1939*, p. 4) were used for conversion into values. For years before 1912 it was assumed that the output of aeroplanes was insignificant; a small but indeterminate output for the census year 1909 was included with the motorcycle and bicycle industry.

Minor Group 36

The interpolating series was based on a combination of state totals (see Note A to Table II 6) and several commodities reported in *Mineral Resources of the United States* (*seriatim*). These commodities included chemical stoneware from the clay-working industries group, and millstones, grindstones, and oilstones from the natural abrasives group.

Construction Materials

From *Mineral Resources of the United States* (*seriatim*), data were taken for roofing slate; building lime; manufactured asphalt; building stone; paving stone; stone curbing; stone flagging; rubble; riprap; crushed railroad ballast, concrete and road metal; building sand; paving sand; sand railroad ballast; gravel; sand-lime brick; common brick; vitrified brick; face brick; fancy or ornamental brick; enameled brick; architectural terra cotta; hollow building tile and fire-proofing; tile, not drain; draintile; sewer pipe; and sanitary ware. Series for products of the clay-working industries (brick through sanitary ware) were usable only from 1899 to 1919. Building lime was estimated for 1889–93 from the movement of total lime. Building stone was estimated for 1889–91 from the movement of all quarried stone.

Softwood production, 1899, 1904–19, was reported in Frank J. Hallauer, *Our National Timber Requirements,* Senate Document 12, Separate 4 (prepared by the Forest Service in response to Senate Resolution 175, 73d Cong., 1st Sess.), Table 1. The derivation of softwood production for 1889–99 and 1899–1904 is described in Note A to Table II 11. Prices used were those per M bd. ft. in eastern United States, average quality, 1 inch softwoods, *American Forests and Forest Products,* Statistical Bulletin 21, Department of Agriculture, 1927, Table 76.

Production of lath and shingles, 1904–19 (except 1913 and 1914), was taken from *Statistical Bulletin 21* and from the *Agricultural Yearbook, 1923,* pp. 1072–6. Quantities of lath for 1913 and 1914 were estimated by straight line interpolation between 1912 and 1915; shingles were estimated from the movement of the production by reporting mills of cypress, white pine, and cedar. Prices for 1904, 1906–11, and 1919 were also taken from the above sources. Prices of lath 1913–18 were estimated from the movement of the BLS wholesale price index for lath; and for 1912 and 1905 were based on the movement of the prices of average quality 1 inch soft woods in eastern markets. Shingle prices for 1905 and 1912–18 were estimated from the movement of the average of the BLS prices for cypress and red cedar shingles.

Lath production was estimated for years before 1904 by means of an interpolating series consisting of the production of lath in the Northwest (*American Lumberman,* Jan. 21, 1905), reported for 1892–99, and production of lath in the Adirondack forest, 1894–1904 (James E. Defebaugh, *History of the Lumber Industry of America,* Chicago, 1907, Vol. 2, p. 405). These series provided estimates back to 1892; estimates for 1890 and 1891 were based on straight line interpolation between the 1889 census figure and the 1892 estimate. Prices for the years before 1904 were derived by adjusting to census levels the prices for average quality 1 inch softwoods in eastern markets.

The production of shingles was estimated for 1889–99 and 1899–1904 by using the cut of shingles in the Northwest, 1889–1904 (*American Lumberman,* Jan. 21, 1905, p. 28); receipts of shingles at San Francisco, 1889–98 (*Annual Report of the San Francisco Chamber of Commerce, seriatim*), and production of shingles in the Adirondack forest, 1894–1904 (Defebaugh, *op. cit.,* p. 405), as interpolating series. Shingle prices were based on BLS prices for cypress and white pine shingles, 1890–1904, weighted 1 and 9 respectively according to approximate importance, and adjusted to census price levels.

Production of iron and steel rails, 1889–1919, is from the *Annual Statistical Report of the American Iron and Steel Institute for 1924* (p. 43). BLS prices for steel rails: Bessemer, used to derive values for 1890–1919, were extrapolated to 1889 by the movement of the price for steel rails: Bessemer (*Wholesale Prices, Wages and Transportation,* Part 2, p. 215).

Production of iron and steel structural shapes, 1892–1919, is from the Institute Report (p. 44). For conversion into values, BLS structural steel prices were used for 1913–19; for years before 1913, prices were estimated from the movement of the BLS price for billets: Bessemer. The estimates for structural shapes, 1889–91, were based upon the movement of the value of iron and steel rails.

Production of concrete bars, 1909–19, is from the Institute Report (p. 52). BLS prices for 1913–19 were extrapolated back to 1909 by the movement of the price for bar iron, Philadelphia.

Production of cut and wire nails, 1889–1919, is from the Institute Report (p. 59); BLS prices for wire nails were used to calculate values.

Production of butt and lap weld pipe, 1914–19, is from *Metal Statistics, 1938* (p. 109); prices for the same period were derived by interpolating census per unit values for pipes and tubes made in rolling mills by the movement of BLS prices for cast-iron pipe.

The sum of the estimated values for all the above mineral, lumber, and metal products was used as the interpolating series for construction materials.

TABLE II 7

Percentage Changes in Census Year Ratios of Interpolating and Complementary Series to Minor Commodity Group Totals

	COMMODITY GROUP	1889 TO 1899	1899 TO 1904	1904 TO 1909	1909 TO 1914	1914 TO 1919	AVG. CHANGE FOR THE 4 PERIODS, 1899–1919
	A	INTERPOLATING SERIES					
1	Food & kindred products	22.5	13.2	6.8	16.9	0.5	9.4
2	Cigars, cigarettes & tobacco	0.5	2.8	8.8	0.8	14.9	6.8
3	Drug, toilet & household preparations	42.2	6.6	8.9	17.0	11.0	10.9
4	Magazines, newspapers, stationery & supplies & misc. paper products	18.8	1.3	12.4	7.7	12.9	8.6
5a	Fuel & lighting products: mfd.*	38.2	20.0	11.3	22.5	11.5	16.3
6	Dry goods & notions	14.0	5.5	9.7	13.4	13.1	10.4
7	Clothing & personal furnishings	5.8	0.5	6.7	2.3	3.9	3.4
8	Shoes & other footwear	18.6	3.8	16.2	1.0	1.5	5.6

* Although coke and petroleum products were estimated separately for all years, the two samples were combined to derive the ratios from which the percentage changes were calculated.

TABLE II 7 cont.

PERCENTAGE CHANGE IN RATIOS FROM

	COMMODITY GROUP	1889 TO 1899	1899 TO 1904	1904 TO 1909	1909 TO 1914	1914 TO 1919	AVG. CHANGE FOR THE 4 PERIODS, 1899–1919
9	House furnishings (semi-durable)	26.4	2.2	5.7	0.9	14.7	5.9
10	Toys, games & sporting goods	37.1	15.5	15.6	5.8	12.5†	12.4
11	Tires & tubes‡		52.7	37.1	94.1	19.8	50.9
12	Household furniture	8.8	2.4	23.2	3.2	29.8	14.6
13a	Heating & cooking apparatus, household appliances except electrical	25.0	31.2	33.3	6.9	12.8	21.0
13b	Electrical household appliances & supplies		20.7	9.6	10.6	22.6	15.9
14a	Floor coverings	11.1	6.4	0.6	8.1	7.0	5.5
14b	Misc. house furnishings (durable)	9.9	3.1	21.5	9.9	16.3	12.7
15	China & household utensils§	12.6	12.2	11.8	6.0	29.1	14.8
16	Musical instruments	70.1	47.1	37.9	19.2	63.3	41.9
17	Jewelry, silverware, clocks & watches	13.9	11.1	6.3	3.8	7.1	7.1
18	Printing and publishing: books	19.3	36.2	7.4	36.8	0.8	20.3
19	Luggage	19.4	7.5	25.3	23.1	10.8	16.7
20a	Passenger vehicles, motorized		‖	1.2	1.3	0.1	0.9
20b	Motor-vehicle accessories		‖	26.3	2.3	19.0	15.9
20c	Passenger vehicles & accessories, horse-drawn	22.0	23.4	20.2	34.2	30.6	27.1
21	Motorcycles & bicycles¶		48.6	31.9	37.9	16.5	33.7
22	Pleasure-craft	23.1	8.0	40.7	30.6	26.5**	26.4
23	Ophthalmic products & artificial limbs††	79.1	22.6	15.8	40.7	29.1	27.0
24	Monuments & tombstones	61.6	19.0	46.8	8.9	14.9	22.4
25	Industrial machinery & equipment	14.3	7.0	3.2	4.7	8.1	5.8
26	Electrical machinery, industrial & commercial	149.2	20.7	16.5	6.9	22.8	16.7
27	Farm equipment	1.6	7.7	26.7	5.4	23.9	15.9

† Although firearms and all other toys, games, and sporting goods were estimated separately, 1914–19, the two samples were combined to derive the ratios from which the percentage changes were calculated.
‡ The interpolating sample was changed in 1899, 1904, and 1914.
§ Although pottery and clay products and all other china and household utensils were estimated separately in all years after 1899, the two samples were combined to derive the ratios from which the percentage changes were calculated.
‖ No percentage change is given for this period because no sample total was available for 1899.
¶ Changes were made in the interpolating series in 1904 and 1914. For years before 1904, exports were used to interpolate for both bicycles and motorcycles; from 1904 to 1914, state totals. From 1914 to 1919, exports were again used, but for bicycles alone; production of the Indian Motorcycle Company was used for motorcycles. The two samples were combined in 1914 and 1919 to derive the ratios from which the percentage change was calculated.
** Change from 1914 to 1916 only; state data were not used in 1917, 1918, or 1919.
†† The interpolating samples for Minor Groups 23 and 34 were changed in 1909.

TABLE II 7 concl.

	COMMODITY GROUP	PERCENTAGE CHANGE IN RATIOS FROM 1889 TO 1899	1899 TO 1904	1904 TO 1909	1909 TO 1914	1914 TO 1919	AVG. CHANGE FOR THE 4 PERIODS, 1899–1919
28	Office & store machinery & equipment	51.8	14.4	45.7	6.3	25.2	22.9
29	Office & store furniture & fixtures	21.5	7.0	2.2	4.7	0.2	3.5
30	Locomotives & rr. cars‡‡	1.8	0.1	45.0	6.3	19.6	17.8
31	Ships & boats	27.9	5.3	33.5	8.9	39.8§§	21.9
32a	Business vehicles, motorized			37.0	29.8	0.2	22.3
32b	Business vehicles, horse-drawn	10.0	16.6	0.2	18.3	9.1	11.0
33	Aircraft					57.7	57.7
34	Professional & scientific equipment††	27.0	9.3	26.8	27.0	21.4	16.1
35	Carpenters' & mechanics' tools	14.6	15.1	5.6	14.0	2.3	9.2
36	Misc. subsidiary durable equipment	26.9	0.0	13.0	34.6	12.9	15.1
	Construction Materials	30.2	9.5	10.2	13.1	12.4	11.3

B COMPLEMENTARY SERIES

1	Food & kindred products	9.6	17.7	4.4	2.5	22.1	11.7
2	Cigars, cigarettes & tobacco	39.8	25.2	16.9	13.1	22.5	19.4
5a	Fuel & lighting products: mfd.		92.6	76.6	80.0	17.0	66.6
9	House furnishings (semi-durable)		31.7	26.7	11.3	47.3	29.2
11	Tires & tubes					46.2	46.2
12	Household furniture		24.9	18.8	13.4	32.8	22.5
14b	Misc. house furnishings (durable)		31.7	6.7	18.6	32.5	22.4
16	Musical instruments				3.1	129.9	66.5
21	Motorcycles & bicycles		42.4	264.8	9.3		37.4
24	Monuments & tombstones		12.3	‖‖	4.9	69.2	28.8
25	Industrial machinery & equipment	51.3	9.1	8.6	24.9	17.0	14.9
26	Electrical machinery, industrial & commercial				7.9	7.9	7.9
27	Farm equipment					19.5	19.5
34	Professional & scientific equipment					89.9	89.9
	Construction Materials	0.2	9.6	3.2	21.7	5.1	9.9

‡‡ Although locomotives and railroad cars were estimated separately for all years, the two samples were combined to derive the ratios from which the percentage changes were calculated.

§§ Census commodity totals were available for 1916 as well as for 1919; the change from 1914 to 1919 is an arithmetic average of the percentage changes from 1914 to 1916 and from 1916 to 1919.

‖‖ Because of a break in the state sample between 1907 and 1908, the 1904 and 1909 ratios were not comparable.

TABLE II 8

Differences in the Year-to-year Percentage Changes in the Interpolating Series Frequency Distribution by Minor Commodity Groups

COMMODITY GROUP	PERCENTAGE CLASS	1889–1899	1899–1904	1904–1909	1909–1914	1914–1919	TOTAL
Food & kindred products	0–4.9	4					4
	5.0–9.9	2					2
	10.0 & over	4					4
	0–4.9		3	3	3	4	13
	5.0–9.9		1	1	2		4
	10.0 & over		1	1		1	3
Cigars, cigarettes & tobacco	0–4.9	4	3	5	2	2	16
	5.0–9.9	4	1		3	2	10
	10.0 & over	2	1			1	4
Fuel & lighting products, mfd.	0–4.9		1			1	2
	5.0–9.9			2		1	3
	10.0 & over		4	3	5	3	15
Housefurnishings	0–4.9		3	3	2	2	10
	5.0–9.9		1		2	1	4
	10.0 & over		1	2	1	2	6
Tires & tubes	0–4.9					1	1
	5.0–9.9					1	1
	10.0 & over					3	3
Household furniture	0–4.9		1	1	2	2	6
	5.0–9.9		2	2		1	5
	10.0 & over		2	2	3	2	9
Misc. housefurnishings	0–4.9		2	2	2	3	9
	5.0–9.9		2	1	2	1	6
	10.0 & over		1	2	1	1	5
Musical instruments	0–4.9				4	1	5
	5.0–9.9				1		1
	10.0 & over					4	4
Motorcycles & bicycles*	0–4.9	1	1				2
	5.0–9.9		1				1
	10.0 & over	3	3				6
	0–4.9			2	1		3
	5.0–9.9				1		1
	10.0 & over			3	3		6
Monuments & tombstones	0–4.9		1				1
	5.0–9.9				4		4
	10.0 & over		4	5	1	5	15
Industrial machinery & equipment—tractors	0–4.9	3	2	3	2	1	11
	5.0–9.9	2					2
	10.0 & over	5	3	2	3	4	17
Electrical equipment, industrial & commercial	0–4.9				5	5	10
	5.0–9.9						
	10.0 & over						

* This commodity group was estimated for only four years before 1899. The bicycle industry expanded rapidly within a few years, then declined almost immediately.

TABLE II 8 *concl.*

COMMODITY GROUP	PERCENTAGE CLASS	1889–1899	1899–1904	1904–1909	1909–1914	1914–1919	TOTAL
Farm equipment	0–4.9					1	1
	5.0–9.9					2	2
	10.0 & over					2	2
Aircraft†	0–4.9				1	2	3
	5.0–9.9						
	10.0 & over				1	3	4
Construction materials	0–4.9		3	3	1	2	9
	5.0–9.9	2	2	1	1	1	7
	10.0 & over	8		1	3	2	14
Total	0–4.9	14	21	24	26	28	113
	5.0–9.9	14	12	7	19	10	62
	10.0 & over	36	27	29	27	42	161

† This group was estimated for two years before 1914.

Table II 9

Value of Nonmanufactured Food Products Destined for Consumption in Farm Households or for Sale to Ultimate Consumers, 1869, 1879, 1889–1919

(thousands of dollars)

	FRUITS, VEGETABLES & NUTS (SEE TABLE II 9A)	WHEAT, CORN, RYE & BUCKWHEAT CONSUMED IN FARM HOUSEHOLDS	FARM BUTTER	FARM CHEESE	FLUID MILK (SEE TABLE II 9B)	EGGS SEE TABLE II 9C	CHICKENS	CATTLE & CALVES, HOGS & SHEEP & LAMBS SLAUGHTERED ON FARMS FOR HOME CONSUMPTION	FISH (SEE TABLE II 9D)	NATURAL MINERAL WATERS	TOTAL
1869	241,822	15,801	151,995*	7,538*	72,459	55,924	56,000	75,176	9,446	no data	686,161
1879	264,259	21,135	108,913	1,851	75,532	63,859	47,000	88,282	29,850	577	701,258
1889	306,855	23,083	171,327	1,441	92,968	114,653	73,000	117,468	33,748	1,748	936,291
1890	320,383	23,498	141,851	1,420	116,501	122,670	80,000	108,151	36,515	2,601	953,590
1891	380,044	25,755	144,614	1,412	123,392	137,099	85,000	114,644	38,259	2,996	1,053,215
1892	336,507	23,436	146,817	1,494	127,361	154,963	86,000	114,312	41,081	4,906	1,036,877
1893	388,618	17,821	158,013	1,234	135,254	167,385	90,000	149,727	41,062	4,247	1,153,361
1894	319,657	17,478	136,795	1,213	119,609	154,507	91,000	118,147	38,474	3,742	1,000,622
1895	376,098	18,673	139,453	964	116,715	156,697	94,000	114,772	36,446	4,254	1,058,072
1896	235,488	16,118	158,854	903	113,819	151,793	92,000	102,969	33,082	4,136	909,162
1897	326,404	19,103	147,605	1,219	128,590	151,018	98,000	110,156	30,449	4,599	1,017,143
1898	370,527	24,339	140,091	1,086	147,285	167,617	99,000	119,193	30,175	8,052	1,107,365
1899	347,869	23,262	150,076	1,365	156,178	182,315	110,000	121,706	41,401	6,948	1,141,120
1900	361,905	26,645	174,340	1,382	169,903	197,161	106,000	150,913	39,577	5,792	1,233,618
1901	461,324	29,407	175,798	1,466	171,850	223,252	112,000	168,915	45,528	7,444	1,396,984
1902	487,838	27,839	166,393	1,375	181,633	252,711	134,000	196,896	38,039	8,634	1,495,358
1903	459,743	27,478	162,910	1,323	213,029	260,859	145,000	173,343	39,507	6,788	1,489,980
1904	555,080	29,959	160,138	1,057	194,329	297,374	147,000	150,913	40,497	6,219	1,582,566
1905	424,445	33,217	188,838	1,256	195,279	299,739	148,000	160,057	48,603	6,491	1,505,925
1906	583,188	32,711	168,181	1,048	184,447	312,720	153,000	195,359	38,688	8,028	1,677,370
1907	560,481	34,460	190,994	1,070	258,003	367,856	167,000	197,549	48,389	7,332	1,833,134
1908	616,908	39,710	233,113	1,002	227,546	355,271	162,000	184,859	42,259	6,713	1,869,381

TABLE II 9 concl.

	FRUITS, VEGETABLES & NUTS (SEE TABLE II 9A)	WHEAT, CORN, RYE & BUCKWHEAT CONSUMED IN FARM HOUSEHOLDS	FARM BUTTER	FARM CHEESE	FLUID MILK (SEE TABLE II 9B)	EGGS (SEE TABLE II 9C)	CHICKENS	CATTLE & CALVES, HOGS & SHEEP & LAMBS SLAUGHTERED ON FARMS FOR HOME CONSUMPTION	FISH (SEE TABLE II 9D)	NATURAL MINERAL WATERS	TOTAL
1909	656,197	42,318	222,720	1,117	295,169	363,837	188,000	230,044	50,860	6,894	2,057,156
1910	724,936	37,645	260,757	1,298	302,963	409,178	197,000	270,598	41,414	6,358	2,252,147
1911	843,266	35,563	231,019	1,067	261,032	358,990	183,000	210,305	52,173	6,838	2,183,253
1912	898,105	37,935	213,352	1,238	344,563	404,755	194,000	215,788	35,552	6,616	2,351,904
1913	768,318	38,012	214,451	1,216	343,392	384,216	210,000	244,739	45,923	5,631	2,255,898
1914	825,515	38,550	220,934	1,216	317,157	407,883	214,000	247,464	37,169	4,892	2,314,780
1915	792,997	41,267	239,603	1,380	290,759	431,540	213,000	229,306	36,740	5,139	2,281,731
1916	999,013	46,747	257,547	1,526	304,709	472,939	248,000	273,605	41,290	5,735	2,651,111
1917	1,545,672	81,497	278,110	2,132	437,414	663,980	316,000	439,068	63,205	4,932	3,832,010
1918	1,460,867	93,627	266,261	1,870	629,422	731,545	408,000	556,561	59,357	4,533	4,212,043
1919	1,634,048	87,653	346,104	2,231	631,200	932,377	448,000	572,320	55,443	4,880	4,714,256

*The values for 1869 include both farm and factory output.

TABLE II 9a

Value of Fruit, Nut, and Vegetable Crops Produced and Destined for Consumption in Farm Households or for Sale to Ultimate Consumers, 1869, 1879, 1889–1919

(thousands of dollars)

	CITRUS FRUITS	ORCHARD FRUITS	GRAPES	POTATOES	SWEET POTATOES	DRY EDIBLE BEANS	NUTS	FRUITS, VEGETABLES & NUTS ESTIMATED DIRECTLY	SMALL FRUITS‡	VEGETABLES RAISED FOR SALE & FARM GARDEN CROPS‡	TOTAL PRODUCED	USED IN MFG.	DESTINED FOR CONSUMPTION IN FARM HOUSEHOLDS OR FOR SALE TO ULTIMATE CONSUMERS
1869	4,991*	47,335	no data	57,690	25,000	5,000	no data	150,727†	16,354	78,559	245,620	3,798	241,822
1879	5,365*	50,876		76,920	19,000	4,000		168,107†	18,240	87,617	273,964	9,705	264,259
1889	8,824	83,683	9,368	65,786	20,000	5,000	4,650	197,311	21,408	102,838	321,557	14,702	306,855
1890	13,497	67,673	7,010	88,053	21,000	5,000	4,399	206,632	22,420	107,697	336,749	16,366	320,383
1891	7,124	80,763	8,178	119,428	21,000	5,000	4,393	245,886	26,679	128,156	400,721	20,677	380,044
1892	10,482	81,824	6,038	91,089	20,000	5,000	3,953	218,386	23,695	113,823	355,904	19,397	336,507
1893	12,690	89,933	7,782	115,379	19,000	5,000	3,224	253,008	27,451	131,868	412,327	23,709	388,618
1894	9,008	65,540	5,553	102,222	19,000	5,000	2,430	208,753	22,650	108,802	340,205	20,548	319,657
1895	5,240	116,873	4,906	94,125	18,000	5,000	2,229	246,373	26,731	128,410	401,514	25,416	375,098
1896	4,822	64,128	6,070	56,678	17,000	4,000	2,060	154,758	16,791	80,660	252,209	16,721	235,488
1897	4,534	97,482	11,272	78,944	18,000	3,000	1,943	215,175	23,346	112,149	350,670	24,266	326,404
1898	9,410	96,741	8,756	105,258	19,000	4,000	1,887	245,052	26,588	127,721	399,361	28,834	370,527
1899	9,798	83,752	11,848	98,174	20,000	5,000	2,211	230,783	25,030	120,282	376,095	28,226	347,869
1900	10,027	89,863	13,974	95,137	21,000	8,000	3,008	241,009	25,113	124,409	390,531	28,626	361,905
1901	15,575	107,631	16,441	133,597	24,000	9,000	2,180	308,424	30,812	157,666	496,902	35,578	461,324
1902	9,530	107,924	29,382	141,694	26,000	9,000	3,879	327,409	31,268	165,767	524,444	36,606	487,838
1903	10,395	94,423	21,362	142,706	27,000	11,000	2,903	309,789	28,253	155,297	493,339	33,596	459,743
1904	16,841	115,911	15,004	183,190	30,000	12,000	2,537	375,483	32,629	186,352	594,464	39,384	555,080
1905	14,980	94,138	16,947	119,428	31,000	10,000	2,519	289,012	23,872	141,992	454,876	30,431	424,445
1906	21,931	148,763	25,582	156,876	32,000	12,000	2,569	399,721	31,298	194,384	625,403	42,215	583,188
1907	22,214	118,991	36,397	155,863	36,000	14,000	3,196	386,661	28,574	186,139	601,374	40,893	560,481
1908	22,173	136,220	21,548	189,263	37,000	17,000	5,221	428,425	29,818	204,102	662,345	45,437	616,908
1909	23,903	140,866	22,028	209,499	37,000	21,000	4,448	458,744	29,975	216,257	704,976	48,779	656,197
1910	30,972	199,935	41,213	169,415	41,000	21,000	5,884	509,419	32,501	239,682	781,602	56,666	724,936
1911	30,246	251,749	27,564	213,572	45,000	21,000	6,462	595,593	37,105	279,631	912,329	69,063	843,266
1912	28,430	241,696	38,161	253,186	45,000	21,000	8,124	637,597	38,766	298,778	975,141	77,036	898,105
1913	33,189	215,789	40,168	188,990	43,000	23,000	6,083	548,219	32,509	256,402	837,130	68,812	768,318
1914	36,495	258,144	30,990	197,445	42,000	21,000	5,992	592,066	34,221	276,376	902,663	77,148	825,515
1915	33,946	259,274	40,540	160,807	43,000	24,000	10,433	572,000	32,261	266,495	870,756	77,759	792,997
1916	48,081	252,816	52,954	271,790	51,000	37,000	11,171	724,812	39,792	336,965	1,101,569	102,556	999,013
1917	46,297	322,058	53,086	528,270	76,000	88,000	14,092	1,127,803	60,225	523,301	1,711,329	165,657	1,545,672
1918	63,084	357,328	78,297	369,339	91,000	86,000	27,090	1,072,138	55,644	496,486	1,624,268	163,401	1,460,867
1919	112,057	431,098	95,586	391,432	112,000	53,000	29,714	1,224,887	61,732	537,915	1,824,534	190,486	1,634,048

* Extrapolated according to orchard fruit movement.
† Raised to include grapes and nuts on the basis of the percentage, in 1889, that the total for crops estimated directly was of the total excluding grapes and nuts.
‡ The values for these crops were not estimated directly; see Note A to Table II 9 for a description of the estimates.

TABLE II 9b

Value of Fluid Milk Produced and Destined for Consumption
in Farm Households or for Sale to Ultimate Consumers
1869, 1879, 1889–1919
(thousands of dollars)

	PRODUCED*	USED IN MFG.*	DESTINED FOR CONSUMPTION IN FARM HOUSEHOLDS OR FOR SALE TO ULTIMATE CONSUMERS
1869	73,000	541	72,459
1879	77,000	1,468	75,532
1889	95,000	2,032	92,968
1890	119,000	2,499	116,501
1891	126,000	2,608	123,392
1892	130,000	2,639	127,361
1893	138,000	2,746	135,254
1894	122,000	2,391	119,609
1895	119,000	2,285	116,715
1896	116,000	2,181	113,819
1897	131,000	2,410	128,590
1898	150,000	2,715	147,285
1899	159,000	2,822	156,178
1900	173,000	3,097	169,903
1901	175,000	3,150	171,850
1902	185,000	3,367	181,633
1903	217,000	3,971	213,029
1904	198,000	3,671	194,328
1905	199,000	3,721	195,279
1906	188,000	3,553	184,447
1907	263,000	4,997	258,003
1908	232,000	4,454	227,546
1909	301,000	5,831	295,169
1910	310,000	7,037	302,963
1911	268,000	6,968	261,032
1912	355,000	10,437	344,563
1913	355,000	11,608	343,392
1914	329,000	11,843	317,157
1915	303,000	12,241	290,759
1916	319,000	14,291	304,709
1917	460,000	22,586	437,414
1918	665,000	35,578	629,422
1919	670,000	38,800	631,200

* Other than to make butter, cheese, and condensed and evaporated milk.

Table II 9c

Value of Eggs Produced and Destined for Consumption in Farm Households or for Sale to Ultimate Consumers, 1869, 1879, 1889–1919
(thousands of dollars)

	PRODUCED	USED IN MFG.	DESTINED FOR CONSUMPTION IN FARM HOUSEHOLDS OR FOR SALE TO ULTIMATE CONSUMERS
1869	57,400	1,476	55,924
1879	66,690	2,831	63,859
1889	119,470	4,817	114,653
1890	127,728	5,058	122,670
1891	142,648	5,549	137,099
1892	161,134	6,171	154,963
1893	173,925	6,540	167,385
1894	160,427	5,920	154,507
1895	162,582	5,885	156,697
1896	157,380	5,587	151,793
1897	156,479	5,461	151,018
1898	173,552	5,935	167,617
1899	188,630	6,315	182,315
1900	203,995	6,834	197,161
1901	231,014	7,762	223,252
1902	261,497	8,786	252,711
1903	269,957	9,098	260,859
1904	307,738	10,364	297,374
1905	310,707	10,968	299,739
1906	324,702	11,982	312,720
1907	382,586	14,730	367,856
1908	370,113	14,842	355,271
1909	379,652	15,815	363,837
1910	427,072	17,894	409,178
1911	374,768	15,778	358,990
1912	422,588	17,833	404,755
1913	401,228	17,012	384,216
1914	426,029	18,146	407,883
1915	451,307	19,767	431,540
1916	495,224	22,285	472,939
1917	696,069	32,089	663,980
1918	767,865	36,320	731,545
1919	979,944	47,567	932,377

Table II 9d

Value of Fish Catch Destined for Sale to Ultimate Consumers
1869, 1879, 1889–1919
(thousands of dollars)

	TOTAL CATCH	USED IN MFG.	DESTINED FOR SALE TO ULTIMATE CONSUMERS
1869	10,510	1,064	9,446
1879	33,656	3,806	29,850
1889	37,757	4,009	33,748
1890	41,252	4,562	36,690
1891	43,406	4,992	38,414
1892	46,810	5,589	41,221
1893	46,993	5,818	41,175
1894	44,222	5,669	38,553
1895	42,076	5,579	36,497
1896	38,359	5,255	33,104
1897	35,464	5,015	30,449
1898	35,325	5,150	30,175
1899	48,717	7,316	41,401
1900	46,870	7,293	39,577
1901	54,265	8,737	45,528
1902	45,627	7,588	38,039
1903	47,696	8,189	39,507
1904	49,212	8,715	40,497
1905	58,927	10,324	48,603
1906	46,798	8,110	38,688
1907	58,398	10,009	48,389
1908	50,884	8,625	42,259
1909	61,098	10,238	50,860
1910	50,715	9,301	41,414
1911	65,151	12,978	52,173
1912	45,284	9,732	35,552
1913	59,694	13,771	45,923
1914	49,326	12,157	37,169
1915	50,332	13,582	36,740
1916	58,435	17,145	41,290
1917	92,513	29,308	63,205
1918	89,975	30,618	59,357
1919	87,139	31,696	55,443

Note to Table II 9
Derivation of the Estimates
1 Fruits, vegetables, and nuts

Citrus fruits, orchard fruits, grapes, potatoes, sweet potatoes, dry edible beans, nuts, vegetables raised for sale, products of farm gardens, and small fruits are included in this classification.

a *Citrus fruits*

The method of estimate was suggested in *Gross Farm Income, Indexes of Farm Production, and Indexes of Farm Prices in the United States, 1869–1937*, Frederick Strauss and Louis Bean (Department of Agriculture, Washington, D.C., 1939), hereafter referred to as Strauss and Bean. Because of minor improvements, our estimates do not correspond exactly with those of Strauss and Bean.

Crop year shipments of both California and Florida oranges and lemons were available 1889–1918. California figures in boxes, 1901–18, were taken from the *Annual Report of the State Board of Agriculture, 1918*, p. 178; *1919*, p. 161; before 1901 the figures were given in carlots, *ibid., 1921*, p. 237. The carlot data were converted to boxes on the basis of 374 boxes of oranges and 313 boxes of lemons to a car. Florida shipments in boxes are given for the entire period in Strauss and Bean, p. 85.

California orange prices, 1895–1918, were computed by dividing f.o.b. income (Strauss and Bean, p. 85) by the number of boxes shipped. The level of this series was then adjusted to the calendar year census[a] prices of California oranges and lemons. Prices, 1889–95, were estimated by using the Strauss and Bean price index for orchard fruits, citrus fruits, and grapes (p. 147) to interpolate between the 1889 census price and the previously derived 1895 price. A similar procedure was followed with the Florida data except that prices could be computed only to 1909; prior to that year the Florida price series was extrapolated by the movement of the series previously estimated for California oranges.

Crop year shipments were converted to calendar year by distributing them 25 and 75 percent (Strauss and Bean, p. 83) and multiplying the calendar year estimates by the appropriate price series. The resulting values were combined and raised to cover all lemons and oranges grown in the United States and to include other citrus and subtropical fruits by straight line interpolation of census year ratios.

b *Orchard fruits*

Apples, peaches, pears, and plums and prunes were estimated separately:

Calendar year production of apples since 1899 (*Yearbook of Agriculture, 1928*, p. 764) was multiplied by an estimated apple price series (Strauss and

---

[a] Reference to 'census' means that figures were obtained from the *Census of Agriculture*, taken decennially from 1869 to 1919.

Bean, p. 82) which had been adjusted to the level of the census prices for 1909 and 1919.

Calendar year peach production since 1899 (*Yearbook of Agriculture, 1923,* p. 745, and *1928,* p. 778) was extrapolated to 1889 by the Department of Agriculture 'condition of crop' or yield percentages (*ibid., 1923,* p. 746). The 1889 and 1899 census quantities were raised to full crop estimates by dividing by these percentages, then interpolating along a straight line. The resulting full crop estimates were multiplied by the yield percentages to derive actual crop estimates. For 1910–19 (*ibid.,* p. 747) the 1919 census price was extrapolated by a weighted average of farm prices per bushel of peaches. Prior to 1909 the 1909 census price for peaches was extrapolated by the Strauss and Bean apple price series. Values were then calculated by multiplying the production data by the derived prices.

Calendar year production of pears (*ibid.,* p. 748, and *1928,* p. 781) was multiplied by the weighted average price per bushel of pears (*ibid., 1923,* p. 750) for 1910–19. Because the level of this series was extremely close to the 1919 census price it was not adjusted.

Calendar year production of plums and prunes in California 1890–1917 (*Annual Report of the California State Board of Agriculture, 1919,* p. 165) was adjusted to the level of census totals by extrapolating forward to 1917 using the 1909 ratio, by straight line interpolation of the census year ratios for the intercensal period 1899–1909, and by extrapolating backward to 1890 using the 1899 ratio. A figure for 1918 was obtained by straight line interpolation between the 1917 estimate and the 1919 census total. The average price per pound for California prunes, in boxes, 1890–1919 (Bureau of Labor Statistics, *Bulletin 320,* pp. 116–7) was converted to a per bushel basis, adjusted to census price levels, and used to translate the production estimates into values. The estimated 1890 price was used also for 1889.

The aggregates of the above orchard fruits were raised, by straight line interpolation of census year ratios, to cover all orchard fruits. For 1879 and 1869 census value for all orchard fruits were used directly.

c *Grapes*

The estimates of grape production are based on data for California, Ohio, and the Chatauqua-Erie district of New York state. California production of table and raisin grapes, 1899–1919, and wine grapes, 1890–1919, are from S. W. Shear and H. F. Gould, *Economic Status of the Grape Industry* (University of California College of Agriculture, Agricultural Experiment Station, *Bulletin 429,* 1927), p. 122, and S. W. Shear and G. G. Pearce, *Supply and Price Trends in the California Wine Grape Industry* (*ibid.,* Giannini Foundation, mimeographed report 34, June 1934), Table 42. The Ohio grape crop, 1889–1918, is from the *Annual Report of the Secretary of State to the Governor of Ohio, 1890–1914,* and *Ohio Agricultural Statistics, 1914–20.* A figure for 1919 was obtained by correspondence with P. P. Wallrabenstein, Department of Rural Economics, Ohio State University. Production in the Chatauqua-Erie district, 1900–18, is from H. D. Phillips, *Cooperative Marketing in the Chatauqua-*

ESTIMATES OF THE VALUE OF OUTPUT   255

Erie Grape Industry (Cornell University, Agricultural Experiment Station, *Memoir 28,* Sept. 1919), p. 14. Data for 1919 (Shear and Gould, *op. cit.,* p. 89), reported in carlots, were converted to tons by using the Shear and Gould conversion factor of 10 tons per car. An 1899 estimate was based on the movement of the California and Ohio series.

To estimate total grape production 1899–1919 the three series were combined and raised to census levels by straight line interpolation of the census year ratios. The 1899 census total was extrapolated 1890–98 by the two available series.

F.o.b. shipping point, average prices per ton, for California Malaga and Tokay grapes 1910–19 are from Shear and Gould, *op. cit.,* p. 86; also, the estimated prices per ton paid to California growers for wine grapes 1889–1910 (Table 25). Prices for dry and sweet wine grapes are reported separately; averages were calculated by weighting the prices 6 and 4 respectively. Finally, the average prices per ton of Chatauqua-Erie grapes, 1900–19, were calculated by dividing the reported values by the derived tonnage figures.

For 1910–19 the California Malaga-Tokay prices were weighted 9 and the Chatauqua-Erie prices 1 on the basis of approximate production in census years. The 1919 census price was extrapolated to 1910 by the resulting average. The 1909 census price was extrapolated to 1900 by the average of the California wine grape price, weighted 4, and the Chatauqua-Erie price, weighted 1. For years before 1900 the movement of the California series alone was used.

d *Potatoes*

Crop year sales of potatoes and the value of those used in farm households 1909–19 (*Disposition of Potatoes, Crop Years 1910–37,* Department of Agriculture, Agricultural Marketing Service, Sept. 1939, p. 8) were adjusted to calendar years on the basis of the ratios of calendar year gross income from potatoes to crop year gross income (Strauss and Bean, p. 53). The series were extrapolated beyond 1909 by the Strauss and Bean calendar year gross income figures.

e *Sweet potatoes and dry edible beans*

Calendar year estimates of gross income received by farmers for these crops were taken from Strauss and Bean, pp. 55, 73.

f *Nuts*

California production of walnuts and almonds, 1899–1918, was taken from the *Annual Statistical Report of the California State Board of Agriculture, 1918,* pp. 217, 218, and *1917,* p. 191. For 1899–1909 the series was raised to cover all walnuts and almonds grown in the United States by straight line interpolation of the census year ratios. For 1909–18 the 1909 ratios were used. Average calendar year import prices for almonds, 1889–1919, and walnuts, 1901–19, were taken from the *Monthly Summary of Foreign Commerce (seriatim).* For 1909–19 these prices were adjusted to census levels by straight line interpolation of the census year ratios; for years before 1909 the 1909 ratios were used. Walnut prices before 1901 were estimated from the movement of almond prices.

Values, calculated by multiplying the almond and walnut production estimates by the adjusted import price series, were raised to include all nuts by straight line interpolation of the census year ratios for 1909 and 1919, and by using the 1909 ratios for 1899–1909.

For 1889–98 the 1889 and 1899 census quantities of almonds, walnuts, and pecans were interpolated along a straight line. The census year quantities were divided into the estimated 1899 value for all nuts and the 1889 census value in order to get per pound prices which, when multiplied by the estimated production of almonds, walnuts and pecans, gave estimates of the value of all nuts. The prices for 1899 and 1889 were then interpolated by the movement of the almond import price series, and the resulting series used to convert the previously derived quantities into values.

g *Small fruits*

Census values for 1899, 1909, and 1919 were used directly. Estimates were made for 1910–18, 1900–08, 1879–98, and 1869 from the movement of the aggregate estimates for all fruits, vegetables, and nuts, excluding small fruits, vegetables raised for sale, and farm garden crops.

h *Vegetables raised for sale and farm garden crops*

Census values for 1899, 1909, and 1919 were used directly. Vegetables raised for sale were estimated for 1918 from the movement of the value of commercial truck crops in *Agricultural Statistics, 1939*, p. 258; farm garden crops were estimated for 1918 from the movement of the aggregate estimates for all fruits, vegetables, and nuts, excluding small fruits, vegetables raised for sale, and farm garden crops. For 1899–1918 estimates for the combined value of vegetables raised for sale and farm garden crops were based on straight line interpolation of the ratios of the 1918 total and the 1909 and 1899 census values to the aggregate estimates excluding small fruits. For years before 1899, 1899 ratios were used.

Apportionment of Fruits, Vegetables and Nuts

The estimates of unfinished fruits, vegetables, and nuts were based on the materials consumed method. The limitations of this method, which is used also for other nonmanufactured foods below, are described in Note A to Table II 2.

Census data were reported for fruits and vegetables consumed in the canning and preserving industry (1899, 1904), nuts in the chocolate and cocoa products industry (1919), fruits and nuts in the confectionery and ice cream industry (1919), fruits in the flavoring extracts industry (1929), potatoes in the glucose and starch industry (1899–1919), and grapes in the liquors, vinous industry (1899). Estimates for the other census years were based upon the ratios of these materials to the total cost of materials, excluding fuel and rent of power, for the respective industries. The census year estimates were then totaled and expressed as a percentage of the estimates of the aggregate value of all fruits, vegetables, and nuts for those years; intercensal estimates

ESTIMATES OF THE VALUE OF OUTPUT

were based on straight line interpolation of census year ratios. Estimates for finished fruits, vegetables, and nuts, are the differences between the estimates for unfinished and aggregate values.

2 *Wheat, Corn, Rye, and Buckwheat consumed in farm households*

Farm household consumption of each crop was estimated separately.

For the calendar years 1910–19 the annual values were taken from *Income Parity for Agriculture,* Part I, Farm Income (Department of Agriculture, Bureau of Agricultural Economics), Sec. 5, *Income from Wheat,* p. 7; Sec. 7, *Income from Corn,* p. 12; Sec. 10, *Income from Rye and Buckwheat,* pp. 11, 81.

Values were estimated for the years before 1910 by using the calendar year gross incomes for each crop as extrapolators (Strauss and Bean, pp. 36, 39, 40, 48–50).

3 *Butter and cheese*

Total production of butter and cheese, farm and factory, was taken from Strauss and Bean, pp. 94–5. Farm production was computed by applying unpublished percentage allocations prepared by E. E. Vial of the Department of Agriculture. Census prices of butter and cheese were interpolated by the butter prices and Wisconsin cheese prices given in Strauss and Bean, pp. 94–5. Farm values were then calculated by multiplying the quantity estimates by the derived prices.

Since all unfinished butter and cheese, except unfinished butter for 1869, had been estimated previously (Note A to Table II 2) it was unnecessary to apportion the estimates of farm value between finished and unfinished. Unfinished butter for 1869 was estimated on the basis of its percentage relation in 1879 to the total value of farm and factory butter.

4 *Fluid milk*

Gross income from the production of fluid milk was taken from Strauss and Bean, p. 98. Since the data excluded milk used in the production of butter, cheese, condensed and evaporated milk, it was necessary to estimate only the value of fluid milk consumed in other manufacturing industries. Such estimates, made by using the materials consumed method, were based on milk consumed in the bread and bakery products industry (1923), the oleomargarine industry (1899), the ice cream industry (1929), and the confectionery industry (1929). Consumption in other census years was estimated from the ratios of the value of milk consumed to the total cost of materials, excluding fuel and rent of power, in the census years for which specific industry data were available. Consumption in the ice cream industry was estimated for 1914 and 1919 alone since the industry was not included in the census before 1914. The census year aggregates of milk consumed were expressed as a percentage of total farm production of fluid milk, and intercensal consumption was based upon straight line interpolation of the resulting ratios.

5 Eggs

For census years, figures adjusted for varying amounts of census underreporting were taken from Strauss and Bean, p. 103. Intercensal interpolation was based on the marketings of eggs, 1891–1919, in Boston, Chicago, Milwaukee, New York, St. Louis, and San Francisco (*Yearbook of Agriculture, 1912*, p. 688, and *1919*, p. 666) ; and on the production of eggs in Ohio, 1889–1917 (Annual Reports of the Ohio Board of Agriculture, *Ohio Agricultural Statistics, seriatim*). The Ohio series was extended to 1919 by the movement of the marketing totals in seven cities, the six listed above and Cincinnati. Since an indeterminate amount of the Ohio production was duplicated in the marketings, the marketing series was weighted 2 and the Ohio series 1 in combining the two samples. Ratios of the combined sample to the census year figures were computed and intercensal estimates based on straight line interpolation of these ratios. The resulting estimates were multiplied by the annual price of eggs (Strauss and Bean, p. 103).

The allocation of eggs between finished and unfinished was estimated by the materials consumed method. Census year estimates of consumption in the bread and other bakery products industry were based on the 1923 ratio of the cost of eggs to the total cost of materials, excluding fuel and rent of power. This series was then raised to cover consumption in all industries on the basis of data for 1929. Total consumption by manufacturers (*Materials Used in Manufactures: 1929*, p. 45) was expressed as a percentage of 1929 consumption in the bread and bakery products industry. Intercensal estimates were derived by straight line interpolation of the census year ratios of the estimated cost of eggs used in all manufacturing to the estimated values for total egg production.

6 Cattle and calves, hogs, sheep and lambs slaughtered for home consumption

Quantities and values of cattle and calves, hogs, and sheep and lambs slaughtered for home consumption were reported for 1909–19 in *Income Parity for Agriculture*, Part I, Farm Income, Sec. 4, *Income from Cattle and Calves*, pp. 12, 13; Sec. 3, *Income from Hogs*, pp. 11, 12; and Sec. 6, *Sheep and Lambs, Wool and Mohair*, pp. 17, 18. Quantities were extrapolated to 1899 by the movement of the farm slaughter series (*Agricultural Statistics, 1939*, pp. 318, 329, and 347). Estimates for 1869, 1879, and 1889–98 were based upon the movement of the total slaughter series (Strauss and Bean, pp. 110, 114, 119, 122–3).

Prices with which to translate the estimated quantities into values were calculated by extrapolating the 1909 prices per unit slaughtered for home consumption. The cattle and calf price was extrapolated by the average of beginning and end of year farm values for cattle other than milk cows (*Agricultural Statistics, 1939*, p. 308) ; the hog price and the sheep and lamb price were extrapolated by series given in Strauss and Bean, pp. 119, 122–3.

ESTIMATES OF THE VALUE OF OUTPUT

7 Fish

United States totals for fish were built up from annual estimates of the catch in four important regions—New England, Middle Atlantic, Lake, and Pacific—and from occasional figures reported by the Bureau of Fisheries for other regions.

The quantity and value of the New England catch were given for 1889, 1898, 1902, 1905, 1908, and 1919 in *Fishery Industries of the United States, 1929* (Bureau of Fisheries, Document 1095), p. 825. Interpolating series included the value of landings at Boston and Gloucester in 1891 and 1893–1919 (*Annual Report of U. S. Commissioner of Fisheries, seriatim*); and the Connecticut shad and lobster catch for 1905–19 (*Biennial Report of Connecticut State Board of Fisheries and Game, seriatim*).

For 1905–19 the two samples were combined and ratios to the New England catch in 1905, 1908, and 1919 computed; intercensal estimates were then based upon straight line interpolation of the ratios. For years before 1905 the Boston and Gloucester sample alone was used. Ratios to total catch were computed and estimates for 1891 and 1893–1905 based on the various ratios. Estimates for 1890 and 1892 were calculated by straight line interpolation of the catch for 1889 and the estimates already made for 1891 and 1893.

The quantity and value of the Middle Atlantic catch were given for 1889–91, 1897, 1901, 1904, and 1908 in *Fishery Industries*, p. 859. Interpolating series included the landing of mackerel along the Atlantic coast, 1908–19 (*ibid.*, p. 856) and the value of landings, excluding mackerel, at Boston and Gloucester (for years reported, see above). For 1908–19 the mackerel series, multiplied by the average price per pound for mackerel landed at Boston and Gloucester, was combined with the Boston and Gloucester series; and the total used to extrapolate the 1908 value for the Middle Atlantic catch. Estimates for all earlier years except 1892 were based upon the ratios of the Boston and Gloucester data, including mackerel, to the Middle Atlantic catch. That for 1892 was derived by straight line interpolation of the figures for 1891 and 1893.

The quantity and value of the Lake catch were reported for 1890, 1899, 1903, and 1908, and quantity alone for 1913–19 in *Fishery Industries*, p. 1,038. A value for 1917 was estimated by using the per pound price calculated from the Great Lakes quantity and value figures (*Statistical Abstract of the United States, 1924*, p. 674). Values for 1913–16 were estimated by using prices obtained by extrapolating the 1917 price by the price per pound of the Lake Erie catch (*Biennial Report of Pennsylvania Department of Fisheries, 1916–17*, p. 26; *1915–16*, p. 31; *1914–15*, p. 17; *1913–14*, p. 13; *1912–13*, p. 18).

Estimates for 1909–12 were based upon the movement of the value of the catch in Lakes Michigan, Superior, and Green Bay (*Biennial Report of Wisconsin Commissioners of Fisheries, 1913–14*, p. 11; *1911–12*, p. 34; *1909–10*, p. 29). No estimates were made for the years missing before 1908.

The quantity and value of the Pacific catch were given for 1892, 1895, 1899, 1904, 1908, and 1915 in *Fishery Industries*, p. 1,007. Interpolating series,

1889–1919, included the Pacific cod catch in pounds (J. N. Cobb, *Pacific Cod Fisheries,* Department of Commerce, Bureau of Fisheries, Document 1,014, p. 464), and the Pacific salmon pack, excluding Alaska and British Columbia (J. N. Cobb, *Pacific Salmon Fisheries, ibid.,* Document 1,092, pp. 553–55). Quantities for the entire Pacific catch were interpolated by the total of these two series.

Prices were calculated by interpolating the available per pound figures for the entire catch by annual salmon prices. The salmon series was for opening prices of 1 pound tall cans for the different varieties given, together with pack data, in *Pacific Salmon Fisheries,* pp. 586–88. For 1906–19 the pack data, also reported by varieties, were used as weights to derive a single composite series. Before 1906 the separate prices were combined by using weights approximated from an average of the 1906–10 figures: Chinock, 1, Puget sockeye, 1, Alaska red, 5, and Alaska pink, 5.

The values of the catch in the South Atlantic and Gulf regions were reported for 1889, 1890, 1897, 1902, 1908, and 1918 in *Fishery Industries,* pp. 910, 967. No estimates were made for intervening years.

Censuses of the fishery industries of the United States were taken in 1869, 1879, 1889, and 1908. All products except food fish, edible crustaceans and mollusks, and oysters were eliminated from the totals reported for those years. Estimates for the years in which the South Atlantic and Gulf catches were available as well as that for other regions were based upon straight line interpolation of census year ratios between 1889 and 1908 and 1908 ratios for 1918. Estimates for all other years except 1919 were based upon straight line interpolation of the ratios of the sample data to the previously derived totals for the specified years; that for 1919 was based upon the 1918 ratios.

The apportionment of fish between finished and unfinished was based upon the materials consumed method. Total consumption of fish in food manufacturing industries in 1929 (*Materials Used in Manufactures: 1929,* p. 45) was extrapolated to all other census years except 1879 by the movement of the cost of materials, excluding fuel and rent of power, in the fish canning and preserving industry. Ratios of estimated census year consumption to total catch were then calculated and intercensal estimates based upon straight line interpolation.

Since the fish canning and preserving industry was not included in the 1879 census, a more complicated method had to be employed. First an 1879 commodity total for the industry was estimated by applying the 1889 ratio of the commodity total for the fish canning industry to the fish catch for that year. An 1879 cost of materials estimate was calculated by applying the 1889 ratio of cost of materials to the commodity total; this estimate was then adjusted to include all fish consumed in food manufacturing industries. Finally, the estimated consumption figure was subtracted from the value of the fish catch; the estimated commodity total for the fish canning industry was added. This provided an 1879 total roughly comparable with the sum of the fish canning figures in Table I and the estimates of the finished part of the fish catch in other census years.

ESTIMATES OF THE VALUE OF OUTPUT

8 *Natural mineral waters*

Annual values of natural mineral waters, 1889–1919, were taken from *Mineral Resources of the United States,* Part II, *1914,* p. 218; *1918,* p. 499, and *1921,* p. 231. A figure for 1879 was estimated from the ratio in 1889 of the value of natural waters to the census value of manufactured mineral and soda waters.

Table II 10

Value of Nonmanufactured Fuels Destined for Sale to Ultimate Consumers, 1869, 1879, 1889–1919

	ANTHRACITE COAL, DOMESTIC SIZES			BITUMINOUS COAL			FUEL BRIQUETS			TOTAL $000
	SHIPMENTS 000 NET TONS (1)	PRICE PER NET TON $ (2)	VALUE AT MINE $000 (3)	DESTINED FOR SALE TO ULTIMATE CONSUMERS $000 (4)	AV. PRICE PER NET TON PREPARED SIZES AT MINE $ (5)	VALUE AT MINE $000 (6)	PRODUCTION 000 NET TONS (7)	VALUE $000 (8)	(3) + (6) + (8) (9)
1869	13,014	3.484	45,341	2,101	2.092	4,395			49,736
1879	24,537	2.015	49,442	4,975	1.210	6,020			55,462
1889	33,617	1.902	63,932	12,452	1.069	13,311			77,243
1890	34,385	1.884	64,779	14,405	1.069	15,399			80,178
1891	37,595	1.929	72,505	15,290	1.069	16,345			88,850
1892	39,072	2.071	80,936	16,418	1.069	17,551			98,487
1893	39,809	2.098	83,528	16,513	1.037	17,124			100,652
1894	37,818	1.991	75,298	15,308	0.983	15,048			90,346
1895	41,100	1.866	76,695	17,422	0.929	16,186			92,881
1896	38,320	1.982	75,955	17,743	0.897	15,915			91,870
1897	36,357	1.991	72,390	19,027	0.875	16,649			89,039
1898	36,202	1.866	67,555	21,383	0.864	18,475			86,030
1899	40,376	1.929	78,561	24,747	0.940	23,262			101,823
1900	38,036	1.964	74,714	26,967	1.124	30,311			105,025
1901	45,000	2.205	99,242	28,852	1.134	32,718			131,960
1902	25,414	2.429	61,720	33,429	1.210	40,449			102,169
1903	49,558	2.696	133,629	36,319	1.340	48,667			182,296
1904	47,282	2.509	118,627	35,528	1.188	42,207			160,834
1905	50,001	2.420	120,985	40,181	1.145	46,007			166,992
1906	44,529	2.446	108,937	43,701	1.199	52,397			161,334
1907	53,417	2.518	134,497	50,105	1.232	61,729	67	258	196,484
1908	51,799	2.509	129,960	42,126	1.210	50,972	90	323	181,255
1909	49,297	2.429	119,721	48,138	1.156	55,648	140	453	175,822
1910	51,873	2.509	130,145	52,944	1.210	64,062		631	194,838
1911	56,013	2.571	144,035	50,928	1.199	61,063	218	809	205,907
1912	52,566	2.714	142,679	56,642	1.242	70,349	220	952	213,980
1913	58,052	2.723	158,088	59,784	1.275	76,225	182	1,007	235,320
1914	57,299	2.768	158,596	53,143	1.264	67,173	251	1,155	226,924
1915	55,042	2.768	152,350	55,000	1.221	67,155	222	1,036	220,541
1916	53,787	3.179	170,695	62,787	1.426	89,534	295	1,446	261,675
1917	60,502	3.723	225,263	57,104	2.441	139,391	407	2,234	366,888
1918	58,762	4.330	254,460	57,000	2.787	158,859	477	3,213	416,532
1919	55,537	5.366	298,018	53,611	2.690	144,214	296	2,301	444,533

Note to Table II 10
Derivation of the Estimates
Anthracite Coal

Annual shipments of domestic sizes, pea and larger, were given for 1913–19 in *Mineral Resources of the United States, 1926,* Part II, p. 574, and *1924,* Part II, p. 575. Data excluding pea were also shown for 1890–1912; for these years pea was estimated upon the basis of the 1913 ratio of pea to total pea and steam. Shipments of domestic sizes in 1869, 1879, and 1889 were estimated from the 1890 ratio to all anthracite shipments.

A composite price of domestic sizes, calculated by weighting prices of lump, broken, egg, stove, chestnut, and pea (reported for 1910–19 in *Mineral Resources*) by the quantity of each type shipped, was extrapolated to 1909 and the earlier years through 1880 by the average value at mine per net ton of all anthracite (*Mineral Resources, 1921,* Part II, p. 534). The 1879 and 1880 relative prices for stove, egg, and chestnut (Aldrich Report, Part I, p. 39) were weighted similarly in order to extrapolate the estimated 1880 price to 1879. To get a price for 1869 the movement of bituminous prices shown in the Aldrich Report was used.

The estimates of values, obtained by multiplying the estimated shipments of domestic sizes by the derived prices, are slightly high because of the inclusion in domestic sizes of a small but indeterminate amount intended for business or industrial use.

Bituminous Coal

Total United States consumption was given for 1913–19 in *Mineral Resources of the United States, 1923,* Part II, p. 504. For years before 1913 production figures (*Mineral Resources, 1921,* Part II, p. 482) were adjusted for calendar year exports and imports on the basis of data compiled from *Monthly Summary of Commerce and Finance* (seriatim).

Domestic or household consumption was estimated by applying varying percentages to total consumption. For 1919, 12 percent, the approximate percentage for 1923, the nearest postwar year for which data were available, was used; for 1918, 10 percent, 1917, 11, and 1915, 13 were used, on the basis of figures in *Report of Distribution Division, 1918–1919,* Part I, *The Distribution of Coal and Coke* (United States Fuel Administration) p. 12; for 1916 and the years before 1915, the 1915 percentage was applied. These obviously crude estimates should be considered merely as usable approximations.

The average value at mine, 1880–1919 (*Mineral Resources, 1921,* Part II, p. 482), raised on the basis of the average ratio for 1917–20 of the wholesale prices of prepared sizes, southern Illinois field, to the wholesale prices of mine run, same field (Bureau of Labor Statistics, *Bulletin 320,* p. 16) was used as a price series. A price was estimated for 1869 and 1879 by means of the movement from 1880 to 1879 of the relative prices for bituminous coal (Aldrich Report, p. 39).

Fuel Briquets

Annual values were reported for 1907–09 and 1911–19 in *Mineral Resources of the United States, 1919*, Part II, p. 35. A figure for 1910 was estimated by straight line interpolation of the 1909 and 1911 figures. Prior to 1907 production was apparently so negligible as not to be compiled separately.

TABLE II 11

Value of Nonmanufactured Construction Materials
1869, 1879, 1889–1919
(thousands of dollars)

	LUMBER DESTINED FOR DIRECT USE IN CONSTRUCTION	CROSSTIES	SAND-BUILDING, PAVING, RR. BALLAST & GRAVEL	CRUSHED STONE	TOTAL
1869	43,503	5,707		no	49,210
1879	67,083	11,037		data	78,120
1889	106,034	18,374		4,309	128,717
1890	123,826	19,565		4,388	147,779
1891	116,340	16,913		3,913	137,166
1892	146,175	22,704		4,031	172,910
1893	119,809	21,117		2,812	143,738
1894	120,856	19,871		3,067	143,794
1895	128,950	21,764		2,870	153,584
1896	112,328	19,901		2,593	134,822
1897	127,664	20,970		2,984	151,618
1898	126,268	22,943		3,176	152,387
1899	131,419	28,394		3,697	163,510
1900	157,780	30,533		5,142	193,455
1901	161,079	32,618		6,744	200,441
1902	184,926	38,562	133	8,820	232,441
1903	190,619	48,751	122	9,327	248,819
1904	191,125	44,188	1,784	11,071	248,168
1905	202,390	40,230	6,086	11,540	260,246
1906	244,527	48,819	7,798	11,477	312,621
1907	267,221	78,959	8,680	15,390	370,250
1908	245,021	58,932	9,332	14,435	327,720
1909	233,257	60,721	12,959	17,067	324,004
1910	243,019	68,483	15,085	18,308	344,895
1911	230,174	60,909	15,091	18,868	325,042
1912	244,038	59,898	16,380	18,334	338,650
1913	254,501	54,540	18,138	20,759	347,938
1914	216,262	54,626	18,533	19,437	308,858
1915	197,656	49,288	17,909	19,434	284,287
1916	226,650	54,582	22,216	17,593	321,041
1917	271,200	49,946	25,135	16,185	362,466
1918	304,586	57,690	24,796	14,941	402,013
1919	379,222	75,722	34,773	18,654	508,371

NOTE TO TABLE II 11

DERIVATION OF THE ESTIMATES

Lumber

The production of soft- and hardwoods in 1899 and 1904–19 was taken from Frank J. Hallauer, *Our National Timber Requirements,* Senate Document 12, Separate 4 (prepared by the Forest Service in response to Senate Resolution 175, 73d Cong., 1st Sess.), Table 1. Total production, given also for 1869, 1879, and 1889, was apportioned according to the division in 1899.

Softwood production for intercensal years prior to 1904 was estimated from the following samples:

1 Production of white pine in the Northwest, 1889–1904 (*American Lumberman,* Jan. 21, 1905, p. 27).
2 Pine, spruce and hemlock surveyed at Bangor, Me., 1889–1904 (J. E. Defebaugh, *History of the Lumber Industry of America,* Vol. 2, Chicago, 1907, pp. 58–9).
3 Spruce, pine and hemlock, product of the Adirondack forest, 1889–1904 (*ibid.,* p. 405).
4 Arrivals of redwood, pine, and fir at California points, 1899–1904 (*Monthly Summary of Finance and Commerce, seriatim*).
5 Receipts of lumber at Norfolk, Va., 1889–99 (*ibid.,* Nov. 1900, p. 1,089).
6 Shipments of lumber from Savannah, Ga., 1889–99 (*ibid.,* p. 1,092).

For 1899–1904 estimates were based upon the movement of the aggregate for the first four series; for 1889–99 the sum of all the series except that of arrivals at California points was used.

Since no satisfactory hardwood samples were available, hardwood production for intercensal years was estimated from the movement of the derived softwood figures.

The allocation of production between unfinished and construction materials was based upon the quantities of wood, by species, used in all industries engaged primarily in the manufacture of wooden products (J. C. Nellis, *Lumber Used in the Manufacture of Wooden Products,* Department of Agriculture, *Bulletin 605,* Feb. 27, 1918, Table 1). Totals for soft and hardwoods were calculated by summation. Although the Nellis compilation was built up from state reports for several years, the majority were for 1911 and we used the figures to represent consumption in that year. The percentages that consumption of soft- and hardwoods constituted of total production were computed and applied to the production totals for all other years. Application of constant percentages undoubtedly affects the reliability of the estimates, especially during the War years. But the error introduced is perhaps not as serious as might be supposed. A similar compilation for 1928 (*Lumber Used in Manufacture,* 1928, Department of Agriculture, *Forest Service,* Table 1), shows that the lumber consumed in that year was between 50 and 60 percent of total production. For 1911 the roughly comparable percentage was 57.1. These over-all percentages, however, conceal an apparent trend toward greater consumption of hardwoods and less consumption of softwoods.

The annual output of lumber destined for use in construction without further processing, obtained by subtracting the consumption estimates, was converted into values by data from *American Forests and Forest Products,* Statistical Bulletin 21 (Department of Agriculture, 1927). Table 74 of that bulletin gives average mill prices per M board feet, by kinds of wood, for 1899, 1904, 1907, 1909–11, and 1915–19. To derive a composite price series for softwoods the individual prices for 10 important species—cedar, cypress, Douglas fir, hemlock, redwood, spruce, western yellow pine, eastern yellow pine, white pine, and larch—were weighted by annual production figures. Similarly, a composite hardwood price was obtained by weighting the prices for oak, maple, gum, chestnut, birch, beech, yellow poplar, elm, basswood, cottonwood, ash, and hickory by annual production figures. To interpolate for the missing years and to extrapolate for the years before 1899, the average prices per M board feet, in eastern markets, of first and average quality 1 inch soft- and hardwoods (*ibid.,* Table 76) were used. For both soft- and hardwoods the prices for average quality were given a weight of 2 and those for first quality a weight of 1.

The price series thus derived are at levels determined by the weights of the total production of the different species; they should be at levels determined by the amount of each species used directly for construction. For 1911 composite prices were estimated by applying approximately correct weights, calculated by raising the total production of the woods listed above to allow for underreporting,[a] and subtracting the amount of each species consumed in manufacturing. The 1911 composite prices thus estimated were compared with the prices first estimated for 1911 and the levels of the original prices adjusted accordingly. The same proportionate adjustments were applied to all years.

The values of lumber destined for direct use in construction, calculated from the above production and price data, include lath and shingles. Since these products are already included with manufactured construction materials (see Table I 4 for census year values and Note B to Table II 6 for a description of the derivation of intercensal estimates) they were subtracted from the total lumber figures. The differences, the final estimates, are probably too high. First, data on lumber consumption apparently do not include lumber used for boxes and crates in establishments whose chief products are not wooden. Second, even though we made crude adjustments we are not sure that the levels of the price series are low enough. There is reason to believe that lumber used in manufactures is usually superior in quality to that used directly for construction; if so, average prices received for the total production of each species overstate the values destined for construction. Finally, our estimates probably include small but indeterminate amounts of sawed ties, the values of which are included also in the estimates of railway ties (see below). To the extent that lumber pro-

[a] The Forest Service revised the total estimates of soft- and hardwoods for 1911 (*Our National Timber Requirements,* Table 1), but did not revise the estimates for the different species (*Statistical Bulletin 21,* pp. 62–3). To compute revised figures for each species we applied ratios based upon the revision of the soft- and hardwood totals.

duced on farms (not included in the total production on which we based our estimates) is used directly for construction, the preceding biases may be compensated.

Crossties

Purchases of crossties by steam and electric railroads for 1906–11 and 1915 were reported in *Statistical Bulletin 21,* Tables 186 and 188. A 1905 figure for steam railroads alone was raised to include electric roads by using 1906 percentages. Estimates for 1904, 1912–14, and 1916–19 were based upon the production of the three types of wood most commonly used in making crossties; southern pine, oak, and cedar *(ibid.,* Table 55). An extrapolating series for 1890–1904 was constructed from the track mileage data for steam railroads *(Statistics of Railways, 1926,* p. XCVIII). Additions to mileage for the fiscal year following the calendar year were multiplied by 3,000, the approximate number of ties required per mile of new construction *(Our National Timber Requirements,* p. 272). Approximate renewals were calculated by multiplying the total track mileage of the fiscal year preceding the calendar year by 261 ties per mile, the average figure for renewals on principal roads 1910–15 *(ibid.,* p. 271). The sum of these two series was used to extrapolate the 1905 figure for total purchases. Estimates for 1889, 1879, and 1869 were also based upon track mileage, but the mileage data had first to be adjusted. Total mileage for the year ending June 30, 1889 was estimated from the movement of operated mileage *(Report on the Transportation Business in the United States at the Eleventh Census: 1890,* Part I, *Transportation by Land,* p. 53). A total mileage figure for the year ending June 30, 1880 was given in the *Report of the Agencies of Transportation in the United States* (Tenth Census, Washington, D.C., 1883), p. 292; a figure for the fiscal year 1879 was estimated from the movement of operated mileage (p. 290, and the *1890* report, p. 53).

Values of purchased crossties for 1906 and 1907 and an average price for 1909 were reported in *Statistical Bulletin 21,* Table 189. A partial value reported for 1905 was raised to cover electric railroads by applying the average price per tie paid by steam railroads to our estimate of the number of ties purchased by electric roads. Approximate average prices for 1918 and 1919 were published in the *Annual Report of the Director General of Railroads, 1919, Division of Purchases,* pp. 6, 7. Finally, an average price for 1889 was calculated by using the partial data on quantities and values from the *Report on Manufacturing Industries in the United States at the Eleventh Census: 1890,* Part III, *Selected Industries,* pp. 620, 639. For all other years prices were interpolated and extrapolated by the movement of the average price in eastern markets of first quality hard- and softwoods, weighted equally *(Statistical Bulletin 21,* Table 76).

Other Lumber Products

Other lumber products used directly for construction include round timbers for mining, round timbers for bridge building and construction other than mining, poles, and an indeterminate amount of the forest products of farms. Because data are not continuous and an interpolation would be unsatisfactory, we did not make estimates for these products; our estimates of lumber used directly for construction are incomplete.

The magnitude of the deficiency is suggested by the figures for single years. The cost to mines of round timbers was approximately $9 million in 1905 and $18.5 million in 1923 (*Statistical Bulletin 21,* Table 182). No figures on round timbers used for other construction are reported, but it is likely that the value is considerably smaller. Purchases of poles by telephone and telegraph companies and railroads were about $9 million in 1906 and $10 million in 1907 (*Poles Purchased, 1907,* Bureau of the Census, Forest Products, No. 9, Table 1). Although the total value of forest products produced on farms is reported for three census years: 1899, $110 million; 1909, $195 million; and 1919, $394 million (*Fourteenth Census,* V, *Agriculture,* pp. 881–3), little information is given concerning their distribution. Approximately one-half is consumed on farms and the other half cut for sale; but how much is destined for direct use in construction is difficult to determine. The greater part of farm output is used for fuel; some is undoubtedly sold to manufacturing concerns. Perhaps 10 percent, representing chiefly the amount used for fence posts and other farm construction, would be a plausible estimate.

The total of the omitted products probably ranges between $25 and $100 million. Although these are sizable figures, they are only 1 or 2 percent of the estimated totals for all construction materials. Consequently, their inclusion, were satisfactory estimates possible, would have no appreciable effect upon the movement of the totals.

Sand-building, Paving, Railroad Ballast, and Gravel

Values of building sand were reported for 1905–19 and in part for 1902–04, of paving sand for 1911–19, of railroad ballast for 1913–19, and of gravel for 1905–19 in *Mineral Resources of the United States* (*seriatim*). Since the output of these materials was relatively small and satisfactory extrapolation was impossible, no attempt was made to extend the various series beyond the earliest year reported. The comparability of the construction material totals is thus affected very slightly.

Crushed Stone

Values were reported in *Mineral Resources of the United States* (*seriatim*).

PART III

Exports and Imports

PART III describes the derivation of the export and import data that make it possible to pass from value of output to value of output destined for domestic consumption. In it we review the limitations inherent in the data and discuss the importance of the export-import adjustments.

A   EXPORTS

Exports, including exports to noncontiguous territories, were compiled by commodity groups for 1893–1919 from the detailed statistics in the *Monthly Summary of Foreign Commerce,* December issues.[1] For 1869 and 1879 and for 1889–93 calendar year totals were summated from the *Quarterly Report of the Chief of the Bureau of Statistics,* United States Treasury Department (Table III 1).

There are several deficiencies in the export statistics: the incomplete presentation of exports by rail to Canada and Mexico before 1915, the probable failure to include all parcel post shipments, the peculiar timing of the monthly data, which in many instances are not the values of goods exported within a given month but the values the Section on Custom Statistics had time to compile, and the possible inaccuracies of many of the early export returns and their effects on quantity-value comparisons. These and other limitations are described by Dudley J. Cowden, *Measures of Exports of the United States* (Columbia University Press, 1931), and Laurence F. Schmeckebier, *The Statistical Work of the National Government* (Johns Hopkins Press, 1925). We did not attempt to allow for the various deficiencies because accurate data with which to make corrections were not available.

The basic export statistics were modified in two ways. The first had to do with the allocation of commodities among the minor groups. For most years exports were reported in sufficient detail to admit of a fairly good allocation. When, in the earlier years, some commodities had been combined, apportionment between finished and unfinished or among two

[1] Also called at various times the *Summary Statement of Imports and Exports; Finance, Commerce, and Navigation; Monthly Summary of Finance and Commerce;* and *Monthly Summary of Commerce and Finance.*

or more groups was based on the nearest year for which detailed figures were given.

The second modification involved the determination of the price level at which exports were valued. For our present purpose exports had to be valued at prices comparable with the output data, which were in manufacturers' or producers' prices. Consequently, the problem was to determine not only whether export prices differed from manufacturers' prices but also how much.

Per unit census and export prices for 1914 and 1919 were compared for as many finished commodities and construction materials as possible. As it was difficult to get prices for qualitatively similar commodities and reliability of the per unit export prices is uncertain, we do not present the comparisons in detail.[2] In more than half of 97 commodities distributed fairly evenly among the various commodity groups export prices were higher than manufacturers' prices. The exceptions—the groups included under producer durable other than miscellaneous subsidiary equipment and the following consumer durable groups: heating and cooking apparatus, household appliances, and electrical supplies; books; passenger vehicles and accessories; motorcycles and bicycles; and pleasure craft—can usually be explained by the nature of the commodities. Some—mechanical items such as machinery and transportation equipment—are usually exported directly by the manufacturer; others—for which foreign competition is keen—are often reduced in price to meet such competition. Books, which do not belong to either category, are usually subject to trade discounts as large as or larger than the reduction in price to meet foreign competition. In any event it was assumed that export values did not have to be modified for these groups.

For the other commodity groups it was necessary to estimate how much export values had to be trimmed to make them comparable with the value of output destined for domestic consumption. Since the per unit price comparisons were inadequate for purposes of precise measurement they had to be supplemented with more comprehensive data. From the *Census of Distribution: Wholesale Trade 1929*,[3] Table 5, 6, 7, the expense ratios of exporters and export agents were calculated for groups of establishments

---

[2] See comments in Cowden, *op. cit.*, pp. 18–25 and 36–9, regarding the accuracy of per unit export prices.

[3] Although this is a 1929 reference, the operating expense data are probably sufficiently similar to corresponding data for early years to justify their use in arriving at *approximate* reduction percentages.

EXPORTS AND IMPORTS

roughly comparable with our minor commodity groups.[4] Reduction percentages were based on these ratios in conjunction with our per unit price comparisons. The accompanying table gives the final percentages applied in all years (all are rounded to the nearest 5).

COMMODITY GROUP	REDUCTION PERCENTAGE
1a Manufactured foods and kindred products	5
b Nonmanufactured foods	10
2 Cigars, cigarettes and tobacco	10
3 Drugs, toilet and household preparations	10
4 Magazines, newspapers, stationery	20
5a Manufactured fuel and lighting products	10
6 Dry goods and notions	10
7 Clothing and personal furnishings	15
8 Shoes and other footwear	15
9 Housefurnishings (semidurable)	20
10 Toys, games and sporting goods	15
11 Tires and tubes	5
12 Household furniture	20
14a Floor coverings	20
b Miscellaneous housefurnishings (durable)	20
15 China and household utensils	20
16 Musical instruments	20
17 Jewelry, silverware, clocks and watches	15
19 Luggage	5
36 Miscellaneous subsidiary durable equipment	10
Construction materials	10

A tabulation of the percentages that exports constituted in 1909 of the total output of the five major commodity groups before and after the application of the reduction percentages suggests the effects of applying them. The differences between the two sets of figures reveal that in no major group was the reduction as much as .005 of total output. An error in the reduction percentages as high as 50 percent would thus have no appreciable effect on the estimated amounts destined for domestic consumption.

	BEFORE	AFTER
Consumer perishable	3.77	3.53
Consumer semidurable	1.90	1.66
Consumer durable	2.96	2.87
Producer durable	9.57	9.55
Construction materials	4.17	3.76

A similar test can be made for the minor groups by comparing the export values in Tables III 2 and I 1. Such a test for 1909 shows that in only six groups (21, 25, 26, 27, 28, and 35) would the effect of a 50 percent error be as much as 1 percent.[5]

---

[4] See Simon Kuznets, *Commodity Flow and Capital Formation,* Vol. One, pp. 199–201, for the groups utilized.

[5] In minor groups where no reduction percentage was applied, a 10 percent reduction was assumed. All six groups fall in this class.

B Imports

As our chief interest is in the cost of commodities to the United States economy at the time they enter it, i.e., when the commodities are delivered to importers, we use imports for consumption including duties. To the extent that even imports for consumption may be re-exported and duties refunded, this series is unsatisfactory because re-exports are not included in our export figures; but the amount of re-exports is extremely small.

Fiscal year imports for consumption including duties were compiled by commodity groups from detailed annual data in *Foreign Commerce and Navigation*. Since comparable figures for calendar years were not available, approximate adjustments were based on the relations between fiscal and calendar year general imports (the latter taken from the sources used for exports).[6] Calendar year imports from noncontiguous territories, also taken from the sources used for exports, were added to the resulting totals.

A minor inadequacy in the reported figures is that they are based on the value and rate of duty claimed by the importers; revisions made by the customs authorities do not appear in the figures. Despite these faults, and even if other slight defects in our import correction, such as the failure to include ocean freight, are considered, we believe that for all practical purposes the import values used approximate the values desired. For a discussion of the general reliability of import statistics see Schmeckebier and Cowden, *op. cit*.

Nor is a correction for level analogous to that made for exports needed. In the period under consideration most finished commodities were imported by wholesalers; and it is reasonable to assume that the level of prices paid corresponds roughly to manufacturers' prices.

C Changes in Relative Importance of Exports and Imports

The following tabulation, based on Table I 1, shows the importance of the adjustments for exports and imports. A percentage less than 100 indicates that exports exceeded imports: one more than 100 that imports exceeded exports. The greater the deviation from 100 the greater the influence of the foreign trade adjustment and thus the greater the difference between total domestic output and the value of output destined for

---

[6] General imports are articles entered for immediate consumption and for warehouse. Since duties are not fully determined on the latter, the general import data exclude duties. Imports for consumption—articles entered for immediate consumption and withdrawals from warehouse—include duties. The two series thus differ by the amount that entries for warehouse exceed or are less than withdrawals.

domestic consumption. To reveal possible trends, percentages are computed for three periods.

Percentage that Value Destined for Domestic Consumption Constitutes of Total Value of Domestic Output
Major and Minor Commodity Groups, Three Periods

	MAJOR AND MINOR COMMODITY GROUPS	1869, 1879, 1889–99	1900–13	1914–19
1	Food & kindred products			
	a Manufactured	89.7	95.2	90.4
	b Nonmanufactured	102.1	102.3	101.4
2	Cigars, cigarettes & tobacco	101.2	101.7	99.6
3	Drug, toilet & household preparations	98.5	97.5	95.9
4	Magazines, newspapers, stationery & supplies, & misc. paper products	102.4	101.5	98.0
5	Fuel & lighting products			
	a Manufactured	99.6	99.8	100.2
	b Nonmanufactured		Not estimated	
	Consumer Perishable, Total	95.6	98.1	94.7
6	Dry goods & notions	124.0	112.0	92.5
7	Clothing & personal furnishings	106.2	102.7	99.7
8	Shoes & other footwear	99.5	97.5	95.4
9	Housefurnishings	102.2	103.3	101.2
10	Toys, games & sporting goods	113.6	113.5	81.1
11	Tires & tubes	97.1*	92.5	94.4
	Consumer Semidurable, Total	108.2	103.0	97.0
12	Household furniture	97.7	98.0	99.2
13	Heating & cooking apparatus, household appliances & electrical supplies			
	a Heating & cooking apparatus & household appliances except electrical	99.0	98.7	98.5
	b Electrical household appliances & supplies	100.0†	100.0	101.4
14	Housefurnishings			
	a Floor coverings	110.1	116.3	106.8
	b Misc. housefurnishings	100.0	99.4	99.1
15	China & household utensils	159.6	130.7	102.0
16	Musical instruments	102.4	98.0	96.6
17	Jewelry, silverware, clocks & watches	117.7	123.2	122.9
18	Printing & publishing: books	102.0	99.7	97.3
19	Luggage	99.3	99.7	98.8
20	Passenger vehicles & accessories			
	a Motor vehicles	100.0†	95.3	94.7
	b Motor vehicle accessories	....	93.5‡	79.3
	c Carriages & wagons	98.2	93.4	97.1
21	Motorcycles & bicycles	82.0§	83.8	77.5
22	Pleasure craft	100.0	100.0	100.0
23	Ophthalmic products & artificial limbs	100.0	100.0	100.0
24	Monuments & tombstones	100.0	100.0	100.0
	Consumer Durable, Total	106.0	104.3	98.5
	Consumer Commodities, Total	99.5	99.9	95.7
25	Industrial machinery & equipment & tractors			
	a Industrial machinery & equipment	92.8	88.8	84.6
	b Tractors	....	61.9‖	85.5
26	Electrical equipment, industrial & commercial	97.5	88.0	84.1

MAJOR AND MINOR COMMODITY GROUPS	AVERAGE PERCENTAGE 1869, 1879, 1889–99	1900–13	1914–19
27 Farm equipment	92.3	82.7	84.7
28 Office & store machinery & equipment	90.7	77.4	87.4
29 Office furniture & fixtures	99.3	98.1	96.8
30 Locomotive & railroad cars	95.3	94.8	90.7
31 Ships & boats	100.0	100.0	100.0
32 Business vehicles			
a Motor	....	96.9‡	84.1
b Wagons	100.0	100.0	100.0
33 Aircraft	....	100.0‖	97.2
34 Professional & scientific equipment	79.2	83.4	92.6
35 Carpenters' & mechanics' tools	92.5	84.7	86.1
36 Misc. subsidiary durable equipment	99.5	98.3	95.7
Producer Durable, Total	94.8	90.3	88.6
Construction materials			
Manufactured	100.6	98.7	96.6
Nonmanufactured	96.9	91.7	96.5

* 1895–99.   † 1899.   ‡ 1904–13.   § 1889, 1895–99.   ‖ 1912–13.

For all consumer commodities the export-import adjustments tend to balance. The sizable excess of exports in such groups as manufactured food and kindred products, tires and tubes, passenger vehicles and accessories, and motorcycles and bicycles are compensated by the excess of imports in several of the semidurable groups and in such durable groups as floor coverings, china and household utensils, and jewelry, silverware, clocks, and watches.

Comparison of the averages for 1869, 1879, 1889–99 with those for 1900–13 suggests a declining trend in the importance of food exports and a rising one in the importance of exports in many other commodity groups.[7] In part, this shift reflects a transition from an agricultural to an industrial economy. But the food average for 1914–19, influenced as it was by the war and its immediate aftermath, reverses the trend of that group. Moreover, during this period the United States became an importer of semidurable commodities. Even its imports of consumer durables, always large, were drastically reduced.

As exports of producer durable commodities and construction materials have usually exceeded imports, output destined for domestic consumption has been smaller than total output. The trend in these groups seems clearly to be toward greater excesses of exports.

[7] If 1869 and 1879 were averaged separately the trend would be even more pronounced.

Table III 1

Classification of Import and Export Series by Minor Commodity Groups

IMPORTS — *EXPORTS*

1 Food and Kindred Products

Imports: Bread, biscuits & wafers; macaroni, vermicelli, & all similar preparations; rice flour & meal; wheat flour; all other breadstuffs (dutiable); cocoa & chocolate, prepared or mfd.; edible substances, n.s.p.f.; meat & dairy products, excl. sausage casings; salt; malt liquors; brandy; cordials, liqueurs, etc.; gin; whisky; wines; other beverages; sugar, candy, & confectionery; vinegar; all other spirits; beverages, n.e.s.; ginger ale or ginger beer; fish; fruits & nuts, excl. coconut meat, not shredded, & palm nut kernels; spices, ground; tea; vegetables; honey; eggs of poultry

Exports: Bran & middlings; bread & biscuits; buckwheat; corn meal & corn flour; all other cereal preparations; oatmeal & rolled oats; rye flour; wheat flour; all other breadstuffs; baking powder; infants' food; chewing gum; cocoa & chocolate, mfd. or prepared, excl. confectionery; coffee, roasted or prepared; confectionery; flavoring extracts & fruit juices; butter; cheese; condensed & evaporated milk; all other milk; meat products (finished); salt; spices; malt liquors; rum; whisky; all other distilled liquors, excl. alcohol & cologne spirits; wines; other beverages; sugar, refined; vegetables; vinegar; brandy; fruits & nuts; fish; egg yolks; canned eggs, etc.; honey

2 Cigars, Cigarettes and Tobacco

Imports: Tobacco mfrs.; pipes & smokers' articles

Exports: Cigarettes; cigars & cheroots; plug tobacco; smoking tobacco; all other tobacco mfrs.

3 Drug, Toilet and Household Preparations

Imports: Medicinal preparations; coal-tar preparations; perfumeries, cosmetics & all toilet preparations; soap, castile, medicinal, powder, toilet & all other

Exports: Blacking & polishes; washing powder & fluid; druggists' sundries (rubber); perfumeries, cosmetics, toilet preparations; soap, toilet or fancy; soap, all other; surgical appliances, excl. instruments; medicines, patent or proprietary

4 Magazines, Newspapers, Stationery and Supplies, and Miscellaneous Paper Products*

Imports: Pencils & pencil leads; penholders & pens, incl. fountain & stylographic; maps, music engraving; photographs & etchings; lithographic prints, incl. postcards, souvenir; charts; newspapers & periodicals; other printed matter, incl. booklets

Exports: Ink, except printers'; mucilage & paste; carbon paper; playing cards; adding machine paper; writing paper & envelopes; pencils & lead; pens, fountain; stationery, except paper

5a Manufactured Fuel and Lighting Products

Imports: Matches: friction or lucifer

Exports: Matches; candles

5b Coal
Not compiled

---

* The exports of books, music, maps, engravings, etchings, photographs, and other printed matter were combined in all years during the period under consideration. The 1922 ratio of books and music to the total was used to estimate the export totals for Minor Group 18. The balance was assigned to Minor Group 4.

The import totals for Minor Group 18 are the portion of the total for books, music, maps, engravings, etchings, photographs and other printed matter on which no duties were paid. The portion on which duties were paid was assigned to Minor Group 4.

TABLE III 1 cont.

IMPORTS | EXPORTS

6 Dry Goods and Notions†

Statuary & art works; bone & horn, mfrs. of, incl. combs; buttons, pearl or shell & all other; dyed, colored, stained, painted or printed cotton cloth; cotton embroideries, incl. edgings, insertings & galloons; cotton laces & lace articles, incl. lace edgings, insertings & galloons; cotton nets & nettings; feathers & downs, on the skin or otherwise, dressed, colored, & mfd., not suitable for millinery ornaments; feathers for millinery ornaments; flowers, fruit, etc., artificial or ornamental; hair & mfrs. of; all other leather mfrs., excl. bags, satchels, shoes, gloves; silk fabrics, woven in the piece; silk laces, embroideries & articles made thereof (excl. wearing apparel); silk plushes, velvets, chenilles, or other pile fabrics; silk ribbons, not exceeding 12 inches in width; woolen & worsted cloths; wool dress goods, women's & children's; cotton veils & veiling | Statuary & art works; buttons, pearl & all other; printed, dyed-in-the-piece colored & other cotton cloths; cotton laces & embroideries; cotton sewing & crochet thread; feathers; cut flowers; all other leather mfrs.; silk dress goods; all other mfrs. of silk; wool cloth and dress goods; all other mfrs. of wool

7 Clothing and Personal Furnishings

Cotton handkerchiefs or mufflers; knit goods, incl. gloves, stockings, hose & all other; all other cotton wearing apparel; fibers, woven: handkerchiefs; fibers, woven: wearing apparel; fur hats, bonnets & hoods; hats, bonnets & hoods; household & personal effects & wearing apparel in use; leather gloves; silk handkerchiefs & mufflers; silk wearing apparel; umbrellas & parasols; wool wearing apparel; wool shawls; wool knit gloves; corsets; silk hosiery; clothing—ready to wear | Cotton wearing apparel; hats, & materials for; leather gloves; silk wearing apparel; hosiery, artificial silk; suspenders and garters; umbrellas & parasols; wool wearing apparel; other wearing apparel

8 Shoes and Other Footwear

Leather boots & shoes | India rubber: boots and shoes; leather boots & shoes; leather slippers

9 Housefurnishings (semidurable)

Brushes, feather dusters & hair pencils; cotton lace window curtains | Brooms; brushes; cotton blankets & comforts

10 Toys, Games and Sporting Goods

Fishhooks, rods & reels, artificial bait; photographic goods—cameras & parts of; toys; firearms | Athletic & sporting goods; billiard tables & accessories; firearms; photographic goods—cameras; toys

11 Tires and Tubes

None | India rubber: tires for automobiles & all other tires

† The import totals for Minor Group 6 were reduced on the basis of the census year breakdowns at the manufacturing stage of the totals between finished and unfinished commodities. The intercensal year breakdowns were estimated by straight line interpolation of the census year ratios.

Table III 1 cont.

IMPORTS	EXPORTS
12 Household Furniture	
Wood furniture	Chairs; all other wood furniture, except store & office
13a Heating and Cooking Apparatus and Household Appliances, Except Electrical	
None	Stoves and ranges; refrigerators
13b Electrical Household Appliances and Supplies	
Electric lamps: incandescent	None
14a Floor Coverings	
Matting & mats for floors, of cocoa fiber, rattan, straw, etc.; oilcloth & linoleum for floors; wool carpets & carpeting	Oilcloth & linoleum for floors
14b Miscellaneous Housefurnishings (durable)	
Cotton tapestries & jacquard & figured upholstery goods; wool blankets	Oilcloth & linoleum other than for floors; wool blankets
15 China and Household Utensils	
Earthen, stone & chinaware: china, parian, porcelain & bisque; earthen & crockery ware; glass decanters, bottles & other glassware, cut or ornamented; cutlery; table, kitchen & other utensils, or hollow ware, enameled or glazed with vitreous glasses	Chinaware; earthen and stoneware; cut or engraved glassware; all other glassware; iron and steel cutlery
16 Musical Instruments	
Musical instruments, & parts of, incl. strings; phonographs, graphophones & parts	Musical instruments; phonographs, graphophones, records & accessories
17 Jewelry, Silverware, Clocks and Watches	
Clocks, & parts of; watches, & parts of; gold & silver, mfrs. of; jewelry; diamonds, corals, rubies, cameos, pearls & other precious stones, cut but not set, & suitable for use in the manufacture of jewelry	Clocks, & parts of; watches, & parts of; gold & silver, mfrs. of; jewelry; silver plated ware; all other plated ware
18 Printing and Publishing: Books*	
Bibles; books & music, in raised print used exclusively by the blind; books & pamphlets printed wholly or chiefly in languages other than English; textbooks, used in schools & other educational institutions	Books & pamphlets; music in books or sheets
19 Luggage	
None	Trunks, valises & traveling bags
20a Motorized Passenger Vehicles	
Automobiles	Automobiles, passenger
20b Motor Vehicle Accessories	
Automobile parts (not incl. engines & tires)	Automobile parts (not incl. engines & tires)
20c Horse-Drawn Passenger Vehicles and Accessories	
Cars, carriages & parts of: all except automobiles	Carriages; wagons; parts

Table III 1 *cont.*

IMPORTS   *EXPORTS*

21 Motorcycles and Bicycles

Bicycles, motor & other cycles, & parts of — Bicycles, tricycles, etc.; motorcycles

22 Pleasure Craft

None — Motorboats

23 Ophthalmic Products and Artificial Limbs

None — None

24 Monuments and Tombstones

None — None

25 Industrial Machinery and Equipment

Machines, machinery, & parts of, n.e.s. — Machinery, n.e.s., excl. adding machines, calculating machines, cash registers, locomotives, electrical machinery & typewriters

25a Tractors

None — Engines, traction

26 Electrical Equipment, Industrial and Commercial

Electric arc lamps; all other electric lamps, excl. incandescent — Electrical machinery & appliances, excl. locomotives; instruments, electrical for scientific purposes, incl. telephone & telegraph equipment

27 Farm Equipment

Agricultural implements — Agricultural implements; horseshoes; barbed wire; woven wire fencing

28 Office and Store Machinery and Equipment

None — Adding & calculating machines; cash registers, & parts; scales & balances; typewriters

29 Office and Store Furniture and Fixtures

None — Metal furniture; safes; wood furniture, store & office

30 Locomotives and Railroad Cars

None — Cars for railways: passenger, freight & other; cars for other railways; locomotives

31 Ships and Boats

None — None

32a Motorized Business Vehicles

None — Automobiles, commercial; motor warehouse & station trucks

32b Horse-Drawn Business Vehicles

None — None

33 Aircraft

None — Aeroplanes; parts of aeroplanes

34 Professional and Scientific Equipment

Philosophical & scientific apparatus; optical instruments — Instruments for scientific purposes

35 Carpenters' and Mechanics' Tools

Files, file blanks, rasps & floats; saws & tools — Tools, n.e.s.; saws; all other tools

Table III 1 concl.

IMPORTS — EXPORTS

36 Miscellaneous Subsidiary Durable Equipment

None — Emery & other abrasive wheels; wheelbarrows, pushcarts & hand trucks; fire extinguishers; rubber belting, hose & packing; leather harness & saddles

Construction Materials

Imports: Cement: Roman, Portland, & other hydraulic; cement, all other; glass, cylinder, crown & common window glass; plate glass, cast, polished, silvered & unsilvered; iron & steel building forms & all other structural shapes; iron & steel rails for railways; paints, pigments, colors & varnishes; stone, marble & mfrs. of; stone, all other, incl. slate; wood, cedar, mahogany & all other; logs & round timber; boards, planks, deals & other sawed lumber; laths, shingles

Exports: Asphaltum: mfrs. of; brass pipes & fittings; cement, hydraulic; sanitary ware—closet bowls, lavatories, sinks, etc.; tiles, except drain; brick, building; brick, fire; glass, common window; plate glass, unsilvered; iron & steel bolts, nuts, rivets & washers; castings, n.e.s.; enamel ware—bathtubs; lavatories & sinks, all other; hardware; nails; pipes & fittings; radiators & house-heating boilers; rails of steel; structural iron & steel; lime; paints, colors & varnishes; plaster, builders' & common; roofing felt & similar materials; stone-roofing slate; doors, sash & blinds; wood trimmings, moldings & other house finishings; sand & gravel; stone, unmfd.; wood: logs; timber; railroad ties; boards, planks, etc.; shingles; all other lumber

Table III 2

Export Values before Application of Reduction Percentages
1869, 1879, 1889–1919
(thousands of dollars)
Major and Minor Commodity Groups

	1a	1b	*PERISHABLE* 2	3	4	5a	TOTAL
1869	52,548	1,888	1,604	1,273	360	376	58,049
1879	148,651	2,092	2,214	1,881	736	232	155,806
1889	220,232	12,829	3,833	2,906	1,237	142	241,179
1890	249,211	8,914	4,019	3,308	1,285	157	266,894
1891	244,189	11,478	4,279	3,057	1,185	164	264,352
1892	236,353	11,722	3,872	3,465	1,107	217	256,736
1893	198,091	8,086	4,021	3,425	1,471	238	215,332
1894	221,705	22,663	3,837	3,536	1,543	272	253,556
1895	183,131	11,793	4,190	4,392	1,497	288	205,291
1896	189,470	13,691	4,719	4,375	1,576	322	214,153
1897	207,756	15,543	4,966	4,535	1,593	290	234,683
1898	252,479	16,797	5,136	4,710	1,497	321	280,940
1899	258,975	18,119	5,201	5,994	1,828	360	290,477
1900	259,052	21,126	5,737	6,165	2,298	304	294,682
1901	278,224	17,854	5,376	6,103	2,631	325	310,513
1902	282,581	25,426	5,524	6,663	3,286	439	323,919
1903	241,633	29,917	6,057	8,009	3,287	564	289,467
1904	216,540	30,387	6,295	8,465	4,118	698	266,503
1905	242,033	28,278	6,643	9,931	4,575	687	292,147
1906	266,726	29,636	6,960	10,728	5,006	632	319,688
1907	260,281	30,031	6,442	11,714	5,632	537	314,637
1908	240,859	30,111	5,808	12,081	5,091	294	294,244
1909	204,063	35,215	6,030	11,715	5,548	353	262,924
1910	185,196	40,241	5,716	12,787	6,284	291	250,515
1911	214,937	54,117	5,775	14,645	6,192	278	295,944
1912	216,716	57,399	6,807	16,031	7,039	257	304,249
1913	236,895	58,183	8,200	16,977	8,719	253	329,227
1914	238,897	57,499	8,304	17,700	7,627	308	330,335
1915	438,202	76,298	7,622	22,933	7,999	497	553,551
1916	523,054	85,894	12,349	23,788	12,006	1,195	658,286
1917	712,688	91,139	18,463	30,190	14,579	1,321	868,380
1918	1,312,374	106,006	32,462	39,434	17,604	1,756	1,509,636
1919	1,671,231	239,290	49,652	44,930	31,622	2,364	2,039,089

1a Food and kindred products, mfd.
1b Food and kindred products, nonmfd.
2 Cigars, cigarettes, & tobacco
3 Drug, toilet, & household preparations
4 Magazines, newspapers, stationery & supplies, & misc. paper products
5a Fuel & lighting products, mfd.

TABLE III 2 cont.

SEMIDURABLE

	6	7	8	9	10	11	TOTAL
1869	2,524	813	442	154	2,051	...	5,984
1879	3,732	772	441	112	2,400	...	7,457
1889	3,860	529	770	154	949	...	6,262
1890	3,766	618	795	152	826	...	6,157
1891	3,513	768	823	157	846	...	6,107
1892	3,106	607	1,042	210	830	...	5,795
1893	5,023	805	932	216	830	...	7,806
1894	5,178	779	1,091	187	741	...	7,976
1895	4,966	988	1,480	152	1,015	...	8,601
1896	5,887	1,090	1,764	182	866	720	10,509
1897	6,429	1,314	1,926	184	781	642	11,276
1898	6,854	1,547	2,169	162	828	609	12,169
1899	7,224	2,043	3,995	235	1,080	624	15,201
1900	7,068	2,332	5,347	241	1,665	659	17,312
1901	10,823	2,980	7,064	267	1,193	738	23,065
1902	12,534	3,823	7,774	277	1,279	851	26,538
1903	11,071	5,223	8,859	312	1,537	1,063	28,065
1904	10,874	5,841	9,254	318	1,954	990	29,231
1905	12,334	6,908	10,939	393	2,323	1,199	34,096
1906	13,530	8,198	12,084	413	3,249	1,389	38,863
1907	13,325	9,296	14,768	505	3,904	1,668	43,466
1908	12,824	7,361	12,539	525	3,136	1,515	37,900
1909	15,158	8,818	14,566	569	4,281	1,867	45,259
1910	19,276	10,711	17,177	719	4,357	2,532	54,772
1911	21,358	12,145	18,489	818	4,788	3,424	61,022
1912	23,916	15,629	20,898	755	6,145	4,444	71,787
1913	24,264	16,649	22,409	695	7,792	5,263	77,072
1914	27,899	22,112	20,961	566	7,351	4,488	83,377
1915	69,540	54,444	43,442	1,155	15,397	14,259	198,237
1916	83,083	53,646	48,759	1,273	47,177	18,975	252,913
1917	105,222	40,409	43,545	2,335	102,069	17,966	311,546
1918	110,152	50,487	39,671	3,884	35,530	17,090	256,814
1919	153,130	100,375	83,914	5,430	22,343	32,557	397,749

6   Dry goods & notions
7   Clothing & personal furnishings
8   Shoes & other footwear
9   Housefurnishings
10 Toys, games, & sporting goods
11 Tires & tubes

Table III 2 cont.

CONSUMER DURABLE

	12	13a	14a	14b	15	16	17	18
1869	1,246	102	...	...	749	268	679	165
1879	1,604	83	...	...	867	757	1,862	313
1889	2,992	283	...	39	1,191	1,052	3,155	891
1890	3,008	232	...	36	1,132	1,293	2,817	950
1891	3,068	253	...	31	1,274	1,224	2,946	876
1892	2,973	205	...	14	1,305	1,653	2,120	834
1893	3,335	236	...	45	1,284	1,244	2,657	1,131
1894	3,241	241	...	42	1,200	1,068	2,200	1,183
1895	3,152	289	...	33	1,298	1,153	2,515	1,153
1896	3,434	304	...	48	1,459	1,269	2,738	1,222
1897	3,889	361	...	55	1,586	1,284	2,931	1,228
1898	3,418	449	29	137	1,691	1,595	3,109	1,172
1899	3,877	524	40	158	2,444	1,960	3,343	1,326
1900	4,126	567	52	266	2,814	2,113	3,915	1,577
1901	4,123	656	89	233	2,827	3,599	4,105	1,750
1902	4,332	869	48	196	2,984	3,451	4,128	2,129
1903	5,017	1,057	83	295	3,233	3,427	4,511	2,095
1904	4,567	898	71	279	3,518	3,201	4,543	2,285
1905	5,232	1,115	86	274	3,993	3,255	5,106	2,592
1906	5,535	1,441	90	338	4,539	3,256	5,901	2,837
1907	6,409	1,490	135	345	5,011	3,571	6,081	3,309
1908	5,001	1,142	131	240	4,305	2,932	4,425	3,012
1909	5,406	1,300	172	338	4,630	3,158	4,777	3,147
1910	6,617	1,474	149	405	5,631	6,195	5,611	4,091
1911	6,737	1,820	197	390	6,349	6,808	6,554	4,047
1912	7,732	2,266	191	679	8,374	6,512	6,874	4,666
1913	8,023	2,166	153	703	5,296	6,771	6,374	4,794
1914	4,980	1,663	109	565	4,345	4,629	4,444	4,312
1915	3,398	2,081	151	937	7,842	4,699	5,795	3,902
1916	4,039	2,113	349	1,210	12,235	7,029	7,820	4,913
1917	4,751	2,783	490	1,376	13,206	9,645	8,662	5,389
1918	3,585	2,134	1,426	3,973	12,837	9,168	8,283	5,552
1919	4,786	3,124	1,796	2,761	21,590	13,410	14,036	8,809

12 Household furniture
13a Heating & cooking apparatus & household appliances, except electrical
14a Floor coverings
14b Misc. housefurnishings
15 China & household utensils
16 Musical instruments
17 Jewelry, silverware, clocks & watches
18 Printing & publishing: books

Table III 2 cont.
CONSUMER DURABLE

	19	20a	20b	20c	21	22	TOTAL
1869	75	...	...	445	...	...	3,729
1879	163	...	...	892	...	...	6,541
1889	189	...	...	2,004	...	...	11,796
1890	223	...	...	1,898	...	...	11,589
1891	179	...	...	2,094	...	...	11,945
1892	160	...	...	1,610	...	...	10,874
1893	137	...	...	1,654	...	...	11,723
1894	110	...	...	1,601	...	...	10,886
1895	110	...	...	1,626	...	...	11,329
1896	103	...	...	1,912	3,796	...	16,285
1897	103	...	...	1,851	6,903	...	20,191
1898	112	...	...	1,586	7,092	...	20,390
1899	142	218	...	2,158	4,820	...	21,010
1900	112	297	...	2,773	3,061	...	21,673
1901	109	367	...	2,667	2,599	...	23,124
1902	189	1,070	...	2,987	2,581	...	24,964
1903	179	1,643	...	3,514	2,099	...	27,153
1904	201	1,898	...	3,255	1,622	...	26,338
1905	233	2,824	...	3,697	1,320	...	29,727
1906	260	4,481	...	4,270	1,405	...	34,353
1907	314	5,489	677	4,462	1,083	...	38,376
1908	219	4,769	666	3,883	702	303	31,730
1909	261	7,224	1,016	3,864	681	437	36,411
1910	...	11,688	2,136	5,051	729	407	50,184
1911	...	16,257	3,435	5,471	962	544	59,571
1912	443	23,840	4,808	5,205	1,211	881	73,682
1913	548	26,741	6,423	2,251	1,499	711	72,453
1914	334	20,890	5,841	1,550	1,753	505	55,920
1915	447	37,260	16,935	1,047	3,432	844	88,770
1916	446	46,482	24,399	817	4,313	518	116,683
1917	496	55,173	32,219	997	4,470	1,514	141,171
1918	359	37,997	34,220	576	3,710	3,664	127,484
1919	742	76,813	43,248	863	9,922	359	202,259

19 Luggage
20a Motor vehicles
20b Motor vehicle accessories
20c Carriages & wagons
21 Motorcycles & bicycles
22 Pleasure craft

TABLE III 2 *cont.*

PRODUCER DURABLE

	25a	25b	26	27	28	29	30	32a
1869	4,456	...	...	1,068	117	...	876	...
1879	5,296	...	...	2,656	195	...	1,265	...
1889	11,715	...	...	4,589	335	...	3,545	...
1890	13,532	...	...	3,696	307	...	4,416	...
1891	14,560	...	...	3,760	314	...	3,901	...
1892	14,282	...	...	4,722	359	...	2,080	...
1893	14,156	...	...	5,700	372	...	3,746	...
1894	13,803	...	...	5,426	292	...	2,264	...
1895	15,952	...	...	6,016	388	...	3,132	...
1896	22,103	...	...	5,549	1,063	...	3,814	...
1897	24,631	...	917	6,494	1,936	46	4,304	...
1898	30,807	...	2,524	10,610	2,406	177	7,255	...
1899	37,821	...	3,143	16,392	3,684	453	7,350	...
1900	42,872	...	5,286	18,310	4,141	415	9,032	...
1901	32,880	...	7,499	19,146	4,397	395	9,334	...
1902	37,230	...	10,043	20,601	5,304	294	7,534	...
1903	38,961	...	10,030	25,789	7,135	355	6,397	...
1904	44,005	...	11,133	24,693	6,633	413	7,821	...
1905	52,538	...	13,216	25,750	8,066	594	11,795	...
1906	62,710	...	16,841	29,259	9,335	705	16,225	...
1907	71,234	...	17,760	30,295	10,169	889	21,172	...
1908	55,306	...	12,773	28,999	9,437	683	6,844	...
1909	55,427	...	13,211	31,351	11,057	716	6,822	427
1910	74,155	...	17,235	35,874	12,771	801	9,502	695
1911	87,290	...	19,936	41,615	16,383	1,045	14,325	987
1912	97,557	5,001	24,137	46,433	18,095	1,343	16,355	1,470
1913	106,764	3,802	29,430	58,293	18,193	1,427	22,059	1,687
1914	79,967	972	21,085	27,367	12,852	1,004	8,118	8,986
1915	118,076	1,303	25,342	30,959	10,089	1,006	21,833	59,839
1916	201,112	6,209	41,644	55,084	15,438	1,767	40,097	52,948
1917	233,675	16,521	57,339	55,695	14,202	2,055	57,206	36,755
1918	227,419	24,402	61,699	58,091	11,304	2,731	41,121	27,164
1919	309,953	20,026	90,948	54,531	27,972	4,514	89,487	35,918

25a Industrial machinery & equipment
25b Tractors
26 Electrical equipment, industrial & commercial
27 Farm equipment
28 Office & store machinery & equipment
29 Office & store furniture & fixtures
30 Locomotives & railroad cars
32a Business vehicles, motor

TABLE III 2 *cont.*

PRODUCER DURABLE

	33	34	35	36	TOTAL
1869	...	9	310	81	6,917
1879	...	42	898	165	10,517
1889	...	571	1,975	368	23,098
1890	...	616	1,831	416	24,814
1891	...	642	1,901	467	25,545
1892	...	468	1,838	811	24,560
1893	...	658	1,886	389	26,907
1894	...	664	2,019	409	24,877
1895	...	882	2,012	442	28,824
1896	...	1,117	2,353	501	36,500
1897	...	1,268	2,377	473	42,446
1898	...	1,364	2,636	442	58,221
1899	...	2,341	3,479	575	75,238
1900	...	2,790	3,714	1,007	87,567
1901	...	2,638	3,629	954	80,872
1902	...	1,384	4,358	1,078	87,826
1903	...	1,996	5,292	1,486	97,441
1904	...	1,865	5,726	1,764	104,053
1905	...	2,085	6,772	2,195	123,011
1906	...	2,937	7,252	2,565	147,829
1907	...	3,174	9,635	2,771	167,099
1908	...	2,215	7,553	2,374	126,184
1909	...	1,278	7,100	3,148	130,537
1910	...	1,684	8,703	3,917	165,337
1911	...	1,850	10,749	4,233	198,413
1912	113	1,972	12,554	4,891	229,921
1913	61	1,804	12,516	4,876	260,912
1914	253	1,782	8,864	6,696	177,946
1915	2,960	3,722	11,551	21,867	308,547
1916	114	7,427	17,583	14,409	453,832
1917	1,100	5,138	24,947	11,772	516,405
1918	607	4,557	21,206	11,309	491,610
1919	215	6,092	33,205	11,975	684,836

33 Aircraft
34 Professional & scientific equipment
35 Carpenters' & mechanics' tools
36 Misc. subsidiary durable equipment

TABLE III 2 *concl.*

CONSTRUCTION MATERIALS

	TOTAL FINISHED COMMODITIES	Mfd.	Nonmfd.	Total	TOTAL ALL COMMODITIES
1869	74,679	648	5,337	5,985	80,664
1879	180,321	1,013	4,879	5,892	186,213
1889	282,335	3,840	11,951	15,791	298,126
1890	309,454	4,860	12,488	17,348	326,802
1891	307,949	4,671	11,680	16,351	324,300
1892	297,965	4,842	15,768	20,610	318,575
1893	261,768	4,692	15,251	19,943	281,711
1894	297,295	4,871	15,690	20,561	317,856
1895	254,045	5,435	15,447	20,882	274,927
1896	277,447	7,228	19,280	26,508	303,955
1897	308,596	9,940	22,508	32,448	341,044
1898	371,720	14,882	21,104	35,986	407,706
1899	401,926	21,378	26,200	47,578	449,504
1900	421,234	23,321	31,229	54,550	475,784
1901	437,574	20,166	28,575	48,741	486,315
1902	463,247	22,967	29,218	52,185	515,432
1903	442,126	24,427	40,603	65,030	507,156
1904	426,125	27,135	39,742	66,877	493,002
1905	478,981	31,807	37,477	69,284	548,265
1906	540,733	35,952	53,190	89,142	629,875
1907	563,578	43,378	60,037	103,415	666,993
1908	490,058	33,103	46,161	79,264	569,322
1909	475,131	35,649	47,502	83,151	558,282
1910	520,808	45,523	53,666	99,189	619,997
1911	614,950	54,456	66,549	121,005	735,955
1912	679,639	64,723	74,739	139,462	819,101
1913	739,664	74,527	82,891	157,418	897,082
1914	647,578	47,302	54,012	101,314	748,892
1915	1,149,105	59,415	35,194	94,609	1,243,714
1916	1,481,714	101,003	36,109	137,112	1,618,826
1917	1,837,502	133,876	45,288	179,164	2,016,666
1918	2,385,544	126,490	58,207	184,697	2,570,241
1919	3,323,933	174,938	82,175	257,113	3,581,046

PART IV

Price Indexes

A Problems of Constructing Price Indexes

THE VALUE of output in constant prices can be measured by counting the actual quantities of commodities produced and multiplying by appropriate base period prices or by deflating the current dollar values of the different classes of commodities by representative price indexes. Lack of adequate quantity data for most commodities make the second method alone feasible in this study. Even if this were not true, there would be reason to prefer the second method since most quantity series do not reflect changes in quality.[1]

Nearly all price indexes attempt to measure price changes for qualitatively constant articles; thus deflation of current dollar values by these indexes makes the deflated series reflect qualitative as well as purely quantitative changes.

Of course, for such indexes to give meaningful results, there must be a continuous core of homogeneity in the series being deflated. If, to cite the extreme, a commodity changes so drastically from Period I to Period II that as produced in Period I it may be said to have disappeared, deflation by an hypothetical price index for the commodity that has disappeared would have no meaning. In fact, the problem of continuous deflation could hardly be solved.

So far as possible, a price index was constructed for each minor group. This usually involved combining two or more series. Since the group indexes are intended to serve as deflators of current dollar values, the most appropriate weights are clearly the corresponding value data for the individual commodities. And since the weights used by the Bureau of Labor Statistics, the chief source of the basic indexes, approximate the most appropriate weights, we simply adopted them to calculate composite indexes for many of the groups. When indexes were taken from other sources, the weights utilized are indicated in the detailed notes below.

Weighting, of course, involves more than a decision concerning the

---

[1] A change in quality is just as much a change in physical output, as defined here, as a change in units produced.

most appropriate weights. Of considerable importance is whether to use fixed or variable weights. It is hardly necessary here to go into the ramifications of this perennial index problem.[2] Although fixed weights were deemed simplest and therefore preferable, the length of the period and the marked changes in the composition of output following World War I led us to use two sets: one for the period since 1919 based on the weights in *Wholesale Price Bulletin 512* (Bureau of Labor Statistics) and reflecting proportionate values of output in the late 1920's; and one for the period before 1919 based on the weights in *Bulletin 269* and reflecting proportionate values of output in 1909. Occasional modifications and exceptions to this general rule are mentioned specifically in the detailed notes below.

B Adequacy of the Price Indexes

Series not taken from the Wholesale Price Bulletins were assembled from the Presidents' Conference Committee (on Railroads), the Bureau of Valuation, Interstate Commerce Commission, the Bureau of Corporations, the Federal Trade Commission, the Automobile Manufacturers' Association, and *Wholesale Prices, Wages and Transportation* (Senate Report 1394, Finance Committee, 52d Cong., 2d Sess., Part V, Washington, D. C., 1893), hereafter called the Aldrich Report.

All series suffer from defects inherent in their origin. Those from the Bureau of Labor Statistics usually reflect list price quotations for specific grades of commodities in certain areas. Moreover, despite attempts to obtain quotations on commodities qualitatively comparable over time, many of the indexes reflect both price and quality changes. In some series from other sources—e.g., the per unit price of automobiles, which we had to use for the years before 1913—we could not differentiate between price and quality changes. Yet it is unlikely that these defects, ubiquitous as they are, seriously impair the usefulness of the indexes.[3]

Of graver import is the lack of any price series whatever for many commodities. Some of the gaps were filled by using indexes of the chief ma-

---

[2] For comprehensive discussions of indexes see Irving Fisher, *The Making of Index Numbers* (Houghton Mifflin, 1925) and *Wholesale Price Bulletin 284* (Bureau of Labor Statistics). Part I of the latter contains an excellent summary of the various factors that should be considered in constructing indexes.

[3] For an appraisal of the BLS wholesale price series, see Saul Nelson, A Consideration of the Validity of the Bureau of Labor Statistics Price Indexes, *The Structure of the American Economy* (National Resources Committee, 1939), App. 1.

terials that enter into a commodity, for example, women's dress goods to represent women's dresses. In this respect our indexes are more comprehensive than those in *Commodity Flow and Capital Formation,* Vol. One. Kuznets used only price series directly measuring finished commodities. The use of indirect series tends to make the composite indexes fluctuate a little more than they would if based on direct series alone, for it is generally recognized that prices of materials usually fluctuate more than prices of end products. We believe, however, that the better trend representativeness more than compensates for this slight cyclical defect.

But even the use of indirect indexes did not provide enough series to ensure complete coverage; and for no minor group is there a series for every commodity in it. For many, enough series are included to warrant an assumption of representativeness; but for some, including several durable groups, coverage is less than 25 percent and representativeness uncertain. Finally, for groups accounting in 1909 for 3.1 percent of the total value of semidurable commodities, 22.8 of consumer durable, and 23.4 of producer durable, we could not find any series at all.[4] To derive estimates in 1913 prices for these groups we had to use either an index for a related group or an average index based on the minor groups, within the apposite major group, for which we were able to compile separate indexes.

Table IV 1 shows the price indexes computed for each commodity group. The note to the table describes the composition of each index.

[4] For the groups for which indexes could not be derived as well as the data from which similar percentages can be computed for any year, see Tables I 3 and IV 1.

TABLE IV 1

Price Indexes 1869, 1879, 1889–1939 (1913: 100)

Major and Minor Commodity Groups

	PERISHABLE													*SEMIDURABLE*			
	1	2	3	4	5a	5b	IMPLICIT INDEX[a]	6	7	8		9	10	11	IMPLICIT INDEX[b]
1869	143.8	96.7	No Index	No Index	263.0		141.2	225.9	177.1	105.4		191.7	No Index		158.5
1879	84.9	93.7			154.4		86.6	107.0	106.7	89.5		91.5			102.2
1889	89.5	82.6	80.2	138.8	60.1		88.3	108.2	101.3	75.5		91.5			95.6
1890	86.4	87.2	87.6	131.3	59.6	Different Method of Estimates. See Notes	86.1	100.2	101.7	78.2		91.1			94.9
1891	85.3	86.9	87.4	129.2	49.7		84.8	92.0	101.7	76.9		88.5			92.6
1892	79.4	84.2	82.0	129.2	44.0		79.8	95.9	100.6	76.3		84.2			92.6
1893	85.1	86.5	94.0	127.8	43.5		84.7	94.7	96.7	75.4		86.6			90.5
1894	75.1	86.7	86.9	129.4	48.4		76.3	78.9	84.2	75.0		79.0			80.5
1895	73.6	85.6	76.1	126.9	68.8		75.0	77.0	79.9	75.4		76.6			77.1
1896	68.7	82.6	83.5	121.2	66.2		70.9	73.4	76.1	75.5		79.1			75.5
1897	70.8	81.4	78.5	120.5	51.6		72.0	74.1	77.2	72.8		77.4			75.5
1898	74.3	87.0	75.0	95.4	55.4		74.9	76.4	80.5	71.7		75.1			77.3
1899	74.3	88.9	73.3	91.1	70.1		75.4	85.3	84.2	71.0		80.0			81.0
1900	79.0	90.8	76.2	109.1	76.2		80.2	91.8	91.0	72.4		89.3			86.7
1901	78.6	91.7	72.7	101.9	69.0		79.6	83.9	85.7	71.8		83.6			81.9
1902	83.0	92.5	85.3	104.1	69.2		84.1	87.4	87.1	71.9		84.3			83.5
1903	81.0	93.8	84.6	109.7	84.8		83.3	91.3	89.9	73.0		89.1			86.0
1904	84.0	95.1	82.1	112.7	85.3		85.5	90.8	89.7	73.9		91.5		114.8	86.0
1905	85.8	97.8	85.2	107.6	75.2		86.9	94.9	94.5	78.0		85.9		173.4	90.5
1906	83.2	98.1	87.3	100.4	82.1		84.9	102.8	102.1	85.1		93.5		201.3	98.2
1907	88.7	97.2	88.0	106.5	87.5		89.7	113.8	105.9	86.0		104.5		231.7	102.6
1908	91.4	98.1	95.1	105.6	89.6		92.3	98.2	100.0	83.9		90.0		231.6	96.0
1909	97.4	98.5	98.8	94.8	83.7		96.9	101.4	102.6	88.6		93.0		140.1	99.3
1910	101.1	98.5	104.3	95.0	71.7		100.0	103.7	104.7	88.2		103.1		129.4	100.9
1911	96.5	99.6	104.0	97.1	67.2		96.2	98.5	100.1	87.8		98.4		122.8	97.4
1912	104.0	100.0	101.7	98.4	79.5		102.8	101.1	100.5	92.7		92.4		102.3	98.6
1913	100.0	100.0	100.0	100.0	100.0		100.0	100.0	100.0	100.0		100.0		100.0	100.0

290

Year	1	2	3	4	5a	5b	6	7	8	9	10	11
1914	101.8	100.3	101.8	100.1	90.1	101.4	94.8	96.3	100.0	103.3	83.5	96.5
1915	104.5	102.0	107.1	99.8	82.8	103.7	94.9	97.0	102.4	92.4	74.9	96.5
1916	121.2	102.0	125.7	149.5	113.4	120.6	129.4	121.7	111.9	120.8	77.4	117.6
1917	167.2	108.4	155.2	189.2	127.3	161.1	185.0	171.8	151.5	189.9	95.6	161.0
1918	188.4	146.7	170.4	194.6	147.1	182.8	262.2	233.3	172.0	272.0	110.6	206.2
1919	206.6	176.4	173.0	221.7	140.5	199.9	254.6	227.0	236.6	262.3	101.0	212.4
1919	201.7	175.0	199.9	221.3	135.6	196.5	246.1	239.2	247.2	266.5	101.0	219.0
1920	214.0	186.9	212.8	297.0	185.3	213.4	311.9	312.8	277.2	310.1	112.2	265.6
1921	141.1	183.1	167.1	206.4	114.9	146.5	170.5	182.7	204.6	192.1	86.3	173.8
1922	136.4	182.5	146.9	180.1	121.8	141.2	179.3	183.9	180.0	192.3	55.7	163.2
1923	144.4	182.5	149.5	190.6	106.0	147.7	202.5	205.7	181.8	222.7	52.8	177.6
1924	141.7	161.3	148.5	202.1	98.8	143.5	199.0	201.7	180.6	233.5	44.7	164.9
1925	156.1	159.5	151.6	214.2	105.2	154.3	197.8	202.9	184.4	217.6	47.6	160.0
1926	155.8	159.5	155.8	201.7	109.3	154.3	178.6	188.6	183.5	195.1	48.3	150.4
1927	150.6	159.5	148.4	176.1	85.2	146.9	174.4	179.0	188.1	183.2	36.1	137.4
1928	157.3	157.0	140.2	174.8	86.7	150.0	179.2	174.6	201.7	184.1	30.6	131.7
1929	155.6	156.5	138.7	174.8	82.7	147.4	169.5	169.2	195.0	182.8	26.3	130.7
1930	141.0	157.4	133.8	174.8	71.1	135.1	149.5	154.1	187.2	164.5	24.8	122.0
1931	116.2	153.4	120.4	164.5	54.2	114.1	123.7	139.9	191.9	133.8	22.2	109.2
1932	95.0	147.4	106.1	158.2	58.1	96.7	104.9	115.6	158.0	113.7	19.8	93.6
1933	94.2	132.2	101.2	149.4	56.5	95.0	129.3	131.1	165.5	139.1	20.3	105.0
1934	109.8	138.0	114.1	148.2	62.7	107.8*	149.5	148.2	180.0	168.4	21.7	120.6*
1935	130.4	137.4	116.2	148.2	63.2	122.4	142.4	144.3	179.8	152.7	22.1	119.2
1936	127.9	137.1	122.3	149.1	68.8	122.6*	140.5	145.6	183.1	155.8	22.8	120.6*
1937	133.2	138.0	135.9	150.7	72.2	126.4	151.0	157.3	192.7	217.4	26.9	132.6
1938	114.6	137.7	134.0	157.6	66.1	114.6*	124.7	147.7	187.5	182.4	27.9	122.7*
1939	109.7	137.7	132.2	155.1	64.7	110.6*	128.1	146.9	188.3	189.6	28.7	123.1*

a For Total Perishable.
1 Food & kindred products—mfd. & nonmfd.
2 Cigars, cigarettes & tobacco.
3 Drug, toilet, & household preparations.
4 Magazines, newspapers, stationery & supplies, & misc. paper products.
5a Fuel & lighting products, mfd.
5b Fuel & lighting products, nonmfd.

b For Total Semidurable.
6 Dry goods & notions.
7 Clothing & personal furnishings.
8 Shoes & other footwear.
9 House furnishings.
10 Toys, games, & sporting goods.
11 Tires & tubes.

*Implicit indexes for these years derived by weighting the individual group indexes by the average current price estimates for 1933, 1935, and 1937. The composite indexes thus calculated were used to interpolate and extrapolate the implicit indexes for 1933, 1935, and 1937.

CONSUMER DURABLE

	12	13a	13b	13c	14a	14b	15	16	17	18	19	20a	20b	20c	21	22	23	24	IMPLICIT INDEX
1869	81.8				168.0	186.3	263.4												119.4
1879	54.0				104.0	96.6	128.9												83.2
1889	55.9				82.1	86.4	125.7	89.6											81.9
1890	54.9				82.0	85.6	124.1	87.4	127.3										82.3
1891	54.9		No Index		87.5	83.9	123.8	85.5	127.3										82.1
1892	54.9	No Index		No Index	81.1	82.6	120.5	93.1	115.8										79.2
1893	50.9				82.3	84.0	120.2	90.6	104.0										74.8
1894	50.0				77.2	77.8	118.0	83.8	98.6										72.3
1895	45.8				69.8	71.3	113.8	75.1	98.6										67.4
1896	41.0				68.9	71.8	111.2	75.2	98.6										63.8
1897	40.7				71.8	69.3	101.2	75.9	90.5										63.0
1898	45.5				76.9	67.7	101.4	74.6	96.8										67.5
1899	47.0				76.0	67.8	104.4	80.6	100.0			129.0							70.0
1900	53.0				79.4	78.7	110.1	87.1	100.0			129.0							77.0
1901	52.3				78.6	74.0	125.8	88.3	109.5	No Index		129.0	Index of Minor Group 20a		No Index	Index of Minor Group 31	No Index	No Index	75.5
1902	54.5				79.0	76.2	126.1	96.8	109.5			127.4							79.9
1903	56.4				83.9	80.5	124.8	97.6	109.5			127.6							82.7
1904	56.6				85.0	86.7	119.1	95.6	111.7			116.4		95.8					83.5
1905	57.1				89.7	80.7	112.2	102.5	112.0			175.9		99.9					85.3
1906	60.2				90.9	91.3	111.9	102.4	105.6			204.2							89.1
1907	67.3				94.9	97.6	113.0	109.4	109.4			235.1							97.7
1908	66.0				91.6	82.9	110.4	105.2	95.7			235.0							96.6
1909	64.8				89.6	86.7	106.9	104.2	90.5			142.2		100.9					90.4
1910	70.3				89.9	93.9	104.4	103.2	90.5			131.3		101.4					93.5
1911	80.0				89.9	96.5	98.3	105.6	90.5			124.6		100.0					95.8
1912	88.2				95.6	95.1	98.7	97.6	94.1			103.8		100.0					66.2
1913	100.0	100.0			100.0	100.0	100.0	100.0	100.0		100.0	100.0		100.0					100.0
1914	99.8	100.0			97.5	98.2	104.2	94.1	101.4		100.0	84.7		98.3					94.4
1915	100.0	99.8			100.7	92.3	104.6	101.0	100.0		106.0	78.3		95.9					90.3
1916	102.5	103.2			123.2	122.3	119.5	95.8	118.2		138.1	72.9		98.2					90.4
1917	113.4	115.9			146.7	212.4	165.2	97.2	165.4		181.4	74.8		109.1					100.8
1918	131.5	141.5			192.2	284.3	208.7	117.0	198.2		221.5	82.0		150.1					121.9
1919	168.2	154.9			230.6	254.8	224.9	141.0	213.9		263.2	96.6		171.1					136.4

Year										
1919	168.2	154.9			222.4	216.4	144.0	213.9	263.2	96.6	134.5
1920	252.3	184.8			291.6	252.2	170.4	243.0	263.2	108.9	157.8
1921	195.3	178.0			228.0	245.1	159.9	230.1	245.5	97.2	139.8
1922	173.2	176.0			199.3	210.3	144.0	197.1	233.5	79.0	113.4
1923	178.6	199.2			217.9	253.7	160.7	237.7	189.4	73.7	108.2
1924	165.0	194.3			206.4	255.3	166.5	240.8	189.4	72.9	108.5
1925	158.7	190.6			214.0	236.7	155.3	220.6	187.6	71.4	103.3
1926	153.7	187.5			209.8	227.5	158.8	207.4	174.1	67.8	98.8
1927	149.7	186.0			206.2	224.7	162.6	207.4	184.6	69.5	104.0
1928	148.9	178.0			200.8	223.6	163.4	207.4	194.8	72.5	105.4
1929	147.1	180.0			195.4	220.2	161.9	207.4	189.8	75.2	106.4
1930	146.4	177.8			195.5	225.5	166.3	207.4	188.4	70.8	104.3
1931	137.6	168.5			160.0	225.3	138.5	207.4	162.8	67.1	99.8
1932	119.3	155.9			146.5	224.0	147.4	201.0	145.3	66.8	98.0
1933	119.2	140.9			151.3	230.4	124.6	193.7	137.1	66.7	96.8
1934	122.6	147.8			165.2	261.7	141.1	193.7	145.1	70.0	98.5*
1935	118.2	151.1			168.5	262.0	105.0	193.7	146.8	68.9	93.6
1936	117.2	153.1			172.2	262.9	127.2	193.7	158.6	67.8	90.8*
1937	132.1	165.0			201.2	285.1	113.5	198.2	192.2	63.4	91.9
1938	132.2	166.0			193.5	285.2	117.9	198.2	186.4	67.2	92.8*
1939	130.1	167.3			200.1	283.4	116.4	185.0	180.8	65.6	92.1*

c For Total Consumer Durable.

12 Household furniture.
13a Heating & cooking apparatus & household appliances, except electrical.
13b Electrical household appliances & supplies.
13c Radios.
14a Floor coverings.
14b Misc. house furnishings.
15 China & household utensils.
16 Musical instruments.
17 Jewelry, silverware, clocks & watches.
18 Printing & publishing: books.
19 Luggage.
20a Motor vehicles.
20b Motor vehicle accessories.
20c Carriages & wagons.
21 Motorcycles & bicycles.
22 Pleasure craft.
23 Ophthalmic products & artificial limbs.
24 Monuments & tombstones.

PRODUCER DURABLE

	25a	25b	26	27	28	29	30	31	32a	32b	33	34	35	36	IMPLICIT INDEX	C.M.ᵉ
1869	No Index		No Index	No Index		No Index	No Index	No Index					204.8	129.7	163.8	107.4
1879													132.5	79.9	95.4	81.4
1889	87.3		76.6	116.6		61.5	82.7	77.1					97.1	91.0	88.2	85.0
1890	88.6		77.8	118.4		60.4	82.7	77.1					93.0	83.4	87.7	84.3
1891	80.6		70.8	113.9		60.4	81.2	75.7					90.4	72.3	81.1	80.2
1892	79.8		70.0	112.3		60.4	80.2	74.8					90.1	71.2	80.0	75.9
1893	79.9		70.1	110.6		56.0	78.5	73.2					89.7	66.1	78.4	75.4
1894	84.9		74.5	106.8		55.0	76.9	71.7					87.6	60.2	78.2	71.6
1895	69.9		61.4	103.9		50.4	74.7	69.7					86.1	70.3	72.2	70.7
1896	62.0		54.4	100.7		45.1	74.2	69.2					85.9	65.9	66.1	71.8
1897	85.0		74.6	97.9		44.8	75.3	70.2					86.1	59.5	75.9	67.1
1898	91.5		80.3	94.4		49.7	79.0	73.7					85.7	71.9	82.5	69.9
1899	98.1		86.1	97.3		50.3	82.9	77.3					91.2	81.3	88.1	80.7
1900	96.9		85.1	101.0		56.5	84.0	78.4					97.9	87.3	90.0	85.8
1901	95.9		84.2	101.7		55.2	86.2	80.4					98.5	80.7	88.9	80.7
1902	93.9		82.4	102.6		57.2	87.2	81.3					99.4	87.1	89.7	82.5
1903	88.2		77.4	103.1		59.1	87.2	81.3					99.9	81.9	86.2	84.5
1904	94.7		83.1	102.0		59.0	88.3	82.4	97.1				97.2	80.5	88.8	81.7
1905	94.4		82.9	102.0		59.7	90.1	84.0	94.7				98.1	83.4	89.7	87.0
1906	93.0		81.6	99.6		63.1	92.3	86.1	96.1				100.0	91.0	90.6	96.6
1907	97.3		85.4	99.6		69.7	93.6	87.3	95.1				102.6	92.3	93.6	101.0
1908	90.0		79.0	103.1		68.0	95.0	88.6	90.8				101.2	81.8	89.3	93.3
1909	100.6		88.3	102.6		66.8	96.6	90.1	86.4				100.6	82.3	94.3	94.8
1910	100.7		88.4	100.4		72.1	98.2	91.6	86.0				100.5	83.0	95.3	97.6
1911	111.4		97.8	100.0		81.9	90.9	94.2	105.0				101.4	81.2	99.1	97.0
1912	104.2	97.1	91.5	100.0		89.8	94.4	96.7	104.4				100.6	86.6	97.6	97.9
1913	100.0	100.0	100.0	100.0		100.0	100.0	100.0	100.0				100.0	100.0	100.0	100.0
1914	106.7	96.6	100.2	100.2		100.3	91.8	101.8	94.9				99.0	95.6	100.3	93.1
1915	120.3	92.6	105.6	98.4		100.4	93.3	107.3	90.8				98.6	102.5	106.4	94.6
1916	131.8	91.0	124.7	98.3		103.3	126.9	125.4	93.3				117.3	119.0	120.5	119.0
1917	162.1	74.5	152.6	97.1		113.9	162.7	164.5	92.1				158.9	171.1	145.5	154.9
1918	200.8	89.2	173.2	128.7		131.8	213.7	227.7	102.0				191.8	192.0	175.7	174.5
1919	209.2	87.1	182.5	127.6		170.4	235.1	245.7	88.3				200.4	242.9	185.0	202.7

Index of Minor Group 25a (col. 28)
Index of Group 20c (col. 32b)
No Index (col. 33)
No Index (col. 34)

1919	209.2	87.1	182.5	127.6	168.1	235.1	245.7	88.3	199.2	242.9	184.1	202.7
1920	219.7	78.0	197.0	121.8	242.6	259.8	239.7	70.2	221.3	265.2	181.0	262.0
1921	207.1	89.0	181.3	135.2	190.2	180.9	200.6	59.9	191.1	204.5	164.5	172.2
1922	181.0	66.6	169.0	104.4	167.9	159.1	175.5	44.7	173.2	193.6	135.2	170.7
1923	191.4	66.0	181.1	104.7	171.1	194.1	170.5	40.3	186.3	196.4	138.7	190.4
1924	193.5	63.0	178.4	109.1	158.0	178.0	170.5	40.8	188.6	193.1	134.8	179.5
1925	193.5	65.2	175.4	107.4	153.4	169.0	170.5	46.1	188.0	204.0	135.0	178.5
1926	194.6	66.4	178.9	108.3	146.5	170.5	170.5	46.7	189.8	201.0	138.4	175.6
1927	195.6	66.3	173.8	108.3	146.5	179.2	170.5	42.8	187.5	205.9	138.5	166.6
1928	197.7	65.7	173.2	107.3	146.4	169.7	170.5	39.7	187.3	210.5	136.5	165.6
1929	199.8	65.3	173.8	106.2	145.8	182.0	170.5	41.1	187.7	206.7	131.1	167.8
1930	184.1	64.5	164.1	104.4	145.6	181.1	165.5	38.3	185.0	199.0	125.6	158.4
1931	173.6	60.3	150.4	101.3	137.3	166.3	158.5	35.7	179.5	181.5	117.2	140.2
1932	162.1	57.1	140.8	97.3	127.3	149.9	148.4	34.7	175.5	170.4	112.9	126.8
1933	162.1	56.7	146.2	95.0	116.6	149.3	148.4	31.4	166.8	165.2	104.6	136.0
1934	187.2	57.1	155.2	97.0	123.6	165.7	158.5	32.6	175.9	164.8	107.6*	151.4
1935	187.2	59.9	149.0	99.2	117.9	177.1	160.5	31.4	173.6	164.3	99.6	149.8
1936	187.2	60.4	151.8	100.0	117.6	178.3	160.5	31.3	173.4	178.4	102.0*	152.2
1937	207.1	62.6	157.4	103.6	129.0	191.2	171.5	33.1	186.5	191.2	112.1	167.3
1938	209.2	62.6	154.6	105.0	128.3	190.6	171.5	36.5	191.1	190.0	112.8*	159.0
1939		58.5		102.5	130.0			36.3	190.9	185.1	110.4f	159.0

d For Total Producer Durable.
e Construction Materials.
f Based on the movement of the NBER price index for processed capital equipment goods.

25a Industrial machinery & equipment.
25b Tractors.
26 Electrical equipment, industrial & commercial.
27 Farm equipment.
28 Office & store machinery & equipment.
29 Office & store furniture & fixtures.
30 Locomotives & railroad cars.

31 Ships & boats.
32a Business vehicles, motor.
32b Business vehicles, wagons.
33 Aircraft.
34 Professional & scientific equipment.
35 Carpenters' & mechanics' tools.
36 Misc. subsidiary durable equipment.

NOTE TO TABLE IV 1

Composition of the Price Indexes,
Minor Commodity Groups

1 *Food and kindred products:* Since 1890 the Bureau of Labor Statistics wholesale price index for foods, a composite of manufactured and nonmanufactured foods, was used. For years before 1890 the following appropriate series (Aldrich Report, Part I) were combined, using 1909 BLS weights: beans; butter and cheese; coffee; eggs; codfish; mackerel; flour and meal; currants; lard; meat and meat products; fresh milk; molasses; rice; salt; spices; refined sugar; potatoes; livestock; and raisins. The composite index was then linked to the BLS index for 1890.

2 *Cigars, cigarettes and tobacco:* Since 1926 BLS series for cigarettes; cigars; plug tobacco; snuff; and safety matches were combined, using 1926 BLS weights (*Wholesale Prices, 1931,* Bull. 572, Bureau of Labor Statistics, Washington, D.C., 1933). For 1919–25 BLS series for plug and smoking tobacco were combined and linked to the index compiled for later years. For 1890–1919 the BLS series for plug and smoking tobacco were combined with series for cigarettes and little cigars (weighing less than 3 lb. per thousand). The latter series, developed from data in *Prices of Tobacco Products* (Federal Trade Commission, Jan. 1922); *Prices of Tobacco and Tobacco Products,* Lloyd L. Shawnlis (Bull. 19, War Industries Board, Washington, D.C., 1919); and *Report of the Commissioner of Corporations on the Tobacco Industry, Part III, Prices, Costs and Profits* (1915), are described more fully in Part II, Table II 6, Note B. Plug and smoking tobacco were first combined by using 1909 BLS weights; then combined with the cigarette and little cigar series, using census production values for 1909 as weights. For years before 1890 prices of tobacco leaf used for binders, fillers, smokers, and wrappers (Aldrich Report) were weighted equally and linked to the index compiled for later years.

3 *Drug, toilet and household preparations:* Since 1926 the BLS index for drugs and pharmaceuticals was combined with the series for soap chips, laundry soap, laundry powder, and toilet soap, using 1926 BLS weights. For 1919–25 a similar combination, but including fewer series, was made and linked to the index compiled for later years. For 1913–18 indexes for drugs and pharmaceuticals; proprietary medicine; soap; hot water bottles; and ice bags (*Prices of Drugs and Pharmaceuticals* and *Prices of Proprietary Preparations,* W. Lee Lewis and F. W. Casserbeer, Bull. 54 and 55, War Industries Board, 1919; and *Prices of Soap and Glycerin,* H. L. Trumbull, Bull. 49, *ibid.*) were combined, using the average value of production of these commodities in 1914 and 1919 as weights. For 1890–1912 and 1919 BLS series for opium, natural; quinine; and bicarbonate of soda were combined, using 1909 BLS weights, with an index of the average annual export price of soap (*Monthly Summary of Foreign Commerce, seriatim*). The composite index was then linked to the War Industries Board composite for 1913–18. Extension to 1889 was based on

the movement of the opium and castile soap series (Aldrich Report). For years before 1889 no index could be constructed.

4 *Magazines, newspapers, stationery and supplies, and miscellaneous paper products:* Since 1919 BLS series for newsprint and wrapping paper were combined, using 1926 BLS weights. For 1890–1919 the same series were combined, using 1909 weights. For years before 1890 no index could be constructed.

5a *Fuel and lighting products, manufactured:* Since 1926 BLS series for byproduct coke, Newark, N.J.; fuel oil, Pennsylvania; gasoline, California, North Texas, Oklahoma, and Pennsylvania; kerosene, standard and water white; regular matches; and oil, neutral, Gulf coastal, and Pennsylvania were combined, using 1926 BLS weights. For 1919–25 such of the above series as were available were similarly combined and linked to the index constructed for later years. For 1913–18 series for gasoline; kerosene; lubricating oil; and matches (*Prices of Petroleum and Its Products,* J. E. Pogue and I. Lubin, and *Prices of Matches,* Mary L. Danforth, Bull. 36 and 37, War Industries Board, 1919) together with a BLS series for byproduct coke, Newark, N.J., were combined, using the average value of production in 1914 and 1919 as weights. For 1919 a BLS composite, based on 1926 weights, of byproduct coke, Newark, N.J.; fuel oil, Pennsylvania; gasoline, Oklahoma; and kerosene, standard and water white, was linked to the War Industries Board index for 1913–18. For 1890–1912 a BLS composite, based on 1909 weights, of matches; candles; crude petroleum; and kerosene, standard and water white, was linked to the War Industries Board index. For years before 1890 series for candles and matches (Aldrich Report) were used to extrapolate the index for later years.

5b *Fuel and lighting products, nonmanufactured:* Quantity data for anthracite and bituminous coal, and fuel briquets were multiplied by the respective prices for 1913. See Note to Table II 10 for sources.

6 *Dry goods and notions:* Since 1926 BLS indexes for cotton goods and woolen and worsted goods, together with the separate index for cotton thread, were combined, using 1926 BLS weights. For 1919–25 the cotton and woolen and worsted group indexes, after the removal of series for cotton blankets, hosiery, and underwear, and for woolen blankets and underwear, were combined and linked to the index for later years. For 1890–1919 BLS series for colored cotton flannel, denims, cotton thread, drillings, ginghams, print cloths, raw silk, all wool flannels, woolen dress goods, overcoatings, suitings, trouserings, and broadcloth were combined, using BLS 1909 weights. For years before 1890 prices for drillings, denims, print cloths, ginghams, cotton thread, and cassimeres (Aldrich Report) were combined, using BLS 1909 weights, and linked to the index for later years.

7 *Clothing and personal furnishings:* Since 1926 BLS indexes for clothing, men's and women's cotton and silk hosiery, cotton and woolen underwear and gloves were combined, using 1926 BLS weights. For 1919–25 BLS indexes for ginghams, hosiery, overcoatings, shirtings, suitings, trouserings, underwear, women's dress goods, and broadcloth were combined and linked to the index

for later years. For 1913–18 an index for clothing products excluding boots and shoes (*Prices of Clothing,* John M. Curran, Bull. 5, War Industries Board, 1919) was used. The boots and shoes components were removed by using weights based on the average census values of production for 1914 and 1919. For 1890–1912 and 1919 the composite BLS series listed above for 1919–25, but combined, using 1909 BLS weights, was linked to the War Industries Board index. For years before 1890 series for shirtings, hosiery, cassimeres, shirts and drawers, suitings and dress goods (Aldrich Report) were combined, using 1909 BLS weights, and linked to the index for later years.

8 *Shoes and other footwear:* Since 1919 the BLS index for boots and shoes was used. For 1913–18 composite prices for men's, women's, boys', misses', and children's shoes, rubber arctics and boots (*Prices of Clothing*) were combined, using average census production values in 1914 and 1919. The composite index for 1913–18 was extrapolated to 1919 by the movement of the BLS index for boots and shoes. For 1890–1912 BLS series for men's brogans, men's vici kid shoes, men's calf bluchers, and women's solid grain shoes were combined, using 1909 BLS weights, and linked to the 1913–18 index excluding rubber shoes. For years before 1890 series for men's brogans and women's solid grain shoes (Aldrich Report) were combined and linked to the index for later years.

9 *Housefurnishings (semidurable)*: Since 1926 BLS indexes for blankets, comforters, table oilcloth, pillowcases, shades, sheets, tablecloths, and mirrors were combined, using 1926 BLS weights. For 1919–25 the BLS index for blankets was linked to the index for 1926 and later years. For 1890–1919 BLS indexes for cotton blankets, sheetings, and tickings were combined, using 1909 BLS weights. For years before 1890 series for blankets and sheetings (Aldrich Report) were combined and linked to the index for later years.

11 *Tires and tubes:* Since 1913 the BLS index for tires and tubes was used. For years before 1913 the index for Minor Group 20a was used to extrapolate the tire and tube index.

12 *Household furniture:* Since 1913 BLS indexes for wooden beds, bedroom chairs, dressers, and rockers; dining room buffet chairs and tables; kitchen chairs and tables; and living room davenports and tables were combined, using 1926 BLS weights. For 1890–1912 BLS indexes for bedroom sets, bedroom chairs, and kitchen chairs and tables were combined, using similar weights (no satisfactory 1909 weights were available), and linked to the index for later years. For years before 1890 series for bedroom chairs, kitchen tables and chairs (Aldrich Report) were combined and linked to the index for 1890 and later years.

13a *Heating and cooking apparatus and household appliances except electrical:* Since 1913 BLS composite indexes for coal, gas and oil cooking stoves were combined, using 1926 BLS weights. For years before 1913 no index could be constructed.

14a and 14b *Floor coverings and housefurnishings (durable)*: Since 1919 BLS indexes for Axminster, Brussels, and Wilton carpets, all wool blankets, wooden beds, and tickings were combined, using 1926 BLS weights. For 1890–1919 BLS indexes for Axminster, Brussels, and Wilton carpets were combined, using 1909 BLS weights, to derive a separate floor coverings index. For years before 1890 series for Brussels, Lowell, and Wilton carpets (Aldrich Report) were combined and linked to the index for later years. A separate index for housefurnishings (durable) 1890–1919 was computed by combining, using 1909 BLS weights, BLS indexes for all wool blankets, bedroom sets, and tickings. For years before 1890 series for blankets and tickings (Aldrich Report) were combined and linked to the index for later years.

15 *China and household utensils:* Since 1919 BLS indexes for carvers, knives and forks, pails, napkins, pitchers, tumblers, white plates, and teacups and saucers were combined, using 1926 BLS weights. For 1890–1919 the same indexes were combined, but using 1909 weights. Series unweighted in 1909 were arbitrarily assigned a weight of .01. For years before 1890 series for glass pitchers and tumblers, and wooden pails and tubs (Aldrich Report) were combined and linked to the index for later years. Pitchers and tumblers were assigned 1909 BLS weights; wooden pails and tubs, weights based on their 1909 production value relative to that of glass products.

16 *Musical instruments:* The price index compiled for this group was based chiefly on per unit export price series (*Foreign Commerce and Navigation of the United States* and the *Monthly Summary of Foreign Commerce*). Since 1919 export prices of pianos and phonographs were first adjusted to the census year per unit price, then combined, using the average values of output in 1927 and 1929 as weights. For 1913–19 export prices of player pianos, other pianos, and organs were adjusted to 1914 and 1919 census prices, then combined, using the average values of output in 1914 and 1919 as weights. For 1904–12 a similar compilation was based on export prices for *all* pianos and organs. For 1889–1903 an index based on the export prices of organs was linked to the index for later years. For years before 1889 no index could be constructed.

17 *Jewelry, silverware, clocks, and watches:* Since 1890 BLS indexes for carvers and knives and forks were combined, using 1926 BLS weights. For years before 1890 no index could be constructed.

19 *Luggage:* Since 1913 BLS indexes for suitcases and traveling bags were combined, using 1926 BLS weights. For years before 1913 no index could be constructed.

20a *Passenger vehicles, motorized:* Since 1913 the BLS index for passenger cars was used. For 1900–12 an index derived from the per unit prices of passenger cars sold in the United States (*Automobile Facts and Figures, 1941*, Automobile Manufacturers' Association, p. 4) was linked to the index for later years.

20b *Motor vehicle accessories:* The index derived for passenger vehicles, motorized, was used.

20c *Passenger vehicles, horse-drawn:* As this group is included with the farm equipment group since 1919, no separate index had to be constructed for these years. For 1913–19 the revised BLS index for wagons (*Wholesale Prices,* Bureau of Labor Statistics, Jan. 1936, p. 22) was used. For 1911–12 an index of prices paid by farmers for farm machinery and motor trucks (*Income Parity for Agriculture,* Part III, Sec. 4, *Prices Paid by Farmers for Farm Machinery and Motor Vehicles, 1910–38,* Bureau of Agricultural Economics, May 1939) was linked to the index for later years. For 1907–10 prices received by the International Harvester Company for two-horse wagons (U. S. Bureau of Corporations, *The International Harvester Company,* March 1913, p. 248) were linked to the index for later years. For years before 1907 no index could be constructed.

22 *Pleasure craft:* The index derived for Minor Group 31 was used.

25a *Industrial machinery and equipment:* Since 1915 the maintenance account index for shop machinery (Interstate Commerce Commission, Engineering Section, Bureau of Valuation, mimeographed release, July 1, 1940) was used. For 1889–1914 an index of shop machinery costs (*Trend of Cost of Shop Machinery,* President's Conference Committee, Eastern Group Pamphlet 314, Jan. 1926) was linked to the index for later years. The President's Conference Committee index was based on railroad purchase of 1,091 machines representing 288 types, sizes, or kinds of machines—air compressors, pressure blowers, bolt cutters, bolt headers, boring mills, car wheel borers, car borers, centering machines, flue cutters, metal cutters, drill presses, flangers, flue welders, forging machines, grinders, hammers, jacks, lath axles, lath engines, lath turrets, lath wheels, milling machines, mortisers, pipe threaders, planers, press bushings, hydraulic presses, power presses, press wheels, punches and shears, boiler feed pumps, band saws, rip saws, hack saws, crank shapers, slotters, surfacers, and welders and rappers. For years before 1889 no index could be constructed.

25b *Tractors:* Since 1913 BLS indexes for tractors, 2-plow; tractors, 3-4 plow; and tractors, crawler (*Wholesale Prices,* Jan. 1936 and subsequent Dec. issues) were combined, using 1926 BLS weights.

26 *Electrical equipment, industrial and commercial:* Since 1915 a combination of Interstate Commerce Commission indexes (*op. cit.*) for the following accounts: telephone and telegraph lines (26), signals and interlockers (27), power transmission systems (31), power distribution systems (32), power line poles and fixtures (33), underground conduits (34), power plant machinery (45), and power substation apparatus was used. For years before 1915 the index derived for Minor Group 25a was linked to the index for later years.

27 *Farm machinery and equipment:* Since 1913 the revised BLS index for farm machinery (*Wholesale Prices,* Jan. 1936 and subsequent Dec. issues) was used. For 1911–12 the index of prices paid by farmers for farm machinery and motor trucks (*Income Parity for Agriculture,* Part III, Sec. 4) was linked to the index for later years. For 1903–10 prices received by the International Harvester Company (*op. cit.*) for grain binders, 5, 6, and 7 feet; grain binders, 8 feet; mowers; rakes; tedders; corn binders; disk harrows; manure spreaders; and cream separators were combined, using 1913 BLS weights, and linked to the index for later years. For 1900–02 the index for Minor Group 35 was linked to the index for later years. For 1890, 1895, and 1900 prices for hay carriers,

churns, condensers, cradles, cultivators, cutters, diggers, drills, fertilizer distributors, forks, gins, harrows and pulverizers, harvesters, hullers, markers and furrows, mills, mowers, planters, plows, rakes, reapers, rollers, scythes, seeders and sowers, shellers, stackers, stump pullers, tedders, threshers, and windmills (*Course of Prices of Farm Implements and Machinery for a Series of Years,* George K. Holmes, Department of Agriculture, Division of Statistics, Misc. Series, Bull. 18, Washington, D.C., 1901) were combined, using BLS 1913 weights. Items for which no weights were reported were arbitrarily given weights of .01. The composite index was linked to the index for later years. An index for the intervening years and for 1889 was constructed on the basis of the index for carpenters' and mechanics' tools. For years before 1889 no index could be constructed.

28 *Office and store machinery and equipment:* The index for Minor Group 25a was used.

29 *Office furniture and fixtures:* Since 1926 BLS indexes for four types of office furniture—side and swivel armchairs, flat-top and typewriter desks—were combined, using 1926 BLS weights. For 1919–26 the BLS index for household furniture was linked to the index for later years. For 1890–1919 the index for Minor Group 12 was combined with an index of the per unit export prices of safes, using 1909 census values for all other office furniture and safes and vaults as weights. For 1889 the index for household furniture was linked to the index for later years.

30 *Locomotives and railroad cars:* Since 1915 a combination of Interstate Commerce Commission indexes (*op. cit.*) for the following accounts: steam locomotives (51), other locomotives (52), freight train cars (53), and passenger train cars (54) was used. For 1910–14 indexes for locomotives; freight cars: all steel; freight cars: wood and steel; freight cars: all wood; and passenger cars, all steel (*Trend of Prices for Locomotives, Freight and Passenger Train Cars and Floating Equipment,* President's Conference Committee, Eastern Group Pamphlet 138-6, Aug. 15, 1930) were combined, using Interstate Commerce Commission weights. The total weight for freight train cars was split among the different types on the basis of average census values in 1914 and 1919. For years before 1910 the index for Minor Group 31 was used to extrapolate the index for later years.

31 *Ships and boats:* Since 1915 the Interstate Commerce Commission (*op. cit.*) index for floating equipment was used. For 1889–1914 two indexes of the cost to railroads of floating equipment were reported in *Cost of Floating Equipment* (President's Conference Committee, Eastern Group Pamphlet 290). One was prepared by the Committee from shipbuilders' reports of estimated prices to railroads; the other by the Cost Section, Bureau of Valuation, Interstate Commerce Commission, from actual prices to railroads for more than 1,500 units of floating equipment. It was indicated in Pamphlet 290 that an average of the two series would probably be more reliable than either separately. The average was linked to the index for later years.

32a *Business vehicles, motorized:* Since 1927 the BLS index for motor trucks was linked to the index for earlier years. For 1904–26 an index was constructed from the per unit prices for motor trucks (*Automobile Facts and Figures, 1941,* Automobile Manufacturers' Association, p. 4).

32b *Business vehicles, horse-drawn:* The index for Minor Group 20c was used.

35 *Carpenters' and mechanics' tools:* Since 1890 BLS indexes for augers, chisels, files, hammers, planes, cross-cut saws, handsaws, shovels, vises, axes (1922 and subsequent years), and hatchets (1926 and subsequent years) were combined, using 1926 BLS weights. For years before 1890 series for handsaws, cross-cut saws, and shovels (Aldrich Report) were combined and linked to the index for later years.

36 *Miscellaneous subsidiary durable equipment:* Since 1913 BLS indexes for Manila rope and leather harness were combined, using 1926 BLS weights. For 1890–1912 the leather harness index was first extrapolated by the BLS index for oak harness leather, then combined with that for Manila rope. For years before 1890 series for manila rope and harness leather (Aldrich Report) were combined and linked to the index for later years.

Construction materials: Since 1913 BLS index for lumber and building materials and BLS index for steel rails were combined using 1926 weights. For 1890–1913 a similar composite, using 1909 weights, was combined with an index of structural steel prices computed from data in *Metal Statistics, 1938* (p. 95) by means of weights suggested by comparing the 1909 production values of steel rails and structural steel. For years before 1890 series for lead pipe, cut nails, brick, cement, lime, maple boards, pine boards, pine flooring, spruce shingles, window glass, and plate glass (Aldrich Report) were combined, using 1909 BLS weights, and linked to the index for later years.

Index

(Tables and notes following the introductory text to each Part are not indexed;
for descriptive titles, see the Contents.)

AGRICULTURAL STATISTICS, use for estimates since 1933, 105
ALDRICH REPORT, 288
AUTOMOBILE FACTS AND FIGURES, use for estimates since 1933, 107

BARGER, HAROLD, 2, 102
BEAN, LOUIS, 101
BUREAU OF LABOR STATISTICS WHOLESALE PRICE BULLETINS, 269, 284 and 512, 288
BURNS, ARTHUR, 22, 25

Capital formation, 1, 4
CENSUS OF AGRICULTURE, 101
CENSUS OF DISTRIBUTION: WHOLESALE TRADE, 270
CENSUS OF MANUFACTURES
  Adjustments to commodity data, 81, 82
  Comparison of commodity total and industry total, 82
  Deficiencies, 80
  Description, 79, 80
  Use for estimates since 1933, 105
CLARK, J. M., 6
Comparison of 1919 estimates with those of Kuznets, 89
Comparison of value of output with value destined for domestic consumption, 273, 274
Construction materials
  Derivation of estimates since 1919, 105, 107
  Evaluation of interpolating series, 101
  Importance of mixed commodities, 83
  Non-manufactured, 104
  Percentage that exports constitute of value of output in 1909, 271
  Relation of value of output to value destined for domestic consumption, 273
  Use of series, 4, 7
Consumer commodities
  Definition, 5, 6
  Relation of value of output to value destined for domestic consumption, 273
  Use of detailed series, 3

Consumer durable commodities
  Comparison of 1919 estimate with that of Kuznets, 89
  Decade variations, 16–18
  Definition, 5
  Derivation of estimates since 1933, 106
  Importance of mixed commodities, 83
  Indexes of conformity, 26, 27, 29
  Percentage of 1909 total for which direct price indexes are not available, 289
  Percentage that exports constitute of value of output in 1909, 271
  Rate of growth, 9, 28
  Relation of value of output to value destined for domestic consumption, 273
  Variations in cyclical amplitude, 24, 29
Consumer expenditures, 1
Consumer perishable commodities
  Comparison of 1919 estimate with that of Kuznets, 89
  Decade variations, 16, 17, 29
  Definition, 5
  Derivation of estimates since 1933, 105, 106
  Importance of mixed commodities, 83
  Indexes of conformity, 26, 27
  Percentage that exports constitute of value of output in 1909, 271
  Rate of growth, 9
  Relation of value of output to value destined for domestic consumption, 273
  Variations in cyclical amplitude, 24
Consumer semidurable commodities
  Comparison of 1919 estimates with that of Kuznets, 89
  Decade variations, 16, 17, 29
  Definition, 5
  Derivation of estimates since 1933, 106
  Importance of mixed commodities, 83
  Indexes of conformity, 26, 27
  Percentage of 1909 total for which direct price indexes are not available, 289
  Percentage that exports constitute of value of output in 1909, 271

Rate of growth, 9
Relation of value of output to value destined for domestic consumption, 273
Variations in cyclical amplitude, 24
COUNTRYMAN, W. A., 92
COWDEN, D. J., 269, 270

Decade variations
Behavior of measures for major commodity groups, 15–18, 28, 29
Method of measurement, 14, 15
DEPARTMENT OF AGRICULTURE, 101–3
DEPARTMENT OF COMMERCE, 7, 107
DOMESTIC COMMERCE, use for estimates since 1933, 106, 107
DUN'S REVIEW, use for estimates since 1933, 106, 107

Exports
Adjustments in data, 269–71
Changes in relative importance, 272–4
Deficiencies of data, 269
Percentages that exports constitute of value of output in 1909, 271
Per unit prices compared with census prices, 270, 271
Sources of data, 269

FABRICANT, SOLOMON, 2
Finished commodities
Changes in importance of minor groups, 12, 14, 28
Decade variations, 15–18, 28, 29
Definition, 4–6
Importance, 1
Indexes of conformity, 25–8, 29
Rate of growth, 8, 9, 28
Variations in cyclical amplitude, 22–4, 29
FISHER, IRVING, 288

Gross national product, 1

Imports
Changes in relative importance, 272–4
Deficiencies of data, 272
Definition, 272
Derivation of calendar year figures, 272
Source of data, 272
Indexes of conformity
Behavior of indexes for major commodity groups, 25–28
Method of calculating, 25
Indexes of industrial production
Agricultural output, 2, 3
Approximation of by total output of finished commodities and construction materials in constant prices, 1
Comparison with total output in 1913 prices, 2, 3
Manufacturing output, 2, 3
Mining output, 2, 3

KUZNETS, SIMON, 4, 7, 79, 83–5, 89, 104, 105, 271, 289

LANDSBERG, HANS, 2, 102

Manufactured food and kindred products, detailed evaluation of estimates, 97–100
Measures of cyclical amplitude
Behavior of measures for major commodity groups, 22–24
Limitations of annual measures, 22
Method of calculating, 18, 22
MINERAL RESOURCES of the UNITED STATES, 103, 104
MINERALS YEARBOOK, use for estimates since 1933, 105
Minor commodity groups
Changes in importance, 12, 14, 28
Comparison of estimates for 1919 with those of Kuznets, 85–88
Criteria for grouping, 6
Derivation of estimates since 1919, 104, 105
Effect of errors in export adjustments, 271
Final rating of interpolating series, 101
Procedure when direct price indexes could not be computed, 289
Reduction percentages applied to export prices, 271
Relation of values of output to values destined for domestic consumption, 273–4
Selection and evaluation of interpolating series, 97–101
Sources of data for intercensal estimates, 92–7
MITCHELL, W. C., 22, 25
Mixed commodities
Definition, 82, 83
Relative importance of in major commodity groups, 83
MOORE, G. H., 2

NELSON, SAUL, 288
Net value of manufactures
Approximation of by total of manufactured finished commodities and construction materials, 1

INDEX

Comparison with . . . in 1899, 89–92
Definition, 89
Non-manufactured foods, 101–3
Non-manufactured fuels, 103

Output of finished commodities and construction materials in constant prices
Approximation of composite index of industrial production, 1
Comparison with indexes of industrial production, 2, 3
Output of manufactured finished commodities and construction materials
Approximation of net value of manufactures, 1
Comparison with net value of manufactures for 1899, 89–92
Output in constant prices, problem of measuring, 287

Population
Increase from 1879 to 1939, 9, 28
Rate of growth, 9
Price indexes
Adequacy, 288, 289
Deficiencies, 288, 289
Evaluation, 289
Problems of constructing, 287, 288
Weights, 287, 288
Price indexes for finished commodities
Decade variations, 16
Indexes of conformity, 25–28
Long term rises, 9
Reliability, 8
Variations in cyclical amplitude, 22–24
Prices
Export, 270, 271
Use of material prices to represent end-product prices, 289
Producer durable commodities

Comparison of 1919 estimate with that of Kuznets, 89
Decade variations, 16, 18
Definition, 4, 5
Derivation of estimates since 1933, 106, 107
Importance of mixed commodities, 83
Indexes of conformity, 26–29
Percentage of 1909 total for which direct price indexes are not available, 289
Percentage that exports constitute of value of output in 1909, 271
Rate of growth, 9, 28
Relation of value of output to value destined for domestic consumption, 273
Use of series, 4
Variations in cyclical amplitude, 24

Rates of growth
Differences among major commodity groups, 9, 28
Finished commodities, 8, 9
Population, 9
Reference cycle dates, 25

SCHMECKEBIER, L. F., 269
SCHURR, SAM, 2
STATISTICS of INCOME, use for estimates since 1933, 105–7
STRAUSS, FREDERICK, 101
SURVEY of CURRENT BUSINESS, use for estimates since 1933, 106

TERBORGH, GEORGE, 4

Unfinished commodities, definition, 5, 6

WILLIS, H. PARKER, 80

Relation of the Directors to the Work and Publications

of the

National Bureau of Economic Research

1. The object of the National Bureau of Economic Research is to ascertain and to present to the public important economic facts and their interpretation in a scientific and impartial manner. The Board of Directors is charged with the responsibility of ensuring that the work of the Bureau is carried on in strict conformity with this object.

2. To this end the Board of Directors shall appoint one or more Directors of Research.

3. The Director or Directors of Research shall submit to the members of the Board, or to its Executive Committee, for their formal adoption, all specific proposals concerning researches to be instituted.

4. No report shall be published until the Director or Directors of Research shall have submitted to the Board a summary drawing attention to the character of the data and their utilization in the report, the nature and treatment of the problems involved, the main conclusions and such other information as in their opinion would serve to determine the suitability of the report for publication in accordance with the principles of the Bureau.

5. A copy of any manuscript proposed for publication shall also be submitted to each member of the Board. For each manuscript to be so submitted a special committee shall be appointed by the President, or at his designation by the Executive Director, consisting of three Directors selected as nearly as may be one from each general division of the Board. The names of the special manuscript committee shall be stated to each Director when the summary and report described in paragraph (4) are sent to him. It shall be the duty of each member of the committee to read the manuscript. If each member of the special committee signifies his approval within thirty days, the manuscript may be published. If each member of the special committee has not signified his approval within thirty days of the transmittal of the report and manuscript, the Director of Research shall then notify each member of the Board, requesting approval or disapproval of publication, and thirty additional days shall be granted for this purpose. The manuscript shall then not be published unless at least a majority of the entire Board and a two-thirds majority of those members of the Board who shall have voted on the proposal within the time fixed for the receipt of votes on the publication proposed shall have approved.

6. No manuscript may be published, though approved by each member of the special committee, until forty-five days have elapsed from the transmittal of the summary and report. The interval is allowed for the receipt of any memorandum of dissent or reservation, together with a brief statement of his reasons, that any member may wish to express; and such memorandum of dissent or reservation shall be published with the manuscript if he so desires. Publication does not, however, imply that each member of the Board has read the manuscript, or that either members of the Board in general, or of the special committee, have passed upon its validity in every detail.

7. A copy of this resolution shall, unless otherwise determined by the Board, be printed in each copy of every National Bureau book.

(*Resolution adopted October 25, 1926 and revised February 6, 1933 and February 24, 1941*)

National Bureau Publications Still in Print

BOOKS

GENERAL SERIES

9 *Migration and Business Cycles* (1926)
Harry Jerome — 256 pp., $2.50

10 *Business Cycles: The Problem and Its Setting* (1927)*
Wesley C. Mitchell — 510 pp., $5.00

12 *Trends in Philanthropy* (1928)
W. I. King — 78 pp., $1.00

16 *Corporation Contributions to Organized Community Welfare Services* (1930)
Pierce Williams and F. E. Croxton — 348 pp., $2.00

22 *Seasonal Variations in Industry and Trade* (1933)
Simon Kuznets — 480 pp., $4.00

25 *German Business Cycles, 1924–1933* (1934)
C. T. Schmidt — 308 pp., $2.50

26 *Industrial Profits in the United States* (1934)
R. C. Epstein — 692 pp., $5.00

27 *Mechanization in Industry* (1934)
Harry Jerome — 518 pp., $3.50

28 *Corporate Profits as Shown by Audit Reports* (1935)
W. A. Paton — 166 pp., $1.25

29 *Public Works in Prosperity and Depression* (1935)
A. D. Gayer — 482 pp., $3.00

30 *Ebb and Flow in Trade Unionism* (1936)
Leo Wolman — 272 pp., $2.50

31 *Prices in Recession and Recovery* (1936)
Frederick C. Mills — 602 pp., $4.00

33 *Some Theoretical Problems Suggested by the Movements of Interest Rates, Bond Yields and Stock Prices in the United States Since 1856* (1938)
F. R. Macaulay — 612 pp., $5.00

The Social Sciences and the Unknown Future, a reprint of the introductory chapter to Dr. Macaulay's volume — .25

38 *Residential Real Estate, Its Economic Position as Shown by Values, Rents, Family Incomes, Financing, and Construction, Together with Estimates for All Real Estate* (1941)
D. L. Wickens — 330 pp., $3.50

39 *The Output of Manufacturing Industries, 1899–1937* (1940)
Solomon Fabricant — 710 pp., $4.50

* Listed also as the first volume under Studies in Business Cycles.

41 *Employment in Manufacturing, 1899–1939: An Analysis of its Relation to the Volume of Production* (1942)
Solomon Fabricant — 382 pp., $3.00

44 *National Product in Wartime* (1945)
Simon Kuznets — 174 pp., $2.00

46 *National Product since 1869* (1946)
Simon Kuznets — 256 pp., $3.00

47 *Output and Productivity in the Electric and Gas Utilities, 1899–1942* (1946)
J. M. Gould — 208 pp., $3.00

48 *Value of Commodity Output since 1869*
W. H. Shaw — 320 pp., $4.00

STUDIES IN BUSINESS CYCLES

1 *The Problem and Its Setting* (1927)
Wesley C. Mitchell — 510 pp., $5.00

2 *Measuring Business Cycles* (1946)
A. F. Burns and Wesley C. Mitchell — 592 pp., $5.00

TWENTY-FIFTH ANNIVERSARY SERIES

1 *National Income: A Summary of Findings* (1946)
Simon Kuznets — 160 pp., $1.50

2 *Price-Quantity Interactions in Business Cycles* (1946)
Frederick C. Mills — 160 pp., $1.50

3 *Economic Research and the Development of Economic Science and Public Policy* (1946)
Twelve Papers Presented at the Twenty-fifth Anniversary Meeting of the National Bureau of Economic Research — 208 pp., $1.00

4 *Trends in Output and Employment* (1947)
George J. Stigler — 80 pp., $1.00

CONFERENCE ON RESEARCH IN INCOME AND WEALTH
Studies in Income and Wealth, Vol. I (1937) — 370 pp., $2.50

FINANCIAL RESEARCH PROGRAM

I A PROGRAM OF FINANCIAL RESEARCH

1 *Report of the Exploratory Committee on Financial Research* (1937) — 96 pp., $1.00

2 *Inventory of Current Research on Financial Problems* (1937) — 264 pp., $1.50

II STUDIES IN CONSUMER INSTALMENT FINANCING

2 *Sales Finance Companies and Their Credit Practices* (1940)
Wilbur C. Plummer and Ralph A. Young — 324 pp., $3.00

3 *Commercial Banks and Consumer Instalment Credit* (1940)
John M. Chapman and Associates — 342 pp., $3.00

4 *Industrial Banking Companies and Their Credit Practices* (1940)
R. J. Saulnier   216 pp., $2.00

6 *The Pattern of Consumer Debt, 1935–36* (1940)
Blanche Bernstein   256 pp., $2.50

7 *The Volume of Consumer Instalment Credit, 1929–38* (1940)
Duncan McC. Holthausen in collaboration with
Malcolm L. Merriam and Rolf Nugent   158 pp., $1.50

8 *Risk Elements in Consumer Instalment Financing* (1941)
David Durand   128 pp., $1.50
Technical edition,   186 pp., $2.00

10 *Comparative Operating Experience of Consumer Instalment Financing Agencies and Commercial Banks, 1929–41* (1944)
Ernst A. Dauer   240 pp., $3.00

III STUDIES IN BUSINESS FINANCING
Term Lending to Business (1942)
Neil H. Jacoby and R. J. Saulnier   184 pp., $2.00
Accounts Receivable Financing (1943)
R. J. Saulnier and Neil H. Jacoby   176 pp., $2.00
Financing Equipment for Commercial and Industrial Enterprise (1944)
Neil H. Jacoby and R. J. Saulnier   112 pp., $1.50
Financing Inventory on Field Warehouse Receipts (1944)
Neil H. Jacoby and R. J. Saulnier   108 pp., $1.50
The Pattern of Corporate Financial Structure: A Cross-Section View of Manufacturing, Mining, Trade, and Construction, 1937 (1945)
Walter A. Chudson   164 pp., $2.00
Corporate Cash Balances, 1914–43 (1945)
Friedrich A. Lutz   148 pp., $2.00
Business Finance and Banking (1947)
Neil H. Jacoby and R. J. Saulnier   208 pp., $3.50

OCCASIONAL PAPERS

1 Manufacturing Output, 1929–1937 (Dec. 1940)
Solomon Fabricant   .25

3 Finished Commodities since 1879, Output and Its Composition (Aug. 1941)
William H. Shaw   .25

4 The Relation between Factory Employment and Output since 1899 (Dec. 1941)
Solomon Fabricant   .25

5 Railway Freight Traffic in Prosperity and Depression (Feb. 1942)
Thor Hultgren   .25

6 Uses of National Income in Peace and War (March 1942)
Simon Kuznets .25
10 The Effect of War on Business Financing: Manufacturing and Trade, World War I (Nov. 1943)
R. A. Young and C. H. Schmidt .50
11 The Effect of War on Currency and Deposits (Sept. 1943)
Charles R. Whittlesey .35
12 Prices in a War Economy: Some Aspects of the Present Price Structure of the United States (Oct. 1943)
Frederick C. Mills .50
13 Railroad Travel and the State of Business (Dec. 1943)
Thor Hultgren .35
14 The Labor Force in Wartime America (March 1944)
Clarence D. Long .50
15 Railway Traffic Expansion and Use of Resources in World War II (Feb. 1944)
Thor Hultgren .35
16 British and American Plans for International Currency Stabilization (Jan. 1944)
J. H. Riddle .35
17 National Product, War and Prewar (Feb. 1944)
Simon Kuznets .50
18 Production of Industrial Materials in World Wars I and II (March 1944)
Geoffrey H. Moore .50
19 Canada's Financial System in War (April 1944)
B. H. Higgins .50
20 Nazi War Finance and Banking (April 1944)
Otto Nathan .50
22 Bank Liquidity and the War (May 1945)
Charles R. Whittlesey .50
23 Labor Savings in American Industry, 1899–1939 (Nov. 1945)
Solomon Fabricant .50
24 Domestic Servants in the United States, 1900–1940 (April 1946)
George J. Stigler .50

TECHNICAL PAPERS

3 Basic Yields of Corporate Bonds, 1900–1942 (June 1942)
David Durand .50
4 Currency Held by the Public, the Banks, and the Treasury, Monthly, December 1917—December 1944 (Jan. 1947)
Anna Jacobson Schwartz and Elma Oliver .75
5 Concerning a New Federal Financial Statement (in press)
Morris A. Copeland

NATIONAL BUREAU OF ECONOMIC RESEARCH
1819 Broadway, New York 23, N. Y.